> "The events as tol
> have a value quite apart from their religious significance: a value as literature. They tell of mankind's experience at its most moving and most memorable in words that go beyond mere chronicle: words that strike the heart and light up the vision."
>
> —from the Introduction

In this superb new translation, Paul Roche brings you the timeless stories of the Bible in fresh and lucid modern English. Here are the great tales of life, death, and rebirth, of love, war, and destruction, of envy, greed, and heroism that form such an important part of our literary and cultural heritage. Combining a scholar's knowledge with a poet's sensitivity, Paul Roche's eloquent retelling preserves all the drama of the great biblical stories while capturing the rhythm, cadence, and balance of the original text.

THE BIBLE'S GREATEST STORIES

PAUL ROCHE is a distinguished poet and translator. His translations include *The Oedipus Plays of Sophocles* and *The Orestes Plays of Aeschylus*, both available in Mentor editions.

 (0451)

ENLIGHTENING READING

☐ **THE UPANISHADS:** ***Breath of the Eternal*** **translated by Swami Prabhavananda and Frederick Manchester.** Concerned with the knowledge of God and the highest aspects of religious truth, these ancient Hindu scriptures are presented in a readable translation. (626079—$4.50)

☐ **THE MEANING OF THE GLORIOUS KORAN:** ***An Explanatory Translation*** **by Mohammed Marmaduke Pickthall.** The complete sacred book of Mohammadanism, translated with reverence and scholarship. (627458—$5.99)

☐ **UNDERSTANDING ISLAM:** ***An Introduction to the World*** **by Thomas W. Lippman.** An invaluable primer on one of the world's most powerful religions—from its founding in the seventh century to today's headlines. (627601—$4.99)

☐ **THE SONG OF GOD: BHAGAVAD-GITA with an Introduction by Aldous Huxley.** The timeless epic of Hindu faith vividly translated for Western readers by Swami Prabhavananda and Christopher Isherwood. (627571—$4.50)

☐ **THE SAYINGS OF CONFUCIUS Translated by James R. Ware.** The philosophy of one of the greatest wise men of ancient China, teaching the ageless virtues of civilized man. (627636—$4.50)

Prices slightly higher in Canada.

Buy them at your local bookstore or use this convenient coupon for ordering.

NEW AMERICAN LIBRARY
P.O. Box 999 – Dept. #17109
Bergenfield, New Jersey 07621

Please send me the books I have checked above.
I am enclosing $__________ (please add $2.00 to cover postage and handling). Send check or money order (no cash or C.O.D.'s) or charge by Mastercard or VISA (with a $15.00 minimum). Prices and numbers are subject to change without notice.

Card #________________ Exp. Date ________
Signature____________________
Name____________________
Address____________________
City __________ State ________ Zip Code ________

For faster service when ordering by credit card call **1-800-253-6476**

Allow a minimum of 4-6 weeks for delivery. This offer is subject to change without notice.

THE BIBLE'S GREATEST STORIES

Paul Roche

A MENTOR BOOK

MENTOR
Published by the Penguin Group
Penguin Books USA Inc., 375 Hudson Street,
New York, New York 10014, U.S.A.
Penguin Books Ltd, 27 Wrights Lane,
London W8 5TZ, England
Penguin Books Australia Ltd, Ringwood,
Victoria, Australia
Penguin Books Canada Ltd, 10 Alcorn Avenue,
Toronto, Ontario, Canada M4V 3B2
Penguin Books (N.Z.) Ltd, 182–190 Wairau Road,
Auckland 10, New Zealand

Penguin Books Ltd, Registered Offices:
Harmondsworth, Middlesex, England

First published by Mentor, an imprint of New American Library,
a division of Penguin Books USA Inc.

First Printing, May, 1990
10 9 8 7 6 5 4 3

Library of Congress Cataloging Card Number: 90-60113

Printed in the United States of America

for

VANESSA ARIADNE JANE

in Vanessa veritas et amor:
flore stirpite fruge.

ἐν βανεσσᾳ ἡ ἀληθεια ἀγαπη τε

κατ' ἀνθος καυλον καρπον

Contents

PART II
THE EMERGENCE OF ISRAEL
(c. 1700 to 1200 B.C.)
Stories from the Books of Exodus, Numbers, and Deuteronomy

PART III
SETTLEMENT IN THE PROMISED LAND
(1200 to 1000 B.C.)
Stories from the Books of Joshua, Judges, Ruth, and Samuel

PART IV
THE DAVIDIC KINGDOM
(c. 1000 to 900 B.C.)
Stories from the Books of Samuel 1 & 2 and 1 Kings

PART V
THE DIVIDED KINGDOM: ISRAEL AND JUDAH
(c. 933 to 800 B.C.)
Stories from the Books of 2 Chronicles and 1 & 2 Kings

PART VI
PALESTINE DURING THE ASSYRIAN, BABYLONIAN, PERSIAN, AND GREEK DOMINATION
(c. 842 to 4 B.C.)
Stories from the Apocrypha and the Books of Jonah, Job, Esther, Ezekiel, and Daniel

PART VII
PALESTINE UNDER THE ROMANS IN THE HELLENISTIC AGE
(c. 4 B.C. to A.D. 67)
Stories of Jesus and the Apostles from the Four Gospels and Acts

Acknowledgments

First of all, I am beholden to Hugh Rawson, my perceptive and patient editor at New American Library, who combed through the massive manuscript, suggesting, emending, correcting; without his help the whole endeavor would have been seriously flawed. My gratitude here must include my admiration for the copy-editing job done by John Paine. Then I owe a debt of thanks to Pat Gilbert-Read, who weeded out many a gauche phrase and typographical error. And to William Lemieux of Milwaukee, who housed and fed me in princely fashion while much of the translation was being done. Who also made it possible for many of the blessings of America to be showered upon me. As did, too, Muriel Pollia, Dame of the ancient and august Military and Hospitaler Order of St. Lazarus of Jerusalem, who first encouraged me to accept the challenge of making my own translation of the biblical texts. I must thank Frances Lucas of Albion College, Michigan, who lent me her precious copy of that perennial children's classic, *Hurlbut's Story of the Bible*, which I often found gave me more feeling for the biblical background than hours of research. I cannot be grateful enough to Isaac Asimov, whom I have never met but whose two-volume *Asimov's Guide to the Bible* I could not have done without. I must thank too the scholars of the *Anchor Bible*, several of whose masterly studies I depended on; and J. G. Williams for his most helpful exposition *Understanding the Old Testament*, which is full of indispensable insights; and the authors of *The Gospels: Interpreter's Concise Commentary*, who pack essential information into a brief handbook. Then there is *Fauna and Flora of the Bible* (published by the United Bible Societies), which stimulated and went a long way toward satisfying my curiosity about biblical plants and animals. As to the translation itself, my three main texts were: the Greek Septuaginta in the 1979 edition published by Deutsche Bibelgesellschaft Stuttgart, the Latin Vulgate of St. Jerome, *Biblia Sacra Vulgata* in the 1983 edition put out by the same publishers, and the Greek New Testament in the 1975 edition of the United Bible Societies. All the way through preparing my own rendition I was inspired, helped, and steadied by the Authorized Version (also known as the King James Bible), by the Douay Bible (on which I was brought up), the Revised Standard Version, the Jerusalem Bible, and by The Living Bible. Finally, when I was at a loss for basic information, *Harper's Bible Dictionary* often came to my rescue. I thank the compilers of that monumental work.

—P.R.

Introduction

In many ways the Bible is a shocking book, abounding in tales of wars, murders, mutilations, pestilences, and famines (not to mention a chauvinism both sexual and racial hardly to be equaled in all literature). And yet the Bible is a monument to our humanity: our humanity at its worst and at its best, with no other purpose than to warn us how evil we can be, yet to show us also how sublime; as if our worst were on display as a foil to turn us toward our best.

We proceed from the parable of Creation, through the historical defeats and triumphs of the Children of Israel, to the coming of Jesus; and all the while we cannot but notice an evolution of human awareness toward the more humane and the more spiritual. Our consciousness mellows from elemental ruthlessness to selfless devotion, and so does our concept of Godhead, until finally all things are seen to move within that divine flow, whereby the finite is carried toward its celebration with the infinite.

The ultimate purpose of the Creator is then seen in all its beauty, and the Creator himself changes in our conception from the stance of arbitrary champion of a primitive people to the all-embracing Father of the gospels.

But the Bible is not simply a record of humanity's progress and regressions: it is a treasury of maxims, proverbs, wisdom, of the loftiest inspiration. The psalms alone search our perceptions to the core and have sustained untold generations.

However, the reason for this anthology of Bible stories, in an age when even in schools the Bible is absent, is to make it easier for a wider public to become acquainted with its chief episodes and characters.

Much of the Bible is difficult to read, much of it hardly relevant to our present needs, and much of it beset with interpretive and textual problems. To single out the stories just because they make good reading and to leave out the rest might not seem to be a satisfactory way of proceeding;

but to ignore the stories as well as the rest is even worse. Moreover, the events as told in the Scriptures have a value quite apart from their religious significance: a value as literature. They tell of mankind's experience at its most moving and most memorable in words that go beyond mere chronicle: words that strike the heart and light up the vision.

Translator's Foreword

It may be wondered why I have gone to the trouble of setting forth these stories in a new translation when I could have chosen from the many new translations that have sprung up in the last forty years. My answer is that though the best of these have indeed done wonders for our understanding of the Bible by their scholarship and clarity, none of them quite fitted my designs.

I wanted a version couched in contemporary English which paid consistent attention to the way the Bible not merely informs us but moves and illuminates. Clarity of information by itself does not achieve this, though who shall say what does?

This much is certain, that both the Old and the New Testaments, in all their original texts and all their greatest versions, choose words, choose the rhythm and cadence of words—with their varied inflections, repetitions, incantations, and antitheses—so to fall upon the ear as to go beyond the mere meaning of words and lift them to a new level of experience. Such precisely is the power of poetic illumination: to lift knowledge beyond the bounds of knowledge and engage the whole sentient self.

Of course, it would be absurd to suggest that biblical language does this all the time. Whole sections of it are as prosaic and dull as the pages of a telephone directory. But it is not these passages that move us. On the other hand, what shall we say of this single sentence from the King James Bible: "Babylon is fallen, is fallen that great city"? Why does this stir the heart at once and affect us more than the flat assertion: "The great city of Babylon has fallen"? Is it because the stresses are on all the important words: Babylon, fallen, city? Partly so, but also because of the incantatory power of rhythm and repetition which propels the words into the bloodstream almost before and beyond the point at which they are understood. In the Hebrew, the Greek, and the Latin the language is equally beautiful and moving.

Or listen again to the tender lilt of Christ's farewell address to his disciples at the Last Supper: the words are so simple and artless that one wonders (as with late Sophocles and Shakespeare) where the poetry is coming from.

> Now is the Son of Man
>   glorified, and God
> is glorified in him.
>   If God is glorified
> in him, then God will also
>   glorify him in himself.
> And God will glorify him soon.
> Only a little longer,
>   children, am I with you;
> then you will look for me,
>   and as I told the Jews,
> where I am going, you
>   cannot come after me . . .
> A new commandment I
>   leave with you: love
> one another; yes
>   you must love each other
> just as I loved you.

Here in an accumulation of swift, gentle strokes the words go mysteriously beyond communication and into communion. They transcend mere information and begin to rekindle and recreate.

"Oh, but the people who wrote the Bible," I can hear someone saying, "weren't trying to write literature. Take the Apostles: they were simple men, no doubt uneducated, and perhaps even illiterate."

True enough, though I doubt that either Matthew or Luke was uneducated; and Mark and John were far from being illiterate. The point is that, simple people or not, they wrote a masterpiece—perhaps because of their simplicity. Whoever the writers of the four gospels were—and likewise the authors of the Old Testament—they were men still very much in tune with the rhythms that flowed through their being. However much their styles differed, each achieved an immediacy of contact that has seldom been surpassed.

It goes without saying that a translation forms a bridge from one age and culture to another. The translator therefore has a double allegiance: that of truth to the original and truth to his own time and tongue. He owes an equal duty to both. If he is true to the original but meaningless to his own people, he has not made a bridge. Conversely, even if he be brilliantly readable in his own time but untrue to what the original said, he has not made a bridge either. His duty is to make readable only that which was originally said and, as far as possible, the very way in which it was said.

I have based my translation of the following stories on the Septuagint and the Vulgate, that is, they are from the Greek and the Latin. The Septuagint was a translation from Hebrew and Aramaic texts undertaken about 250 B.C. for the sake of the Greek and Egyptian Jews living in and around Alexandria. The Pharaoh Ptolemy II sequestered seventy-two Hebrew scholars from Jerusalem on the island of Pharos in the bay of Alexandria to do the work. The number was later altered by tradition to a round seventy, and legend also has it that it took them seventy or seventy-two days. These figures gave the Septuagint, or LXX, its name, *septuaginta* being the Latin for seventy.

The Vulgate is St. Jerome's direct translation into Latin of Hebrew and Aramaic texts, undertaken for the general Christian public of the Roman empire in A.D. 382 and completed toward A.D. 400. The word *vulgatum* denotes that which is spread abroad or made common.

As to the Masoretic text (the Hebrew), my own Hebrew not being up to scratch, I have depended on a plethora of translations, as I have acknowledged: especially the King James Bible, which came out in 1611, and the Douay-Rheims Bible, which appeared between 1582 and 1610.

On the occasions when the New Testament quotes the Old, I often use the King James so that young ears may catch something of the cadences which have helped to shape our language. I have also retained some of the key phrases that have become household words. Joseph's "coat of many colors," for instance, which his father, Jacob, gave him and which led to such jealousy from his brothers, does not become "a multicolored tunic." (A long-sleeved dalmatic reaching to the ground is a poetic garment and needs a poetic name.) So too, "The voice is the voice of Jacob but the hands are the hands of Esau" does not become: "It is Jacob's voice but Esau's hands." The reader will find many a well-known phrase which I could not bring myself to jettison.

When it comes to the matter of scholarship, every scholar of the Bible will acknowledge that no book in the world so bristles with problems and unsolved questions. In compiling this anthology I have not presumed to shoulder the burden of biblical exegesis; I have not written for scholars, although

I hope that what I have attempted is not unscholarly. I made a distinction which I think is valid between the truth of scholarship and the truth of fact, supposing that the duty of the first is toward the text itself, which must be regarded as sacred and an end in itself; whereas the duty of the second is to that which the text implies, i.e., to that which actually happened. And the search for this is guided by common sense and the historical imagination.

To make the distinction clear, let us suppose that the Our Father had come down to us only in the following disjointed fragments:

> Our Father who art . . . . . . hallowed . . . thy . . . . .
> thy will . . . done . . . . in heaven. Give us
> this day our . . . . daily . . . .
> trespasses . . . . . . forgive those that trespass against
> us. Lead us . . . into temptation . . . deliver us . . . evil.

In these fragments the Lord's Prayer says the opposite of what Christ enjoined his disciples to say, and yet the truth of scholarship must insist that any departure from these words is pure conjecture. It would be the task of the enlightened restorer, using every scrap of internal and external evidence, and all his common sense and imagination, to find out what Christ actually said.

If this is an extreme and somewhat crude example, let us take 2 Kings 9:31. Here Queen Jezebel, sitting at a high window just before she is hurled to her death, looks down and sees the hated Jehu entering the city in triumph after having murdered her husband. The Bible scene opens with the words: "As Jehu entered the gates, she said . . ." and her insult follows. These are the words of the text which the truth of scholarship must keep, but the alert translator knows full well that Jezebel did not simply *say* her insult—it would not have been heard—she shouted it. That is what I mean by the truth of fact.

As to the insult itself, the truth of scholarship renders it in all exactness: "Is all well, Zimri, you murderer of your master?" which to the modern ear is no insult at all but an enigma. One needs to know that Zimri was a captain of King Elah's chariots early in the ninth century B.C. who led a coup against his master and murdered him. One week later Zimri committed suicide and his name became a byword of treachery and regicide. So what Jezebel is really shouting down to her enemy is: "Having a nice day? You king-murderer! You Zimri!" Such a rendering may border on pharaphrase, but, so far as the modern reader is concerned, it represents the truth of what actually happened, and, with legitimate license, makes the bridge from then to now. On the same principle, whenever I have added a word or a phrase not shown literally in the original, this is because its intent is so strongly implied that to omit it would be tantamount to pedantry and even mistranslation.

Another point is this: a reader coming upon a sentence or a passage not found in other versions need not assume that I have invented it. Sometimes the Septuagint or the Vulgate give touches missed by the Masoretic text, and when these add clarity and color to the story I have used them. Note also that I have not always adhered to those successive repetitions of a word in the manner of the ancient writers. This compulsion goes so much against the grain of modern English as to be merely tiresome.

As to my selection of tales, I am well aware that an anthology suffers from the limitations of its compiler. Doubtless there are stories absent which should have been included, and others that are included which could have been omitted. I know only that there are many for which I would like to have found room, and others which, however shocking, I could not leave out without falsifying the record of our human regresses, recovery, and advance.

Lastly, let me aver that I am not so sanguine as to dare guarantee that I have escaped falling into errors. The biblical field is too heavily mined with booby traps for that. In all humility I stand to be corrected and promise to amend every lapse in any subsequent editions of *The Bible's Greatest Stories*.

—P.R.

NOTE TO THE READER

Square brackets enclosing a word or phrase in the biblical text indicate an interpolation put in by the translator either for the sake of clarity or because it is implied.

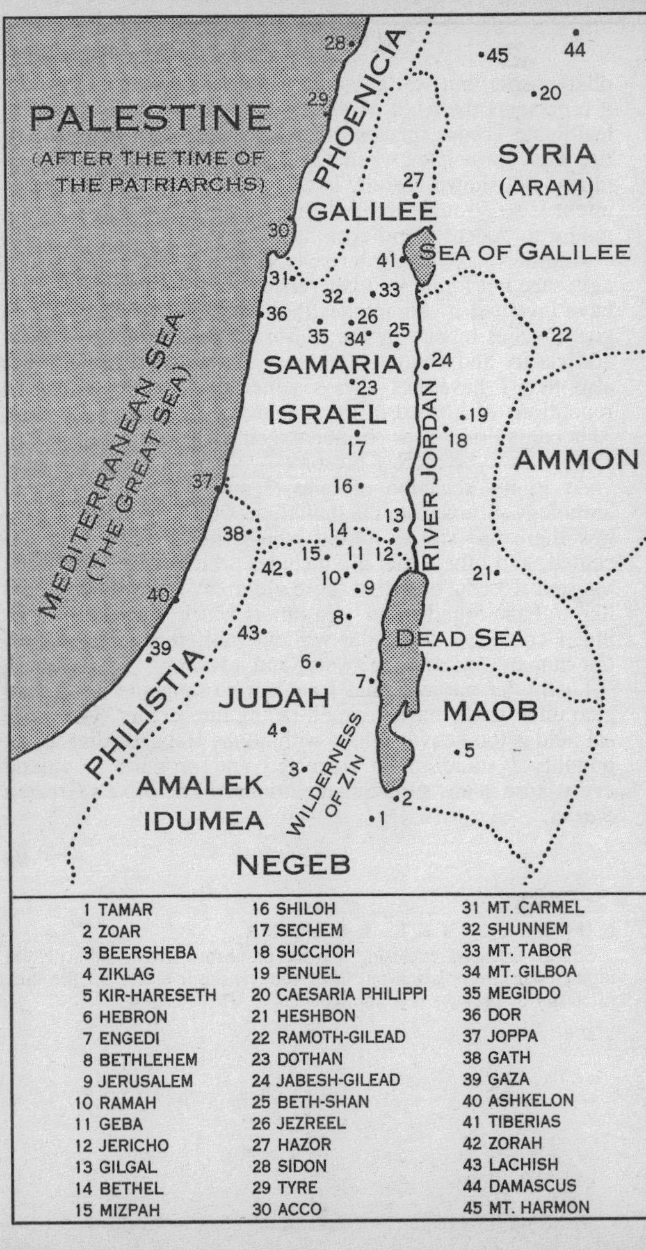
PALESTINE
(AFTER THE TIME OF THE PATRIARCHS)
MEDITERRANEAN SEA (THE GREAT SEA)
PHOENICIA
GALILEE
SYRIA (ARAM)
SEA OF GALILEE
SAMARIA
ISRAEL
RIVER JORDAN
AMMON
DEAD SEA
PHILISTIA
JUDAH
MAOB
WILDERNESS OF ZIN
AMALEK
IDUMEA
NEGEB
1 TAMAR
2 ZOAR
3 BEERSHEBA
4 ZIKLAG
5 KIR-HARESETH
6 HEBRON
7 ENGEDI
8 BETHLEHEM
9 JERUSALEM
10 RAMAH
11 GEBA
12 JERICHO
13 GILGAL
14 BETHEL
15 MIZPAH
16 SHILOH
17 SECHEM
18 SUCCHOH
19 PENUEL
20 CAESARIA PHILIPPI
21 HESHBON
22 RAMOTH-GILEAD
23 DOTHAN
24 JABESH-GILEAD
25 BETH-SHAN
26 JEZREEL
27 HAZOR
28 SIDON
29 TYRE
30 ACCO
31 MT. CARMEL
32 SHUNNEM
33 MT. TABOR
34 MT. GILBOA
35 MEGIDDO
36 DOR
37 JOPPA
38 GATH
39 GAZA
40 ASHKELON
41 TIBERIAS
42 ZORAH
43 LACHISH
44 DAMASCUS
45 MT. HARMON

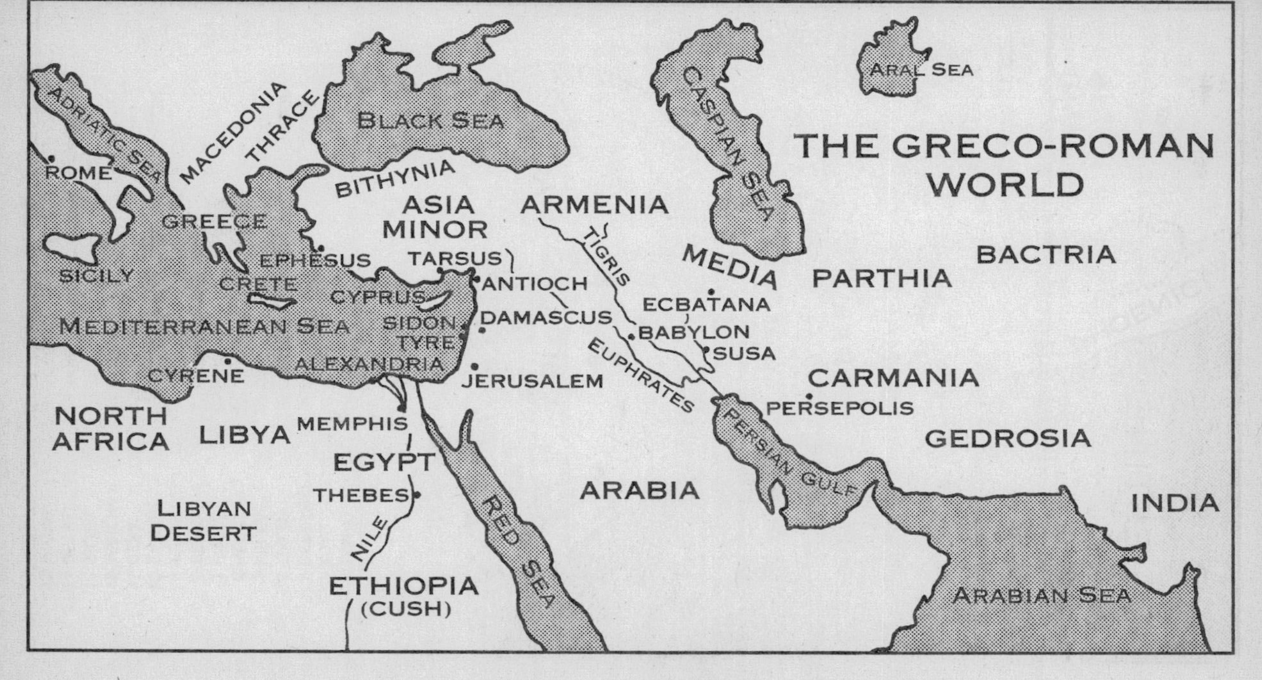
THE GRECO-ROMAN WORLD
ADRIATIC SEA
ROME
SICILY
MACEDONIA
THRACE
GREECE
BLACK SEA
BITHYNIA
ASIA MINOR
EPHESUS
TARSUS
CRETE
CYPRUS
ANTIOCH
MEDITERRANEAN SEA
SIDON
TYRE
DAMASCUS
ALEXANDRIA
JERUSALEM
CYRENE
NORTH AFRICA
LIBYA
MEMPHIS
EGYPT
THEBES
LIBYAN DESERT
NILE
ETHIOPIA
(CUSH)
RED SEA
ARMENIA
TIGRIS
EUPHRATES
CASPIAN SEA
ARAL SEA
MEDIA
ECBATANA
BABYLON
SUSA
PARTHIA
BACTRIA
CARMANIA
PERSEPOLIS
PERSIAN GULF
GEDROSIA
ARABIA
INDIA
ARABIAN SEA

PART I

IN THE BEGINNING

(c. 40,000 TO 1700 B.C.)

Stories from the Book of Genesis

Introduction

Genesis is the Greek word for "coming into being." Nobody knows who or how many authors wrote the Book of Genesis, though scholars today agree that it was not Moses, the author by tradition. Rather it was put together by several different hands, all relying on ancient sources—one of them Moses—and received its final shape after the return of the Jews from their exile in Babylon, i.e., about 538 B.C.

Genesis is the first of the five books known as the Pentateuch (Greek for "five-volume work"). The other books of the Pentateuch are: Exodus, Leviticus, Numbers, and Deuteronomy.

Genesis is not only the beginning of the Bible but the beginning of the biblical process: that record of our humanity at its worst, best, most mediocre, and most noble. A record in which we see the mind of humankind wrenching itself away from the advanced but polytheistic cultures of primordial Mesopotamia, and then slowly and often painfully evolving the concept of God as a loving Father: a father whose designs for the brotherhood and sisterhood of mankind go far beyond the stereotyped problem of evil and are every moment triumphant.

The Creation

The Bible creation story is thought by some to be a Hebrew version of an earlier Babylonian creation myth purged of its polytheism. It opens like a hymn to creation and should be read more as a poem than as an attempt to account scientifically for the origin of the universe. The writer is singing in praise of Elohim: one of the Hebrew names of God, meaning the "Powers" who cause everything to be.

(Genesis 1:1-31, 2:1-3)

IN the beginning when God created the heavens and the earth, the earth was a chaos empty of form, and darkness shrouded the abyss. Then the spirit of God stirred over the dark waters and God said, "Let there be light." And there was light. God saw the benediction of the light and God divided the light from darkness, calling the light Day and the darkness Night. Dusk and dawn were the first day.

Then God said, "Let there be a vault of space parting the waters." So God created a vault of space that parted the waters, dividing the sky above from the waters beneath. It was done. God called the skies above Heaven. Dusk and dawn were the second day.

Then God said, "Let the waters under the heavens amass together and let dry land appear. It was done. God called the dry land Earth and the massed waters Sea. And God saw that this was good.

Then God said, "Let the earth sprout green with plants all crowded with seeds, and every fruit tree after its kind. It was done. The earth sprouted green with every seed-bearing plant and every fruit tree according to its kind. God saw that this was good, and dusk and dawn were the third day.

Then God said, "Let there be lights in the upper skies to mark out day from night. Let these be bearings to fix the days, seasons, and years. Let them illumine the vault of heaven and shine down on earth. It was done. God made two great lights: the larger light to rule the day, and the smaller to rule the night. And he created the stars, which he set in the expanse of the sky to shine upon the earth and keep light apart from dark. God saw that this was good. Dawn and dusk were the fourth day.

Then God said, "Let the waters teem with life, and let winged creatures fly through the vault of heaven." It was done. God created sea monsters of enormous bulk and every kind of living, swimming thing with which the waters teem, as well as every kind of winged fowl. God saw that this was good, and he blessed them, saying: "Be fruitful and multiply, fill the seas, and let winged fowl throng the air." Dusk and dawn were the fifth day.

Then God said, "Let the land engender every sort of living creature: cattle, animals that crawl, and the beasts of the wild." It was done. God created all kinds of wild beasts and every sort of animal that crawls. God saw that this was good.

Then God said, "Let us make mankind in our own image, in our own likeness. Let them have dominion over the creatures of the sea, over all cattle, birds of the air, beasts of the wild, and every ground-creeping thing."

So God created man in his own image. In the image of God he created him. Male and female he created them.

God blessed them and said, "Be fruitful and multiply. Fill the world and tame it. Be master over the creatures of the sea, the birds of the air, and every living animal that moves on the face of the earth."

Then God said, "See, I have given you every seed-bearing plant that grows and every fruit-bearing tree for your food. And to the wild beasts of the world, the birds of the air, and every creeping thing that has the breath of life, I have given green herbage for fodder."

And so it was. God saw that everything he had created was supremely good. Dusk and dawn were the sixth day.

So the heavens and the earth were perfected in all their array and on the sixth day God completed the work he had begun. On the seventh day he rested from his great endeavor. The seventh day he blessed and made holy, resting from his labors of creation.

Adam and Eve

The word "Adam" is the Hebrew word for "man" or "mankind," both male and female, in the sense of Homo sapiens. In the interests of not making too distracting a break with the traditional English of the Bible, which has played such an important part in shaping our rich literature, I have throughout this translation retained the generic use of the words "man" and "mankind," which seemed to me too full of resonances to jettison. Their pedigree tells an interesting story. By about the middle of the sixth century A.D. in England three dominant words covered the human species: *wer* for male, *wif* for female, and *man* for human being. It was this generic use of *man* which led to the suffix of *man* in *woman* (originally *wifman*), i.e., female human. As to *human* itself, the suffix there comes from a different source: from the Latin *humanus*, which has the same root as *homo*. In either case, those who condemn sexist language are quite correct in not ostracizing the suffix *man* from woman and human. By the same token the suffix *male* at the end of female is unassailable because it has nothing to do with masculine but comes from the Latin *femella*, a young girl, and is the diminutive of *femina*—woman. As to the word *mankind*, this has been used for the most part generically and even today, unlike *man* by itself, seldom means male and should be retained.

The name "Eve" is derived from the Hebrew word meaning "life-giving." The word "Eden" is the Hebrew for "delight" or "pleasure." "The Garden of Eden" should really read "The Garden in Eden" because Eden was not a place but a territory. Its exact location (in so far as Eden actually existed and is more than metaphor) has been the subject of scores of books and studies. There seems to be little doubt that Eden was in Mesopotamia, somewhere near the head of the Persian Gulf in the fertile valley between the rivers Tigris and Euphrates—the cradle of civilization. As myth, Eden may be a way of saying that before human beings submitted to the labors of an agricultural way of life during the thousands of years of prehistory, they enjoyed a carefree existence roaming where they would and living off a generous and plentiful earth.

God's fashioning of Eve from a rib (i.e., close to the heart) of Adam, is of course a metaphor to show that male and female share their sexuality. In Jungian terms we would say that man has his female complement within him, his anima, and woman her male, her animus.

It is obvious that this whole account comes from a second creation story differing from Genesis 1:27, which says: "male and female he created them."

(Genesis 2:1-9, 15-18, 21-25)

THEN the Lord God fashioned man out of the clay of the earth and breathed into his nostrils the breath of life, and man became a living soul. The Lord God planted a garden in the eastern part of Eden and there he set the man he had made. Out of the ground the Lord caused every kind of tree to grow, both beautiful to see and good to eat. Among them too in the depth of the garden was the Tree of Life, as well as the Tree of the Knowledge of Good and Evil.

The Lord God took the man and settled him in the garden to till and nurture it.

Then the Lord God said, "It is not good for man to be alone. Let me make him a helpmate like himself."

So the Lord God cast the man, Adam, into a deep sleep and while he slept took out one of his ribs, closing up the gap with flesh. The rib which the Lord took from Adam he made into a woman and brought her to him. And Adam said:

> She is now bone of my bone,
> flesh of my flesh.
> She shall be called "wo-man"
> because she was taken from man.

That is why a man leaves father and mother and cleaves to his wife, making two in one flesh. They were both naked, the man and his wife, but they felt no shame.

The Temptation and Fall

Though the Bible does not say in this story that the Serpent is Satan, that is what we are expected to assume. "Satan" is the Hebrew word for "opponent" or "adversary." Snakes were also a symbol of subtlety, cunning, and wisdom.

The idea that Satan is the chief executive of an evil principle constantly warring against the good and getting mankind to sin, is part of a dualistic view of reality which probably entered Jewish thought either during their Babylonian captivity (between 597 and 538 B.C.) or, more probably, during the Persian dominion over Asia (550 B.C. onward), after the Persian prophet Zoroaster (Zarathustra) began to explain the presence of evil in the world by proposing two nearly equal originating principles: the good and the evil.

Simplistic and false though such a solution of the problem of evil is, the tenacity of this dualistic view in all sorts of disguises is amazing, tinging the minds of even the greatest thinkers.

Perhaps mankind's first sin was precisely to judge God's creation as not all good and to see evil in that which in itself and for itself was good. Adam and Eve ate from the Tree of the Knowledge of Good and Evil in a garden where there was not supposed to be anything bad, and their "discovery" may have been the real beginning of the dualistic view of the universe, and of that puritanism which made them ashamed of their sexuality and made them hide from God.

The storyteller here wastes not a word or a moment. With a beautiful irony and sureness of insight he gets to the heart of his characters in the briefest of narratives.

(Genesis 3:1-24)

NOW the serpent was slyer than any creature which the Lord had made and the Serpent said to the Woman; "Did God tell you of any tree in the garden from which you may not eat?"

And the Woman answered the Serpent; "We may eat of all the trees in the garden, but there is one tree in the middle of the garden whose fruit God told us: 'You must not eat, or even touch, or you will die.' "

"Not so," said the Serpent to the Woman. "You will not die. God knows that if you eat it, your eyes will be opened and you will be like God, comprehending good and evil."

The Woman could see that the tree was good to eat from, beautiful to look at, and desirable for the understanding it would give. So she plucked a fruit and ate it, then gave some to her husband and he ate too.

Forthwith the eyes of both of them were opened and they saw that they were naked, so they stitched fig leaves together and made themselves loincloths.

When they heard the voice of the Lord God, who was walking in the garden in the cool of the evening, Adam and his wife hid themselves from God in the bushes of the garden. But the Lord called Adam, asking, "Where are you?" And he answered, "I heard you in the garden, but I was ashamed of being naked so I hid."

"Who told you you were naked?" God said. "Have you eaten from the tree I charged you not to eat from?"

"The woman you made my partner, she gave me fruit from the tree," Adam replied, "so I ate."

Then the Lord God said to the Woman, "How could you do such a thing?"

"The Serpent tricked me," the Woman answered. "That is why I ate."

The Lord God turned to the Serpent: "Because you have done this you are the most damned of animals and of all creatures in the wild. You shall crawl on your belly and swallow dirt for the rest of your life. Between you and the Woman I shall put hate, a war between her seed and your seed. Hers shall crush your head, and yours lie in wait for their heel."

To the Woman he said, "As for you, I shall put labor into your child-bearing and in spasms you shall bring forth your children. Yet you will yearn for your husband, who will be your master."

Then to Adam he said, "Because you have listened to your wife and eaten from the tree I commanded you not to eat from, the very soil is cursed because of you and you shall garner from it in toil all the days of your life. It will reward you with thorns and thistles and you will eat the weeds of the fields. In the sweat of your brow shall you eat your bread until the day you go back to the earth from which you were taken. For you are made of clay and to clay you shall return.

Adam named his wife Eve, because she was the mother of all living. And the Lord God made garments of skin for Adam and his wife and clothed them, saying, "So Adam has become one of us and discerns good from evil! Next perhaps he will reach out a hand for the Tree of Life and take a bite and live forever."

Whereupon the Lord God dismissed him from the Garden of Eden to work that very soil from which he stemmed. He thrust mankind out and posted the cherubim at the gates of Eden with a reeling blade of fire to guard the entrance to the Tree of Life.

NOTES

1. The cherubim (in the Hebrew plural) were high-up angels or minor deities.
2. The reeling or all-revolving blade of fire is typical of the specific magic weapon which this or that ancient Mesopotamian god adopted.

Cain and Abel

In this story we have the beginnings of "religion." When Adam and Eve were at one with God in the Garden of Eden, there was no need for special rites: for altars, sacrifices, and attitudes of appeasement. Now humankind begin the attempt to heal the original estrangement. Ironically and paradoxically, they also begin all those wars of religion that have plagued mankind ever since.

Perhaps it should be pointed out that God's preference for

Abel's sacrifice was prompted not simply by an arbitrary whim, or because the Lord preferred meat to vegetables, but because Abel was living righteously and Cain (we are not told in what way) was not.

Cain's punishment turned out to be not as drastic as he thought it. He became the grand avatar (probably) of the Canaanite race: the gifted developers of farming, husbandry, metalworking, music, and the arts. In the end it was the farmer who made human progress rather than the nomad herdsman.

In later verses of Chapter 4 (which I have not included) we are told about the youngest of the three brothers, Seth. It was through Seth that the people of Israel traced their lineage. After his birth God's name for the first time becomes "Yahweh" ("I-Am-Who-Am"): a title usually translated as "The Lord God" or (erroneously) as "Jehovah."

The name "Cain" is a play on the Hebrew word "to create" or "give birth."

As to the "mark" God gave Cain, nobody knows what this was, or the location of the Land of Nod—which has come to mean Nowhere-in-Particular, as befits the wanderer, which Cain must have been before he settled down as smith and farmer.

(Genesis 4:1-16)

ADAM entered Eve his wife and she conceived and bore Cain, remarking, "The Lord and I have made a man-child." Next she bore his brother Abel.

Now, Abel was a shepherd and Cain a tiller of the soil. In the course of time Cain brought to the Lord an offering from his harvest. Abel too brought choice tenderings from his flock, plump with goodness.

The Lord was pleased with Abel and his offerings, but for Cain and his offerings he had only contempt. Cain was crestfallen and resentful, and the Lord said to him, "Why are you resentful, looking so downcast? If you were living rightly, surely you should look happy. But if you are not living rightly, is not sin crouching on your doorstep? Sin wants you, but you must master it."

Then Cain said to his brother Abel, "Shall we go into the fields?"

As soon as they were in the fields, Cain set on his brother Abel and killed him. When the Lord asked Cain, "Where is your brother Abel?" he answered, "How should I know?

Am I my brother's keeper?" And the Lord said, "What have you done? I tell you, your brother's blood cries out to me from the ground. You are now damned by the very earth which gapes to receive your brother's blood—spilt by your hand. And when you till the land it will return you a meager harvest. You shall wander through the world a fugitive."

Cain cried out to the Lord, "My punishment is too great to bear. You are banishing me today from the good earth, and I must wander through the world hidden from your gaze—a restless fugitive. And whoever comes upon me will kill me."

"Not so," the Lord answered. "Whoever kills Cain shall be punished sevenfold."

Then the Lord put a mark upon Cain so that whoever came upon him would not kill him. Cain went out from the Lord's presence and lived in the Land of Nod, east of Eden.

Noah and the Flood

Noah, who was "five hundred years old" when he begot Shem, Ham, and Japheth, was the great-great-great-great-great-great-great-grandson of Adam. His impressive age (nine hundred and fifty years old when he died) is a fictional exaggeration to bring it into line with the obligatory longevity of Babylonian kings and heroes. So too with the other Patriarchs. One must remember that the compilers of the Pentateuch were putting it together after the end of the Babylonian captivity in 538 B.C. and were necessarily influenced by Mesopotamian culture.

If we take "myth" roughly as meaning a story which has immediate significance and recognition wherever it is told, then the story of the Flood is one of the most universal and persistent myths known to man. It occurs among the Sumerians (the tale of Gilgamesh) and the Egyptians, not to mention the Greeks, the Chinese, and the Incas of Peru. And yet there is no geographical evidence of a *universal* deluge. What there is evidence of are very severe floodings around 3000 B.C., which would be about the time of Noah.

Naturally, a people caught in a flood covering enormous tracts of land and wiping out the inhabitants would think of it as a deluge covering the whole earth. It was not only rain that caused the Flood, but "the fountains of the deep" that were opened (Genesis 7:11). Isaac Asimov makes the fascinating suggestion that a large meteorite landing in the nearly landlocked Persian Gulf would cause quite a splash. Indeed, the Flood could have been caused by "a tidal wave plus rain," with the consequent flooding of the Tigris and the Euphrates.

As to Ararat, where the Ark came to rest, this was not a particular mountain but a range running through a land later called Armenia.

(Genesis 6:15-22, 7:1-24, 8:1-22, 9:12-13)

WHEN Yahweh saw how great was human wickedness on earth and how all man's imagination and thoughts were bent on evil, Yahweh was sorry that he had ever made mankind. Indeed he was sad to the depth of his heart and he said, "I shall wipe out man whom I created from the face of the earth. Yes, and not only man but every beast and creeping thing, even the birds of the air, for I regret that I ever made them."

But Noah was in good favor with the Lord. He was an honest and blameless man in that degenerate age, walking with God. And Noah had three sons: Shem, Ham, and Japheth.

So as the world continued in depravity before God's eyes and he looked down and saw all the violence and how the earth and all flesh was corrupt to its very core, he said to Noah, "I have made up my mind to obliterate all flesh from the earth. The world is full of violence because of it. I shall destroy it and the earth as well. I want you therefore to build an ark of cedar wood, with rooms in the ark. Seal it with pitch inside and out. Make the ark to these dimensions: four hundred and fifty feet long, seventy-five feet wide, and forty-five feet high. Make a skylight all around, a foot and a half from the top. Set a door inside the ark opening onto a first, second, and third deck. . . . Look to it now, for I mean to flood the world and destroy every living creature under heaven. Everything on earth shall perish. But with you I shall make a pact. You are to go into the ark: you, your sons, your wife, and your sons' wives. And you are to bring into the ark and keep alive two of every animal there is, male and female. This includes birds of every kind, different sorts of livestock, and all those creatures that creep upon the ground: two of each are to go in with you and be kept alive.

Also take in with you and store all the food you will need: provisions for both you and them."

Noah did exactly as God commanded him. Then the Lord said, "Now go into the ark, you and all your family. You are the only one I have found to be a good man in this bad age. I want you also to take in with you seven pairs, male and female, of every clean mammal there is [for sacrifices], that is, in addition to the one pair, male and female, of the unclean. And take too, seven pairs of every bird so that their progeny will be preserved on earth. In seven days' time I am going to make it rain on earth for forty days and forty nights. This will wipe out everything that I have created from the face of the earth."

Noah did all that the Lord commanded him. He was in his six hundredth year when the flood broke on the world and the waters came. It was the seventeenth day of the second month exactly. On that day, the fountains of the deep gushed forth and the sluices of heaven were opened. For forty days and forty nights rain fell upon the earth. But on the day it started, Noah and his sons, Shem, Ham, and Japheth, and his wife and the three wives of his sons were safe in the ark. With them had entered every kind of beast, cattle, creeping thing, and every kind of bird and thing that flies. Two by two they had gone into the ark, male and female—every creature endowed with the breath of life—as God had commanded. Then the Lord Yahweh had shut them in.

For forty days the deluge on the earth continued. The waters rose, lifting up the ark and floating it above the ground. The waters welled up and rose still higher over the earth, but the ark drifted free on their wide open surface. Higher and higher still rose the waters till even the peaks of the highest mountains were submerged twenty-two feet down. All flesh perished from the face of the earth: birds, cattle, beasts, the teeming wild, and all mankind. Everything on dry land in which life had breathed died out: all existence was wiped off the earth: people, livestock, reptiles, birds—all erased from the earth. Only Noah and those with him in the ark were left.

For a hundred and fifty days the flood buried the world. But God had not forgotten Noah and all the animals and cattle that were with him in the ark. So God swept a wind over the earth and the waters receded. The fountains of the deep and the windows in the sky were stoppered and the rain from heaven withheld. Little by little the waters began to drain off the land till, after a hundred and fifty days, on the seventeenth day of the seventh month, the deluge had so gone down that the ark came to rest on the mountains of Ararat. As the waters continued to subside, on the tenth day of the tenth month, the tops of the mountains appeared. After another forty days Noah opened a hatch he had made in the ark and let out a raven, which flew back and forth till all the water had dried off the land.

Then he sent out a dove to see if the water had left any dry ground, but the dove finding no footing anywhere (for the flood still covered the earth), returned to him in the ark. He stretched out his hand and caught her back to him. After another seven days he again sent out the dove from the ark and this time the dove returned with a sprig of olive in her beak; so Noah now knew that the waters had shrunk from the earth. He waited another seven days and released the dove, but she did not come back to him again.

It was on the first day of the first month, when the waters had begun to drain from the earth, that Noah (now in his six-hundred-and-first year) removed the covering from the ark and saw that the land was drying. Then, in the second month on the twenty-seventh day, the soil itself was dry and God announced to Noah, "Now you may go from the ark: you and your wife, and your sons and your sons' wives, and bring out every living thing that is with you, all flesh, be it bird, beast or reptile. Let them teem over the earth, breed and multiply."

So Noah came out of the ark with his sons, his wife, and his sons' wives; while from the ark there proceeded group by group all the beasts, birds, cattle, reptiles that stir on the earth. Then Noah built an altar to Yahweh and on it made burnt offerings of every beast and bird that was ritually clean. As Yahweh scented the pleasing aroma, he said to himself, "Never again shall I damn the earth because of mankind, for the human heart is bent to evil from the start. Never again shall I strike down every living thing as I have done. As long as the world lasts, so long will last seed time and harvest, cold and heat, summer and winter, day and night. And I seal this promise with a sign—a sign forever of my covenant with you and me and every living thing: my rainbow, which I have put among the clouds."

NOTE

The Hebrew calendar contained twelve months. The second month, therefore, when the flood broke would be April/May, the first month being March/April.

The Tower of Babel

The descendants of Noah settled in Shinar (Sumeria) in the fertile plain between the two great rivers that run through Mesopotamia: the Tigris and the Euphrates. Whether the events in the story of the Tower of Babel actually occurred or not, the point to be made by the Bible's mythologizing of history is that human beings when they leave out God in their reckonings are apt to be too clever for their own good.

One of the features of the Sumerian city was an edifice known as the "ziggurat," which was a sort of stepped pyramid not unlike those found in Mexico. The ziggurat seems to have served as part temple and part town hall, and is described as "reaching to heaven." There was one such ziggurat in Babylon begun by a Sumerian king and never finished. Perhaps this ziggurat served as the model for the biblical Babel. Ironically, many centuries later this ziggurat *was* finished just about the time Genesis was being written. Sumer and the other cities of the kingdom of Ur, which were mankind's first really civilized centers, were destroyed toward the end of the third millennium by a series of invasions from both East and West.

As to the name "Babel," the sacred authors apparently thought that this was akin to the Hebrew word *balal*, meaning "muddled," whereas the word was more probably derived from the Babylonian "Babilu," meaning "the Gate of God," which was the name the Babylonians gave Babylon.

(Genesis 11:1-9)

THE whole world then shared a single language, a single tongue, and as people moved in from the East they came upon a plain in the land of Shinar and there they settled.

"Come," they said to one another, "let us shape bricks and bake them." So instead of stone they had bricks, and pitch for mortar.

Then they said: "Come, now let us build a city with a tower reaching into the sky. This will make our name and also keep us from being scattered all over the earth."

Yahweh came down to inspect the city that the men of earth were building, and Yahweh said, "Look at what they are doing, these people, when they are one with a single tongue. Soon nothing will restrain them. Very well, let us go down and muddle their speech so that they do not understand one another."

Thus did the Lord disperse them in different directions all over the earth, and they never finished their city. That is why it is called Babel ["Babbletown"], because there Yahweh mixed up the speech of the world and scattered people all over the earth.

Abram

Gradually the Bible narrative shifts from the shadowy ground of prehistory and myth to the more recognizable territory of the family saga. Abram (meaning Mighty Father), later to be called Abraham (Father of Multitudes), was the first of the patriarchs and a direct descendant of Shem, the son of Noah.

The time is somewhere between 2000 and 1800 B.C. There had been some kind of collapse of the civilized world in Mesopotamia (mythologically described in the story of the Tower of Babel), and Abram's father moved the family from Ur of the Chaldees to the town of Haran, a busy commercial center in the north of the old Babylonian empire, which would now be placed in the middle of southeastern Turkey. Then when Abram was seventy-five he received a divine call to leave Haran and move with his household, his nephew Lot, and all they possessed to the land of Canaan (Palestine), which God promised to give him and his descendants.

Abram's thousand-mile journey is a momentous step in the history of the world. The command "Go forth" was no mere whim of Yahweh, but the beginning of the biblical process whereby a man, a family, a people, wrested from their cultured but polytheistic background, become the vehicle of the long, painful, often retrogressive evolution toward a divine unfolding of humanity's loftiest ideals.

(Genesis 12:12-20)

THERE was a famine in the land and Abram went down to Egypt and lived there because the famine had devastated the countryside. As he was about to enter Egypt he said to Sarai his wife, "I know what a beautiful woman you are. When the Egyptians see you they will say, 'But she is his wife,' and they will kill me to keep you. So please say you are my sister. In that way I shall be safe on your account and I shall live because of you."

Accordingly, when Abram came into Egypt, the Egyptians indeed saw what a beautiful woman she was, and once Pharaoh's courtiers had seen her they commended her to Pharaoh and the woman was taken into Pharaoh's household. Abram was treated handsomely because of her and became the owner of sheep and cattle, he-asses, men and women slaves, she-asses, and camels.

But the Lord struck Pharaoh and his household with grievous plagues because of Sarai, Abram's wife, and Pharaoh summoned Abram and said: "Look what you have done to me! Why did you not tell me that she was your wife? Why did you say 'She is my sister' and let me marry her? Well, here she is, your wife. Take her and go."

Pharaoh gave his men instructions what to do with Abram. They sent him away: him, his wife, and all that he had.

NOTES

1. The Canaanites were a people of mixed origins who spoke a Semitic language. They had already enjoyed a long history of civilization. The Egyptians too had an advanced culture, as old perhaps as that of Sumeria. Egypt tended to be a land of plenty in times of famine because the fertile Nile valley could nearly always be counted on for crops even when the rainfall elsewhere had plunged to nothing.

2. Abram's behavior toward his wife is not quite as shocking as it might seem if one remembers that to adopt a wife as "sister" was held to give her special status. He was probably trying to protect his wife as much as himself. The Egyptians, however, had no inkling of such a custom.

3. The word "Pharaoh" was the name given to the reigning Egyptian monarch whoever he happened to be.

Sarai and Her Servant Hagar

Abram and his nephew and ward, Lot (an orphan), have separated; it being agreed that the same terrain cannot support the large retinues of each with their multifarious households and their cattle and their flocks.

Abram generously lets Lot, for whom he is ever solicitous, have the first pick, and Lot chooses what he thinks is the richer portion: the fertile valley of the Jordan with its sophisticated (and soon to be doomed) towns of Sodom and Gomorrah.

Abram, after another message from Yahweh, moves to Hebron, an ancient city twenty miles south of Jerusalem, which at that time seems to have been called Salem. Abram sets up his camp among the sacred oak trees of Mamre.

In this story, Sarai's offering her husband her maid was not simply a gesture of personal and unusual altruism but the expected thing in Sumerian society, where an infertile wife must herself find her husband a suitable substitute for the bearing of children.

(Genesis 16:1-16)

ABRAM'S wife bore him no children, but she had a maidservant called Hagar, an Egyptian, and Sarai said to Abram, "Listen, the Lord has kept me from bearing, go therefore into my maid. Perhaps I can get children through her."

Abram heeded Sarai's suggestion, and so it was that after Abram had lived ten years in Canaan, his wife Sarai brought Hagar the Egyptian to him as a concubine. He entered Hagar and she conceived, but when she saw that she was pregnant she began to look down on her mistress. So Sarai spoke out to Abram, "This injustice done me is your fault. I myself gave my maid to your embrace, but as soon as she found she had conceived she began to despise me. The Lord judge between you and me."

"Look, your maid is in your own hands," Abram answered Sarai. "Do what you like with her."

Sarai then treated the girl so harshly that she ran away. The Lord's angel found her sitting by a spring in the desert—the spring on the way to Sur—and he asked her, "Hagar maid of Sarai, where have you come from and where are you going?"

"I am running away from my mistress Sarai," she replied.

"Go back to your mistress," the Lord's angel said, "and submit to her. I shall so multiply your progeny that none shall count them." Then the angel added, "You are now with child and you shall bear a son. You shall call him Ishmael because Yahweh has taken note of your abasement. He will be a wild colt of a man, his hand against everyone and everyone's hand against him. He will pitch his camps with no regard for his kinsmen."

Hagar gave this name to the Lord who had spoken: "Thou-the-God-of-Vision," saying; "Have I really seen him who sees me, and lived?" That is why the well is called Beer-lahai-roi ["The Well of the Living One Who Sees Me"] and it lies between Kadesh and Bered.

Hagar bore Abram a son and Abram called this son that Hagar bore him Ishmael ["God Hears"]. Abram was eighty-six years old when Hagar bore him Ishmael.

The Lord Promises a Son to Abraham and Sarah

Yahweh appeared to Abram once more, now in his hundreth year, and made an everlasting covenant with him in which he promised a mighty posterity to Abram and changed his name to Abraham, "Father of Multitudes." Abraham for his part was to accept Yahweh as the only God and the God of all his generations. Yahweh also insisted on the ritual of circumcision.

Circumcision was an ancient practice, already in use by the Egyptians and the people of Canaan, though not apparently by the inhabitants of Mesopotamia, whence Abraham stemmed. The rite involves cutting away the foreskin around the penis and was not followed absolutely by the Hebrews till the time of their exile in Babylon, when it became almost an emblem of suppressed nationalism.

The reasons for circumcision are lost in antiquity. Some scholars discount hygiene as a reason—for modern notions of cleanliness would have meant little to primitive man—and suggest that the ritual may have had overtones of magic, with designs on fertility.

(Genesis 17:15-25, 18:1-15)

ANOTHER thing God said to Abraham was: "As for Sarai your wife, you must not call her Sarai any more. Her name is to be Sarah ["Princess"]. I shall bless her and give you a son by her, and I shall bless him too. She is to be the mother of nations and out of her shall issue reigning kings."

Abraham threw himself on his face as God was speaking, and he laughed, thinking, "Is a man of a hundred going to make a baby, and the ninety-year-old Sarah bear a child?"

Then Abraham said to God, "All I ask is that Ishmael flourish."

"Be that as it may," God replied, "your wife Sarah is still going to bear a son, and you must call him Isaac ["laughter"]. I shall keep an everlasting pact with him and all his descendants. As for Ishmael—I heard you. I hereby bless him and shall make him fruitful and wonderfully numerous. Twelve princes shall come out of him and I shall make of him a great nation. Isaac, however, is the one with whom I shall establish my covenant and whom Sarah will bear you at this time next year."

At that, God ended his talk with Abraham and was gone.

That same day, Abraham took his son Ishmael and all his slaves whether houseborn or bought, every male in his household, and had the flesh of their foreskins cut away, as God had told him. Abraham was ninety-nine years old when he was circumcised, and his son Ishmael thirteen.

Not long afterward, the Lord God appeared to him by the oaks of Mamre as he was sitting at the entrance of his tent in the heat of the day. Looking up, he saw three men standing not far off and at the sight of them he ran to greet them. "My Lord," he said, bowing low to the ground, "if it please you, I beg you not to pass your servant by. Let a little water be fetched so that you can wash your feet, then rest yourselves under the tree. Meanwhile, let me bring you a morsel of bread so you may refresh yourselves before you go on."

"Thank you," they replied. "Do as you say."

Abraham hurried into the tent, calling to Sarah, "Quick, three measures of our best flour! Knead it and make rolls!"

Then he ran to the herd, picked out a prime, tender calf,

and gave it to the boy, who lost no time in preparing it. Then he took some curds and milk and, with the calf now ready, set these before them; he himself stood under the tree while they ate.

"Where is your wife Sarah?" they asked him. "Why, she is in the tent," he replied. Then one of them said, "Nine months from now when I come to you again, your wife Sarah will have a son."

Sarah was behind him, listening just inside the tent. Now Abraham and Sarah were old—ridden with age—and Sarah no longer had her womanly periods. So she laughed to herself, saying, "Am I, this ancient creature, about to succumb to passion with my ancient consort?"

Yahweh turned to Abraham and asked, "Why did Sarah laugh and say, 'Is this old me really going to have a baby?' Is anything too difficult for Yahweh? I shall be back when her time is come, and Sarah will have borne a son."

Sarah protested, pretending (for she was afraid), "But I did not laugh."

"Yes, you did," he answered.

Abraham Pleads for Sodom and Gomorrah

After the three visitors have finished their meal, they set out for Sodom. Abraham politely escorts them a little way, it having transpired that two of them are angels, and one indeed none other than Yahweh himself.

Yahweh lets the other two go on while he himself pauses in the gathering dusk in front of Abraham. Near them are the oaks of Mamre high up in the Hebron Hills overlooking the Dead Sea. Below them Sodom and the cities of the plain begin to sparkle with lights, and Yahweh asks himself whether he should take Abraham into his confidence and tell him that before sunrise he intends to reduce these lush towns to a heap of smoking ruins. He decides that since Abraham from now on is to be the channel of his large designs for mankind, he will tell him. Yahweh opens the conversation.

(Genesis 18:20-33)

"SODOM and Gomorrah are a disgrace. They are so deep in sin that I must go down to the plain and see for myself whether their behavior is as bad as the terrible rumors that have reached me. Then I shall know."

"Are you really going to obliterate the good with the bad?" asked Abraham, stepping forward. "What if there are fifty in the city who are good? Will you still level the place and not spare it for the sake of those fifty good? Surely you would not do such a thing: destroy the good with the bad? Far be it from you! Ought not the Judge of the World behave with justice?"

"Very well," Yahweh replied, "if I find just fifty good people in Sodom, I shall spare the whole place for their sake."

Abraham spoke up again, "What am I but dust and ashes, yet brazen enough to talk to God! Suppose there be five less than fifty good, would you stamp out the whole city despite those five less?"

"No," said Yahweh, "I would not destroy it if I found forty-five."

"But," persisted Abraham, "what if only forty are found there?"

"No, I will not do it if there are forty," he said.

Then Abraham went on, "Lord, do not be angry with me if I continue. What if only thirty are found there?"

"No, I will not do it if I find thirty," he answered.

"Here am I daring to tell God!" Abraham exclaimed. "What if there are no more than twenty?"

"All right, I will not destroy it for twenty," the Lord replied.

Still Abraham persisted: "Please do not be cross with me, Lord, if I speak once more. What if only ten be found there?"

"No," he answered, "even for only ten I will not bring down destruction."

Having finished his talk with Abraham, Yahweh departed, and Abraham went home.

Lot and His Daughters Escape from Sodom

From the many occasions when angels are mentioned in the Bible, one gets the impression that they appeared as good-looking young men—very different from the simpering creatures found in stained glass windows. Certainly the two angels in this story attracted the lust of the Sodomites.

As to the actual destruction of Sodom, what could it have been? There is no archeological evidence to guide us. An earthquake is possible. So is the strike of a meteorite. In any case, not only were Sodom and Gomorrah destroyed, but also the cities of Admah and Zeboim. There is no trace of any of them and we await reports of a lost civilization under the Dead Sea.

It is clear that the fiancés of Lot's two daughters were not saved, having refused to budge. The daughters' own extraordinary behavior toward their father later was not prompted by lust but by the paramount necessity of maintaining the family line when all the males around them had been destroyed. The girls were not only still unmarried, but they were virgins—as Lot expressly says when he offers them as bait to the Sodomites.

With regard to Lot's wife turning into a pillar of salt (with which the region is dotted), this is a metaphorical way of saying that when she hung back she was asphyxiated.

(Genesis 19:1-38)

LOT was sitting by the city gate of Sodom when two angels arrived there. As soon as he saw them he got up to greet them and, abasing himself to the ground, he said, "Turn aside, my lords, into this your servant's house and bathe your feet. Tomorrow you can make an early start."

"Thank you," they said, "but we shall put up in the public square."

He so urgently pressed them, however, that they turned aside and went into his house, where he prepared a meal for them of flat griddle cakes, which they ate.

They had not so much as lain down when the townspeople, the men of Sodom, young and old from every quarter, began to close in upon the house, clamoring to Lot, "Where are those men who came to you this evening? Bring them out to us. We want to get close to them."

Lot went out to this mob, shutting the door behind him. "Please, brothers," he begged, "don't be wicked. Listen, I have two daughters who have never been with a man. Let me bring them out to you and you can do what you like to them. Only do nothing bad to these men. Why, they have come here under the shelter of my roof."

"Stand back!" they shouted. "This fellow came here as a foreigner, and now just look at him: he wants to play the master. Well, we are going to give you an even harder time than we give them."

With that, they crowded in on Lot and advanced to break down the front door. But the men inside reached out, grabbed Lot, pulled him in, and slammed the door. And the people near the entrance of the house were struck with a light so blinding that they could not even find the door.

The men, who were angels, then asked Lot, "Have you anyone else at home? Sons, daughters, sons-in-law, or anybody who belongs to you in this city? Get them out of the place. We are going to destroy it because the outcry against everyone in it that has reached Yahweh has become so great that he has sent us to demolish it."

So Lot went and found his future sons-in-law and said, "Quick, leave this place, for Yahweh is about to destroy the city."

But the sons-in-law simply stared at him as if he were joking.

Dawn was breaking, and the angels urged Lot on. "Hurry," they said. "Remove your wife and your two daughters, or you will be wiped out in the city's punishment."

But Lot continued to dawdle, so the men seized him by the hand, his wife and daughter by the hand too, and propelled them into safety outside the city. Once they had been gotten outside, they were told, "Flee for your lives, and don't look back or halt anywhere on the plain. Escape to the hills or you will be annihilated."

"Please, my lords, not the hills!" Lot begged. "You have been so kind in saving my life, please indulge me in this too. I'll collapse and die if I have to go to the hills. Can't I just go to that village over there—it's such a tiny one—and be saved there? It's a mere nothing."

"Very well," one of the angels said. "I grant you this favor too. I won't destroy the town you mean. Only hurry to safety there, because I can do nothing till you arrive." (This is how the town got the name Zoar ["Littletown"].)

The sun was just rising over the world as Lot entered Zoar, and Yahweh began to rain down fire and brimstone on Sodom and Gomorrah—right out of the Lord's own skies. He annihilated those cities and the whole plain, together with all their inhabitants and all plant life. But Lot's wife, who was behind him, hung back and was turned into a pillar of salt.

Early that morning, Abraham hurried to the spot where he had stood before Yahweh, and gazing down toward Sodom and Gomorrah along the entire stretch of plain, all he could see were plumes of smoke rising from the earth as from a furnace.

This was the manner in which God was mindful of Abraham when he destroyed the cities of the plain and leveled the very town in which Lot lived, yet saved Lot from the center of the disaster.

Lot left Zoar with his two daughters and settled in the hills because he was afraid to stay in Zoar. So he lived with his two daughters in a cave.

That was when the elder said to the younger, "Our father is getting old and there's not a man in the land for us to marry in the normal way. Come, let us ply our father with wine, then sleep with him, and so make life with our father's seed."

That night they plied their father with wine. Then the elder girl went in and lay with her father, who was unaware of her lying down or getting up. Next morning, the elder said to the younger, "Listen, it was my turn last night to sleep with Father. Let's fill him with wine again tonight, then you can sleep with him and make life through Father's seed."

So they plied their father with wine that night too, and the younger went in and lay with him, without his being aware of her lying down or getting up. That is how both Lot's daughters became pregnant by their father.

The elder gave birth to a son whom she called Moab ["From Father"], and he is the father of today's Moabites. The younger also gave birth to a son, whom she called Ben-Ammi ["Son of My Kin"], and he is the father of today's Ammonites.

The Sacrifice of Isaac

In this strange and vividly disturbing story, in which Abraham, in spite of his unspeakable ordeal, is ready to plunge the sacrificial knife into his adored son, one must remember that he was living in a land, Canaan, where the firstborn son was indeed sometimes sacrificed to deity. We have no way of telling to what extent Abraham was influenced by religions around him.

The Bible, however, wants to make one supreme point. If the divine purpose for humanity through the long and arduous ups and downs of the coming centuries is to be sustained, it can only be if a note of absolute and sublime faith is struck right from the beginning.

There is also perhaps a secondary message to Abraham and his descendants from Yahweh: "You who are the spearhead of my design for mankind must know that from now on human sacrifice is taboo."

The Anchor Bible delicately sets the scene:

> As father and son go off by themselves on the last stage of that melancholy pilgrimage—the boy burdened with the wood for his own sacrificial pyre, and the father fidgeting with the flint and the cleaver—the unwary victim asks but a single question. The father's answer is tender but evasive, and the boy must by now have sensed the truth. The short and simple sentence, "And the two of them walked on together," covers what is perhaps the most poignant and eloquent sentence in all literature.

(Genesis 22:1-13)

SOME time afterward, God put Abraham to the test. "Abraham," he called.

"Yes, I am here."

"Take your son, the very much loved one whom you so adore—yes, Isaac—and go to the land of Moriah and there offer him up as a burnt sacrifice on a hill that I shall designate."

Early next morning Abraham saddled his ass, split wood for the burnt offering, and set off with two young servants and with his son Isaac for the place that God had indicated to him.

On the third day Abraham sighted the spot a long way off, and he said to his young men, "You stay here with the ass while the boy and I go over there to pray, then we'll come back to you."

Abraham took the wood for the burnt offering and laid it on his son Isaac, while in his own hands he carried the flint-and-tinder and the knife. As the two of them walked on together, Isaac broke the silence and said to his father Abraham, "Father."

"Yes, my son."

"You have the flint-and-tinder and the wood, but where is the sheep for the burnt offering?"

"God will provide a sheep for the sacrifice, my son," Abraham replied. And the two of them walked on together.

When they came to the place that God had indicated, Abraham built an altar there and set out the wood on top of it. Then he bound up Isaac his son and laid him on the wood over the altar. Abraham took the knife and lifted his hand to slay his son, but the Lord's angel shouted to him from heaven, "Abraham, Abraham!"

"Yes, I am here," he answered.

"Do not lay a hand on the boy, or do a thing to him. Now I know the depth of your devotion to God, since you would not withhold from me your own very much loved son."

Abraham looked around and he saw a ram snarled by its horns in a thicket. He went and took the ram and sacrificed it as a burnt offering instead of his son.

Finding Isaac a Wife

Sarah has died at the age of a hundred and twenty-seven at Hebron, to where the family seems to have gone back. Abraham "mourns and weeps for her" and buries her in a cave by a field which he has specially bought for the purpose and where he, Isaac, Rebecca, Leah (her sister), and finally Jacob will all be buried in time. In spite of his great age, Abraham marries again and sires six more children; though it is not clear how many years before his own death this was, or whether all this happened a long time before the events of the present story. In any case, Isaac is now forty years old and it is high time that he be married.

As in most early societies, it was the duty of the father to procure a wife for his son. In Hagar's case we saw that because she and her son were separated from Abraham, she had to find a wife for Ishmael on her own. We shall see when we come to Samson that he made the first move, but even so it was up to his father to arrange the marriage.

Abraham, now a hundred and seventy-five years old or thereabouts, and fearful that Isaac might marry a Canaanite girl, charges his most senior and responsible servant to make the month-long journey into Mesopotamia, where Abraham was born and where his brother Nahor's family still lives, to find a bride for Isaac. When the old retainer returns, Abraham will be dead.

The story opens with Abraham about to make the old servant swear that he will not let Isaac marry a local Canaanite girl, but must bring back a bride from among his relatives in Mesopotamia. (Marriages with close relatives were common.) The servant responds with a pertinent question.

(Genesis 24:5-67)

"BUT what if the woman does not want to follow me back to this land? Am I then to return your son to the country from which you came?"

"On no account return my son back there," Abraham replied. "The Lord God of heaven, who took me from my father's house and the land of my birth, made me a solemn promise and declared, 'I shall give this land [of Canaan] to your descendants,' so he will send his angel before you and he will find you a bride there for my son. If the girl refuses to follow you, you are released from your oath to me, but on no account must you take my son back there."

The servant placed his hand under his master's thigh and swore the oath to him in this affair. Then with ten of his master's camels, laden with all kinds of presents from his master, the servant made his way to the town in Mesopotamia where Nahor's family lived.

He arrived there one day toward evening, at a time when the women come to draw water, and he made the camels kneel down by a well outside the city.

"O Yahweh, God of my master Abraham," he prayed, "give me a good omen today and be gracious to my master Abraham. As I stand here at this spring and the girls of the town come out to draw water, if I say to a young woman: 'Please lower your pitcher so that I can have a drink,' and she answers: 'Drink, and I'll water your camels too,' let her be the one you have chosen for your servant Isaac. Please let that be the way I know you have been gracious to my master."

Hardly had he finished his prayer when out came Rebecca with a pitcher on her shoulder. She was the daughter of Bethuel son of Milcah, the wife of Abraham's brother Nahor [so the grandniece of Abraham].

She was a lovely young woman, a virgin untouched by man. She went down to the spring, filled her pitcher, and was just returning when the servant ran over to her, exclaiming, "Could you spare me a sip of water from your pitcher, please?"

"Drink, sir," she answered, immediately lowering the pitcher into her hands to let him drink. When she had finished giving him a drink, she said, "I'll draw water for your camels too and let them drink their fill."

She at once emptied her pitcher into the trough and ran back to the well to draw more until she had given water to all the camels.

During this time the man stood staring, waiting with bated breath to know for certain whether or not Yahweh had made his mission a success. When the camels had finished drinking, the man took out a gold nose ring weighing half a shekel and two gold bangles weighing ten shekels for her arms.

"Tell me, please, whose daughter you are?" he asked. "And is there room for us in your master's house to spend the night?"

"I am the daughter of Bethuel son of Milcah, Nahor's wife," she said. Then she added: "We have plenty of straw and fodder and, yes, there is room for you to spend the night."

The man bowed his head in thanks to Yahweh. "May the Lord be blessed," he murmured, "God of my master Abraham, whose kindness to my master never ceases. Yahweh has led me straight to the house of my master's brother!"

Now Rebecca's brother's name was Laban, and Laban, as soon as he saw the nose-ring and the bangles on his sister's wrists, and had heard his sister say: "So-and-so did the man say to me," he ran out to the well to meet him. He found him still standing by the camels near the spring.

"O blessed of Yahweh, do come in!" he said. "Why stay outside when I have a house ready and a place for the camels?"

So the man went into the house. The camels were unloaded and given straw and fodder. Water was brought for him and his men to wash their feet. But when a meal was set before him, he said, "No, I'll not eat till I have told my tale."

"Tell it," they said.

"I am Abraham's servant," he began. "Yahweh has heaped blessings on my master and made him prosper. He has given him sheep and cattle, men and women slaves, camels and asses. My master's wife Sarah in her old age bore my master a son, to whom he has given everything. Then my master put me under oath and told me, 'You are not to get my son a wife from any of the women of Canaan, in whose land I dwell, but you are to go to my father's family, my own kin, and choose a wife for my son there.'

" 'Master,' I responded, 'suppose the woman won't follow me?'

"He answered, 'The Lord God in whose ways I have walked will send his angel along with you and make your journey a success, and you will find a wife for my son from my own kith and kin.'

"Now today, when I came to the spring, I said, 'O Yahweh, God of my master Abraham, bless the outcome of my mission! As I stand here at this spring, if I say to a young woman who comes to draw water, "Please give me a little water from your pitcher," and she says to me, "Yes, not only for you to drink but I'll draw for your camels too . . ." let her be the one Yahweh has reserved for my master's son.'

"Hardly had I framed the words in my thoughts when Rebecca walked out with a pitcher on her shoulder, and she went down to the well and drew some water.

" 'Give me a drink, please,' I said to her.

"At once she lowered her pitcher and replied, 'Do drink. And I'll give your camels some too.'

"So I drank and she watered the camels.

" 'Whose daughter are you?' I asked her.

" 'The daughter of Bethuel son of Nahor and Milcah,' she said.

"Then I gave her the ring for her nose and put the bangles on her arms, and I bowed my head to Yahweh in praise and thanks to the Lord God of my master Abraham who had led me in a straight path to the daughter of my master's nephew as a bride for his son. So now, please, if you mean to do the true and loyal thing by my master, tell me, or if not, tell me, so that I can stay or go."

Laban, answering for Bethuel [who is presumed deceased], replied, "This proceeds from the Lord. It is not for us to say yes or no. Rebecca is at your disposal. Take her along with you and let her be wedded to your master's son as Yahweh has determined."

On hearing their decision, Abraham's servant bowed low to the ground before Yahweh. Then he brought out jewelry of silver and gold, and fine apparel, presenting these to Rebecca. He gave valuable gifts also to her brother and her mother. Then he and the men with him ate and drank, and they stayed the night.

As soon as they had arisen next morning, he said, "Allow me to go back now to my master."

"We would rather the girl stayed another ten days or so with us," they replied. "After that, of course, go."

"Please don't try to keep me," he said. "The Lord has blessed my errand, so let me go back at once to my master."

"We'll call the girl," they said, "and ask her what she herself wants."

So they called Rebecca and asked her, "Will you go with this man?"

"I will," she said.

"So they [Laban and the rest of the family] sent their sister Rebecca on her way with her nurse and Abraham's servant and his men.

Giving their blessing to her, they said:

> Sister of ours, may you increase
> A thousand times ten thousandfold
> And may all your progeny triumph
> Over the gates of your enemies.

Forthwith, Rebecca and her maids mounted the camels and followed the man. Thus did the servant acquire Rebecca and depart.

Isaac, meanwhile, had returned from the desert neighborhood of Beer-lahai-roi, having settled in the region of the Negeb. And as he was walking in the fields one evening, he sighted camels approaching.

Rebecca's eyes fell on Isaac and she dismounted from her camel, asking the servant, "Who is the man walking through the field toward us?"

"That is my master," said the servant.

At which she covered herself with her veil.

The servant unfolded to Isaac all of his transaction. Then Isaac led Rebecca to his mother's tent, and she was wed and became his wife. His love for her became a comfort after the loss of his mother.

NOTE

The curious gesture of the servant's putting a hand under Abraham's thigh when he swore the oath is a euphemism for touching the testicles. The punishment for breaking such an oath originally implied the death of one's offspring or of one's dying childless. The memory of this is preserved in the word "testimony."

Jacob and Esau

As already stated, Abraham had died by the time his trusted servant returned with Rebecca. The provisions he made for his offspring were generous. He bequeathed everything to Isaac but gave handsome presents to the sons of his concubines, sending them eastward so as not to compete with Isaac.

Isaac's marriage to Rebecca, though idyllic, had thus far failed in one essential aspect: Rebecca was childless. However, after twenty years and fervent entreaties from Isaac to Yahweh, Rebecca conceived twins: sons that were destined to contend through history—Esau to become the ancestor of the Edomites, and Jacob of the Israelites.

Once again the Bible appears to be following its method of mythologizing history. The Edomites and the Israelites did indeed compete through the centuries for the promised land of Canaan. The Edomites were within reach of it first (the elder brother), but by the time of King David, the Israelites (the younger brother) had ousted them and held them in subjection.

Many of the details of this saga reflect ancient customs in the Hurrian society of Sumeria and Mesopotamia whence the Patriarchs stemmed, and have been verified in ancient documents discovered in the Hurrian site of Nuzi (modern Iraq).

The story opens with Rebecca finding herself pregnant.

(Genesis 25:22-24, 27:1-45)

BUT the babies jostled so much inside her that she cried out: "If it's to be like this, is life worth living?" At last, she went to consult Yahweh and Yahweh said to her:

> Two nations are in your womb.
> Two peoples are contending in your bosom.
> One will overcome the other
> and the elder serve the younger.

Sure enough, when she was delivered, there were twins in her womb. The first came out ruddy all over, mantled in hair, so they called him Esau. Next came his brother, holding on to Esau's heel, so they called him Jacob. Isaac was sixty years old when they were born.

The boys grew up: Esau a wily hunter, and Jacob a retiring man who kept to the tents. Isaac's favorite was Esau, but Rebecca favored Jacob.

One day when Jacob was cooking a stew, Esau came in from the field faint with hunger, and he said to Jacob, "Give me a mouthful of that red stuff (which got him the nickname "Edom"): I'm starving."

"First trade me your birthright for it," Jacob responded.

"I'm dying," Esau replied, "what good is a birthright?"

"Swear to me first," said Jacob.

So he swore, surrendering his birthright to Jacob. Then Jacob gave Esau bread and some lentil stew. He ate and drank and went his way, setting no more value than that on his birthright.

In time, when Isaac grew old and his eyes dimmed, he called for Esau his eldest son and said:

"My son."

"Here, sir."

"You see how old I am and there's no telling when I may die. Go into the wild with your gear and hunt me some venison. Then prepare me my favorite festive dish and bring it to me to eat so that I can bless you with my very particular blessing before I die."

Rebecca overheard what Isaac said to his son Esau, and as soon as Esau had left for the wild to hunt venison for his father, she said to her son Jacob, "Listen, I have just heard your father say to Esau, 'Fetch me some venison and make me a special dinner so that when I have eaten it I can give you my blessing, endorsed by the Lord, before I die.' Now, my son, pay attention to what I tell you. Go to the flock and bring me two choice kids. I shall prepare them in your father's favorite festive dish, which you can take to him and get him to bless you before he dies."

"But my brother Esau is a hairy man and I am smooth," Jacob said to his mother. "What if my father feels me? He will think I am making a fool of him and I shall bring down a curse on me, not a blessing."

"I'll take care of the curse," his mother replied. "Just listen to what I say and go and get them."

He went, picked them out, and brought them to his mother. She prepared the special dish his father was fond of. Then Rebecca took out some of Esau's best clothes, which she had in the house, and put them on Jacob her youngest son, covering his hands and the smooth of his neck with the kid skins. Then she put in his hands the special dish and the bread she had prepared, and he went in to his father.

"Father," he said.

"Yes, which son are you?"

"I am Esau your eldest. I did what you told me. So sit up, sir, please, and have some of my venison, then you can give me your very particular blessing."

"But how did you come upon it so quickly, my son?" Isaac asked.

"Yahweh your God put it in my way," he answered.

Then Isaac said to Jacob, "Come closer, my son. I want to feel you and see whether you really are my son Esau or not."

Jacob came up to his father Isaac, who felt him and said, "The voice is the voice of Jacob, but the hands are the hands of Esau."

He did not detect him because of his hairy hands like his brother Esau's. Before he blessed him, however, he asked again, "Are you really my son Esau?"

"Yes, I am," Jacob replied.

"Then put the dish down by me," he said, "and let me eat my son's venison and afterward give you my very particular blessing."

So he served it to him and he ate. Then he brought him wine and he drank. Then his father Isaac said to him, "Come closer, my son, and kiss me."

Jacob went up to him and kissed him, and at last when he got a whiff of his son's clothes, he blessed him, saying:

Ah! the scent of my son
Is like the scent of a field
Which Yahweh has blessed.
God give you the dew of heaven
And a fruitful earth
Rich with grain and wine.
Let peoples serve you
And nations bow before you.
Be you master of your brothers
And let your mother's sons
Bow down to you.
Cursed be they that curse you
And blessed be they that bless you.

Hardly had Isaac finished blessing Jacob and Jacob left his father's side, when in from the hunt came Esau. He too prepared a special dish and brought it to his father.

"Rouse yourself, Father," he said, "and enjoy your son's venison, then you can bless me with your very particular blessing."

"But who are you?" his father Isaac asked.

"Your son Esau, of course, your firstborn."

At which Isaac came all over trembling.

"'Who was it then that brought me game fresh from the hunt? I have only just finished eating before you came, and I blessed him . . . and . . . oh . . . he shall be blessed."

On hearing his father's words Esau let out a great, heart-rending sob.

"Bless me too, Father," he cried.

"Alas," Isaac said, "your brother came slyly and has gone off with your blessing."

"Is that why they called him Jacob?" Esau said. "Must he cheat me a second time? First he took my birthright from me, and now he has filched my blessing. Have you no blessing left for me?"

"I have made him your master," Isaac answered. "And all your clan I have given to serve him. I have pledged him grain and wine. What is there left that I could do for you, my son?"

"Have you only one blessing, Father?" Esau begged. "Bless me too, oh my Father!"

Isaac was stung into silence and Esau broke into sobs.

Then Isaac brought himself to say:

Though far from the fatness of the earth your home lie
And far from the dew of heaven above,
And though by your sword you shall live

And be in servitude to your brother,
A day will come
When you toss his yoke from off your neck.

Esau could not forgive his brother Jacob because his father had blessed him specially, and Esau said in his heart, "When the time of mourning my father is over, I am going to kill my brother Jacob."

When this resolution of Esau her elder son became known to Rebecca, she sent for Jacob her younger and said, "'Listen, your brother hopes to make things even by killing you, so I beg you to follow my advice. Take refuge at once with my brother Laban in Haran. Stay with him awhile till your brother's anger cools and he forgets what you did to him. Then I will send for you and have you back. Why should I lose the two of you in a single day?"

NOTES

1. The words "Edom," "Esau," "Jacob," are all plays on words in the Hebrew, suggesting (rather than always meaning): Edom, "red"; Jacob, "heel-grabber" and also "cheater"; Esau, "hairy."
2. The birthright blessing or *herukah* brought with it the full inheritance. Though it was irrevocable and belonged to the eldest son, a father could bestow it on another son.

Jacob's Dream

Jacob takes to heart his mother's plea and makes the five-hundred-mile trek from Beersheba in Canaan across the Jordan, over the mountains, then down into the great eastern desert, and on toward the city of Haran in Mesopotamia, where his uncle Laban lives.

His father Isaac has also charged him not to marry a Canaanite woman but to look for a wife among his cousins, his mother's nieces.

The place where he has his dream, which he names "Bethel" (meaning "House of God"), is about fifty miles northeast of Beersheba and eleven miles north of Jerusalem.

Jacob's "ladder" up and down which the angels went was almost certainly the stairway of a ziggurat, on top of which the deity dwelt and sacrifices were offered.

The stone he set up as a pillar (having used it as a pillow) fits well into the context of the Middle Bronze Age, when such stones had a ritual significance and can be found to this day all over Palestine. Jacob set up his stone as a memorial, a pledge and symbol of God's presence. In this early stage of the concept of deity, Jacob's sense of religion was probably not all that different from that of the surrounding pagans. Indeed, later, the Israelites came to frown on such memorial pillars as perilously close to idolatry.

(Genesis 28:10-19)

JACOB set out from Beersheba and made for Haran. At sunset he stopped for the night and, putting a stone under his head, lay down to sleep. He had a dream.

A stairway led from the ground right up into the sky, and going up and down this stairway, amazingly, were angels of God. And Yahweh was there standing beside him, saying, "The ground you lie on is ground I am giving you—you and your descendants, who shall be like the dust of the earth, spreading west and east, north and south. In you and your offspring all the nations of the earth shall be blessed. And I am with you wherever you are, and shall protect you wherever you go and bring you back to this land. I will never forsake you till I have done all this that I promise."

Jacob woke up from his sleep, crying out, "The Lord lives in this place and I never knew it." Shocked to the core, he exclaimed, "How awesome is this place! None other than God's own home and the gate of heaven."

Next morning as soon as he was up he took the stone which he had put under his head and set it up as a pillar, pouring oil over the top of it.

He named the place Bethel ["the Lord's Place"].

The Meeting of Jacob and Esau

Jacob has married his cousin Rachel, "earning" her from his uncle Laban in return for seven years' work on Laban's land. At least, it should have been seven years, but Laban tricks him into consummating his marriage not with Rachel but with her elder and less beautiful sister, Leah, and then extracts another seven years of labor out of Jacob for Rachel.

Rachel at first is barren and Jacob fathers six sons and one daughter (Dinah) by Leah, as well as two sons by Rachel's maid Bilah and two sons by Leah's maid Zilpath. All this activity on her husband's part prods Rachel into fertility and she bears him a son whom she names Joseph. (Many years later, after Jacob's return to Canaan, she is to bear him a second son and call him Benjamin.)

The twelve sons of Jacob become the ancestors and eponyms of the twelve tribes of Israel.

After serving Laban for twenty years and building up his uncle's and his own livestock into impressive herds, Jacob breaks away from the crafty and mean-minded Laban, and taking Rachel, Leah, his eleven children, and his considerable flocks and droves, travels toward the land of Edom. He is full of apprehension, knowing that he must pass by his estranged brother Esau's territory southeast of the Jordan.

(Genesis 32:4-33, 33:1-11)

Jacob dispatched messengers ahead of him to his brother Esau in the region of Seir, the land of Edom, with this message: "To my lord Esau from his servant Jacob: I have been living with Laban and remained there till now. I own oxen and asses and sheep, menservants and maidservants, and I send this news hoping for your gracious favor."

The messengers returned to Jacob, saying, "We reached your brother Esau, and he himself is coming to meet you with a retinue of four hundred men."

Jacob in a panic divided his people (together with the flocks, cattle, and camels) into two camps, reckoning, "If Esau advances on one camp and attacks, at least the other will be saved."

Then he made this prayer.

"O God of my father Abraham, and God of my father Isaac, the very Yahweh who told me: 'Go back to your native land and I will look after you,' I am not worth the smallest of your mercies and the constant care you have lavished on your servant. I crossed the Jordan [and left home] with nothing more than my staff, and now look at me with my two divisions. . . . Save me, I beg you, from the hands of my brother Esau, for I am afraid he is coming to kill me and the mothers with their little ones. Remember, it was you who pledged: 'I shall look after you and make your progeny as uncountable as the sands of the sea.' "

After passing the night there, Jacob selected a present for his brother Esau from the stock he had with him:

two hundred she-goats
twenty he-goats
two hundred ewes
twenty rams
thirty milking camels with their calves
forty cows
ten bulls
twenty she-asses
ten he-asses

These he committed to the charge of his servants, keeping each drove separate, and he told them: "Go on ahead of me and leave a gap between each drove." Then he gave these instructions to the lead men: "If my brother Esau meets you and asks, 'To whom do you belong? Where are you going, and whose beasts are these you are driving before you?' you are to say, 'They belong to your servant Jacob and are sent as a present to my lord Esau. And Jacob is just behind us.' "

To the first, second, and third contingent, and to all the rest following their droves, he gave the same message for Esau. "And always add," he told them: " 'your servant Jacob is just behind us.' " His hope was that: "If I disarm him first with gifts that go ahead of me, he may forgive me when we come face to face."

So the presents went ahead of him, while he himself remained in the camp that night. During the night, however, he got up, took his two wives, their two maidservants, and his eleven children, and forded the Jabbok, marshaling them across the stream and then sending over all his possessions.

Now Jacob was left on his own, and a certain Man wrestled with him till daybreak. When this Man found that he could not throw Jacob, he struck him on the hip during the tussle, dislocating his hip.

"Let me go," the Man said. "Dawn has broken."

"I will not let you go till you bless me," Jacob answered.

"What is your name?" asked the other.

"Jacob," he said.

"You are to be called Jacob no longer, but Israel ["God-strong"] because you have striven like a champion with God and with men."

Jacob asked him, "What is your name, please?"

"You must not ask my name," he replied. Then on that

very spot he blessed him farewell. Jacob called the place Peniel ["the Face of God"], meaning "Where I came face to face with deity and lived."

The sun rose as he left Peniel, limping because of his hip. As he gazed out, whom should he see approaching but Esau, accompanied by four hundred men. So he divided the children among Leah, Rachel, and the two maidservants, putting the maids and their children first, then Leah and her children, and last of all Rachel with Joseph. He himself walked in front, bowing to the ground seven times before he reached his brother.

But Esau ran out to meet him, embraced him, fell on his neck, and kissed him. And they wept.

Looking up and seeing the women and children, he asked, "Who are these with you?"

"The children God has been good enough to give your servant," Jacob answered.

At that the maids stepped forward with their children, bowing low. Next came Leah with her children, bowing low. Lastly, Rachel and Joseph came and they bowed low.

Esau asked, "What is the meaning of all those droves I passed?"

"To win your favor, my lord," Jacob answered.

"I have all I need, my brother," Esau said. "Keep them for yourself."

"No, please," Jacob insisted, "do me the favor of accepting this present from me. Seeing you was like having to face God, yet you received me kindly. So please take them—this my act of bounty—for God has been good to me and I have plenty."

He so pressed Esau that he accepted.

NOTES

1. The Jabbok is a tributary that joins the Jordan twenty-five miles north of the Dead Sea.

2. The mysterious wrestling with an angel creates many problems. It may be a mythologizing of a man-to-man combat arranged between Jacob and Esau to avoid out-and-out war. Or it may be the remnant of an older story in which a river god figures.

3. The Anchor Bible notes that Jacob's change of name to Israel ("god-strong") is a symbolic way of saying that the once devious man, the cheater, is now to be a straightforward and stalwart champion.

The Rape of Dinah

Jacob does not follow Esau as the latter suggests, at least he only begins to, then changes course and finally, with his huge retinue of women, children, servants, flocks, and all he possesses, enters the land of Canaan and sets up his camp outside the city of Sechem on ground which he has bought from the ruling family.

Sechem is some thirty miles north of Jerusalem and more than a hundred north of Seir, where his brother is. The town played an important part, both politically and religiously, all through biblical history.

The horror story that follows takes place several years after the Jacob-Esau meeting, because Jacob's sons are now obviously young men and Dinah herself nubile. The whole account may well be another piece of mythologized history. Isaac Asimov in his *Guide to the Bible* suggests that three tribes joined forces in attacking central Canaan sometime before all Israel conquered the land. Dinah's tribe was virtually wiped out in the assault and was then avenged by the tribes of Simeon and Levi.

(Genesis 34:1-31)

WHEN Dinah, Jacob's daughter by Leah, went out visiting some of the women of the region, Sechem the son of Hamor the Hivite saw her, took her, and lay with her by force. But his lust for Dinah, Jacob's daughter, turned to love and he did everything he could to win her affection. And he also said to Hamor his father, "Get me this girl for my wife."

When Jacob learnt that Sechem had deflowered Dinah his daughter, his sons were in the fields with the stock, so he did nothing about it till they came home; and when they heard what had happened, they were horrified and very angry. Sechem's violation of Jacob's daughter was, to Israel, an outrage—a crime not to be borne.

But Hamor reasoned with them, saying, "My son has set his heart on your daughter. I beg you to give her to him in marriage. Intermarry with us. Give your daughters to us, and you take ours. Live among us and the land will be at your disposal. You can dwell and trade and hold property here."

Sechem too addressed Dinah's father and brothers. "Accept me," he said, "and I shall pay whatever you ask. Demand whatever dowry you like and I shall pay it. Only give me the girl to marry."

Jacob's sons, laying a trap—to avenge the violation of their sister—replied, "That we cannot do. We cannot commit our sister to an uncircumcised man. For us that would be a disgrace. On one condition only will we comply with you: that you consent to be like us and have every male among you circumcised. Then we can give you our daughters and take yours, settling among you and becoming one people. But if you do not agree to be circumcised, we shall take our daughter and go."

Their proposal seemed agreeable to Hamor and his son Sechem. The young man was so much in love with Jacob's daughter that he lost no time in acting on their request.

Hamor and his son Sechem went before the city council and said to their fellow citizens, "These men are friendly. Let them settle in our land and trade here. Certainly there is room for them. We can take their daughters in marriage and give them ours. These men, however, will agree to stay with us and become one family only on condition that every male among us is circumcised as they are. Wouldn't their cattle then, their property, and all their animals be as good as ours? So let's yield to them and have them live with us."

Since Sechem was more esteemed than anyone of his father's house, their fellow citizens were persuaded by Hamor and his son Sechem, and every male—every able-bodied man—was circumcised.

Then on the third day, when they were still sore, two of Jacob's sons, Simeon and Levi, brothers of Dinah, took their swords, walked boldly into the city, and began slaying all the males. They put Hamor and his son Sechem to the sword, took Dinah from Sechem's house, and left. Then the rest of Jacob's sons went out, finished off those languishing, and sacked the city; all because Dinah had been defiled. They seized their sheep, their cattle, their asses—whatever was in the city or in the fields—all their wealth. They carried off their children and their women, and looted what was in the houses.

Jacob protested to Simeon and Levi, "You have brought trouble on me and made my name a stench among the people of this country, the Canaanites and Perizzites. I am outnumbered. If they should move against me and attack, I and my house are wiped out."

But they retorted, "Should our sister have been treated like a whore?"

The Selling of Joseph

We are moving steadily from the primordial narrative of early Genesis to the far more historical territory of the Middle Bronze Age. Already in the Abraham saga when we came to Jacob, the mythologizing of history began to yield to a verifiable background; and now with Joseph, the narrative, while still making a mythological point, moves convincingly in the direction of historical realism and beautifully unfolded human drama.

The mythological, or perhaps metaphysical, point which the Bible wants to make in the various episodes of the Joseph story prepares the way for the most focal lesson in all of Exodus, which is that mankind is way off track when it presumes to judge what is good and what is evil. There is no evil out of which God does not bring good, and there is no good, purely in man's esteem, which may not be fraught with the most evil consequences. The point will be made again and again in the Joseph story and all the way through the vicissitudes of Exodus.

Isaac at the age of one hundred and eighty has died at Mamre in the hills of Hebron, attended by his sons Esau and Jacob, who also bury him.

Rachel, too, has died, just after bearing her second son, whom Jacob names Benjamin ("Son of the Right Hand," i.e., joyous), who becomes at once the apple of his father's eye.

Joseph, Rachel's other son, is now a lad of seventeen: a thoughtful but overconfident young man, a little spoilt perhaps by his father's doting, and at the beginning at least, unbelievably tactless.

Jacob has resettled with all twelve sons in Canaan, in the Hebron valley, where Joseph assists his halfbrothers in tending their father's flocks and hardly endears himself to them by bringing home tales of these young men's behavior.

The "coat of many colors" was a long tunic with sleeves, reaching below the knees. Such a garment was a mark of distinction.

The names Midianite and Ishmaelite seem to be used interchangeably. Probably two different accounts have been combined.

(Genesis 37:3-36)

NOW, Jacob loved Joseph more than any of his sons because he was the child of his old age. He made him a coat of many colors, but when his brothers saw that their father loved him more than any of them, they came to hate him and could hardly say a kind word to him.

Once Joseph had a dream and told it to his brothers, and this made them hate him all the more. He said to them, "Listen to the dream I had. We were binding sheaves in the field when all at once my sheaf stood up and remained erect while your sheaves gathered around it bowing."

"Do you mean," his brothers retorted, "that you are going to lord it over us—*you* be our master?"

They hated him all the more because of his boasting of his dreams.

Then he dreamed another dream and told his brothers, "You know, I've had another dream. And what do you think, the sun and the moon and the eleven stars bowed down before me!"

When he told this to his father, Jacob rebuked him. "What is this dream you have had?" he said. "Am I and your mother and your brothers going to bow ourselves double before you?"

Though his brothers were jealous, his father gave the matter thought.

One day when his brothers had gone to graze their father's flocks at Sechem, Jacob said to Joseph, "Listen, your brothers are pasturing the flocks at Sechem. Well, I want you to go to them."

"I am ready," he answered.

"Then go and see if everything is all right with your brothers and the flocks, and come and tell me."

He dispatched him from the valley of Hebron and Joseph came to Sechem. A man found him wandering in a field and asked him, "What are you looking for?"

"I am looking for my brothers," he said. "Could you tell me where they are grazing the flocks?"

"They left here," the man said. "I heard them say, 'Let's move on to Dothan.' "

So Joseph went after his brothers and came upon them in Dothan.

When they saw him in the distance, they began plotting to kill him. "Look," they said, "here the dreamer comes. Let us kill him and throw him into a pit. We'll say that a wild beast devoured him. Then we shall see what his dreams are made of."

When Reuben heard this he tried to save him from them and said: "We must not kill him. We must not shed blood. . . . Throw him into that cistern over there in the desert, but don't hurt him yourselves."

His idea was to get him out of their clutches and restore him to his father.

When Joseph reached his brothers, they stripped him of his tunic—the coat-of-many-colors he was wearing—and flung him into the cistern, which had no water in it. Then they sat down to eat, but, looking up, they saw a caravan of Ishmaelites coming from Gilead on their way to Egypt, the camels laden with incense, spices, and resin. At which Judah said to his brothers, "What do we gain by murdering our brother and concealing his blood. Why not sell him to the Ishmaelites, but not do anything to him ourselves? After all, he is our brother and our flesh."

His brothers agreed, and when the Midianite merchants passed by, they hauled him out of the cistern and sold him to them for twenty pieces of silver, and so Joseph was taken to Egypt.

When Reuben went back to the cistern and saw no Joseph in it, he rent his clothes and returned to his brothers, exclaiming, "The boy is not there. Where in the world can I turn?"

The others took Joseph's tunic, slaughtered a kid, and dipped the tunic in its blood. Then they arranged for the tunic—the coat-of-many-colors—to be taken to their father, with the message: "See whether this be your son's tunic or not."

Jacob recognized it, crying out, "Oh, it is my son's tunic. A wild beast has devoured him. Joseph has been torn to pieces."

Jacob rent his clothes and girded himself in sackcloth. He mourned his son for many days. All his other sons and daughters tried to comfort him, but he would not be comforted. "No," he said, "I shall go down into the next life mourning my son." And his father wept for him.

Meanwhile the Midianites sold Joseph in Egypt to Potiphar, one of Pharaoh's officers, his captain of the guard.

Joseph and Potiphar's Wife

The Book of Genesis does not tell us about Joseph's long southward journey with the Midianites (or Ishmaelites) through the barren tracts of the desert of Sur into Egypt.

The young boy, used to sheep and living in tents, must have been overwhelmed by the grandeur and opulence of Egypt. The date is roughly 1650 B.C. and the pyramids are already a thousand years old. The Nile was then, as it is now, a great ribbon of fertility running through an arid land and thronged on either side by the cities and people that depended on it.

Joseph was probably taken to Memphis, Pharaoh's capital in Lower Egypt at the head of the Nile delta—just after the Nile fans out and irrigates, in its annual flooding, the tracts of land enriched with its silt.

And now some years have elapsed, and Joseph is about twenty-eight years old. He has been extremely successful and become his master Potiphar's right-hand man, in complete charge not only of his household but of all his possessions.

(Genesis 39:7-23)

NOW Joseph was well set up and good-looking, and after a time his master's wife cast her eyes longingly at him. "Sleep with me," she said. He refused. "Look," he told her, "with me here my master is free of every care in this house. He has put everything he owns in my hands and exercises no more authority than I do. He has withheld from me only yourself because you are his wife. How can I, then, commit such an outrage, such a sin against God?"

Day after day she importuned him, but he would not listen to her, either to sleep with her or be with her. One day, however, when Joseph had gone into the house to do his duties and none of the house servants was at hand, she caught hold of him by his coat and said, "Sleep with me." He tore himself away and fled outdoors leaving his coat in her hands.

When she found herself with his coat in her hands and saw that he had fled outside, she called out to the house servants. "See what my husband had to bring in—a Hebrew fellow to make a mock of us. He burst in on me to rape me, but I screamed at the top of my voice, and when he heard me screaming he bolted outside, leaving his coat in my hands."

She kept the coat by her till the master came home, then repeated her story: "The Hebrew slave you brought here burst in on me to have some sport—'I want to make love to you,' he blurted. But I screamed at the top of my voice and he bolted outside, leaving behind his coat in my hands."

On hearing his wife's tale of how "your slave did this and this to me," the master was enraged. He seized Joseph and threw him into the jail where the royal prisoners were kept. There he remained. But Yahweh was good to Joseph and made him a favorite of the warden, who put him in charge of all the prisoners in that jail as supervisor of everything. The warden gave no thought to anything in Joseph's charge because the Lord was with him and made whatever he did prosper.

Joseph and the Royal Head Butler and Head Baker

If we assume that the following episode took place fairly soon after Joseph went to prison, his total prison term would have lasted just over two years.

(Genesis 40:1-23)

SOME time afterward, the royal butler and the royal baker both gave offense to their lord, the king of Egypt, and he imprisoned them in the same jail where Joseph was confined, in the headquarters of the captain of the guard. Potiphar then assigned Joseph to look after them.

They were some days in prison and while still there, both this butler and this baker of the king of Egypt, on one and the same night, had a peculiar dream. When Joseph came to them in the morning he saw that they were dejected and he asked them—these officials of Pharaoh in prison with him in his master's mansion—"Why do you look so sad today?"

"Because we both had dreams and there is nobody to interpret them," they answered.

"The interpretation of dreams is surely God's work," Joseph observed, "but tell them to me."

So the head butler told Joseph his dream. "In my dream," he began, "there was a grapevine in front of me and on that grapevine were three branches. Hardly had they budded but they blossomed and the clusters ripened into grapes. Pharaoh's goblet was in my hand, so I took the grapes and squeezed them into the goblet and gave it into Pharaoh's hand."

"This is what it means," Joseph told him. "The three branches are three days. Within three days Pharaoh will grant you a pardon and restore you to your post. You will be presenting Pharaoh's cup to him just as you did before when you were his butler. . . . Now, when all is well with you, remember me here, please, and do me the favor of mentioning me to Pharaoh, to get me out of this stronghold. I was kidnapped from the land of the Hebrews and have done nothing since coming here which merits being put in a dungeon."

When the head baker saw what a promising interpretation had been given, he said, "In my dream there were three wicker baskets on my head. The top basket contained every kind of pastry that Pharaoh likes, but birds out of the sky came pecking at these from the basket on my head."

"Your dream means this:" Joseph said, "the three baskets are three days. Within three days Pharaoh will take off your head and impale the rest of you on a pole, and birds will come out of the sky to pick off your flesh."

Sure enough, three days later, it was Pharaoh's birthday and he gave a celebration for his whole court. During it, in the presence of all his staff, he reexamined the cases of the head butler and head baker. He reinstated the head butler in his office of presenting the cup to his hand, but the head baker he impaled—just as Joseph had foretold.

The head butler gave no further thought to Joseph. He had already forgotten him.

Joseph's Success With Pharaoh's Dreams

It may be wondered in the following story how an august pharaoh, king of kings and venerated as a god, could heap such favors on a Hebrew slave, and later lean over backward to be kind to his family. Nor does it seem likely that he would delegate plenipotentiary powers to a Semitic alien from Asia.

The answer may well be that he himself was a Semitic alien from Asia. There was a period of a hundred and fifty years in Egyptian history (which would overlap with the Joseph saga) when the Nile delta was ruled by Semitic invaders called Hyksos, founders of the Fifteenth and Sixteenth dynasties.

Potipherah priest of On: On was an Egyptian religious center situated just south of the delta and about twenty-six miles northeast of Memphis. It contained an important temple to the sun god Ra. After the time of Alexander the Great, when all Asia Minor was Hellenized, On became known as Heliopolis—City of the Sun. A priest of On (perhaps high priest of On) would be one of the most important personages in the realm.

(Genesis 41:1-57)

TWO years later Pharaoh himself had a dream. He was standing on the banks of the Nile when right out of the river rose up seven cows, sleek and fat, and they went browsing in the reedy meadows. But seven other cows came up after them, ugly and skinny, and they stood with the first cows on the banks of the river. Then the ugly and skinny cows gobbled up the sleek fat ones. At which Pharaoh awoke.

But he fell asleep again and dreamt a second time. Seven ears of grain, plump and robust, sprouted from a single stalk, but close behind them sprouted seven other ears, spindly and blighted by the east wind. And the seven spindly ears swallowed up the seven plump and robust ears. Then Pharaoh awoke. It was all a dream.

But next morning he was troubled and sent for the magicians and wise men of Egypt. He told them his dream, but none could interpret it. Whereupon the head butler stepped forward and said, "Oh, now I remember the time when I did wrong, and Pharaoh was angry with his servants and placed me under arrest in the headquarters of the captain of the guard, me and the head baker; and we both had a dream on the same night, he and I: a dream with a special significance for each of us.

"There was a young Hebrew there, a slave of the captain of the guard, and we told him our dreams. He interpreted them for us, each with its individual purport; and events turned out exactly as he said. *I* was reinstated in my office, the other was impaled."

Pharaoh sent at once for Joseph and he was hustled from the dungeon. They shaved him, gave him clean clothes, and he came before Pharaoh.

"I have had a dream which none can interpret," Pharaoh said to Joseph. "In my dream I was standing on the bank of the Nile when suddenly up from the river rose seven cows, robust and sleek, and they went browsing in the reedy meadows. Then up came seven other cows right behind them: scrawny and ugly, skin and bone—the poorest cows I have ever seen in the whole of Egypt. The scrawny, ugly cows proceeded to eat up the first seven robust cows. But when they had finished gorging, there was no sign that they had eaten: they looked just as skinny as before. Then I awoke.

"In my second dream I saw seven ears of grain, plump and healthy, sprouting from a single stem. But right after them sprang up seven spindly ears, blighted by the east wind. And the spindly ears swallowed up the seven healthy ears. I told all this to the magicians but none of them could explain it."

Joseph answered Pharaoh, "Pharaoh's dreams are one and the same. God is telling Pharaoh what he is about to do. The seven goodly cows are seven years, and the seven healthy ears are seven years: the dream is all one. The seven scrawny, ugly cows that came up after the others are also seven years, as are the seven hollow ears of grain blighted by the east wind—seven years of famine. It is just as I said to Pharaoh: God is telling Pharaoh what he is about to do.

"There will be seven years of great abundance throughout the land of Egypt, but these will be followed by seven years of famine, when all the abundance in Egypt will be forgotten, for the ensuing famine will be so devastating that no trace of the abundance will be seen.

"As for the dreams being shown twice to Pharaoh, this means that the matter is fixed by God and God will shortly bring it to pass. Let Pharaoh therefore seek out a man who is provident and wise and set him over the land of Egypt, and let Pharaoh take steps to appoint overseers for the land who will organize the country of Egypt during the seven years of plenty. They must garner all the produce of those good years soon to come and lay up grain on Pharaoh's authority and store it in the towns for food: food held in reserve for the country against the seven years of famine that are going to afflict Egypt, to save the land from perishing by famine."

Pharaoh thought well of this advice, and so did his ministers. He said to them, "Can we find another like this one here: a man filled with the divine spirit?"

Pharaoh then addressed Joseph, "Since God has revealed all this to you, there is no one so provident and wise as you are. You shall be in charge of my palace, and all my people shall bow to your command. Only in the throne shall I rank higher than your say-so.

"See," continued Pharaoh as he took the signet ring from off his finger and placed it on Joseph's, "I put you in charge of the whole land of Egypt."

Then he robed him in fine linen and hung a gold chain about his neck. He had him ride in his second chariot with out-criers shouting, "Bow down!" Thus was he invested with the charge of all Egypt. "Pharaoh though I am," the king said to Joseph, "nobody in the land shall stir hand or foot without you."

Pharaoh changed Joseph's name to Zaphnathpaaneah ["God's Living Voice"] and gave him as bride Asenath, daughter of Potipherah, priest of On.

Joseph was thirty years old when he entered the service of the king of Egypt. After he left the royal presence he toured the whole land of Egypt. During the seven years of plenty the earth burgeoned with produce, and he husbanded Egypt's seven years of crops and stored it all in the cities, placing in each city the harvests from the fields around it. Joseph heaped up grain as deep as the sands of the sea, until he gave up measuring it, for it was beyond count.

When the seven years of plenty in the kingdom of Egypt came to an end, the seven years of dearth began—just as Joseph said it would—and there was famine in every country, but in the land of Egypt there was food. When all Egypt, too, began to feel the pinch and the people cried to

Pharaoh for bread, Pharaoh told the Egyptians, "Go to Joseph and do whatever he says."

As the famine spread over the face of the land, Joseph opened up the storehouses and distributed grain to the Egyptians, for the famine held all Egypt in its grip. Peoples from everywhere came to Egypt for supplies while the famine devastated every land.

The First Visit of Joseph's Brothers

Almost twenty-three years since he was sold, Joseph—now the Grand Vizier of Egypt—is about thirty-nine, and Benjamin, Jacob's youngest son, at least twenty-four (assuming that Rachel did die in childbirth). These calculations, however, must not be given too much weight. Indeed, one gets the impression from Judah's heartrending speech in this story that Benjamin, somehow, is still in his teens.

The Bible text has the brothers discover the planted money in their sacks twice. This is not likely and is the result of two different compilations.

(Genesis 42:1-38)

WHEN Jacob learned that there was food to be had in Egypt, he said to his sons, "What are you staring at one another for? Do you know what I have heard? That there is grain in Egypt. Get yourselves down there and buy for us so we may live and not die."

So ten of Joseph's brothers set out for Egypt to buy grain. Benjamin, however, Joseph's full brother, Jacob did not send with the other brothers, "because he might come to harm," he said.

And so it was that among the people who came for supplies during the raging famine in Canaan were Jacob's sons. Joseph as regent of the land did the distributing for the entire population. Accordingly, when Joseph's brothers arrived they bowed low to the ground before him. Joseph recognized his brothers the moment he saw them, but he acted aloofly and spoke to them brusquely.

"Where do you come from?" he demanded.

"From the land of Canaan to obtain food," they said, not recognizing him, though he not only knew them but had fresh in his mind his dreams about them.

"You are spies," he said. "You have come to spy out the land in its nakedness."

"No, not at all, my lord," they replied. "Your servants have come to obtain food. We are all the same man's sons. We are honest people. Your servants are not spies."

"I say you are," Joseph retorted. "You have come to spy out the land in its nakedness."

"No, we are twelve brothers, your servants," they insisted: "sons of one man in the land of Canaan. The youngest is still with his father, and one is no more."

"I tell you you are spies," Joseph repeated, "and the test of it shall be this: I swear to you as Pharaoh lives that you are not to leave this place until your youngest brother comes here. So send one of you to fetch your brother while the rest of you remain under arrest until your statement can be proved. Otherwise, I swear by Pharaoh, you are simply spies."

With that, he locked up the lot of them for three days. On the third day he told them this: "Look, I am a God-fearing man. If you want to live and are honest, do the following. One of you is to be kept in custody, while the rest go back home with food for your starving families. Then you are to return here bringing me your youngest brother. Only so will your claim be verified and you need not die."

They complied, but among themselves they confessed, "Alas, we are being punished because of our brother. We saw the anguish of his soul when he pleaded with us and we paid no heed. So now this ordeal has come upon us."

Reuben reminded them, saying, "Did I not tell you not to harm the boy? But you would not listen. Now comes the reckoning for his blood."*

Of course, they had no idea that Joseph understood them, for he spoke through an interpreter. He had to turn away from them to weep. When he was able to face them again he singled out Simeon and had him bound before their eyes. Then Joseph gave orders to fill their sacks with grain but to put back each man's money in his sack; also, to give them

*Reuben, of course, still believes the story of Joseph's being eaten by a wild animal.

provisions for the road. After this was done, they loaded their asses with the supplies and left.

When they stopped for the night and one of them opened up his sack to give his ass fodder, he caught sight of his money lying in the mouth of the sack. "Fancy that!" he called to his brothers, "my money has been returned. There it is back in my sack!"

Mystified and shaken, they turned to one another, asking, "What is this that God has done to us?"

On reaching their father Jacob in the land of Canaan, they told him everything that had happened to them. "The man who controls the country," they said, "spoke to us in a surly way and accused us of being spies. We told him, 'We are honest people, not spies. We were twelve brothers, sons of the same father, but one of us is no more and the youngest is now with our father in the land of Canaan.'

"But this man who governs the country said, 'Prove to me that you are honest people by leaving one of your brothers here with me while the rest of you go home with food for your starving households. When you bring back your brother to me here, I'll know that you are not spies but honest men. Then I'll return your brother to you, and you can be free to traffic in the realm.' "

When they came to empty their sacks, there in each man's sack was his money bag. The sight of these money bags filled them and their father with dismay.

"So you would leave me bereft!" their father Jacob exclaimed. "Joseph is gone, Simeon is gone, and now you would take Benjamin. Everything is loaded against me."

"Father, you may kill my own two sons," Reuben replied, "if I fail to bring him back to you. Just leave him in my hands and I *will* bring him back to you."

"No," said Jacob, "my son shall not go off with you. His brother is dead and he alone is left. If anything should happen to him on this journey of yours, you would doom my gray old age to sorrow and the grave."

The Second Trip to Egypt of Joseph's Brothers

(Genesis 43:1-34)

THE famine still ravished the land, and when they had consumed all the food they had brought from Egypt, their father said to them, "Go back and get us some sustenance."

"But," replied Judah, "the man solemnly warned us, 'Don't show yourselves again unless with your brother.' If you are prepared to let our brother come with us, we shall go down to Egypt and get you food. But if you are not prepared to let him, we shan't go, because the man insisted, 'Do not appear before me again unless your brother is with you.' "

"Why did you ever make things so difficult for me?" Jacob moaned. "Why did you tell the man you had another brother?"

"He asked us straight out about ourselves and our family," they answered: 'Is your father still alive? Have you another brother?' We had to answer his questions. How could we know that he was going to say: 'Bring your brother here.'?"

Judah proceeded to press his father Jacob: "Send the lad with me and we shall be on our way—if we are to come out of this alive and not all be dead: you, we, and our little ones. I shall vouch for him entirely and you can hold me responsible. If I fail to bring him back and set him right in front of you, I shall carry the blame in your eyes forever. And now we have delayed long enough. We could have gone and come by now."

"If it must be so," responded their father Jacob, "do this: pack some of our land's best produce in your bags and take the man a present: some balm, some honey, incense grains, laudanum, some pistachio nuts, and almonds. Take also twice the money you need, for you must return the money that was replaced in the mouth of your sacks. It may have been an oversight. And take your brother, too, and be off: back to the man. May God Almighty dispose him to leniency toward you so that he lets your other brother go as well as Benjamin. As for me, if I am to be bereaved, then let me be bereft."

The men took their gifts and with double money in hand went off with Benjamin to Egypt and came before Joseph. When Joseph saw Benjamin with them he told his steward, "Conduct these men into the house and have an animal slaughtered for a feast, for they are to dine with me at noon."

The steward did as Joseph bade him and took the men to Joseph's house, where they became nervous on the threshold. "We are being brought here," they murmured, "because of the money that was put back in our sacks the first time. This is an excuse to round us up and make us slaves and take our donkeys too."

So they went up to Joseph's steward and spoke to him at the entrance of the house. "Please, sir," they said, "we came here once before to buy food, but when we reached home and opened our sacks, there in the mouth of our sacks was each man's money in full. We have brought it back with us, as well as other money to buy food. We have no idea who first put the money in our sacks."

"Calm yourselves," he replied, "have no fear. Your God and the God of your fathers must have put treasure in your sacks. I received your payment in full."

Thereupon the steward brought Simeon out to them and took them all into Joseph's house. He gave them water to wash their feet, and fodder for their asses. They got their presents out, ready for when Joseph came home at noon, having learned that they were to dine there.

When Joseph came home they presented him with their gifts, bowing to the ground before him. He asked how they were, then inquired, "Is your father well—the old man you spoke of? Is he still alive?"

"Yes," they replied, "our father your servant is alive and in good health," and they bowed low.

As his eye fell on his brother Benjamin, his own mother's son, he exclaimed, "So this is the youngest brother you told me of?" Then he added, "God be kind to you, my boy."

And Joseph hurried out, so moved by the sight of his brother that he was on the verge of tears; and he went to his room and wept. Then he washed his face, came out again holding himself in check, and gave the order: "Let dinner be served."

Their mutual glances were full of wonder as they were being seated opposite him in order of seniority, from the eldest to the youngest. He was served apart, and they were served apart, as were also his Egyptians guests—for it is taboo for Egyptians to eat with Hebrews. Their helpings came from his own table, and Benjamin's helping was twice as large as any of theirs. And so they feasted with Joseph, and the wine flowed.

Joseph Brings the Testing of His Brothers to a Head

The master storyteller of the Joseph saga allows only a few hours to elapse before he unfolds the next episode: it is the time between the false euphoria of the banquet and the coming of dawn. This gives Joseph time to prime his steward in the part he is to play in the final plot.

The confusion of Judah with Reuben in this account is due to a conflation of two separate versions.

(Genesis 44:1-44, 45:1-15)

AFTERWARD Joseph gave these orders to his steward: "Fill the men's sacks with food, as much as they can carry, and in the mouth of each man's sack put his money, but in the sack of the youngest put also my goblet—my silver goblet—together with the money for the grain."

The steward did as Joseph told him. And at the first light of dawn, the men with their asses were sent on their way. They had not gone far from the town when Joseph said to his steward, "Now, up and chase them, and when you overtake them say, 'Why have you repaid kindness with evil? The silver goblet you've gone off with is the one my master drinks from. And he uses it for divining. You've done a despicable thing.' "

The steward overtook them and said exactly that.

"My lord," they protested, "how can you say such a thing? Far be it from your servants to act in such a way! Why, we even brought back to you from the land of Canaan the money we found in the mouth of our sacks! Is it likely that we would sneak off with silver or gold from your master's house? If the goblet is found with any one of us, that one shall die, and the rest of us become my lord's slaves as well."

Each of them eagerly lowered his sack to the ground and opened it. The man searched through them, beginning with the eldest and ending with the youngest. The goblet was found in Benjamin's sack.

They rent their clothes in despair. Each reloaded his ass and they turned back toward the town. Joseph was still at home when Judah and his brothers reached the house. They threw themselves on the ground before him.

"What a thing to have done!" Joseph said to them. "Didn't you know that a man like me can divine the truth?"

"What can we say to my lord?" Judah answered. "What can we plead? And how clear ourselves? God has uncovered the [past] crimes of your servants. So, take us, my lord, as your slaves: all of us as well as the one with whom the goblet was found."

"Far be it from me to do that!" Joseph replied. "Only the one who was found to have purloined the goblet shall be my slave. The rest of you can go off back to your father."

At that, Judah stepped up to him and said, "Please, my lord, may your servant speak a word in your ear! And do not be angry with your servant, for you are like Pharaoh himself. . . . My lord asked his servants, 'Have you a father or another brother?' And we said to my lord, 'We have a father, an old man, and a child of his old age, the youngest, whose brother is dead, leaving him the only child of his mother; and his father loves him. When you told us your servants to bring him here to you so that you could see him, we explained to my lord, 'The boy cannot leave his father, for if he leaves, his father will die.' But you declared to us your servants, 'Unless your youngest brother comes back with you, you are not to come into my presence again.'

"When we returned to your servant my father, we reported my lord's words to him. Some time later our father said to us, 'Go back and get us something to eat.' 'We can go back only if our youngest brother comes with us,' we reminded him, 'for unless our youngest brother is with us we shall not be allowed in the man's presence again.'

"To which your servant my father replied, 'As you well know, my wife Rachel bore me two sons. One is gone from me and I fear that he has been torn to pieces, for I have not seen him since. If you take this one from me, too, and something happens to him, you will bring down my gray old age sorrowing to the grave.'

"If now I go before your servant my father and the boy is not with us, his life is so wrapped up in the lad's life that when he sees that he is missing, he will die; and your servants will have doomed the gray hairs of your servant our father to sorrow and the grave. What is more, it was I your servant who went surety for the boy to my father, vowing: 'If I do not bring him back to you, I stand condemned before you for the rest of my life.'

"Therefore I now beg you, allow me your servant to remain here in place of the boy as my lord's slave, and let the lad go back with his brothers. For how can I approach my father if the boy is not with me? Never could I face the consequence of my father's anguish."

Joseph could hold himself in check no longer in front of his attendants. "Let everybody leave," he called out. Then, with no one else about, he made himself known to his brothers, sobbing so loudly that the Egyptians heard it, and the news spread to Pharaoh's palace.

"I am Joseph," he declared to his brothers. "Is my father really alive and well?"

But his brothers were too stunned to answer. "Come closer," Joseph said to them. They came closer and he went on, "Yes, I am Joseph, the brother you sold into Egypt. Do not be upset or reproach yourselves for having sold me to this place. It was God who sent me here ahead of you to save your lives. The famine has been raging for two years now and there are five more years to go, when there will be no harvests from the plow. God sent me in advance of you to preserve you on this earth into posterity, saving your lives in a most unexpected way. So it was not you who put me here but God. He has set me up as Pharaoh's right-hand man, master of his household and viceroy over the whole land of Egypt. So hurry back to my father and tell him: 'Your son Joseph sends you news: "God has made me governor of all Egypt. Come to me here. Do not delay. You shall dwell in the province of Goshen and be near me: you, your children and grandchildren, your flocks and herds, and all that you have. Five years of famine are still to come, but here I shall provide for you, and you, your family and all your dependants will want for nothing.' "

"Oh, unbelievable as it is, your eyes and Benjamin's eyes really see *me*! It is I who am speaking to you. Tell my father all about my success in Egypt and what you have seen here. Then hurry back, and bring Father."

When he had finished, Joseph threw himself on the neck of his brother Benjamin and sobbed on his shoulder, as Benjamin sobbed on his. Then he kissed all his brothers, weeping over each of them. Only then did the brothers find their tongues.

The news spread through Pharaoh's palace: "Joseph's brothers are here," and Pharaoh and his court were happy to hear it.

Pharaoh then said to Joseph, "Tell your brothers this: 'Load up your beasts and proceed at once to the land of Canaan. Gather up your father and your households and come back here. I shall allot you the best acres in Egypt, where you will live on the fat of the land.' Tell them also to take wagons from the land of Egypt for their little ones and their wives and to transport your father and come back. Tell them to forget about their belongings: the best of the whole realm of Egypt is theirs.' "

The sons of Jacob did this. Joseph gave them the wagons Pharaoh had ordered and also provisions for the journey. He presented each of them with new clothes; and to Benjamin he gave three hundred pieces of silver and far more than one new set of clothes. Also, to his father he sent ten ass-loads of the good things of Egypt, and ten she-asses laden with grain, bread, and provisions for his father's journey.

So he sent his brothers off and as they departed he quipped: "Mind you don't squabble on the way!"

They left Egypt and came to their father in the land of Canaan.

"Joseph is alive," they announced, "and controls the whole kingdom of Egypt."

But numbness struck the heart of Jacob. He could not believe them. When, however, they had recounted all that Joseph had told them, and when he saw the caravans Joseph had sent to convey him, their father's spirit revived and Jacob said, "I am satisfied. My son is alive. I must go and see him before I die."

The Death of Jacob

Seventeen years have passed since Jacob and his household of seventy persons (not counting wives) entered Egypt. Favored by Pharaoh, and under Joseph's patronage, the whole clan has prospered in spite of the famine. Pharaoh, learning that the Israelites were cattle farmers, has put them in charge of his stock. Jacob is now one hundred and forty-seven years old.

(Genesis 47:29-31, 48:1-4, 8-19, 49:1-33, 50:1-3)

AS the time drew near for Jacob to die, he called his son Joseph and said to him, "If you really esteem me, place your hand under my thigh as a pledge of your constant loyalty and promise not to bury me in Egypt. Let me lie down with my fathers. So carry me out of Egypt and bury me in their sepulcher."

Joseph answered, "I shall do as you say."

"Swear it," said Jacob.

And he swore. Then Jacob let his head drop on his pillow.

Some time afterward Joseph was told, "Your father is failing," so he went to him with his two sons Manasseh and Ephraim. When Jacob was informed that Joseph was come, he summoned his strength and sat up in bed.

"Almighty God appeared to me at Luz in the land of Canaan," Jacob said to Joseph, "and he blessed me with the words: 'I shall make you fruitful and increase you. Out of you I shall gather a great company of tribes and endow this land to your descendants forever.'"

Then, glancing toward Joseph's two sons, Jacob asked, "Who are these?"

"They are my sons whom God gave me here," Joseph said to his father.

"Bring them to me," he said, "and let me bless them."

Now, the eyes of Jacob were dim with age and he could hardly see, so Joseph brought the boys to his side. He kissed them and embraced them, exclaiming to Joseph, "I never thought to see your face again, yet here is God showing me your offspring too!"

Then Joseph retrieved them from Jacob's lap, bowing low to the ground. After which, placing his right hand on Ephraim at Jacob's left, and his left hand on Manasseh at Jacob's right, he led them toward him; but Jacob deliberately stretched out his right hand and laid it on Ephraim's head, the younger, and his left hand on Manasseh's head, the firstborn, thus crossing his hands. Then he blessed them, saying:

The God in whose ways my fathers Abraham and Isaac walked,
The God who has been my lifelong shepherd till this day,
The very angel who has delivered me from every harm,
Bless these boys and let them carry on my name
And the names of my fathers Abraham and Isaac.

And may they grow into a people
Numberless upon this earth.

When Joseph saw that his father had his right hand on Ephraim's head, he thought it a mistake, and he lifted his father's hand to move it from Ephraim's head onto Manasseh's, saying to his father, "No, Father, this is the firstborn here. Put your right hand on his head."

"I know, my son, I know," said his father, resisting. "And he too shall become a tribe, he too shall be great; but his brother will be even greater and his posterity a teeming nation."

Then Jacob called together his sons and said: "Gather round that I may tell you the things that will befall you in days to come.

Gather round and listen, O sons of Jacob.
Listen to your father Israel

You Reuben, my firstborn son:
Strong first fruit of my prime,
First in rank, first in honor—
Unstable as water, you are first no longer.
You mounted your father's bed,
Sullied my nuptial couch.

You, Simeon and Levi: two of the same—
Instruments of lawlessness.
Keep away, my soul, from their fellowship;
Have no commerce with their council.
For they murdered in a mad rage,
And tortured oxen just for sport.
Damned be their anger for its savagery
And their ruthlessness so cruel.
I shall disperse them in Jacob
And scatter them in Israel.

You, Judah, your brothers shall extol:
Your hand pressed hard on the enemy's neck.
Your father's sons shall bow before you.
A lion's whelp is Judah:
You, my son, laced to its prey.
He crouches like a lion,
Like a lion he lies down:
A true-bred lion—and who dare rouse him?

The scepter shall not part from Judah
Nor the ruler's mace from between his feet
Until there comes the rightful one,
To whom all peoples shall pay homage.
He who tethers his colt to the vine's stem,
His pure-bred colt to the choicest vine.
He who in wine washes his clothes—
His garments in the blood of grapes.
He whose eyes are darker than wine
And whose teeth are whiter than milk.

Zebulun shall dwell by the shores of the sea.
He shall be a haven for ships:
His borders stretching into Sidon.

Isachar is a sturdy mule
Resting between his saddlebags.
He saw that the rhythm of life was good:
Rural life in the countryside.
So he bowed his shoulder to the burden,
Serving a master willingly.

Dan shall govern his own kin
As one of the tribes of Israel.
Let Dan be a snake on the road,
A horned adder on the path,
Striking at the horse's heel,
Tumbling the rider on his back.

When marauders swoop on Gad,
Gad will turn on them in triumph.

Fat the produce out of Asher:
He shall cater fit for kings.

Naphtali is a hind let loose,
Giving birth to lovely fawns.

Joseph is an untamed colt,
An untamed colt beside a spring.
Bowmen harried and attacked him
But their bows turned to stone
And their arms dithered loosely
Through the Mighty One of Jacob—
Shepherd—Rock of Israel.

May the God of your fathers succor you,
The Almighty grace you with his blessings:
Blessings from the heavens above,
From the deeps of the earth cradled beneath,
Blessings of breast, blessings of womb,
Blessings of grain, blessings of blossom,
Blessings from the eternal mountains
Beyond the everlasting hills . . .
May all these rest upon the head
Of Joseph, on the crown of him
Who suffered exile from his brothers.

Benjamin is a prowling wolf:
Mornings he consumes his quarry,
Divides at evening what is left.

All these were the twelve tribes of Israel and this is what their father said to them as he bade goodbye. He addressed to each of them his proper blessing. Then he gave them all this charge: "Soon I shall be gathered to my people. Bury me with my fathers in the cave of Ephron the Hittite's field, which is the cave of the field of Macphelah that faces Mamre in the land of Canaan. Abraham bought that field from Ephron the Hittite for a burying place. There they buried Abraham and his wife Sarah; there they buried Isaac and his wife Rebecca; and there I buried Leah. The purchase of the field was from the sons of Heth."

When Jacob ended these instructions to his sons, he curled his feet up in bed, breathed his last, and was gathered to his people.

Joseph flung himself upon his father, sobbing and kissing him. Afterward he gave orders to the embalmers to embalm his father. This they did, taking forty days, which is the required time for an embalming.

The Egyptians mourned him for seventy days.

NOTE

Reduced to prose, Jacob's message to his sons (the twelve tribes of Israel) is:

Reuben: to be punished for his adultery with his father's concubine, Bilah (Gen. 35:22).

Simeon and Levi: reprimanded for their vicious treatment of the citizens of Sechem after the rape of their sister Dinah. They are to be granted no fixed territory. In fact, the tribes of Simeon and Levi, unlike their brother tribes, were never given land holdings, but were spread throughout Israel and became the priestly caste.

Judah: his tribe is given the authority of premier rank until the coming of the Messiah, whose era will be marked by spiritual blessings, symbolized by abundance of wine and by physical beauty.

Zebulun: is to establish a maritime nation bordering the Mediterranean near the important seaport of Sidon.

Isachar: will farm the fertile plain of Esdraelon. He will work stolidly and contentedly.

Dan: will be a successful ruler who knows how to defend himself.

Gad: his tribe too will be astute and valiant.

Asher: his land will be fertile, abundant in every kind of produce.

Naphtali: his tribe will excel in all the liberating forms of art.

Joseph: will be rewarded for his fidelity. His descendants will be numerous and rich. They will hold their own against their enemies.

Benjamin: his will be a warrior tribe.

PART II

THE EMERGENCE OF ISRAEL

(c. 1700 TO 1200 B.C.)

Stories from the Books of Exodus, Numbers, and Deuteronomy

Introduction

As with the Book of Genesis, nobody knows who the authors of the above books were, though here too by tradition it was Moses. Suffice to say that these scriptures are the composite work of several hands, remembering always that long before the Pentateuch was edited and committed to writing, the essential narrative would have been recited, chanted, and known by heart from generation to generation.

Despite the fact that whole sections of the Pentateuch deal with detailed injunctions on ritual and Jewish behavior, these books nevertheless reflect happenings of great antiquity. Moreover, even though the Yahvist concept of divinity is still thoroughly primitive, punitive, prudish, and often unethical, the kernel of Jesus' later teaching and his attitude towards the Father is already blazoned forth in the beautiful passage of Deuteronomy 6:5-9 (King James Bible).

> And thou shalt love the Lord thy God
> with all thine heart and with all thy soul,
> and with all thy might.
> And these words which I command thee this day,
> shall be in thine heart.
> And thou shalt teach them diligently unto thy children,
> And thou shalt talk of them when thou sittest in thy house,
> and when thou walkest by the way,
> and when thou liest down, and when thou risest up.
> And thou shalt bind them for a sign upon thine hand,
> and they shall be as frontlets between thine eyes.
> And thou shalt write them upon the posts of thine house,
> and on thy gates.

I have not included any stories from Leviticus because that book is taken up almost entirely with sacrificial matters and the law of Moses.

The Birth of Moses

The date is early in the thirteenth century B.C. Some four hundred years have passed since Jacob with his eleven sons (and presumably his one daughter) joined Joseph in Egypt. The seventy householders who came with Jacob have now multiplied into several thousand, and the reigning Pharaoh (probably Seti I), alarmed at this sustained fertility, has not only turned the Israelites virtually into slaves, but now orders that all newborn Hebrew boys be tossed into the Nile.

(Exodus 2:1-25)

AND it happened that a man of the house of Levi wedded a daughter of the house of Levi, who when she had conceived and borne a son and seen what a beautiful boy he was, kept him hidden for three months. But when she could hide him no longer she wove him a basket of reeds, sealing it with clay and pitch, and into this she laid the child and put it among the bulrushes by the river's edge. Meanwhile, the boy's sister stationed herself some way off to see what would befall him.

When Pharaoh's daughter came down to the river to bathe and went strolling along the riverbanks with her handmaids, she saw the basket and sent a maid to fetch it. What should she see when she lifted the lid but a baby crying, and her heart was touched. "This must be one of the Hebrew infants," she observed. At which the child's sister spoke up and said to Pharaoh's daughter, "Shall I go and get you a Hebrew woman to nurse the baby for you?" "Yes, go," Pharaoh's daughter replied. So the girl hurried off and called the child's mother.

"Take the baby away and nurse him for me," said Pharaoh's daughter. "I shall pay you a wage."

The woman took the baby home and nursed it till the child grew, then she brought it to Pharaoh's daughter and he became her son. She called him "Moses," [to draw out] "because," she remarked, "I drew him out of the water."

One day when Moses was grown he went out among his compatriots, and as he witnessed their hardships he caught sight of an Egyptian striking a Hebrew, one of his own people.

He looked this way and that to make sure that nobody was watching, then slew the Egyptian, and hid him in the sand.

Next day he saw two Hebrews fighting, and he said to the one who was in the wrong, "Why are you hitting your brother?"

The man retorted, "Who made you our master and judge? Are you going to kill me the way you killed the Egyptian?"

At which Moses was alarmed. "The thing is out," he thought to himself. Sure enough, when Pharaoh heard of it he determined to kill him, but Moses fled and took refuge in the land of Midian.

There, as he sat by a well, seven daughters of the priest of Midian came to draw water and fill the troughs for their father's flock, but some shepherds approached and drove the girls away. Whereupon Moses stood up and came to their help, then he watered their father's flock for them.

When they returned to their father, Reuel, he asked them, "How is it that you have come back so soon today?"

"An Egyptian defended us against some shepherds," they told him, "then he drew all the water we wanted and watered our beasts."

"Where is the man now?" he said to his daughters. "Why have you left him? Call him so that we can invite him to dine."

Moses happily sojourned with Reuel, who gave him his daughter Zipporah for a wife. She bore him a son, whom he called Gershom ["Foreigner"], explaining, "I was a stranger in a strange land."

In time the king of Egypt died, but the children of Israel continued to groan under their bondage and the cry of their slavery went up to God and God heard their crying. He remembered his covenant with Abraham, Isaac, and Jacob, and he looked down on them in pity.

Moses and the Burning Bush

In chapter 3 of the Book of Exodus, God for the first time declares his title as "Yahweh" or "I-Am-Who-Am." The sacred writers, however, had been using it as far back as Genesis 2:4 in the capitalized form of YHVH—it being considered presumptuous to pronounce so great a name. Both the King James Bible and the Revised Standard Version translate YHVH as "Lord" or "the Lord." Another favorite rendering in English has been Jehovah, but scholars are now agreed that this is based on a mistake. I have used both Yahweh and the Lord throughout this translation, favoring Yahweh perhaps when the deity shows himself in an intransigent mood.

(Exodus 3:1-22, 4:1-18)

MOSES tended the flock of Jethro [Reuel] his father-in-law, the priest of Midian. One day he led the flock to the edge of the desert as far as Horeb, "the mountain of God." And there from out of a burning bush an angel of the Lord appeared to him in the flames. He gazed and saw to his amazement that though the bush was on fire it was not consumed. So Moses said to himself, "Let me turn aside and look into this marvel and see why the bush does not burn."

When the Lord saw that he had turned aside to look, he called to him out of the heart of the bush and said:

"Moses, Moses."

"Yes, here I am."

"Come no nearer, but take off your shoes, because where you stand is holy ground."

Then the Lord continued, "I am the God of your father, the God of Abraham, the God of Isaac, the God of Jacob."

Whereat Moses screened his eyes, afraid to look upon God. Then the Lord said: "I see all too well the sufferings of my people in Egypt and I hear how they cry out against their oppressors. I am aware of their sorrows and I come to deliver them from the hands of the Egyptians and to bring them out of Egypt to a good land, a large land, a land flowing with milk and honey: the country of the Canaanites, the Hittites, the Amorites, the Perizzites, and the Jebusites. The wailing of the children of Israel has indeed reached me and I see how the Egyptians oppress them. Make yourself ready therefore, I am sending you to Pharaoh, for you are to lead my people the children of Israel out of Egypt."

"Who am I," remonstrated Moses with God, "to go before Pharaoh and lead the children of Israel out of Egypt?"

"I shall be with you, be sure of that," God replied. "Let this be the pledge of my mission to you: when you have brought your people out of Egypt, you shall worship on this very mountain."

"But," said Moses to God, "when I come to the children of Israel and announce to them, 'The God of your fathers has sent me,' and they ask, 'What is his name?' what should I tell them?"

"Yahweh," ["I-Am-Who-Am"] God said to Moses. "That is what you must tell the children of Israel, 'I AM has sent me to you.' Yes, you must say to them, 'Yahweh, the God of your fathers, the God of Abraham, Isaac, and Jacob, has sent me to you to declare, "This is my everlasting name, this is my symbol of sovereignty from generation to generation." Go and call together the elders of Israel and say to them, 'The Lord God of your fathers, the God of Abraham, Isaac, and Jacob, has appeared to me and said, "Know that I have visited you and seen all that is done to you in Egypt and now promise to lead you out of this land of lamentations to the country of the Canaanites, the Hittites, the Amorites, the Perizzites, the Hivites, and the Jebusites, to a land indeed flowing with milk and honey.

"They will listen to your voice; then you and the elders are to go to the king of Egypt and say to him, 'Yahweh, the God of the Hebrews, has visited us. We ask you therefore to let us make a three days' pilgrimage into the wilderness to sacrifice to the Lord our God.' I know, however," the Lord continued, "that the king of Egypt will not let you go: no, not without a mighty swipe of my hand. So I shall lift my arm and hit Egypt most marvelously with wonders. After that he will let you go. . . . And there is more: I shall make the Egyptians generous toward this people so that when you go you will not go empty-handed. Every woman is to ask her mistress and her Egyptian neighbor for jewelry of silver and gold, as well as the finest apparel. With this plunder from Egypt you will dress up your sons and daughters."

"But," replied Moses, "they will not believe me. They will not listen. They will say, 'Yahweh never appeared to you.' "

"What is that in your hand?" the Lord rejoined.

"A staff," he said.

"Throw it on the ground."

He threw it on the ground and it became a snake. Moses sprang away.

"Stretch out your hand and grasp it by the tail," said the Lord.

Moses reached out and grasped it, and it became a staff in his hand.

"This is to make them believe that Yahweh, the God of

their fathers, the God of Abraham, Isaac, and Jacob, has really appeared to you.

"Now," said the Lord, "put your hand into your bosom."

So he put his hand to his bosom and when he withdrew it his hand was leprous as snow.

"Now put your hand to your bosom again," God said.

He put his hand to his bosom again and when he withdrew it his hand had gone back to being like the rest of his body.

"Should they not believe and be convinced by the first marvel, they certainly ought to be by the second. However, if they are convinced by neither and still refuse to listen to you, scoop up some water out of the river and pour it on the ground. As the water you have scooped falls to the earth, it will turn into blood."

"But, Lord," Moses remonstrated to Yahweh, "I have never been a good speaker, neither before nor since you talked to me. I am slow of speech and clumsy of tongue."

"And who," retorted the Lord, "made man's mouth? Who makes the dumb, the deaf, the seeing, and the blind—who if not I the Lord? Go along. I shall be with your lips and tell you what to say."

"Please, my Lord," expostulated Moses, "I beg you send some other man."

At this Yahweh's anger flared up and he said crossly to Moses, "Don't you have a brother called Aaron? I happen to know that he's an excellent speaker. Very well, he's coming to meet you, and he'll be happy to see you. You are to explain all these matters to him and tell him what the message is. I shall be on your lips and his lips too, telling you what to say. He will be your spokesman to the people. He will be your mouthpiece and you his inspiration. Take your staff with you and use it for the marvels."

So Moses went back to his father-in-law Jethro [Reuel] and said to him, "Allow me to return to my kinsmen in Egypt to see if they are still alive."

"Go in peace," said Jethro to Moses.

The First Plague: The Waters Turn to Blood

In the story of the ten plagues we should perhaps approach them more as metaphors than as scientifically verifiable fact; though there is no reason why most of them could not have been fact too. One cannot, however, construe them too literally without running into incongruities. How, for instance, in the first plague when the water throughout Egypt turned to blood—even the water in the household utensils—were the magicians able to find any unpolluted water to perform their own miracle? And if the magicians were able to simulate this miracle, as well as the miracles of Aaron's snake and Moses' frogs, why did they fail with the lice and the flies? There are unfortunately no records outside the Bible to enable us to separate fact from fancy.

And so now, Moses with staff in hand, and with his wife and young sons, mounted on a donkey, makes his way back to Egypt. As he travels, Yahweh tells him to be sure he works his wonders in front of Pharaoh, at the same time warning him that Pharaoh is not going to listen: "Because I mean to harden his heart." Later it becomes clear that the repeated hardenings of Pharaoh's heart are purposely engendered by Yahweh to make all the extraordinary phenomena necessary, and thus force both the Israelites and the Egyptians to recognize his overwhelming presence and power.

Yahweh meanwhile has told Aaron to go into the wilderness to meet Moses. The two brothers meet and embrace at the foot of Mount Horeb, then proceed into Egypt. There they assemble the people; Moses does his marvels, and Aaron explains that God has taken note of their sufferings and is going to help them. The people believe and bow down in awe.

(Exodus 5:1-23, 7:8-24, 8:1-15)

AFTERWARD, Moses and Aaron said to Pharaoh, "Yahweh, the God of Israel, sends you this message: 'You are to let my people go so that they can worship me at a festival in the desert.' "

"Who is this Yahweh?" Pharaoh retorted. "And why should

I listen to him and let Israel go? I know no such Yahweh and I will not let Israel go."

At which the brothers said, "In very fact the God of the Hebrews has visited us. Please, therefore, let us go to make a three days' pilgrimage into the wilderness to sacrifice to the Lord our God. Otherwise he may strike us all with the plague and the sword."

To which the king of Egypt replied, "What do you mean—you, Moses and Aaron—by disrupting the people from their work? Get back to your tasks. And allow me to point out," Pharaoh went on, "that there are now a great many of your people in this land and yet you want them to be bone idle."

That same day he issued the following orders to the taskmasters and overseers of the people: "You are to stop providing them with straw to make bricks. Let them go and find their own straw. But keep them to the same quotas they had before. Reduce none of it. They are lazy and have time to blabber about 'going off to sacrifice to our Lord God.' So, double their work load. Make them sweat. That will stop this empty chatter."

The taskmasters and overseers of the people came before them and announced, "Pharaoh says, "I will not give you straw. Go and find your own straw. And your work load is not to be lessened."

Then the Israelites' own foremen which Pharaoh's supervisors had set up were whipped and abused. "Why have you not fulfilled your brick quotas?" they bellowed. "Neither yesterday's nor today's."

The Israelite foremen came pleading to Pharaoh. "Why are you treating your servants like this? We are not provided with any straw and yet are ordered to make bricks. And we are beaten. The fault is with your own men."

Pharaoh's only reply was: "Idle, idle—that is what you are. That is why you talk of going off to sacrifice to Yahweh. Get back to your work. Not a wisp of straw shall be given you. But mind you deliver the same number of bricks."

The Israelite foremen realized now that no remission of their daily quotas was to be considered and how impossible their plight was. Meeting Moses and Aaron on their way out from Pharaoh's presence, they declared, "You ought to be tried and convicted in God's sight because you have made us stink before Pharaoh and his ministers. You have put a sword in his hand to wipe us out."

Moses went back to Yahweh and protested, "Lord, how

can you treat your people so badly? Why ever did you send me? Since I went to Pharaoh to speak in your name he has done nothing but hurt this people. And you have done nothing to save them."

Then the Lord said to Moses and Aaron, "When Pharaoh asks you, 'Show me a marvel,' you are to say to Aaron, 'Take your staff and throw it down in front of Pharaoh and it will become a snake.' "

So Moses and Aaron went to Pharaoh and did what Yahweh had commanded. Aaron cast down his staff before Pharaoh and his court, and it became a snake.

Pharaoh then called in his seers and sorcerers, and they proceeded to show that they possessed the same magic, for when each of them threw down his staff it too turned into a snake. Aaron's snake did swallow up the magicians' snakes, but nonetheless, God hardened Pharaoh's heart, as he said he would, and Pharaoh was unmoved. "You see," God told Moses, "how Pharaoh's heart is hardened and he will not let the people go. You must waylay him in the morning as he goes to the river and stand in wait for him on the bank of the Nile. Have in your hand the staff which turned into a snake and say to him, 'The Lord God of the Hebrews has sent me back to tell you this: "Even though you have turned a deaf ear till now, you must still let my people go into the wilderness to worship me. To prove that I am indeed the Lord, Moses is going to smite the waters of the Nile with his staff and the river will turn to blood. The fish will all die and the Nile send up such a stench that no Egyptian will want to drink from it." ' "

When the time came, the Lord instructed Moses, "Tell Aaron to take his staff and stretch out his hand toward all the waters of Egypt—all the streams, rivers, lakes, and every pool—and turn them to blood. Let blood be everywhere throughout the land of Egypt: even in the vessels of wood and stone."

Moses and Aaron did what the Lord commanded. Aaron raised his staff and right in front of Pharaoh and his court struck the waters of the Nile, and the waters of the Nile turned to blood. All the fish in the river perished and such was the stench that the Egyptians could not drink from it. There was blood throughout the land of Egypt.

The Egyptian magicians, however, were able to work the same marvel, so Pharaoh hardened his heart and would not listen to Moses and Aaron—just as the Lord had predicted.

Unmoved, Pharaoh turned and went into his palace. Then the Egyptians dug trenches to collect water to drink because the river water was undrinkable.

NOTES

1. The metaphor of the Nile turning to blood is not all that far-fetched. In flood time the river does indeed run dark red. Nor is the plague of frogs which follows improbable. A polluted or disturbed river might well lead to all the frogs leaving it. And when the frogs died or were killed by the thousand, the third and fourth plagues (mosquitoes and then flies) would be more than likely. Flies in their turn, being well-known carriers of disease, especially in the humid and sweltering Nile valley, would naturally infect first the cattle and then the people (fifth and sixth plague). As to the seventh plague, hail with thunder and lightning, this kind of storm is not infrequent in Egypt. So are swarms of locusts (eighth plague). The ninth plague (three days of darkness) may well have been, as has been suggested, a virulent dust storm covering the sun: and this too is by no means uncommon.

2. If one wants a naturalistic explanation of turning a snake into a stick, Professor Jay G. Williams in his *Understanding the Bible* points out that the Egyptians' use of magic is well attested in much Egyptian literature: In Exodus, "Ch. 7:9-12 indicates that the trick of turning a snake into a rod (perhaps by pressing a nerve to make it rigid) was also known and used by the Egyptian magicians as well. Undoubtedly Moses first learned this as a young man brought up in the Pharaoh's house."

The Plagues of the Frogs, the Lice, and the Flies

(Exodus 7:25 & 8:1-32)

SEVEN days after Yahweh had smitten the river, the Lord said to Moses, "Go to Pharaoh again and tell him that Yahweh declares this: 'You must let my people go to worship me. If you refuse to let them go I shall blight your land from border to border with frogs. The Nile will teem with frogs. They will come up into your palace, into your bedroom, into your bed. They will invade your servants' quarters and your subjects' houses: even their ovens and kneading bowls. Oh yes, the frogs will crowd all over you and over your people and ministers.' "

Then the Lord said to Moses, "Have Aaron stretch out his staff toward the streams, rivers, and ponds to make the frogs advance on the entire kingdom of Egypt."

So Aaron reached out toward all the waters of Egypt and the frogs came up and thronged over Egypt's terrain. But the magicians followed suit with their own magic and produced frogs too all over Egypt. At which Pharaoh summoned Moses and pleaded, "Entreat the Lord to remove these frogs from me and my nation, and I shall let your people go to sacrifice to their Lord."

"When shall we celebrate the event?" Moses replied to Pharaoh. "When am I to plead for you and your servants and subjects that the frogs all around you and in your houses be destroyed and kept to the river?"

"Tomorrow," he said.

"Just as you wish," Moses answered. "And, that you may know there is none like the Lord our God, you, your homes, your servants and subjects will be free of frogs except for those in the river."

Moses and Aaron then left the presence of Pharaoh, and Moses pleaded with the Lord to remove the frogs he had marshaled against Pharaoh. The Lord did just what Moses asked. Frogs expired in house, village, and field. They were collected in heaps and the land stank.

But when Pharaoh saw this respite he again hardened his heart and ignored Moses and Aaron, as the Lord said he would. Then Yahweh said to Moses, "Tell Aaron to stretch out his staff and blight the land with lice all over Egypt."

This they did. Aaron reached out his staff and blighted the land till it teemed with lice—all over man and beast. The earth throughout the country of Egypt was alive with lice. The magicians tried to follow suit with their magic, but this time they could not. Humans and beasts were crawling with lice, and the magicians said to Pharaoh, "This is the finger of God," but once more Pharaoh's heart hardened and he would not listen to them (as the Lord had predicted).

Then the Lord said to Moses, "Get up early in the morning and accost Pharaoh on his way to the river. Say to him, 'Yahweh commands you: "Let my people go to worship me. If you refuse to release them, I shall infest you with flies—flies all over you, all over your ministers and subjects. Your whole palace and the homes of the Egyptians will be alive with flies: even the ground on which you tread. But in Goshen where my people live—that shall be kept apart: there will be no flies there. Which will make you realize that

I am the Lord of the World. Yes, I shall separate your people from my people. This prodigy will happen tomorrow." ' "

Yahweh did precisely that. An horrendous blight of flies swarmed into Pharaoh's palace, into his servants' quarters, and all over Egypt. The land became a putrefaction of flies.

Pharaoh called for Moses and Aaron. "Go," he said, "go and sacrifice to your God, but do it in this land."

To which Moses replied, "It is not feasible to do that because our sacrifices to the Lord our God are an abomination to the Egyptians. Are we really going to perpetrate a ritual of abomination right before their eyes and get ourselves stoned? No, we must make a three days' pilgrimage into the wilderness and sacrifice to the Lord our God in the way he commands."

"Very well," responded Pharaoh. "I shall let you go to sacrifice to your God in the wilderness but do not go very far . . . Now plead for me [against the flies]."

"I am leaving at once," Moses replied, "to beg the Lord to take away tomorrow the swarms of flies from Pharaoh, his servants, and his subjects. Only, Pharaoh must never again deceive us by not letting our people go to make their sacrifice to the Lord."

So Moses and Aaron went out from Pharaoh and prayed to the Lord, and the Lord did what Moses asked; so completely ridding Pharaoh, his servants, and subjects from the infestation of flies that not a single fly was left.

Then once again Pharaoh hardened his heart and would not let the people go.

The Plagues of the Stricken Cattle, of the Boils, and of the Hail

(Esodus 9:1-35)

THE Lord next said to Moses, "Go back to Pharaoh and say, 'Yahweh, Lord God of the Hebrews, commands you: "Let my people go to sacrifice to me. If you refuse and hold on to them, I shall raise my hand and strike your fields with a terrible disease infecting your horses, asses, camels, and all your livestock and sheep.

" 'Besides, Yahweh will make a miraculous distinction between that which belongs to Israel and that which belongs to the Egyptians so that not a thing dies belonging to Israel. The time the Lord has fixed for this is tomorrow.' "

Accordingly, the next day the Lord made it happen. The animals of the Egyptians died but not a single beast of the children of Israel. But even though Pharaoh's inquiries confirmed that not a thing had perished which belonged to Israel, his heart was still hardened and he refused to let the people go.

Yahweh then said to Moses and Aaron, "Grab yourselves some handfuls of ash from the hearth and let Moses scatter this in front of Pharaoh till the whole kingdom of Egypt is smothered in dust and everything in Egypt, both human and beast, is covered in boils and blisters."

So they took ashes from the grate and Moses, right in front of Pharaoh, tossed these into the air till everything human or animal became covered in boils and blisters. Even the magicians could not stand up straight in Pharaoh's presence because of their boils. Boils were everywhere in Egypt. But still the Lord hardened Pharaoh's heart, just as he said he would, and Pharaoh was unmoved.

Next, the Lord said to Moses, "Rise early and go to Pharaoh and tell him: 'The Lord God of the Hebrews insists: "Let my people go and worship me, otherwise I shall blight you to the core with plagues—you, your ministers, and your nation—till you really understand that there is none in this world like me. This time I shall reach out and hit you with a disaster that leaves you stunned. The only reason I brought you into existence was to manifest my power through you and make my name ring throughout the earth. Are you still going to defy me in your arrogance and refuse to let my people go? Very well, tomorrow at this hour I shall rain down a giant hail: a hail unheard of since the foundation of Egypt till this day. Make haste to bring in your cattle and everything else from the fields because whatever is left outside, man or beast, is going to be hammered by the hail and killed.' "

Those among Pharaoh's subjects who respected God's word made their servants and livestock take shelter; but those who paid no attention to God's word left their servants and livestock in the fields.

Yahweh then told Moses, "Raise your hand heavenward and cause hail to fall on the length and breadth of Egypt: on all human beings, all beasts, and every growing thing."

Moses lifted his staff toward heaven and Yahweh mustered his thunder and hail. Lightning raced over the ground. Yahweh really rained down hail on the land of Egypt. Hail mixed with fire drove on together. The hail was of a size never seen in Egypt since its beginning. It annihilated everything in the fields, human and animal. It laid flat every plant. It shattered trees. Only in the region of Goshen, where the children of Israel dwelt, did the hail not fall.

Pharaoh hastily summoned Moses and Aaron. "Yes, I have been remiss again," he said. "Yahweh is right and we are wrong. Plead with Yahweh to stop this hail and I promise to let your people go. You need tarry no longer."

"As soon as I leave the city," Moses answered, "I shall lift my hands toward the Lord and the thunderings will stop and the hail cease. That will prove to you that the earth is Yahweh's. However, even now I know that neither you nor your ministers have any respect for Yahweh our God."

All the flax and barley had been flattened, because the barley was green and the flax in flower. The wheat and other grain, however, were undamaged because these were late.

So Moses went from Pharaoh out of the city and raised his hands toward the Lord till the thunder and hail ceased and not a single pebble of hail fell on the earth.

Pharaoh, seeing that the rain and the hail and the thunder were over, returned to his sinning. He and his officials hardened their hearts till Pharaoh's heart was obdurate beyond belief and, just as the Lord had foretold, he would not let the children of Israel go.

The Plagues of the Locusts and the Darkness

(Exodus 10:1-29)

NEXT, the Lord said to Moses, "Go back to Pharaoh, even though I have hardened his heart and the heart of his ministers so that because of them I can manifest these wonders. And I want you to be able to fill the ears of your sons and grandsons with stories of how I plagued the Egyptians and did all sort of marvels just to show you that I am Yahweh."

So once again Moses and Aaron went before Pharaoh and said to him, "Yahweh, God of the Hebrews, demands to know: 'How much longer before you submit? Release my people now to worship me or else tomorrow I shall let locusts loose on all your coasts. They will blanket the ground and smother all sight of the earth. They will consume whatsoever escaped the hail and devour every tree of the field. They will fill your palace and the homes of your officials and every house in Egypt. Your fathers' fathers from the very beginning will never have witnessed anything like it.' "

Moses turned his back on Pharaoh and walked away.

Pharaoh's ministers now came to him, asking, "How long do you think we can put up with this? At least let the *men* go and worship Yahweh their God. Or are you unaware that all Egypt lies in ruins?"

So Moses and Aaron were called back into Pharaoh's presence and he said to them, "All right, go and worship your God. But who do you want to go?"

"Our young and old we must take," Moses replied: "our sons and daughters, our livestock and herds—for we are to celebrate a feast of the Lord."

"In the name of God," expostulated Pharaoh, "I will not let you go with all your children. This is an obvious trick to work some mischief. So no! Only the adult men can go to sacrifice to Yahweh. That is what you wanted."

Moses and Aaron were driven from Pharaoh's presence. Then the Lord said to Moses, "Stretch out your hand now over the land of Egypt and bring in the swarming locusts to devour everything that the hail has left."

So Moses raised his staff over Egypt and Yahweh blew a burning wind all that day and all that night, and when morning came the burning wind had brought the locusts. They covered the whole country of Egypt. They massed in their thousands from coast to coast: a smothering of locusts such as had never been before and will never be again. They blotted out the sun in a cloud of darkness and consumed every plant and fruit tree left by the hail. Throughout Egypt not a vestige of green remained on the trees or in the fields.

Pharaoh hastily summoned Moses and Aaron and declared, "I have wronged Yahweh your God and I have wronged you. I beg you to forgive me this once and to entreat Yahweh your God to remove this death."

Whereupon Moses left Pharaoh and prayed to the Lord,

and the Lord blew a strong west wind which swept the locusts into the Red Sea. Within all the borders of Egypt not a locust was left.

But God hardened Pharaoh's heart and again he would not let the children of Israel go. "Raise your hand toward heaven," Yahweh said to Moses, "and let a darkness so dense fall over the land of Egypt that one can almost feel it."

Moses lifted his hand toward heaven and for three days the whole of Egypt was plunged in a thick darkness. For three days people could not see one another and nobody stirred. But wherever the children of Israel dwelt there was light.

Then Pharaoh called for Moses and said to him, "Go. Worship Yahweh. Only keep your herds and livestock here. You can take your children."

"But," replied Moses, "you must allow us the wherewithal for sacrifice and burnt offerings. Our flocks must go with us and not leave a hoof behind, for we need them for the worship of our Lord God and cannot tell till we get there what the sacrifice requires."

At that the Lord hardened Pharaoh's heart and he would not let them go. "Get away from me," he shouted, "and never let me see your face again. The day you do, you die."

"Very well," Moses replied, "I shall not come into your presence again."

The Death of the Firstborn

(Exodus 11:1-8, 12:21-42, 13:17-22)

THEN the Lord said to Moses, "I shall bring one more plague upon Pharaoh and Egypt, after which he will let you go. In fact, he will expel you. Tell your people that every man and woman is to ask from their Egyptian neighbors jewelry and articles of silver and gold. (The Lord had made the Israelites popular with the Egyptians. Moses, moreover, was a great man in the eyes of Pharaoh's subjects and ministers.)

So Moses made the following announcement to Pharaoh:

"The Lord declares: 'At midnight I shall pass through Egypt and every firstborn son in the land of Egypt shall die, from the eldest son of Pharaoh who sits on the throne to the eldest son of the young woman who works at the mill—even to the firstborn of beasts. A wail of despair will go up all over Egypt the like of which has never been before and will never be again; but against the children of Israel, man or beast, not even a dog shall bark. That will make you realize how great is the gulf which Yahweh sets between the Egyptians and the Israelites. Your ministers will come to me bowing and scraping, pleading with me to depart and take my followers with me.' "

Moses stomped out raging.

Then he called together the elders of the children of Israel and said to them: "Every family is to select a lamb and kill it for the passover, then dip a sprig of hyssop in a basin of the lamb's blood and mark the lintel of their front door with it and both doorposts. No one is to go out through that door till morning, for the Lord will be passing through, striking down the Egyptians. When he sees the blood on the lintel and doorposts he will pass that door by and not let the destroyer go in to hurt you.

"You and your descendents are to observe this ritual ever afterward on a fixed day of remembrance. Even when you have entered the land which the Lord has promised, you must continue to observe these ceremonies. And when your children ask you: 'What is the meaning of this observance?' you must answer: 'It is the celebration of the Lord's passage when he passed over the houses of the children of Israel in Egypt and struck down the Egyptians, leaving our homes intact.' "

The people bowed their heads and worshiped, then went and did all that Moses and Aaron had commanded.

And so it was that at midnight the Lord struck down every firstborn in the land of Egypt, from the firstborn heir of Pharaoh who sat on the throne to the firstborn of the felon in his dungeon, even to the firstborn of cattle.

Pharaoh arose in the dead of night and all his servants and all the Egyptians, and a great wail went up all over Egypt, for there was not a house without one dead. He summoned Moses and Aaron that same night and pleaded, "Collect yourselves at once and leave my people: you and the Children of Israel. Go and worship your God as you want. Take your flocks and herds as you demanded and go. Only bless me in your going."

The Egyptians could hardly wait to rid themselves of the Israelites, muttering, "We shall all be corpses."

Then the people wrapped bundles of unleavened dough in their clothing and slung these over their shoulders. They also asked from the Egyptians—as Moses told them—jewelry of silver and gold and fine apparel. The Lord had made the Egyptians well disposed toward the Israelites, so they furnished them with whatever they asked for. Thus did the people strip the Egyptians.

The children of Israel set forth on the march from Rameses to Succoth, six hundred thousand strong—not counting women and children. There was, besides, a large mixed crowd of camp followers and there were herds of every kind of livestock and cattle.

The Israelites baked the dough they had brought from Egypt into unleavened loaves, not having had time to do this when the Egyptians were pressing them to depart and thrusting them out of Egypt. Nor had they cooked any food. The children of Israel had sojourned in Egypt four hundred and thirty years to the very day: the day that Yahweh's people in a vast array went out from the land of Egypt. It had been a night of watching for the Lord, watching for the moment of exodus, and so the remembrance of this same night is a night of watching too, held sacred to the Lord by all Israelites through untold generations.

Now that Pharaoh had expelled the children of Israel, God did not lead them through the country of the Philistines, though that was the more direct route. He was afraid that if they encountered resistance they might change their minds and turn back for Egypt. So instead he led them the long way round through the desert toward the Red Sea ["Sea of Reeds"].

They left Egypt fully armed, Moses taking with him Joseph's bones, for Joseph had solemnly sworn to Jacob's children: "God will surely punish you if you do not carry away my bones with you out of Egypt."

Marching from Succoth, they camped at Etham on the edge of the desert. Yahweh went before them and showed the way by day in a pillar of cloud, and by night in a column of fire. Thus they could march night and day: the pillar of cloud never failing in the daytime, nor the column of fire at night.

A Path Through the Red Sea

The surge of euphoria that may well have swept over the Israelites on first being released from their Egyptian captors must soon have spent itself when the sun beat down on the slowly moving caravan in one of the hottest places on earth. Nor would they have derived much consolation on coming within sight of the sea they must cross—the Red Sea: a 1450-mile-long snake of very salty water which crawls between the African and Arabian deserts. As they made their way northward, looking for a place to cross, their hearts quailed when they saw the dust clouds of the pursuing Egyptian army.

(Exodus 14:1-31, 15:1-12)

YAHWEH then spoke to Moses and said, "Tell the children of Israel to turn toward Pihahiroth and to encamp opposite Baalzephon between Migdol and the sea. Pitch your tents near the sea because Pharaoh is saying to himself, 'Those children of Israel are trapped, shut in by the desert.' I am hardening Pharaoh's heart and he is going to pursue you. Pharaoh and all his panoply will redound to my glory and make the Egyptians really believe that I am the Lord."

The Israelites did what they were told. But when it was announced to the king of Egypt that the people had fled for good, the feelings of Pharaoh and his ministers changed toward them and they began to lament, "Whatever were we thinking of to let go of these Israelites who slaved for us?"

So Pharaoh harnessed his chariot, mustered his men, and led the chase with six hundred of his best chariots (not to mention chariots from all over Egypt) captained by his finest officers. The Lord had indeed hardened the heart of the king of Egypt to pursue the Israelites, who had departed with so much wealth.

The Egyptians pressed after them with all Pharaoh's cavalry, chariots, charioteers, and entire army, catching up with them as they encamped by the sea at Pihahiroth opposite Baalzephon. When Pharaoh drew near enough for the children of Israel to see the whole Egyptian host behind them, they panicked and called in desperation on the Lord. And they attacked Moses, saying: "Have you brought us out here to die in the desert just because there were not enough graves for us in Egypt? Was that your intention when you led us out of Egypt? Did we not tell you this in Egypt: to leave us alone and let us serve the Egyptians? For surely it is better to be slaves to the Egyptians than corpses in the desert."

"Have no fear," Moses responded. "Stand firm and you will see Yahweh do something marvelous today. These Egyptians you now gaze on, you will never see again. Yahweh will fight for you while you keep still."

But to Moses Yahweh said, "What! are you still praying? Get the children of Israel to start moving forward. Now stretch your staff over the sea and sever the sea in two to let the Israelites walk dry-shod through the middle. I have stiffened the Egyptians' stubbornness and they will pursue you. Yes, Pharaoh with his great army, his chariots and horsemen, is about to magnify my name. And when Pharaoh with his chariots and horsemen magnifies my name, the Egyptians will indeed know that I am Yahweh."

Then God's angel moved with the pillar of cloud from the front of the Israelites to their rear so that it now stood between the Egyptians' camp and the Israelites': a black cloud to the Egyptians but a bright light to the Israelites, making it impossible for them to be attacked during the night.

When Moses stretched his hand over the sea, the Lord began to blow an east wind all through the night, strong and burning. It shrank the sea inward, dividing the water and drying the ground. Through the middle of this sea on a dry floor the children of Israel walked, with walls of water rising on their right and left.

The Egyptians—Pharaoh's entire cavalcade of horses, chariots, horsemen—started after them through the midst of the sea. And at dawn, Yahweh, looking down on them through the column of fire and the dark cloud, began his harassment of the Egyptian army. He clogged the wheels of the chariots till they went scraping along the ground and the Egyptians cried out, "Away from here, away from these Israelites. Yahweh is fighting for them against Egypt."

Then the Lord said to Moses, "Raise your hand over the sea and make the waters fall back on the Egyptians and their chariots and horsemen."

It was morning when Moses raised his hand over the sea and the sea rushed back to its natural state, catching the

Egyptians in the middle of their flight. The waters flushed over them as the Lord overwhelmed them in the waves. The regathering sea submerged chariots, horsemen, and the whole of Pharaoh's army that had pursued the Israelites into the sea. Not a man was saved.

The children of Israel, meanwhile, passed dry-shod between walls of water on their right and left through the middle of the sea.

Thus did Yahweh that day save Israel from the hands of the Egyptians. The Israelites gazed on dead Egyptians strewn along the seashore, struck down by the mighty hand of Yahweh. The people were in awe of Yahweh and believed in him and his servant Moses.

Then Moses and the children of Israel sang this song to the Lord.

I sing to the Lord
  who has triumphed like a champion.
The horse and the horseman
  he hath tossed to the waves.
The Lord is my powerhouse and my hymn.
He is my salvation and my God:
My father's God
  and him I adore.

The Lord is a warrior,
  Yahweh is his name.
The chariots of Pharaoh and his mighty array
  he hath cast into the sea.
Yea, into the Red Sea he hath drowned
  the elite of his captains.
Into the depths they went
  and sank like a stone.

Magnificent in power, O Lord,
  is thy right hand.
Thy right hand hath shattered the foe.
Thine enormous majesty hath overturned
  them that assailed thee.
The breath of thy wrath
  hath consumed them like stubble.

One snort of thy nostrils
  hath heaped up the seas.
The liquid of water
  stood up like a wall.

The depths were congealed
  in the heart of the sea.

The enemy vaunted:
  "I shall chase. I shall catch.
I shall divide and assign
  and glut on the spoils.
The sword in my hand
  shall split them asunder."

But thou blewest thy wind
  and the sea overwhelmed.
Like lead they sank
  in the tumult of flood.

Who is there like thee,
  Lord of the gods?
Who can match
  thy hallowed estate?
Who is so awesome
  a worker of wonders?
When thou stretched forth thy hand
  the earth gulped them down.

NOTES

The average width of the Red Sea is 150 miles, but it is most improbable that where the Israelites crossed it was anywhere near that wide. There have been many conjectures as to where the spot was. Nobody really knows either why this dangerous arm of water, with its coral reefs and sudden squalls from the north, is called the Red Sea. It seems to have been the Greeks who first named it that, perhaps because at certain times the waters teem with microscopic cells (diatoms) which give the surface a ruddy flush. As a child I remember well how, passing from the Indian Ocean down the Red Sea by ship from India at sunset, I saw not only the whole sea but the hills of Africa turn scarlet and crimson.

Manna from Heaven and Water from a Rock

As stated in the text, the Israelites in their march through the desert to the land of Canaan (from which their forefathers had come) did not take the shortest route, which would have been through the country of the warlike Philistines. Instead, they headed southeast through the wilderness below Mount Sinai: a region Moses knew well because he had once been a shepherd there. It was at Horeb in the Sinai range that he had received his divine mission.

The territory which this unwieldy concourse of thousands of men, women, and children (not to mention their cows, sheep, goats, donkeys, and possibly camels) now had to cover was forbidding: the terrain barren and rocky, food virtually nonexistent, springs of water rare and far apart. One can understand why complaints soon began.

The various miracles recounted in this part of the story can now all be "explained" with some degree of probability. The crossing of the Red Sea itself, for instance, was really the crossing of the Sea of Reeds, a much narrower and shallower horn of water east of the Nile delta and at the top of the Red Sea proper, where a strong wind off the desert could conceivably expose the high parts.

As to the quail, manna, and rock gushing water, each can be accounted for. Migratory flocks of quail do fly over the Sinai peninsula and can be picked up quite easily when they rest from exhaustion. Manna is probably the same sweet substance exuded by certain desert insects which is still gathered and eaten. When the Israelites first saw it lying on the ground they said to one another in wonderment, "*Manhu?*" the Hebrew for "What is this?" Lastly, the limestone rocks of this region often do secrete pockets of water which, with luck, can be found and broken open.

Scholarly opinion is divided on how much of the Exodus account actually happened and how much is later embroidery. What cannot be denied is that the Israelites went through an experience that not only welded them into a nation, but distinguished their monotheism once and for all from the religion of the surrounding pagans. They came out of the furnace of the desert with a burnished faith in a God who cared: perhaps cared too much, but who would steer them through the world with a new spirit of hope.

(Exodus 16:31, 35-36, 17:1-7)

THEY came to Elim, with its twelve wells and seventy palm trees, and they camped there by the waters. Then the entire mass of the children of Israel traveled from Elim and on the fifteenth day of the second month after leaving Egypt came to the wilderness of Sin—between Elim and Sinai—and there in the desert the whole community began to grumble against Moses and Aaron. "Would to God the Lord had killed us in the land of Egypt," they moaned, "where we sat by our fleshpots and ate to the full. Now you have brought us into this wilderness to starve us all to death."

At which, Yahweh said to Moses, "Look, I am going to rain down bread from heaven for you, and every day the people can go out and gather their portion for the day. This will test how much they follow my biddings, because on the sixth day they are to collect and prepare twice as much as they normally gather."

So Moses and Aaron told the Israelites, "This evening you will realize that it was Yahweh who brought you out of the land of Egypt. And in the morning you will see God's glory manifest, for he has heard your grumblings against him—not to mention your grumblings against us."

Then Moses continued, "When Yahweh gives you meat to eat in the evening, and in the morning bread to your heart's content, it means that he has listened to your complaints against him. For, yes, your grumblings against us are not really against us but against the Lord."

Moses then said to Aaron, "Tell all the people to gather around and hear the Lord's response to their complaints. And as Aaron was addressing the whole assemblage of Israel, suddenly, from out of the cloud, as they looked out into the wilderness they beheld the awesome majesty of Yahweh. And Yahweh said to Moses, "I have heard the murmurings of the children of Israel, so tell them this: 'You shall have your meat to eat in the evening and in the morning you can stuff yourselves with bread. And you can acknowledge that I am the Lord your God.' "

And so it happened that in the evening quails flew over and dropped down on the camp; and in the morning the ground all around the camp was wet with dew which, when it was gone, left lying there on the desert floor powdery flakes as fine as hoarfrost. When the Israelites saw it they asked one another, "What is this?" ["Manhu?"], for they had no idea what it was. But Moses said to them, "This is the bread which Yahweh has given you to eat. He enjoins that everyone gather it for his household, reckoning one *omer* per person according to the number of people in his tent."

This the children of Israel did; some gathering more, some less. And when they came to measure it into omers, they found that those who had collected a lot did not have too much, and those who had collected less did not have too little. Every person collected according to his wants. Moses also told them that nobody should keep this food till the next day. But there were some who did not listen and kept it till morning, and it bred worms and stank. Moses was angry with them. Morning after morning they gathered it until everybody had enough to eat, and when the sun waxed strong the manna melted. On the sixth day they gathered twice as much—two omers for each person—and the officers of the assemblage reported this to Moses, who said to them, "Yes, that is what the Lord prescribed. Tomorrow is a day of rest, the Lord's holy Sabbath. Bake today what you have to bake, and boil what you have to boil, and put aside what is left over for tomorrow."

They found that what they put aside for the next day, as Moses told them to, did not go bad or wormy. "This is your fare for the Sabbath," Moses explained, "you will not find any food lying around on the Lord's Sabbath. You have six days for gathering, and on the seventh day, the Sabbath, there will be nothing."

In spite of this, some of the people went out to gather on the seventh day and they found nothing. Which made Yahweh expostulate, "How much longer are you people going to ignore my laws and ordinances? Don't you see that the Lord has given you the Sabbath and that is why he provides you with food for two days on the sixth day? So stay at home on the seventh day and none of you stir."

The people therefore rested on the seventh day. They called this food "manna." It was like coriander seed, but white, and tasted like wafers made with honey. The Israelites fed on manna for forty years. They fed on it until they came to an inhabited land and reached the borders of Canaan.

* * *

From the wilderness of Sin, the whole community of Israel, traveling in easy stages as the Lord instructed, encamped at Rephidim. There, finding no water to drink, they complained to Moses, "Give us water to drink."

"Why complain to me?" Moses answered. "And why must you provoke the Lord?"

But the people, crazy with thirst, shouted at Moses, "So this is why you took us out of Egypt—to have us all die of thirst with our children and our cattle?"

At which Moses appealed to Yahweh, "What am I to do with this people? They are almost ready to stone me."

Yahweh answered, "Go with some of the elders of Israel and confront the populace. And take your staff—the one you struck the river with. I shall meet you at Mount Horeb. I'll be standing by the rock there. Hit the rock. Water will gush out for the people to drink."

Moses did exactly this in front of the elders of Israel. He called the spot Massah, "Yahweh provoking," and also Meribah, "contention," because there the children of Israel grumbled and provoked Yahweh, saying, "Is Yahweh with us or not?"

The Young Joshua

It is not clear why this short account of Israel's first battle should suddenly appear in the middle of Exodus 17. The events it describes are probably misplaced.

Joshua is the shortened form of Jehoshua and also the Hebrew for the name Jesus. It means "Yahweh Saves." Joshua was the son of Nun, one of Moses' right-hand men, of the tribe of Ephraim. We shall hear much more about Joshua later.

Amalek was the grandson of Esau and therefore the great-great-grandson of Abraham. His descendants, the Amalekites, were powerful and troublesome Bedouin nomads, destined to be a nuisance to Israel for the next few centuries.

(Exodus 17:8-13)

BUT now the men of Amalek swept down on Israel at Rephidim, and Moses instructed Joshua to pick out a force to go and fight these Amalekite warriors. "I shall stand on the top of the hill tomorrow with the staff of God in my hand," he encouraged.

Joshua did what Moses told him and engaged Amalek in battle while Moses and Aaron climbed to the top of the hill. As long as Moses held up his hands, the men of Israel had the better of the fight, but whenever he let his hands drop, the men of Amalek did. Moses arms grew heavy, so a stone was rolled out for him to sit on and Aaron and Hur [Moses' brother-in-law] stood on either side of him and held up his arms till the sun set.

And so did Joshua rout the warriors of Amalek with the edge of the sword.

The Ten Commandments

We have now reached a theological turning point. Israel has been saved from bondage, not merely physical but spiritual. If she will accept Yahweh as her only god, he will look after all her interests, and the Israelites will be freed from the trammels of a restrictive, uncertain, and superstitious polytheism. To this end Yahweh designs specifically for Israel the safeguard of the Ten Commandments. These are not meant to be curbs upon her freedom but the fundamental honoring of human nature and the setting up of a humane framework within which that freedom can blossom.

Alas, Israel is not up to it. She is not trusting enough to accept Yahweh's gift of freedom. She trembles before him as if he were an ogre and, like a bird that feels safe only in its cage, hankers after all the strictures of a tight, visible (with priests, vestments, rubrics) ritual-ridden system.

Perhaps this is the tragedy of all institutional religions. They may indeed escape from the bondage of the "Egyptians," with spiritual freedom dangled before them, only to fall victims to the human passion for legislation and cultic restrictions.

(Exodus 19:125, 20:1-26)

ON the first day of the third month of their leaving Egypt, the Israelites entered the wilderness of Sinai. With Rephidim behind them, they reached the desert of Sinai and pitched their tents at the foot of the mountain.

Meanwhile, Moses went up the mountain to meet with God, and Yahweh called out to him, "This is what you must tell the house of Jacob, the children of Israel: 'You have seen what I did to the Egyptians, and how I carried you here to me on eagle's wings; so if you will obey me and keep my covenant, you shall be my own special people; dearer to me than all other nations, for all the earth is mine. And you shall be a priestly kingdom, a holy people.' That is what you must tell the Israelites."

Moses came down from the mountain and called together the elders of the community and told them what the Lord had said. After they had unanimously answered: "Yes, we will do everything that the Lord has asked;" Moses brought back this response to the Lord, who then said to Moses, "Look, I am going to come to you in a dark cloud so that the people can hear me talking to you and strengthen their faith in you. . . . Go down now and have them purify themselves today and tomorrow. Let them wash their clothes and be ready for the third day, because on that day Yahweh will descend on Mount Sinai in the full gaze of the people. You are to set them strict limits around the mountain and warn them on no account to go up the mountain or touch its base, because anyone who lays a finger on the mountain will be put to death. Be he man or beast, he is to be stoned or shot with arrows—not killed by hand."

So Moses came down the mountain back to the people. He had them purify themselves and wash their clothes, instructing them to be ready for the third day and not to go near a woman.

And so it happened on the morning of the third day that there was thunder and lightning, and a dense cloud hung over the mountain. A loud blast on a trumpet made the whole camp tremble. Then Moses led the people out from the camp to meet God and they stood at the foot of the mountain.

The whole of Mount Sinai was wrapped in smoke, for Yahweh had come down upon it in fire. The smoke flew up as if from a furnace and the whole mountainside shook. Long blares on the trumpet became louder and louder as Moses spoke with God and God answered in his voice of thunder. Yahweh had descended onto the summit of Mount Sinai and now he summoned Moses to the top of the mountain, and Moses climbed. Then said Yahweh to him:

"Go down now and keep the people from breaking through

to gaze on the Lord, otherwise many of them will perish. Also, have the priests who approach the Lord purify themselves against the shock of Yahweh's intensity."

"But the people cannot go up to Mount Sinai," Moses protested, "because you yourself charged us to put it out of bounds and make it sacroscant."

"Go on down now," Yahweh repeated, "then come up again bringing Aaron; only do not let the priests and the people break through to come up to the Lord or he will destroy them."

So Moses went down to the people and told them this.

Then God issued the following injunctions:

"I am the Lord thy God who brought thee out of the land of Egypt, and out of the house of bondage.

Thou shalt have no other gods before me.

Thou shalt not make unto thee any graven image or any likeness that is in heaven above, or in the earth beneath, or in the water under the earth. Thou shalt not bow thyself to them, nor serve them: for I the Lord thy God am a jealous God, visiting the iniquities of the fathers upon the children unto the third and fourth generation of them that hate me, and showing mercy to thousands of them that love me and keep my commandments.

Thou shalt not take the name of the Lord thy God in vain; for the Lord will not hold him guiltless that taketh his name in vain.

Remember the Sabbath day, to keep it holy. Six days shalt thou labor and do all thy work, but the seventh day is the Sabbath of the Lord thy God: thou shalt not do any work, thou or thy son, or thy daughter, thy manservant, or thy maidservant, or thy cattle, or thy guest who is in thy house. For in six days the Lord made heaven and earth, the sea, and all that in them is, and rested the seventh day and hallowed it.

Honor thy father and thy mother, that thy days may be long upon the land which the Lord thy God giveth thee.

Thou shalt not kill.

Thou shalt not commit adultery.

Thou shalt not steal.

Thou shalt not bear false witness against thy neighbor.

Thou shalt not covet thy neighbor's house, thou shalt not covet thy neighbor's wife, or his manservant, or his maidservant, or his ox, or his ass, or anything that is thy neighbor's."

When the people witnessed the thunder and lightning, the

noise of the trumpet blasts, and saw the mountain smoking, they stood far off shaking with terror.

They said to Moses; "You be the one who speaks to us and we will listen, but don't let God speak to us, or we'll die."

"There's nothing to be afraid of," Moses replied. "God has come in this way only to challenge you and make you respect him so that you won't sin."

Nevertheless, they kept their distance while Moses went up into the thick darkness where God was. And there God said to him, "Tell the children of Israel: 'Now that you have seen for yourselves that I have spoken to you from heaven, you must remember never to make for yourselves gods of silver, or make for yourselves gods of gold. What you can make for me is an altar of earth, on which you may sacrifice your burnt offerings and your peace offerings of sheep and oxen in the places where I design to be remembered. There I shall come to you and bless you. If you make an altar of stone for me, don't build it of dressed stone, for once you have brought a tool to it you have denatured it. And don't go up steps to my altar, letting people view your nakedness from underneath.' "

Aaron and the Golden Calf

The next three chapters of Exodus, 21 to 23, are taken up with every kind of law and ordinance that Yahweh tells Moses he wants the Israelites to follow. Most of these are humane enough, but a few would strike us as very odd. "If a man sells his daughter as a slave," for instance, "she is not to go free after six years as male slaves do"; and "Whoever strikes his father or mother shall be put to death."

Chapters 25 through 31 go into detail of how the Israelites are to worship: how they are to construct the tent Tabernacle with its wooden portable walls, its roofing of eleven goat-hair mattings, its curtains of blue, purple, and scarlet stuffs; not excluding the size, shape, and materials of the Ark of the Covenant in which the sacred slabs inscribed with the Ten Commandments are to be housed.

The vestments too are described in detail: "The robe of the ephod you shall make of violet-blue cloth . . . Its hem all around the bottom is to be embroidered with pomegranates, blue, purple, and scarlet, with gold bells in between. This is what Aaron is to wear when ministering so that their tinkling can be heard as he enters and leaves the Lord's presence in the Holy Place. Otherwise he will die."

While all these instructions are being given to Moses by Yahweh on the mountaintop (a process that takes forty days and forty nights), Aaron, who is to be the high priest of the whole scheme, has succumbed to the clamoring of the impatient Israelites and is busy arranging for them to have a golden calf that they can worship.

Aaron's docility in the face of the Israelites' demands, together with verse 32:5 ("When Aaron saw this he built an altar before the calf and proclaimed: 'Tomorrow will be a feast to Yahweh' "), suggest that the Israelites never quite intended to set up an idol when they asked for "a god that can go before us," but wanted a visible symbol of Yahweh which could be ever present to them and give them confidence. They were, after all, somewhat unnerved by Moses' absence and Yahweh's silence. They had, however, only recently been forbidden (Exodus 20:40) to represent Yahweh in any visible form.

The punishment meted out to them may seem to us excessively harsh, but one must remember that over a period of four hundred years and more they had only precariously maintained and consolidated a monotheistic theology amid the surrounding welter of the polytheistic cults of their pagan cousins. That they were now flouting the Hebraic sense of modesty by frolicking naked around the golden calf, only shows how near and real was the threat of pagan values.

(Exodus 32:1-35)

WHEN the people saw that Moses lingered on the mountain, they came in a deputation to Aaron and said to him, "Come now, make us a god that can go before us, because this fellow Moses who brought us out of the land of Egypt—we have no idea what has become of him."

Aaron replied, "Take off the golden earrings in the ears of your wives, sons, and daughters and bring them to me."

So the people unfastened the gold earrings which adorned their ears and brought them to Aaron, who took them, melted them down, and out of them tooled a calf.

"Israel, this is your god who brought you out of the land Egypt," they exclaimed.

When Aaron saw this, he built an altar before the calf and proclaimed, "Tomorrow will be a feast to Yahweh."

Early next morning they began to sacrifice burnt offerings and they brought tokens of peace. The people then sat down to eat and drink, and rose up to play.

Whereupon the Lord told Moses, "Quick, go down. Your people whom you led out of the land of Egypt have fallen into depravity. They have lost no time in turning away from the laws I gave them. They have made a molten calf and are worshiping it and sacrificing to it, calling out: 'Israel, this is your god who brought you out of the land of Egypt.' "

Then Yahweh added, "I see now, watching these people, what a stiff-necked race they are. Leave me now. My anger is going to flare out and consume them. I shall make a great nation out of you instead."

But Moses pleaded with his Lord God. "Yahweh," he said, "why are you blazing with rage against your very own people whom you brought out of Egypt with such power and magnificence? Do you now want the Egyptians to jeer: 'So his reason for bringing them out was murderous—to slaughter them in the mountains and wipe them off the face of the earth'? Let your fiery anger cool. Relent in doing such an awful thing to your own people. Remember your servants Abraham, Isaac, and Jacob, to whom you swore by your own self to multiply their posterity like the stars of heaven and to give them the large land you promised for their descendants to possess forever."

So Yahweh relented and did not carry out the destruction he had thought to do his people. Moses turned and went down the mountainside with the two tablets of the Commandments in his arms. The tablets were inscribed on both sides, front and back. They were the work of God, with God's own writing graven on them.

Joshua [who had joined Moses in his descent] heard the clamor of the people shouting and he exclaimed to Moses, "The sounds are like a battle cry coming from the camp." "They are not," said Moses. "What I hear are not sounds of victory or defeat but of people singing."

When they drew near the camp, Moses saw the calf and people dancing. In a burst of anger he hurled the tablets to the ground, smashing them at the base of the mountain. Then he took the calf which they had made, melted it down in the fire, ground it to dust, infused the dust in water, and made the Israelites drink it.

He turned next on Aaron. "What did these people ever do to you for you to encourage them in so great a sin?"

"Please, my lord," Aaron answered, "do not be in such a flaming rage. You know how these people are prone to evil. They said to me, 'Make us a god that can go before us, because this fellow Moses who brought us out of the land of Egypt. . . . We have no idea what has become of him.' So I told them, 'Whoever has any gold jewelry, take it off.' This they gave me, which I cast into the furnace and out came this calf."

When Moses saw that the people were naked and that Aaron (to the shameful amusement of their enemies) had let them run wild, he stood at the head of the camp and proclaimed, "Whoever is on the Lord's side, let him come over here and join me."

All the Levites then rallied to his side. "This is the decree of Yahweh, God of Israel," he announced to them. "Buckle your swords, every man of you, and comb through the camp from gate to gate, killing even your brothers, your friends, your neighbors [if they have worshiped the golden calf].' "

The Levites executed Moses' command and about three thousand men fell that day. Then Moses told the Levites, "You have consecrated yourselves to the Lord today because you were prepared to sacrifice even your sons and brothers. You have brought blessings on yourselves today."

The following morning Moses said to the people, "You have sinned a great sin, but I shall go up to the Lord and perhaps I can make atonement for your sin."

So he returned to Yahweh and said, "I know that this people have sinned a great sin in making themselves an idol of gold, yet now please forgive them or else blot me from your book."

Yahweh made answer: "No, Moses, I will blot out only him who has sinned against me. So go off now and lead the people to the land I told you of. My angel shall go before you. But when I visit this people, I shall visit their sin upon them."

NOTES

1. The ephod was an embroidered vestment without sleeves which reached to the ankle and was fastened at the waste by a girdle. It could be heavily ornamented with jewels to form almost a breastplate.

2. Numbers tended to have symbolic connotations in biblical usage. Both seven and three pointed to perfection and completeness: e.g., God's rest on the seventh day after creation, Pharaoh's

dream of the seven good years and seven lean years, Jacob's working seven years for Rachel and then another seven for her because he had been given Leah; the three parts of creation: the heavens, the earth, and the netherworld, the sanctuary divided into three, the Trinity, Jesus' rising on the third day.

Four, too, and its multiple forty had symbolic overtones. Four seems to have suggested radical structure or arrangement: the four corners of the earth, the four winds, the four rivers of Eden (and for the Greeks, the four rivers of Hades). Forty suggested a large number or a long space of time: forty days and forty nights of rain before the Flood, the Israelites wandering for forty years in the desert, Jesus tempted in the wilderness for forty days. Forty also represented the age of maturity.

3. The cult of the cow, bull, calf, had a long tradition behind it in the Near East, dating back to Neolithic times. And although the Hebrews came to regard the calf as a general symbol of pagan worship, they themselves used it both in sacrifice as a sin offering and as an emblem of festive rejoicing (cf. the killing of the fatted calf for the return of the Prodigal Son in the New Testament).

Moses Sends Scouts into Canaan

Almost a year passed since the Israelites established their camp in the desert at the foot of Mount Sinai, the time being spent in building the Tabernacle and listening to the elaborate code Yahweh laid down for them.

The Tabernacle (Latin word for "tent") was a large structure, half tent, half house, about forty-five feet long, fifteen feet wide, and fifteen feet high. It was placed right in the middle of the Israelite camp. Its walls were made of boards fastened to silver bases and layered in gold. The Tabernacle was roofed with a series of mat coverings, the inner one highly decorated and the outer one made of rams' skins to keep out the weather. The floor was the desert sand.

Surrounding the Tabernacle stood a spacious palisade protecting an open rectangle of about a hundred and fifty feet long by seventy-five feet wide. Near the entrance of this enclosure or court was placed a large portable altar made of thin boards topped with brass or copper into which was let a metal grating for the sacrificial fire on which a burnt offering of a lamb or young bull was offered morning and evening: the animals being first bathed with water from a long trough standing not far from the altar.

It was in the inner chamber of the Tabernacle, called The Holy of Holies, that the Ark of the Covenant rested. The Ark was the visible symbol of Yahweh's presence among the Israelites, and it housed the two stone tablets on which the Lord had graven the Ten Commandments. (God had provided Moses with a second pair to replace the ones Moses had smashed.) The Ark could be carried on poles set through metal rings on each side of it. Everything within the Holy of Holies was made of gold or covered in gold, even the walls. The Holy of Holies could be entered only once a year and then only by the high priest.

The Tabernacle with its costly trappings was Moses' answer to the Golden Calf. Here was a tangible expression of God's presence that sublimated the Israelites' dangerous urges to be like the pagans surrounding them and to adopt a visible god. The Tabernacle, a precursor to the Temple, became the pride and the focus of their highest energies. The dismantling and reassembling of its movable parts each time the congregation struck camp became first on their list of priorities.

So now the Israelites have moved from Sinai and set themselves up in an oasis called Kadesh, between the desert and Canaan, on the very borders of the Promised Land. They are all poised to enter it.

(Numbers 13:1-3, 17-33, 14:1-10)

YAHWEH now instructed Moses, "Send a team to explore the land of Canaan which I am giving the children of Israel. Send one leader from each of the twelve ancestral tribes of Israel."

Moses dispatched them, as the Lord instructed, from the desert of Paran, to search out the land of Canaan. "Go by the southern route over the highlands," he told them. "See what the country is like and whether the people who live there are strong or weak, many or few, and whether the land itself is fair or impoverished, the towns walled or unwalled; also whether the soil is rich or poor, the terrain wooded or treeless. And do not hesitate to bring us back some of the country's fruit." (The first grapes of the season were just ripe.)

Striking up into the highlands the team explored the lay of the land from the desert of Zin to Rehob at the entrance of Hamath. After climbing they descended toward the desert and came to Hebron, pushing onward to the brook of Eshcol.

There they cut down a branch with a single bunch of grapes on it, which they carried on a pole between two of them. They also gathered pomegranates and figs. (It was because of the bunch of grapes that the brook was called Eshcol [i.e., "cluster"].)

After reconnoitering the land for forty days, they returned and in the desert of Paran at Kadesh made their report to Moses and Aaron and to the full community of Israel, displaying before them the fruit of the land. "The country you sent us into is certainly flowing with milk and honey," they said, "as you can see from these fruits here. But the natives are fierce, their cities walled and formidably large. What is more, we saw Anakims there [a race of giants]. The Amalekites live in the south, and Hittites, Jebusites, and Amorites in the highlands, while down by the sea and along the banks of the Jordan live the Canaanites."

Then Caleb [one of the leaders sent out to spy] asked for silence, and to the crowds clustered around Moses, he shouted, "We should march straight in and take this land. We can certainly do it."

"But," countered the others who had gone exploring with him, "we can't possibly march against a people much stronger than we are," and they began to spread discouraging reports among the Israelites about the region they had reconnoitered. "The land we scouted is a man-eating land," they told the Israelites. "The people we came across are enormous. We even saw those monsters of men bred from the giant race of Anak. Before them we felt and looked like grasshoppers."

The entire community set up a wail, and all that night they went on wailing. Then they began to find fault with Moses and Aaron. "If only we had died in Egypt!" they whined. "Or if only we had died even in this desert! Has Yahweh brought us out here simply to be put to the sword and have our wives and children pillaged? Would it not be better to go back to Egypt?"

Then they huddled together and said, "We must choose a leader to take us back to Egypt."

Whereupon, Moses and Aaron prostrated themselves before the assembly of Israel, and Joshua the son of Nun and Caleb the son of Jephunneh (who were in the team which had gone out exploring), tore their clothing in protest. Then they harangued the whole assembly. "The land we went through and researched," they declared, "is a lovely land. If Yahweh is pleased with us, he will bring us there and give it to us: a land really flowing with milk and honey. So do not rebuff Yahweh, and do not be afraid of the inhabitants. They are there for the taking. Their defense is gone because the Lord is with *us*, so do not be afraid of them."

The only answer the assembly gave was to threaten to stone them.

NOTE

The desert of Zin is not the same as the wilderness of Sin. Zin stretched along the southern borders of Palestine. The wilderness of Sin lay along the foot of the Sinai massif.

Balaam and His Ass

Yahweh punished the Israelites for refusing to advance on Canaan by decreeing that none of those then living would ever enter it. They would drop dead in the desert after forty years of wandering. Moses and Aaron too would not be allowed to set foot in the Promised Land because they doubted Yahweh's word at a place called Kadesh, where the Lord told them to strike a rock and make water gush out for the thirst-stricken and grumbling people.

Now, however, despite these strictures, the conquest of Canaan under Moses' direction has at last begun. It is made easier by the fact that in the late thirteenth century Palestine, far from being a unified nation, was made up of a number of city-states, each with its own ruler.

Moses, still without himself setting foot in the Promised Land, has sent out victorious armies subjugating the Amorites and commanding the lands east of the Dead Sea along the fertile Jordan valley. Now, however, the Israelites find themselves neighbors to the people south of them, the Moabites: a Midianite race whose origin five hundred years ago stemmed from the partriarch Lot, the nephew of Abraham.

(Numbers 22:1-41, 23:1-30, 24:1-19 & v.25)

THE children of Israel now moved on, encamping in the plains of Moab, east of the Jordan opposite Jericho. When Balak, the son of Zippor, saw what they had done to the Amorites and how numerous they were, he and his people—who hated the Israelites—were filled with apprehension. "This horde will chew up everything around us like an ox in a field chewing up grass," he exclaimed to the elders of Midian (Balak the son of Zippor was king of the Moabites at that time). Accordingly, he sent messengers to Balaam, the son of Beor, who lived with his people at Pethor on the Euphrates, saying, "Look, a mass of populace has arrived out of Egypt and is swarming all over the land. They are now on my borders. Please come and lay a curse on them because they are too strong for me. Perhaps I can hit them hard and drive them from the land, because I know that whomsoever you bless is blessed and whomsoever you damn is damned."

The elders of Moab and Midian set out with handsome fees for divination in their hands and delivered Balak's message to Balaam.

"Stay the night here," he told them, "and I shall let you know whatever the Lord directs."

So the Moabite ambassadors stayed with Balaam. Meanwhile, God came to Balaam, asking, "Who are these men?"

"Balak son of Zippor, king of Moab, has sent them to me with this message," Balaam answered. " 'A horde of people has arrived out of Egypt and is swarming all over my land. Come and lay a curse on them. Perhaps I can join battle and drive them out.' "

"You must not go," God told Balaam. "You must not curse these people; they are blessed."

So when Balaam arose next morning he said to Balak's ambassadors: "Go back home. The Lord will not let me come with you," and the Moabite ambassadors returned to Balak, announcing, "Balaam refuses to come with us."

Then Balak sent further ambassadors, more numerous and distinguished, who approached Balaam and said, "Balak son of Zippor insists: 'Nothing must stop you coming. I shall reward you with great honors and do whatever you tell me. Please come and lay a curse on this people.' "

Balaam's answer to the ambassadors of Balak was: "Even if Balak were to give me his palace stuffed with silver and gold, I cannot add or subtract one single word beyond what the Lord God tells me. However, you too stay the night here till I see if the Lord tells me anything else."

During the night God came to Balaam and said, "When these men come for you, get up and go with them, but only if you make sure to do only what I tell you."

So next morning Balaam arose and saddled his ass and set off with the ambassadors of Moab. But God was angry that he had gone off so readily, and as Balaam was riding along on his ass accompanied by his two young men, God's angel came and stood in his path, blocking it. When the ass saw the Lord's angel standing in the way with drawn sword, she shied into a field and Balaam [who could not see the angel] beat her back onto the road again. Then the Lord's angel stood in a narrow lane between some vineyards, with a wall on either side, and when the ass saw the angel she brushed up against the wall, crushing Balaam's foot. So Balaam hit her again. Then the angel took up a position in an alley so narrow that there was no room to pass either right or left, and seeing the angel standing there, the ass simply collapsed under Balaam, who was now so angry that he beat her with his stick.

Then the Lord opened the ass's mouth and she asked Balaam, "You have now beaten me three times. What have I done to deserve it?"

"You have made a fool of me," Balaam replied to the ass, "and if I had a sword in my hand I would run you through."

"Am I not your faithful beast?" the ass retorted. "On which you have ridden from the very first day you owned me. Did I ever do this to you before?"

"No," he replied.

Then the Lord opened the eyes of Balaam, and he saw the angel standing in his way with drawn sword and he dropped to his knees and bowed to the ground.

"Why did you beat your ass three times?" the angel of the Lord asked him. "I stood there on purpose to block your way, because your way is not the Lord's way. Your ass saw me and swerved three times. If she had not turned to avoid me, I would have killed you by now—though not her."

At which Balaam confessed to the Lord's angel, "I have sinned, although I did not know you were standing in my way. So if this displease you, I shall turn back."

"No," replied the angel of the Lord. "Go with the men but speak only the words I give you to speak."

So Balaam continued with the ambassadors of Balak, and when the king heard that Balaam was coming, he went out to meet him at the town of Moab on the river Arnon at the edge of his kingdom.

"I sent for you. Why did you not come at once?" he said to Balaam. "Did you think I could not heap you with honors?"

"Well, now that I am here," Balaam answered, "do you think I have the slightest power to say anything? I can utter only what God puts into my mouth."

Then Balaam went with the king to Kiriathhuzoth, where Balak sacrificed oxen and sheep, giving portions to Balaam and the ambassadors with him.

The next morning, the king took Balaam up to Mount Bamoth-Baal, whence he could look down on the whole array of the Israelite camp. "Build me here seven altars," Balaam said to him, "and make ready seven bullocks and seven rams."

Balak did what Balaam asked, and the king and Balaam sacrificed a bullock and a ram on every altar. After which Balaam said to him, "You stay by your burnt offering while I go and see if the Lord will meet me. Then I shall tell you whatever he says."

Balaam then went up to an abandoned height, where God met him and Balaam said, "I have set up seven altars and on every altar I have sacrificed a bullock and a ram."

Whereupon the Lord told him what to say on his return to Balak. And when he returned, the king was standing by his burnt offerings together with all the nobles of Moab. Then the spirit of God came down upon Balaam and he uttered this oracle:

> Balak king of Moab has brought me
> all the way from the eastern mountains of Aram.
> "Come," he said: "curse for me Jacob.
> Come, damn for me Israel."
>
> How can I curse whom God has not cursed,
> damn whom God has not damned?
>
> From the topmost crags I see him.
> From the tallest peaks I watch him:
> a nation set apart,
> a nation not to be reckoned among nations.
>
> Oh, who has ever counted the pollen of Jacob?
> Or numbered the wind-borne spore of Israel?
> May I too die the death of the Just!
> May my last hours be like his!

"What have you done to me?" cried out Balak. "I hired you to curse my enemies and you have just blessed them."

"But," replied Balaam, "am I not to speak scrupulously only that which the Lord puts into my mouth?"

"Come with me, please, to another spot," Balak asked him. "Perhaps God will allow you to curse them from there."

So Balak led him to the field of Zophim on the plateau of Mount Pisgah, where he built seven altars and sacrificed a bullock and a ram on every altar. Balaam then said to the king, "Stand here by your burnt offering while I go a little farther to meet the Lord."

The Lord met Balaam and put into his mouth the words he was to say, then told him to return to Balak, who with all the nobles of Moab was standing by his offerings when Balaam approached.

"So, what did the Lord say?" King Balak inquired.

And he replied, "Rouse yourself, Balak, and hear my oracle. Listen hard, you son of Zippor:

God is not a man. He does not lie,
Nor like a human change his mind.
Has he ever promised and not fulfilled?
Ever proposed and not made good?
Understand, I am here to bless.
So I shall bless and cannot undo.

Without a pang shall Jacob be,
Without a burden, Israel.
For Yahweh his God is with him.
Like the shout of a king in triumph, strong
As a rhinoceros, Yahweh brought them
Out of Egypt. There is no spell
Against Jacob, nor no doom
Against Israel . . . It shall be said
Of Jacob and of Israel:
'See what God has wrought:
A people like a lioness rearing,
Oh, like a lion rampant which
shall not lie down
Until it has devoured its prey
and drunk the blood of the slain.' "

"Please," remonstrated Balak, "if you cannot curse them, at least do not bless them."

"But did I not warn you that I can say only what the Lord tells me?"

To which Balak replied, "Well then, let me take you to another spot. Perhaps God will not mind your cursing them from there." And he took Balaam to the top of Mount Peor, which looks down on the valley of Jeshimon.

"Build me seven altars here," Balaam said to the king, "and prepare seven bullocks and seven rams."

Balak did what Balaam asked and sacrificed a bullock and a ram at every altar. And Balaam, now convinced that it was the Lord's will to bless Israel, did not bother to go aside and seek an omen, but turned his eyes toward the plain where the whole Israelite camp, tribe by tribe, was open to his gaze. There and then the spirit of God came upon him and he began to utter this prophecy.

Balaam the son of Beor says . . .
The man whose eyes are opened says . . .
He who has heard God speaking says . . .
He who knows what the Most High knows,
He who sees what the Most High sees
(With unwrapped eyes and vision rapt):

"Oh, how goodly are thy tents, O Jacob,
And thy tabernacles, O Israel!
As the valleys are they spread forth,
As the gardens by the riverside,
As the avenue of aloes which the Lord hath planted,
And as the cedar trees beside the waters.
From living wells shall he pour his waters,
And his seed shall be loosed over many nations.

His king shall be loftier than Agaz
And his kingdom shall be exalted.
God brought him forth out of Egypt
And he has as it were the strength of a unicorn.
He shall eat up the nations his enemies,
He shall break their bones
And pierce them through with his arrows.
He couched and lay down like a lion
Or like a lioness, and who shall rouse him?
Blessed is he that blesseth thee,
And cursed is he that curseth thee."

King Balak's rage now flared up against Balaam. He clapped his hands together, shouting, "I called on you to curse my enemies, and you have blessed them—yes, three times. Get out of here. Go home. I thought to heap you with honors, but your Yahweh has quite blocked you from honor."

"But," remonstrated Balaam, "did I not make it clear to your messengers that even if King Balak gave me his palace stuffed with silver and gold, I still could not go against the Lord's command to do either good or bad of my own choosing? Only that which the Lord tells me can I utter. And now that I am about to return to my own place, let me give you warning of what this people will do to your people in days to come."

Then transported by the spirit of prophecy, he uttered:

Balaam the son of Beor says . . .
The man whose eyes are opened says . . .
He who has heard God speaking says . . .
He who knows what the Most High knows,
He who sees what the Most High sees
(With unwrapped eyes and vision rapt):

"I shall behold him, but not now.
I shall perceive him, but not near.
There shall come a star out of Jacob,
And a scepter shall rise out of Israel.
It shall smite the corners of Moab
And destroy the children of Sheth.
Israel shall possess all Edom,
And Seir fall to her foes.
Israel shall do valiantly
And out of Jacob shall come the conqueror."

Then Balaam turned his back and set out for home; and Balak too went off to his own.

The Death of Moses

Moses is now one hundred and twenty years old and still in perfect health, but Israel's victorious armies are poised to lead the children of Israel into the Promised Land, which Moses by God's express command is not to enter.

Moses has prepared the people thoroughly for his departure, rehearsing them to the minutest detail in the way Jewish life is to be lived to please the Lord. Most important, he has laid the foundation for a new concept of Yahweh, who up till now has been pictured as a primitive tribal power whose anger is easily aroused and who punishes with swift and unrelenting severity. Moses reminds the Israelites of all the forty years in which Yahweh has unswervingly supported them, thus manifesting a steadfast love, to which they must respond with total love: "Thou shalt love the Lord thy God with all thy heart and with all thy soul and with thy whole mind."

It was not yet time to stress Christ's crowning injunction: "Thou shalt love thy neighbor as thyself."

The Israelites are gathered on the plains of Moab, on the threshold of Canaan, where Moses has been delivering to them a series of discourses.

(Deuteronomy 31:30, 32:1-13, 45-52, 34:1-12)

THEN Moses recited to the whole congregation of Israel the words of this song from beginning to end.*

Open your ears, O you heavens, while I speak,
And you, O Earth,
  Listen to the words from my lips.

My discourse shall drop like the rain.
My speech shall distill like the dew:
Oh, like the shower on the grass
And the flurry of snow on the corn.
For I shall sing of the fame
Of the Lord and proclaim our God.

He is the rock—intact,
Perfect in all his deeds:
A God of truth, beyond
Evil; just and right.

But he has been disgraced
By his children: crooked
And degenerate race.

Is this how they repay
The Lord? Oh, foolish people,
Foolish and unwise!

Is he not your father
He who created you?
Made you? Left you strong?

Think of the days of old,
Reflect on age upon age.
Ask your father, he
Will tell you. Ask your elders.

*Only the first few verses are given here.

They will show you how
The Most High parceled out
The nations' heritage:
Sorted out the sons
Of Adam; set the bounds
According to their numbers.
How to himself he gave
Jacob's portion, making
Israel his own.

He found them in a desert,
A howling wilderness.
He shielded them and taught them:
The apple of his eye.
As an eagle hovers
Above her brood to tempt them
Into the air, he hovered
Over them. He bore
Them on his wings. The Lord
Was alone their keeper
With no stranger gods.

They rode the high savannas,
Fed from fertile fields.
Out of the rock they sucked
Honey, and out of granite, oil.

When Moses had finished reciting his song to all the people, he admonished them, "Lodge these words of mine in your hearts, and impress on your children every item of the Law I have given them. This is not an empty formula. This is your life. Through it you will live long days in that land you are about to possess beyond the Jordan."

That very same day, Yahweh said to Moses, "Go up into the range of Abarim in the land of Moab and climb Mount Nebo, which overlooks Jericho. Gaze from there over the land of Canaan, my bequest to the children of Israel. On that mountain you have climbed, you must die and be gathered to your ancestors, just as Aaron your brother died on Mount Hor and was gathered to his own. Because you both failed me in front of the children of Israel at the waters of Meribah-Kadesh in the desert of Zin and did not hallow my name before the people, you may only gaze out upon the land I am giving them but never enter it."

* * *

So from the plains of Moab, Moses climbed Mount Nebo, up to the summit of Pisgah overlooking Jericho. From there the Lord showed him all the land of Gilead as far as Dan: there was all Naphtali and the land of Ephraim and Manasseh; there was the whole stretch of Judah reaching to the sea; then southward, the plain and city of Jericho—that city of palm trees—as far as Zoar.

"This is the land I promised Abraham, Isaac, and Jacob," the Lord said to him, "when I told them, 'This is for your descendants.' I have let you enjoy the sight of it, but you shall not enter."

So, there in the land of Moab, as the Lord had said, Moses, Yahweh's faithful servant, died. And the Lord buried him in a valley of Moab near Bethpeor, but no one knows to this day the site of his tomb.

Moses was one hundred and twenty years old when he died: his vision undimmed, his vigor unabated. For thirty days the children of Israel wept for Moses on the plains of Moab till the prescribed time for weeping and mourning was over.

Joshua the son of Nun was full of the spirit of wisdom, for Moses had laid his hands on him, and the Israelites listened to him and followed the commandments which the Lord had given Moses.

Never again has there risen in Israel a prophet the like of Moses, to whom Yahweh talked face to face. Never again, the like of the signs and wonders which Yahweh sent him to perform in the land of Egypt against Pharaoh and all his servants and nation; nor of the magical and mighty hand he wielded in the sight of all Israel.

PART III

SETTLEMENT IN THE PROMISED LAND

(C. 1200 TO 1000 B.C.)

Stories from the Books of Joshua, Judges, Ruth, and Samuel

Introduction

Except for the short Book of Ruth, which is a welcome tale of great humanity amid the welter of blood and struggle in the other books, the general movement of this section of the Old Testament is toward showing how Yahweh championed Israel and, like a commander in the field, enabled her to take possession of the Promised Land, but how Israel time and time again failed him and had to be punished.

Although it is difficult to separate folk legend and embellished history from what actually happened, the finds of modern archeology clearly vindicate the authenticity of the historical background.

What becomes clear is that Israel's conquest was a checkered and piecemeal affair, with the twelve tribes seldom or never acting in unison. Indeed, the disunity of Israel reached such a pitch that kingship became inevitable. And that is where the Book of Samuel takes us.

It is also clear that as the Israelites conquered Canaan, so were they in turn more and more affected and tempted by the thought and culture of the conquered.

As to the authorship of these books, once again nobody really knows and scholars discuss. Certainly they are based on several very ancient sources stemming from before the exilic period (i.e., before 597 B.C.), and were probably compiled and edited by Jewish scribes in Babylon round about 562 B.C. (except for the Book of Ruth, which may well have been written much earlier).

Many of these stories have the classic "Just so" small fable form found in ancient tales designed to explain cultural phenomena or oddities (almost like "And that is how the camel got his hump!"), and they frequently end with formulas like that of the pile of stones "which remain there to this day," or like the Gibeonites, who "are hewers of wood and carriers of water to this day."

Help from a Prostitute

The mantle of Moses has now fallen on Joshua. Under his leadership the Israelites are to cross the swollen waters of the Jordan and press on with the conquest of the Promised Land.

The biblical acccount telescopes history into a mythological focus in which facts are arranged to symbolize the great central truth that just as Yahweh conquered chaos and darkness when he created the universe, so now his championing the Israelites (who are no better and no worse than their enemies) represents the triumph of good over evil. Failure to keep in mind this mythological intent of the books of Joshua and Judges leaves one with little more than a record of distorted history and a bloodthirsty and prejudiced deity.

Present-day archeology both confirms and refutes much of the historicity of the biblical account, which is clearly oversimplified and "written up" in order to make a point more important than factual accuracy. At the sites of Lachish, Debir, and Hazor, for instance, as Professor Jay G. Williams points out in his *Understanding the Old Testament,* excavations have proved that these cities were indeed attacked and destroyed, very probably by the Israelites. Archeologists have noted that beneath the relatively primitive burnt-out debris of invading tribes lie artifacts of a more sophisticated Canaanite culture. "At the same time," comments Williams, "it is equally clear that the description of the conquest of Jericho and Ai are, if not entirely fictitious, at least highly embellished and misplaced historically."

As for the Israelites' miraculous crossing of the Jordan, if one wants to explain this, one can, but at the cost of neutering a symbol. Landslides into the Jordan do occur and can block the river's flow till it breaks through the dam.

With regard to the story of Rahab the harlot, whom the Israelites save when Jericho is destroyed, she was married later to a nobleman of the tribe of Judah, called Salmon, and thus became the ancestress of a line from which was to stem David the king (she was his great-great-great-grandmother) and later, of course, Christ.

* * *

The story opens with the Israelites being encamped at Shittim on the east bank of the river Jordan, which flows into the Dead Sea.

(Joshua 2:1-24, 3:1-17, 4:1-24, 5:1-12, 6:1-27)

JOSHUA the son of Nun now sent out two young men from Shittim with instructions to spy out the land, especially Jericho.

When the two young men got to Jericho they put up in an inn run by a harlot named Rahab, but when news reached the king of Jericho that two Israelites had arrived that evening from Israel and were surveying the region, the king sent to Rahab and demanded, "Bring out the men who have come and lodged in your house, for they are here to spy out the land."

The woman, who had taken the two men and hidden them, replied, "Yes, two men did come to me, but I have no idea from where. However, after dark, about the time the gates shut, they went away—I do not know where. If you hurry you may catch them."

In point of fact, she had taken them up onto the roof of her house and concealed them under some bales of flax which were laid out there [to dry]. The pursuers went after them as far as the fords over the Jordan, and the city gates were shut as soon as they left.

The two on the roof had not yet fallen asleep when Rahab came to them and said, "I know very well that Yahweh is going to give you this land. In fact, you fill us all with fear. Everybody in the country is terrified of you; for we have heard how Yahweh dried up the waters of the Red Sea for you when you fled from Egypt, and also what you did to the two Amorite kings, Sihon and Og, on the other side of the Jordan: how you utterly destroyed them. The very news of it turned our hearts to water and there was no fight left in us. For Yahweh your God is certainly the God in heaven above and on the earth beneath . . . So I ask you this: swear to me by the Lord that just as I have shown you kindness, you too will show kindness to my father's house and make me a promise that you will spare my father and mother, my brothers and sisters, and all that they have, and save us from death."

"We pledge our life for yours," the men answered her, "and if you do not betray our mission, we shall treat you kindly and justly when the Lord gives us the land."

Then she let them down by a cord from the window (she lived in a house built into the town wall), saying to them, "To escape your pursuers when they come back for you, go and hide in the hills for three days till they return here. Then you can be on your way."

The men explained to her, "We are not to be held to the oath you made us swear unless, when we invade your land, you have tied to the window the scarlet cord you let us down by and have brought into your home your father and mother, your brothers, and all your family. Anybody leaving the house and going outside into the street is responsible for his own death and we cannot be blamed. But we shall be responsible for anything that happens to all those who stay in the house with you. Of course, if you give away our mission, we are free of the oath you made us swear."

"Be it as you say," she replied. Then bidding them farewell, she made sure when they were gone that the scarlet cord was still tied to the window.

Meanwhile, the two men set out for the hills and stayed there three days until their pursuers (who had searched everywhere along the road and not found them) returned to the city. Then the two scouts came back down from the hills, forded the Jordan, came to Joshua the son of Nun, and reported to him all that had happened to them.

The Crossing of the Jordan

The river Jordan, with its headwaters among the slopes of Mount Hermon, is the world's lowest river with a bed eight hundred and fifty feet below sea level. It flows north of and into the Sea of Galilee, then continues its course for two hundred miles between steep mountain walls to the Dead Sea. In places the Jordan valley widens into a fertile plain with a semitropical temperature, while the river meanders between banks dense with tamarisk (a small, feathery tree with olive-green foliage). The cutting down of the forests has given the region a desert climate, though the broad valley surrounding Jericho is still cultivated and during biblical times its rich vegetation earned the town the title of "city of palms."

We do not know at what point Joshua's forces made their famous fording of the Jordan.

(Joshua 3:1-17, 4:1-24)

VERY early the next morning, Joshua struck camp and moved all the Israelites from Shittim to the Jordan. There they stayed three days before crossing the river. At which time criers went through the camp, announcing, "When you see the Ark of the Covenant of the Lord your God being carried forward by the Levite priests, you must stir yourselves and proceed also, keeping about a hundred yards behind it. You have not gone on this route before and the Ark will lead the way. Do not come too near it."

Then Joshua told the people, "Sanctify yourselves because tomorrow Yahweh will work wonders among you." To the priests, he said, "Lift up the Ark of the Covenant and carry it before the people."

Obeying this order, they took up the Ark and carried it ahead of the people. Then Yahweh said to Joshua, "Today I shall exalt you in the sight of all Israel and make the people know that as I was with Moses, so I shall be with you. Now tell the priests who are carrying the Ark of the Covenant to halt at the edge of the river and wait."

Whereupon Joshua proclaimed to the Israelites, "Come and listen to this message from Yahweh your God. It will make you realize that the living God is in your midst and that he will not fail to quell the Canaanites, Hittites, Perizzites, Girgashites, Amorites, and Jebusites against whom you advance. See, there is the Lord's Ark of the Covenant—the Lord of all the earth—ready to go before you when you ford the Jordan. The moment the priests who are carrying the Ark of the Lord of all the earth touch the waters of the Jordan with the soles of their feet, the river will be cut off from its flow, and the waters upstream will pile up in a mass behind."

The people accordingly struck camp ready to cross the Jordan, and the priests carried the Ark of the Covenant before them. The moment the bearers of the Ark dipped their feet in the brimming river (the Jordan overflows its banks during the entire period of the harvest), the flow of waters from upstream stopped and backed up into a massive heap not far from the town of Adam and all the way to Zaretan, while the waters downstream flowing toward the sea (that is, the Dead Sea) were starved of water and trickled away, enabling the people to cross over right opposite Jericho. The priests carrying the Ark stood firmly on dry ground in the bed of the river till all the people had got clean across the Jordan.

When the whole nation had crossed over, Yahweh said to Joshua, "Pick out twelve men, one from each tribe of Israel, and tell them to collect twelve stones from the spot where the priests stood and to carry these with them to wherever you camp tonight and there deposit them."

So Joshua summoned the twelve he had chosen from each tribe of Israel and gave them these instructions: "Enter the bed of the Jordan, past the Ark of your Lord God, and hoist each man a stone onto his shoulders to equal the number of tribes of Israel. This is to be a memorial among you so that when in time to come your children ask their fathers the meaning of these stones, you will be able to tell them that the flow of the Jordan was interrupted and its waters cut off to let the Lord's Ark of the Covenant cross over. These stones are to be an everlasting memorial for the children of Israel."

The twelve men of Israel did what Joshua told them. They lifted out twelve rocks from the bed of the Jordan exactly as bidden (to represent the twelve tribes of Israel) and carried these with them to their next campsite, where they laid them down. Joshua himself also erected twelve rocks in the bed of the Jordan on the spot where the feet of the priests who carried the Ark had stood. They are there to this day.

So the priests carrying the Ark halted in the middle of the river till everything was done which Yahweh had commanded Joshua to tell the people. The people scurried across and when the entire nation had gone over, the Ark of the Lord with its priests crossed too and took up its place in front of the people. The tribe of Reuben, the tribe of Gad, and half the tribe of Manasseh, marched in full armor in the van of the Israelites (as Moses had ordained). About forty thousand men armed for battle made the crossing before the Lord on to the plains of Jericho. Yahweh had exalted Joshua on that day in the sight of all the Israelites, and they respected him for the rest of his life just as they had respected Moses.

Then the Lord told Joshua to order the priests who were bearing the Ark of the Covenant to come up out of the bed of the Jordan, and he shouted, "Come up out of the Jordan," and as soon as the bare feet of the carrying priests touched dry land, the waters of the Jordan flushed back into place, overflowing the riverbanks as before.

The date was the 25th of March when the people crossed the Jordan and camped at Gilgal on the eastern edge of Jericho. The twelve stones which Joshua had lifted from the bed of the Jordan, he set up in Gilgal. Addressing the

Israelites, he said, "When your children in time to come ask the meaning of these stones, you can tell them, 'Israel forded the Jordan dry-shod because Yahweh your God drained away its waters for their passage, just as your Lord God did to the Red Sea when he drew it up for us to go through; which manifests to everyone on earth what a mighty power the Lord is, of whom we should be forever in awe.' "

The Fall of Jericho

Jericho, a fortified city in the Jordan valley about fifteen miles northeast of Jerusalem, was already several thousand years old when Abraham entered Canaan; and at the time Joshua attacked it there had been at least two earlier cities stretching back to 5000 B.C. and before. All that remains of the city of Old Testament times is a mound seventy feet high occupying some ten acres.

That Jericho was highly fortified there can be no doubt. The ruins of what are purported to be its walls are up to fourteen feet thick. There is some doubt, however, that when Joshua made his famous assault toward the end of the thirteenth century B.C. the city was still standing. Archeological excavations at the site suggest that the city had been laid waste at least two hundred years before. If this is so, some scholars think that the biblical account is the dramatizing of a creation myth in which historical ingredients are scrambled to illustrate a cultic ritual (circumambulation, blowing the ram's horn, seven days, shouting), in which the divine creative act is pitted against the evil forces (of nothingness).

Be that as it may, apart from a miracle, the crumbling of the walls of Jericho takes some explaining. Isaac Asimov suggests that while the Israelites were whipping up terror in the hearts of the besieged by their noisy processions, Joshua's sappers were quietly undermining the foundations.

(Joshua 6:1-25)

AT this time Jericho was sealed up tight: fortified against the Israelites. No one went in and no one came out. "You see, I have put Jericho into your hands," the Lord said to Joshua. "Yes, with its king and all its mighty men of valor. Have your soldiers encircle the city and parade around it once a day for six days while seven priests carrying seven ram's horn trumpets walk ahead of the Ark. On the seventh day, while the priests blare on their ram's horns, parade around the city seven times. Then when you hear one long loud blast on the ram's horn, have all the people together raise a mighty yell, and the city walls will fall flat and every man can walk straight into it from where he stands."

So Joshua the son of Nun called the priests and ordered them to take up the Ark of the Covenant and seven priests to carry the seven trumpets of ram's horn, walking ahead of the Lord's Ark. Then he commanded the people to advance and begin their parade around the city.

When he had finished addressing the people, the seven priests bearing the seven ram's horns proceeded before the Lord blowing their trumpets while the Lord's Ark followed them, and the picked troops marched ahead of the trumpeters, who kept up their trumpeting as the rest of the people walked behind.

Joshua had given strict instructions that nobody was to shout, raise his voice, or let a syllable pass his lips: "Nobody, till I give the word is to shout, then *shout*. The city is doomed by the Lord with everything in it except Rahab the harlot and all those with her in the house, because she hid our scouts. Keep for yourselves nothing from the doomed place, because anything you take will doom you too and bring misery on our whole camp. As for their silver and gold and vessels of bronze and iron, these are sacred to the Lord and will be lodged in Yahweh's treasury."

So the Ark of the Lord was paraded once that day around the city, after which the people retired to their camp for the night.

Next morning while it was still dark Joshua arose and the priests took up the Ark of the Lord as the seven trumpet-bearing priests walked ahead blowing their ram's horns. In the vanguard marched the picked soldiery, while the rest of the people followed behind the Ark, the trumpets blaring all the time. On the second day, they again processed around the city once and then returned to base. This they did for six days.

On the seventh day, rising at dawn, they again marched around the city, but this time they did it seven times, and on the seventh time around when the priests blared on the trumpets Joshua yelled, "Shout. The Lord has given you the city."

The moment the people heard the blast of the ram's horn, they raised a mighty shout. With the people shouting and the trumpets blaring, the city walls began to collapse, and the Israelites stormed in from where each man stood and they took the city.

Observing Joshua's ban, they destroyed everything in the city: men, women, the young and the old, cattle, sheep, asses—all were put to the sword. Joshua, however, had ordered the two young men who had acted as scouts to go into the harlot's house and bring out Rahab and everyone with her as they had sworn to. So the two young men went in and rescued Rahab with her father and mother, her brothers, and all her kin. They brought out the entire family and set them up outside the Israelite camp.

But the city and all it contained they consumed with fire, saving only the silver and gold and articles of bronze and iron, which they consigned to Yahweh's treasury in the house of the Lord.

As to Rahab the harlot and all her father's family, whom Joshua had saved because she had hidden the scouts sent by Joshua to spy out Jericho, they are alive in Israel to this day.

The Sin of Achan and the Sack of Ai

Ai was a city two miles northwest of Jericho. Present-day archeological finds confirm that Ai, like Jericho, had long been a ruin when Israel invaded Canaan in the thirteenth century. Indeed, the name Ai means "the ruin." It has been suggested that a much earlier pre-Israelite attack has been incorporated into the biblical story for mythological purposes. As to Achan, whose name probably means "Troublemaker," his punishment seems to us cruel beyond measure, but once again we must remember that the whole account of Achan and the sack of Ai is a symbol of the intransigence of righteousness in its fight against evil (even though to us the evil is set up as a dummy evil).

(Joshua 7:1-26, 8:1-29)

THE children of Israel, unfortunately, violated the ban against looting. Achan, the son of Carmi (grandson of Zabdi and great-grandson of Zerah) of the tribe of Judah, purloined articles under the ban and Yahweh's anger flared up against Israel.

Joshua had dispatched some scouts from Jericho to Ai (which is near Bethaven east of Bethel) to explore the territory. This they did, coming back with the report: "There is no need to muster the whole army to go and attack Ai: about two or three thousand will do. Do not bother the rest with it. The inhabitants are few."

So an Israelite contingent of some three thousand went and they were soundly thrashed by the men of Ai, who killed about thirty-six of them and chased them from the city gates as far as Shebarim, slaughtering them on the slopes.

At this the people melted away with fear and their hearts turned to water. Joshua rent his garments and lay prostrate on the ground till evening—he and the elders of Israel with him. And they covered their heads in ashes.

"O Lord God," Joshua pleaded, "why did you bring this people across the Jordan only to hand us over to the Amorites to be destroyed? Would that we had been content to dwell on the other side of the river! Lord, what can I say, now that Israel turns her back to her enemies? When the Canaanites and other natives hear of it they will encircle us and wipe us from the earth. Then what will you do to save your great name?"

"Get to your feet," Yahweh said to Joshua. "Why are you lying there on your face? Israel has sinned and disobeyed my command by taking forbidden loot. Yes, they have stolen and lied and hidden things among their belongings. That is why the children of Israel cannot stand up against their enemies and have turned their backs. They are under a curse and I refuse to be with them any longer until you root out the culprit. So get up now and purify the people. Tell them this, 'You are to sanctify yourselves for tomorrow. The Lord God says, "A curse lurks at your core, Israel, and you cannot withstand your enemies until you expunge a crime from among you. In the morning you are to present yourselves tribe by tribe. The tribe which Yahweh exposes is to file by clan by clan. The clan which Yahweh exposes is to file by family by family. And the family which Yahweh exposes is to come forward one by one. The person found to have committed this sacrilege will be burnt with everything he possesses because he has violated the Lord's decree and brought disaster on Israel." ' "

Early next morning Joshua reviewed the Israelites tribe by tribe and the tribe exposed was Judah. So he made the clans of Judah file by clan by clan and the clan exposed was Zerah. He made Zerah's clan file by family by family and the family exposed was Zabdi. Finally, going through Zabdi's family person by person he lighted on Achan son of Carmi (grandson of Zabdi and great-grandson of Zerah) of the tribe of Judah.

Joshua said to Achan, "My son, give honor to the Lord God of Israel today and confess. Tell me what you have done. Hide nothing from me."

"I have indeed sinned against the Lord God of Israel," Achan replied to Joshua. "What I did was this: when I saw among the spoils a beautiful colored robe from Babylon and two hundred shekels of silver, as well as a bar of gold weighing fifty shekels, I wanted them so much that I took them. They are now hidden in the ground in the middle of my tent, with the silver at the bottom."

Joshua dispatched messengers on the double to the tent, and there in Achan's tent were the stolen goods with the silver at the bottom. They took these from the tent and brought them to Joshua and the Israelites, laying them out before the Lord.

Then Joshua seized Achan the great-grandson of Zerah with his silver, his robe, his gold bar, together with his sons and daughters, his cattle, his asses, his sheep, even his tent— everything he had—and took the lot to the Valley of Achor. All Israel accompanied him.

"Why have you brought trouble upon us?" Joshua asked him. "Today Yahweh will bring trouble on you."

The Israelites then stoned him to death and made a bonfire of him and everything he possessed. They heaped a pile of stones over him which is there to this day.

Yahweh then said to Joshua, "Do not be afraid or cast down. Mobilize all your forces and march on Ai . . . You see, I have delivered the king of Ai into your hands, with his people, his city, his country. You must do to Ai and its king what you did to Jericho and its king, but this time you may keep the spoils and livestock as booty. Set up an ambush behind the city."

Joshua mustered the main body of the army to advance on

Ai, having picked five thousand of his most valiant warriors to go off by night with the following orders: "Set up an ambush behind the city, not too far from it, and all of you keep alert. I with the rest of the army will make a frontal attack, and when the Aians come out against us we shall do as we did before: turn our backs and run. We shall let them pursue us till we have drawn them away from the city, for they will be thinking: 'Ah, so the Israelites are running away again as they did the first time! Let us press after them.' At which point, break from your ambush and take the city, for Yahweh will put it into your hands. When you have taken the city set it alight. Those are my orders. See that you carry them out."

Joshua accordingly sent out a detachment to lie in ambush. The men took up their position between Bethel and the west side of Ai, while Joshua himself spent the night with the rest of the army.

Early next morning, having taken the roll call, Joshua marched at the head of his army toward Ai, accompanied by the elders of Israel. He drew his troops up opposite the city and encamped on the plain north of Ai with a ravine in between. The contingent he had sent out as ambush were between Bethel and Ai and numbered about five thousand. Once the army was set up north of the city and the ambush west of it, Joshua himself settled down for the night in the valley.

The king of Ai, seeing how things were, hurriedly mustered all his forces and early next morning came out on to the plain to engage, not realizing that an ambush was lying in wait behind the city.

Joshua and the main Israeli army began to yield as if they had panicked, and they fled toward the desert, with the cheering Aians in furious pursuit. This left the city completely unguarded. Not a single soldier was left in Ai or Bethel. They were all chasing after the Israelites.

Whereupon Yahweh said to Joshua, "Raise the spear in your hand and point it toward Ai. I am about to give it to you."

So Joshua stretched out the spear in his hand toward the city, and as soon as the men in ambush saw the signal of the pointing spear they leapt up on the run, captured the city, and set it on fire.

When the men of Ai looked behind them and saw the smoke of the burning city rolling up into the sky, they did not know which way to turn because the Israelite army which had fled into the desert now doubled back on its pursuers.

Once Joshua and his main troops saw that the city had been taken by the ambushers and was now going up in smoke, they wheeled around and began to strike down the Aians. Meanwhile, the Israelites inside the city poured out to join the attack so that the men of Ai were hemmed in by Israelites on both sides, who slaughtered them to a man, not leaving one fugitive.

They took the king of Ai alive and thrust him before Joshua, and when they had finished running their swords through the Aians who had pursued them into the desert, the main Israelite force turned to strike Ai itself.

There perished that day twelve thousand men and women: the entire population of Ai. Joshua did not lower the spear in his hand till every single inhabitant was destroyed. The livestock and loot, however, the Israelites divided among themselves in accordance with Yahweh's instructions to Joshua.

Joshua burnt Ai to the ground, reducing it to a heap of rubble, which is there to this day. The king of Ai he hanged from a tree, leaving him there till evening, but at sunset he had the body removed and thrown down in front of the city gates, where a pile of stones was heaped over it which remains to this day.

NOTE

The Hebrew text gives the number of Joshua's advance guard as thirty thousand, which is almost certainly a copyist's error. VB:12 says "about five thousand." There is also a variant Septuagint reading of "three thousand." In general, one must be on one's guard against the often inflated numbers of the text.

Joshua Is Tricked by the Citizens of Gibeon

After the destruction of Jericho and Ai, the Israelites, still encamped at Gilgal between Jericho and the Jordan, make ready for their next inroad into Canaan. Not surprisingly, the surrounding tribes are full of alarm.

(Joshua 9:3-27)

WHEN the inhabitants of Gibeon heard what Joshua had done to Jericho and Ai, they had recourse to a ruse. They came in a deputation with old sacks on their donkeys and old wineskins torn and patched. The sandals on their feet were antiquated and cobbled, their clothes ragged. The bread they brought with them was dry, worm-eaten, and moldy.

They came thus to Joshua in the camp at Gilgal, explaining to him and the Israelites: "We have come from a long way off to make an alliance with you."

The Israelites replied to this Hivite embassy, "What if you are really living in the land that is going to be ours? How could we then make an alliance with you?"

"Let us be your servants," they replied to Joshua.

"But who are you and where do you come from?" Joshua retorted.

"We, your servants, have come from a very far country," they replied, "and all because of the name of the Lord your God. We heard of his fame and power and the things he did in Egypt, and of what he did to the two Amorite kings on the other side of the Jordan: King Sihon of Heshbon and King Og of Bashan at Ashtaroth. So our elders and our people agreed that we should take provisions for a journey and go to meet you with this proposition: 'we are your servants, make peace with us.' . . . Look at the bread which we took hot from the oven on the day we departed. It is now dry and moldly. These wineskins which were full and new are punctured and patched. Our clothes are shabby, and the sandals on our feet almost worn to nothing by the journey."

The Israelite leaders sampled their provisions without consulting the Lord, and Joshua made a peace treaty with them guaranteeing their lives, which the leaders of the nation ratified with an oath.

Three days after they had made this agreement, the Israelites discovered that these people were their neighbors and would be living among them. So they set off for their towns (the towns of Gibeon, Chephirah, Be-eroth, and Kirjath-jearim). These the Israelites did not assault because the nation's leaders had sworn an oath in the name of the Lord God of Israel.

All the people then complained to their elders, who replied, "We have sworn an oath in the name of the Lord God of Israel, so we cannot touch them. However, though we let them live—so as not to incur Yahweh's wrath for perjury—they can live for our benefit and be hewers of wood and drawers of water."

After this decision of the leaders, Joshua summoned the Gibeonites and demanded, "Why did you trick us by saying you lived far away, when you really live next door? You have condemned yourselves and your whole tribe to servitude in the household of the Lord as our hewers of wood and drawers of water."

To which they answered, "We, your servants, did what we did out of fear for our lives when we heard that Yahweh your God had promised his servant Moses that you were to be given the whole of this territory and its inhabitants destroyed. And now that we are in your power, do with us whatever you think is good and right."

Joshua acted accordingly. He saved them from death at the hands of the Israelites, but decreed that from that day onward they were to be at the service of the people of Israel as woodchoppers and water carriers, and to serve the Lord's altar at whatever place Yahweh chose. And they are still.

When the Sun Stood Still

Several cities now combine to fight off the invading Israelites: a struggle which terminates in the greatest battle of biblical times at Bethhoron: a battle that heralds a whole series of Israelite victories and slaughterings, with the eventual dividing up of the land among the Hebrew tribes.

As to the sun standing still, the present world came to know twenty-five centuries later with Copernicus that this is what the sun always does in relation to the earth—except of course that the sun is actually racing away through space at enormous speed. We must find some other way of understanding the mysterious metaphor by which the day was lengthened to allow the Israelites to consummate their victory at Bethhoron. A suggested eclipse of the sun followed by a hailstorm seems most unlikely. Moreover, as we now know, the earth would have to stop turning to make the sun seem to stand still. To have the earth stop without most of its crust flying off into space would be quite a feat.

(Joshua 10:1-27)

WHEN Adonizedec, king of Jerusalem, heard how Joshua had taken Ai and sacked it, and done to that city and its king what he had done to Jericho and its king, and also how the citizens of Gibeon had made a peace treaty with the Israelites and were living among them, he was extremely alarmed, especially as Gibeon was as large as one of the royal cities, even larger than Ai, and its men brave fighters.

So Adonizedec, king of Jerusalem sent messages to Hoham king of Hebron, Piram king of Jarmuth, Japhiah king of Lachish, and Debir king of Eglon, saying, "Join with me and help me to crush Gibeon, which has made an alliance with Joshua and the Israelites."

Whereupon, these five Amorite kings—the kings of Jerusalem, Hebron, Jarmuth, Lachish, and Eglon—united and marched with their combined forces against Gibeon, setting up their seige before it.

The people of Gibeon forthwith sent an appeal to Joshua at his camp in Gilgal: "Do not fail to support your comrades. Come quickly to our rescue. The Amorite kings from the hills have joined forces against us."

So Joshua took his whole army and with his most valiant fighters marched up from Gilgal.

"Have no fear of these kings," the Lord assured Joshua, "for I have delivered them into your hands. Not one of them will be able to stand up against you."

Joshua, after an all-night march from Gilgal, fell upon them suddenly and Yahweh threw them into disarray before the Israelites, who completely demolished them at Gibeon, pursuing them all the way to Bethhoron and hacking them down as far as Azekah and Makkedah. As they fled before the Israelites down the slopes of Bethhoron toward Azekah, Yahweh struck them from out of the sky with enormous hailstones and more died from the hailstones than by the swords of the Israelites.

It was then—on the day when Yahweh delivered up the Amorites to the children of Israel—that Joshua uttered his famous prayer before all Israel:

> Sun, stand thou still upon Gibeon,
> And thou, Moon, in the valley of Ajalon.
> And the sun stood still,
> And the moon dallied,
> Until the people had avenged themselves
> Upon their enemies.

The sun stood fixed in the middle of the sky and made no move to set for a whole day. Never before or since has there been a day like that, when Yahweh obeyed the voice of a single man.

Meanwhile, the five kings had fled and hidden themselves in a cave at Makkedah. When news reached Joshua that the five kings had been found hiding in a cave at Makkedah, he ordered, "Roll great rocks against the mouth of the cave and post guards to keep the kings inside. But do not linger there yourselves. Go after your enemies and strike them in the rear. You must not allow them to reach their cities because the Lord your God has given them to you."

When Joshua and the Israelites had dealt their final blows in this overwhelming slaughter and the enemy was all but exterminated, the remnant took refuge behind the walls of their cities. The army returned to base at Makkedah—where Joshua was—whole and intact, and nobody dared to criticize the Israelites.

Joshua now gave orders to his men to unblock the mouth of the cave and bring out the five kings to him. This they dutifully did, and as soon as the kings were brought out, Joshua summoned the Israelites and said to the commanders of the troops that had marched with him: "Step forward and plant your feet on the necks of these kings."

When they approached and planted their feet on the victims' necks, Joshua said to them, "From now on have no fear, no hesitation. Be strong and full of courage, because this is how Yahweh will treat all the enemies you fight."

Whereupon Joshua lunged at the kings, killing each of them, then he had the bodies strung up on five trees. They remained dangling on the trees till evening, and when the sun sank Joshua ordered them to be taken down and thrown into the cave where they had hidden. Large rocks were placed against the cave to seal it. They are there to this day.

The Strength and Wisdom of Deborah

Between the end of the thirteenth and the middle of the twelth century B.C. the conquest of Canaan was only in theory complete, for though the various lands were apportioned by Joshua among the eleven tribes (the tribe of Levi was given only cities), these territories were by no means conquered. In fact, their occupancy remained precarious. Jerusalem (given to the tribe of Benjamin) was not held by Israel until the time of David—some hundred and forty years later. More than half the tribes of Israel had failed to capture the cities assigned to them.

Meanwhile, on the coastal plains to the west, a mysterious and powerful people called the "Philistines" were in complete control. Nevertheless, the entire land of Canaan, whether conquered or not, became known as "Israel" or "Palestine": a name derived from the Philistines and later adopted by the Romans for the whole region.

Joshua, now a very old man, in a great farewell address to all Israel, reminds the people of everything that Yahweh has done for them, and he exhorts them never to succumb to foreign gods. Then at the age of one hundred and ten he dies and is buried at Timnasthserah, in the central north of Palestine. A new age has begun and Israel is to be ruled over by a series of judges: not merely judges in our sense but champions and legislators.

The first judge chosen to lead Israel in its fight against the Canaanites was Judah. In a victory at Bezek he slew ten thousand of them, and then pursued and captured their king, Adonibezek. When the Israelites cut off Adonibezek's thumbs and his two big toes, the king's only comment was: "I have had seventy kings, with thumbs and big toes cut off, scrabbling for crumbs under my table. So, as I have done, God now does to me."

The five stories that follow are all part of a loosely put-together saga of the characters and events of the next hundred and fifty years under the judges. The pattern throughout these years is the same: periods of infidelity to Yahweh when the Israelites, living cheek by jowl with polytheists, give way to idolatry (and are immediately punished by failing before their enemies), followed by periods of salvation when a new hero arises to make them repent and lead them to victory.

In the story which follows the parenthetical allusion to Herber the Kenite is put in to show that just as he was a traitor to the cause of Israel, his wife Jael was a traitor to him, though a heroine to the Israelites. Whether she acted from a spirit of patriotism or from some suppressed fury, we are not told, nor whether the tent in which she perpetrated her deed was hers or her husband's. The judge before Deborah was Ehud, who rescued Israel from the thralls of a Moabite king called Eglon—also through an act of treachery.

(Judges 4:1-22, 5:1 onward)

AFTER Ehud's death the children of Israel began again to do evil in the sight of the Lord, so the Lord let them fall a prey to Jabin, king of Canaan, who reigned in Hazor. The commander of his army was Sisera, who lived in the gentile city of Harosheth [or Harosheth-ha-goiim].

The children of Israel appealed to the Lord because Sisera had chariots of iron—nine hundred of them—and for twenty years he had oppressed the Israelites.

At that time the judge presiding over Israel was a woman, a prophetess called Deborah, the wife of Lapidoth. She held her sessions under Deborah's Palm Tree in the hills of Ephraim, between Ramath and Bethel, and there the Israelites came for judgment.

Deborah sent for Barak the son of Abinoam at Kedesh and said to him, "Yahweh, God of Israel, orders you to march with an army of ten thousand taken from the tribes of Naphtali and Zebulun to Mount Tabor. Yahweh says, 'I mean to draw Sisera, commander of Jabin's army, to the river Kishon and with all his chariots and all his men to put him in your power.' "

"I will go if you come with me," Barak answered. "But if you do not come with me I shall not go."

"I *will* go with you," she said, "but this mission you are undertaking is not going to redound to your own glory, because the Lord will let Sisera fall by the hand of a woman."

Deborah arose and proceeded with Barak to Kedesh, where Barak, having mustered the men of Zebulun and Naphtali, marched off at the head of an army of ten thousand accompanied by Deborah.

(Now Heber the Kenite from the clan of Hobab—Moses'

father-in-law—had severed himself from his own people, the Kenites, and pitched his tent on the plain of Za-anannim near Kedesh.)

When Sisera was informed that Barak the son of Abinoam was encamped on Mount Tabor, he deployed all of his nine hundred iron chariots and his whole army along the stretch between Harosheth-ha-goiim and the river Kishon.

"Get ready," Deborah said to Barak. "Today Yahweh has delivered Sisera into your hands and he marches at your head."

Barak swept down from the heights of Tabor with his ten thousand and under his onslaught the Lord sent panic into the heart of Sisera with all his chariots and all his men. Sisera himself leapt from his chariot and ran.

Barak pursued the fleeing chariots and troops as far as Harosheth-ha-goiim till the entire army had been put to the sword and not a man was left.

In the meantime, Sisera had escaped on foot to the tent of Jael, wife of Heber the Kenite (there was an alliance between King Jabin of Hazor and the clan of Heber the Kenite), and Jael came out to meet Sisera, saying:

"Turn in here, my lord. Turn in here with me. There is nothing to fear."

So he followed her into the tent and she covered him with a fur rug.

"Give me some water, please," he said to her. "I am so thirsty."

She opened a flask of milk and gave him some. He drank it and she covered him again.

"Stand at the door of the tent," he told her, "and if anybody comes asking if there is a man in here, say 'No.' "

She covered him once more with the fur rug and then she—Jael, Heber's wife—went and got a tent peg and, approaching him softly with a mallet in her hand as he lay sunk in exhausted slumber, she pounded the tent peg into his temples: right through them into the ground. So he died.

When Barak came by in hot pursuit of Sisera, Jael went out to meet him.

"Come," she said. "I will show you the man you are after."

He followed her into the tent, and there lying with a tent peg through his temples was Sisera.

Deborah and Barak the son of Abinoam celebrated that day singing the following canticle [a few verses in the King James version]:

Praise ye the Lord for the avenging of Israel,
When the people willingly offered themselves.
Hear, O ye kings; give ear, O ye princes;
I, even I, will sing unto the Lord.
I will sing praise to the Lord God of Israel.

Lord, when thou wentest out of Seir,
When thou marchedst out of the field of Edom,
The earth trembled, and the heavens dropped.
The mountains melted from before the Lord.

Speak, ye that ride on white asses,
Ye that sit in judgment and walk by the way.
Awake, awake, Deborah; awake, awake,
Utter a song: arise, Barak,
And lead thy captivity captive,
Thou son of Abinoam.
O my soul, thou hast trodden down strength.
Then were the horse hoofs broken by means of the prancings,
The prancings of their mighty ones.

Blessed above women shall Jael
The wife of Herber the Kenite be.
Blessed shall she be above women in the tent.
He asked for water, and she gave him milk;
She brought forth butter in a lordly dish.
She put her hand to the nail,
And her right hand to the workman's hammer;
And with the hammer she smote Sisera.

At her feet he bowed, he fell, he lay down:
At her feet he bowed, he fell:
Where he bowed, there he fell down dead.

The mother of Sisera looked out at a window,
And cried through the lattice:
"Why is his chariot so long in coming?
Why tarry the wheels of his chariots?
Have they not sped? Have they not divided the prey:
To every man a damsel or two;
To Sisera a prey of divers colors of needlework,
Of divers colors of needlework on both sides,
Meet for the necks of them that take the spoil?"

So let all thine enemies perish, O Lord;
But let them that love him be as the sun
When he goeth forth in his might.

NOTE

We might wonder at first at the apparent stress the Bible account puts on the fact that the Canaanites had "chariots of iron." The truth is that the Bronze Age, which had begun in the Near East about 2500 B.C., did not progress into the Iron Age till sometime in the thirteenth century, when the Israelites were still slaves in Egypt. The Israelites, innocent of iron, may have been at a disadvantage in their first encounters with the more sophisticated Canaanites; though it is also possible that late Bronze Age weapons may have been better than early iron, which could have been too soft to hold a hard edge.

The Call of Gideon and the Miracle of the Fleece

It must not be supposed because the Bible uses such a blanket epithet as the "Children of Israel" or the "Israelites" that Israel at this date was a social or political unity. Far from it. Israel was more like a loose confederation of the twelve tribes all looking after their own interests. On no occasion did all the tribes defend Israel as a unit. The "Judges" too were local rather than national champions of the people.

One might also wonder how the Israelites, after so many lessons from the Almighty and his servants, could repeatedly fall into idolatry. The reason is that they were living in the midst of it. The question was not one simply of religion but of a whole surrounding culture, social life, and worldview, from which it was very difficult for them to isolate themselves.

The two chief pagan deities, male and female, were Baal and Astoreth (or Asherah). Baal originally simply meant "Lord" and only later became the generalized title of Semitic deities. Astoreth, in the guise of Astarte, was the Syrian model of the Greek Aphrodite and the Roman Venus. Long after the period we are covering here, she had a famous temple at Hierapolis in Syria served by three hundred priests.

As to the Midianites, the bane of Israel in this story, they were an association of various nomadic tribes east of the Jordan, stemming originally from the land of Midia in northwest Arabia.

(Judges 6:1-40)

AGAIN the children of Israel did evil in the sight of the Lord, so for seven years he let them be seriously harassed by the Midianites. Indeed, to escape from the Midianites the Israelites had to take refuge in caves and mountain dens. When the Israelites sowed their fields, the Midianites, Amalekites, and other nomad marauders from the east, plundered the Israelite crops, leaving nothing as far as Gaza: not a sheep, not an ox, not an ass.

With their cattle and their tents and their uncountable camels, they would descend like locusts and settle on the land, utterly consuming it.

Reduced to misery by these Midianites, the children of Israel went pleading to Yahweh. In reply to their pleas Yahweh sent them a prophet who told them, "This is what the Lord God of Israel says: 'I brought you out of Egypt and out of the house of bondage. I saved you from the oppression of the Egyptians and the cruelty of others. I drove out your enemies for you and gave you their land. But when I insisted, "I am the Lord your God. Have no truck with the gods of the Amorites in whose land you dwell," you did not listen.' "

A little later, an angel of the Lord came and sat under the oak tree at Ophra, in the compound of Joash the Abiezrite, while his son Gideon was threshing wheat in the winepress (to hide it from the Midianites).

The angel appeared to Gideon and said, "You, mighty man of valor, the Lord is with you."

"Sir, if the Lord is with us," rejoined Gideon, "why is all this happening to us? Where are all those miracles our ancestors talked of when they told us, 'The Lord brought you out of Egypt, didn't he?' No, the Lord has deserted us and given us up to the plague of the Midianites."

The Lord's angel turned to him and said, "Go in the full prowess of your manhood and save Israel from these Midianites. Know it is Yahweh who sends you."

"And with what, sir, am I to save Israel?" Gideon answered. "My family is the poorest in Manasseh and I am the least in my father's house."

"Yahweh himself will be with you," the angel answered. "You will knock all of Midian down like a single man."

Gideon then addressed himself to the Lord: "If I really have found favor in your sight," he said, "give me a sign to prove it. But please stay now till I go and get a present for you."

"We will wait till you return," the angel said.

Gideon ran home, roasted a kid, and baked some small unleaven loaves from a bushel of flour. Putting the roast in a basket and the gravy in a pot, he carried these out to the angel under the oak tree and presented them.

"Lay out the meat and the unleaven loaves on this rock," the angel said to him, "and pour on the gravy."

He did so. Then the angel, reaching out, touched the meat and the loaves with the tip of his staff, and immediately flames burst out of the rock and consumed them. But the angel was nowhere to be seen. Then Gideon knew that this was an angel of the Lord and he cried out, "Oh, my Lord God, I have talked with an angel of Yahweh face to face!"

"Calm yourself and do not be frightened," Yahweh answered: "you are not going to die."

Gideon built an altar there to the Lord and called it "Yahweh-Shalom" ("Yahweh Is Peaceful"). It is still there in Ophrah, in the land of the Abiezrites.

That same night the Lord said to him, "Take the seven-year-old ox and use him to pull down your father's altar to Baal. When you have cut down the wooden idol of Asherah beside it, build a proper altar to the Lord out of solid stone. Then sacrifice the young ox (which you have also led out) as a burnt offering to the Lord, using the wood of the dismantled idol."

So Gideon went with ten servants and did as the Lord commanded. Because of his fear of his family and the townspeople, however, he did not carry out this mission by day but did it at night.

Early next morning, what should greet the eyes of the townspeople but the altar of Baal in pieces and the image beside it cut down! There, on a brand-new altar, lay a sacrificed calf.

"Who can have done this?" they asked one another. On inquiry they discovered that Gideon the son of Joash had done it.

"Bring out your son," the townspeople demanded. "He

has to die. He has thrown down the altar of Baal and cut down the image of Asherah."

"So Baal has to be rescued, does he?" retorted Joash as the mob pressed around him. "Really! Anyone who insults Baal like that deserves to die this very morning. If Baal is a god and his altar has been dismantled, he can look after the matter himself, surely."

This quip about Baal looking after himself when his altar was dismantled got Gideon the nickname of "Jerubaal" ("Let Baal Take Action").

Meanwhile, the Midianites, Amalekites, and other intruders from the east had swarmed across the Jordan in one mass into the valley of Jezreel, pitching their tents there.

It was then that the spirit of the Lord came upon Gideon. With a bugle blast he called to arms the clan of Abiezer. Then he sent heralds all through Manasseh, and the clan rallied around him; then through Asher, through Zebulun, through Naphtali, and they all rallied to his side.

Nonetheless, Gideon said to God, "If you really mean to save Israel through me, as you said, let me put out this woollen fleece on the threshing floor, and if dew settles only on the fleece, leaving the ground around it dry, then I shall know for certain that you want to save Israel through me." It happened exactly so.

When he rose early next morning and squeezed the fleece, he wrung out enough dew from it to fill a basin. But Gideon still said to God, "Lord, do not be angry with me but, please, let me ask once more . . . about the fleece . . . just one more test. Can the fleece this time be dry and all the ground around it wet?"

That is precisely what God did that night. The fleece only was dry, and there was dew all over the ground.

Gideon and the Three Hundred

The spot in the valley of Jezreel where Gideon prepares to engage the Midianite forces is near a river that leads into the Jordan, about fifteen miles south of Galilee. As to the surprising criteria which Yahweh lays down by which he is to select his warriors, there seems to be some textual confusion in verses 5 and 6, and this is reflected in all the versions.

There can be no real doubt, however, as to the meaning. The three hundred who lap the water like dogs are obviously not the ones who cup their hands to drink. One does not lap from a cupped hand. The distinction is between those who drink straight from the stream, lapping, and those who cup the water in their hands.

(Judges 7:1-25)

EARLY the next morning Jerubaal—that is, Gideon—moved with his entire army to camp at the well of Harod, so that now the Midianite forces were entrenched to his north down in the valley beneath the hill of Moreh.

Yahweh, however, said to Gideon, "You have too many men with you, and if I deliver the Midianites to you, Israel will boast that she liberated herself by her own power. So I want you to make this announcement to your troops: 'Anyone who has qualms and is fearful can leave Mount Gilead and go home.' "

Twenty-two thousand men left. Only ten thousand stayed. Nevertheless, the Lord said to Gideon, "There are still too many of you. Take them down to the water and I shall sort them out for you there. 'This one goes, that one does not,' I shall tell you, and the ones of whom I say 'That one does not' must on no account accompany you."

When Gideon had led his soldiers down to the water, the Lord said to him, "Stand to one side all those who lap the water with their tongues like a dog. Place on the other side all those who go down on their knees to drink."

The number of those who lapped with their tongues came to only three hundred; all the rest went down on their knees to drink. Then Yahweh said to Gideon, "To save Israel and put Midian in your power, I need only the three hundred who lapped. Let the rest go home."

The three hundred Gideon retained were given their rations and also bugle horns. The rest were sent back to their tents. The Midianite camp lay below his own in the valley.

In the middle of that same night the Lord roused Gideon, saying, "The time has come to descend and attack them. But if you are nervous, go down into their camp with your orderly, Purah, and when you have overheard what they are saying you will be greatly encouraged to begin the onslaught on their camp."

So Gideon slipped out with Purah his orderly down into

the outposts of the enemy barracks. There before him the whole Midianite-Amalekite army, with all its eastern reinforcements, was spread out over the valley like a swarm of locusts. Their camels were as uncountable as the sands of the seashore.

Then as Gideon crept up to listen he overheard one soldier telling another his dream. "Listen to what I have just dreamt," the man said. "A barley loaf came tumbling down into the Midianite camp. It hit our tent and knocked it flat."

"That can mean only one thing," the other responded: "the sword of Gideon the Israelite, son of Joash. God has put the whole Midian army at his mercy."

When Gideon heard this dream and how it was interpreted, he gave great thanks to God and hurried back to the Israelite camp. "Up and out!" he shouted. "The Lord has put the whole Midian army into our hands."

Then, dividing his three hundred into three companies, he equipped every man with a bugle horn and an empty earthenware pitcher with a torch inside.

"Watch me," he told them, "and do as I do. Wait till I get to their outposts, then follow my actions exactly. When I and my hundred with me begin to blast on our horns, you must blast on yours on all sides of the camp, yelling: 'For God and for Gideon.' "

It was the beginning of the middle watch, soon after midnight and the guards had just been changed, when Gideon and his hundred reached the fringes of the Midianite camp and began to blare on their horns and batter the pitchers in their hands. Then all three companies were blaring away and smashing their pitchers. In their left hands they held up their torches, using the right to blow on their horns, as they yelled, "A sword for the Lord and for Gideon!"

The whole enemy camp fell into a pandemonium of rushing and shouting and fleeing, while Gideon's men simply stood their ground in a circle around the camp. Yahweh set all the Midianites running one another through with their own swords as the three hundred kept up their blaring. The whole army fled, going as far as Bethshittah and toward Zererah, even to the borders of Abelmeholah near Tabath.

Then the Israelites from Naphtali were mustered, and from Asher and the whole of Manasseh, to join in pursuing the Midianites. Gideon sent a call to arms all through the hills of Ephraim, summoning their men to enlist against the Midianites and cut them off before they reached the water courses by Bethbarah and the Jordan. The Ephraimites came and captured the water courses as far as Bethbarah and the Jordan. They also took captive two of the Midianite commanders, Oreb and Zeeb. They killed Oreb at the rock called Oreb, and Zeeb at the winepress called Zeeb. Then, concluding their pursuit of the Midianites, they crossed the Jordan and brought Gideon the heads of Oreb and Zeeb.

Following Gideon's Victory

Gideon's victory over the Midianites was complete. Only fifteen thousand out of an allied army of some hundred and thirty-five thousand remained. Now he pursues this remnant as it makes for the desert and utterly destroys it, capturing the two kings, Zebah and Zalmuna.

Next, he returns to the town of Succoth and punishes the leading citizens (who had refused to feed his troops during the pursuit of the two kings) by throwing them into a pit of desert thorns.

Having likewise punished the neighboring town of Penuel by demolishing the city tower and killing all the males, he now turns his attention to the two captive kings, Zebah and Zalmuna.

(Judges 8:18-32)

"WHAT were they like, the men you put to death at Tabor?" he asked Zebah and Zalmuna.

"Very much like you," they answered, "obviously of royal stock."

"They were my brothers," Gideon replied, "my mother's sons. I swear by the Lord if you had spared their lives I should not kill you."

Turning to Jether, his eldest son, he said, "Get up and kill them." But the lad had not the nerve to draw his sword: he was only a boy. At which Zebah and Zalmuna said, "Get up yourself and kill us. You have the strength of a grown man."

So Gideon rose and slew Zebah and Zalmuna. Then he removed the crescents from their camels' necks.

The Israelites now asked him, "Rule over us, you, your son, and your son's son, because you have saved us from the power of the Midianites."

"No," said Gideon, "neither I nor my son shall rule over you: let only the Lord be your ruler."

Then he said, "I have a request to make you: will each of you give me the earrings from your booty?" (The enemy, being Ishmalites, wore gold earrings.)

"Willingly," they replied, and spreading out a cloak they all threw in the earrings from their booty.

The weight of these gold earrings he had asked for came to one thousand, seven hundred gold shekels. There were besides crescents and pendants, costumes of royal purple worn by the Midianite kings, and the gold caparisons adorning the necks of their camels.

Out of these Gideon made an ephod and displayed it in his city of Ophrah, where it became an object of idolatrous pilgrimage among the Israelites: a bad thing for Gideon and his family.

Anyway, this is how the Midianite menace was crushed by the children of Israel, never to rear its head again, and the land enjoyed forty years of peace under Gideon.

So Jerubaal (or Gideon) son of Joash, retired and lived at home. From his numerous wives he begot seventy sons. His concubine too in Sechem bore him a son whom he called Abimelech.

Gideon died at a ripe old age and was buried in the tomb of his father Joash in the Abiezrite city of Ophrah.

Jephthah's Dilemma

It becomes clear as one reads the stories of Israel during the two hundred years of the rule of the Judges how disunited she really was, living untrammeled in some parts but subject to alien nations in others. Not only was the religious focus of the Tabernacle in Shiloh remote from most of the tribes, but they were all of them beleaguered by neighbors whose culture and customs it was impossible to avoid. That human sacrifice was practiced among these alien nations there can be little doubt, but that the Israelites succumbed to human sacrifice we can only say for certain that it happened once. Possibly the sacrifice we read of in this story was not of actual life but of someone dedicated to the Lord by renouncing the normal vocation of a young woman—so important to the Jews—of marrying and having children.

(Judges 11:1-11, 29-40)

Jephthah from the land of Gilead was a strong man and a brave one, but he was the son of a prostitute and his father Gilead had a wife who gave him other sons. When these sons of his wife were grown up they threw Jephthah out.

"You are not going to inherit a thing from our father," they said to him. "You son of a whore!"

Jephthah fled from his brothers and lived in the land of Tob, where a gang of ne'er-do-wells attached themselves to him, and with him went raiding.

Later, when the Ammonites made war on Israel and attacked, the elders of Israel went to bring Jephthah back from the land of Tob. "Come and be our commander," they begged him, "and help us to fight off these Ammonites."

"What! Did you not hate me?" Jephthah responded. "And thrust me out of my father's house? Why do you come to *me* now that you are in trouble?"

"Because we must turn to you," they answered. "Please go with us to fight the Ammonites and we will make you chief of all Gilead."

"Do you mean," said Jephthah, "that if I go with you and fight the Ammonites—with the Lord's help—I am really going to be your chief?"

"We swear exactly that," replied the elders of Gilead. "The Lord be our witness."

So Jephthah went back with the elders, and the people made him their commander-in-chief and head. He took the oath at Mizpah.

Then the spirit of the Lord came upon Jephthah and he marched through Gilead and Manasseh, on past Mizpah, and invaded the Ammonites. He had made a vow to Yahweh, saying, "If you promise to deliver the Ammonites into my hands, when I return in triumph from Ammon, the first person who comes out of my house to greet me shall be the Lord's, and I shall sacrifice whoever it is as a burnt offering."

He invaded and attacked the Ammonites, and Yahweh did indeed put them in his power. He beat them soundly from Aroer all the way to Minnith (comprising twenty cities) and as far as Abel in its great plain of vineyards.

However, when Jephthah returned to Mizpah and approached his house, who should run out to welcome him home but his daughter—playing the tambourine and dancing. She was his only child. He had no other sons or daughters.

When Jephthah saw her he rent his clothes in agony. "Oh, my poor daughter!" he groaned. "You have stabbed my eyes. Alas, my lips uttered a vow to Yahweh and it is about you. I cannot undo it."

"Father," she answered him, "if your lips have uttered a vow to Yahweh, do to me whatever your lips have said, because the Lord has paid back your enemies and defeated the Ammonites . . . There is, however, one thing I ask. Let me go away for two months into the hills to walk and wander with my dearest companions, lamenting my maidenhood."

"Go," he said, and he sent her away for two months with her comrades to bewail her virginity among the hills. When the two months were over and she came back to her father, he submitted her to his vow, untouched by man still as she was.

In time it became a tradition for Israelite girls to come together for four days in the year to mourn for the daughter of Jephthah the Gileadite.

The Shibboleth Incident

The tribe of Ephraim, which saw its military hegemony over Israel slipping and which had threatened to give trouble before (coaxed out of it only by Gideon's brilliant diplomacy—Judges 8:1-3), now comes out in open revolt, crosses the Jordan, and invades the land of Gad.

The reason I include this story is that it gives the origin of a Hebrew word which has become a useful word in English. *Shibboleth* has come to mean a test-word or password whereby the true identity of a person is uncovered. In Hebrew *Shibboleth* merely meant "stream," also an "ear of grain."

(Judges 12:1-7)

THE tribe of Ephraim mustered and marched north. They demanded of Jephthah, "Why did you not call on us when you went to attack the Ammonites. Now we are going to burn down your house over your head."

To which Jephthah replied, "My people and I were in a death struggle with the Ammonites, but when I called on you to rescue us you did nothing. So when I saw that you were not going to help, I took my life in my hands and invaded the Ammonites, whom the Lord delivered into my power. Why do you then come and attack us?"

Jephthah forthwith mobilized the Gilead army and struck at Ephraim. He fought and defeated them, furious at the Ephraimite taunt that they, the Gileadites, were only outcasts living in land belonging to Ephraim and Manasseh.

The men of Gilead had seized the fords of the Jordan, thus cutting off the Ephraimite retreat. When escaping Ephraimites asked permission to cross over, the Gileadites challenged them, "Aren't you an Ephraimite?"

If they said no, they next asked them, "Say *Shibboleth.*" If they said *Sibboleth,* unable to pronounce it properly, they were taken and killed right there by the fords of the Jordan. Forty-two thousand were slain at that time.

Jephthah the Gileadite was judge over Israel for six years, and when he died he was buried in his own city of Gilead.

Samson and His Disastrous Marriage

It has been suggested that the whole Samson saga is a folk legend historicizing a pagan sun myth. The word "Samson" itself means the "sun," and Samson's birthplace, Zorah, was near Beth Shemesh ("House of the Sun"), Shamash being the name of a sun god. Samson's unshorn locks symbolize the rays of the sun and signify his strength. When those locks are shorn and he loses the emblem of his potency, the sun's rays are put out and he goes blind. The one weakness of this virile man is women—as it is with many a pagan god—and when Delilah deceives him (her name too echoing the Hebrew word *lilah,* "night"), the metaphor is completed: the night overwhelms the light of the sun and cuts off its rays.

Be that as it may, Samson, though a Judge, never rules or organizes the Israelites to withstand their enemies, the Philistines. He is more of a danger to them than an asset, and his mentality and temperament are those of a schoolboy. How he could ever have been the "brown-eyed-boy" of the Almighty is one of the Bible's thousand enigmas. Perhaps it was because of the very simplicity of his character.

As to the Philistines, who came to dominate the whole coastal plain of Palestine, nobody knows for certain who they were or where they came from. It is possible that they came from post-Minoan Crete and were therefore of Greek origin. Like the Greeks, and unlike most of the Semites and the early Egyptians, they were uncircumcised. Their civilization seems to have been more sophisticated than that of the Israelites, and one of their advantages was that they knew the uses of iron.

The word "Nazarite" means "one who is set apart," that is, one who separates himself from the common run of humanity and dedicates his life to the Lord. The Nazarites never cut their hair, thus symbolizing that every item of their person was sacred to the Lord. Samson was a Nazarite: a vocation he never seems to have taken very seriously.

There was no Israelite impediment to a Hebrew's marrying a Philistine, though this was frowned on. There were, however, impediments to mixed marriages with other native peoples.

In the following account I have followed the Vulgate rather than the Greek and Hebrew texts, because it seems to me to make more sense. Samson could hardly himself have set up a wedding banquet lasting seven days if this was simply to be a stag party for the thirty young men who were his escort. In any case, marriages in most primitive societies were arranged by both sets of parents. There are, however, scholars who think that the seven-day banquet was a *premarital* celebration and that consequently the marriage was never consummated.

(Judges 14:1-20)

ONE day when Samson was visiting the town of Timnath he saw a young Philistine woman there whose whole bearing pleased him. So when he came home he said to his father and mother, "There is a Philistine girl I have seen in Timnath. Get her for my wife."

"What?" said his father and mother. "Is there no young woman from our own clan or from all our people you could choose for a wife instead of someone from these uncircumcised Philistines?"

"Just get her for me," Samson repeated to his father. "I like what I see."

(His father and mother had no idea that the Lord was arranging matters to counter the Philistines, who at that time controlled Israel.)

So Samson went with his father and mother down to Timnath and on the outskirts of Timnath in the vineyards a young lion came roaring toward him. At that moment the whole strength of the Lord's spirit came upon Samson and he ripped the beast apart with his bare hands as easily as he would a baby goat. This deed he did not divulge to his father and mother. And on arriving at Timnath he talked with the young woman and she delighted him.

Some time later, on his way back there for the wedding, he turned aside to look at the skeleton of the lion, and what should he see inside the lion's mouth but a hive of bees with honey. He took some honeycomb in his hands and ate is as he walked. Catching up with his father and mother, he gave some to them and they ate too. He did not, however, tell them that he had taken the honey out of a lion's carcass.

His father made arrangements for the bride and for a wedding banquet for his son to last seven days, which was the custom then to give young men. The local citizens in turn assigned an escort for Samson of thirty young men, his peers. It was to them that Samson propounded a riddle. He said, "If during the seven days of celebration you are able to solve this riddle, I shall give you thirty bolts of fine cambric and thirty tunics. If you fail to solve the riddle, then you must give me thirty bolts of cambric and thirty tunics."

"Let us have your riddle, then," they shouted. "We are all ears."

"This is it," he said:

"Out of the devourer came forth provender
And out of the strong came forth sweetness."

After three days they had still not solved the riddle. On the fourth day they came to Samson's wife. "Coax your husband and get the riddle out of him," they ordered. "Otherwise, we are going to burn down your father's house with you in it. Or were we invited to this wedding to be ruined?"

Samson's wife proceeded to hang on him in tears. "You hate me," she sobbed. "You do not love me at all. You tell my people a riddle and will not tell me the answer."

"I have not even told my father and mother," he replied. "Why should I tell you?"

She kept up her weeping for the remaining seven days of the nuptials, and on the seventh day he could stand her needling no longer, so he told her the answer. She immediately went and told her fellow people, and just before sunset on the evening of the seventh day these sons of her countrymen proclaimed:

"What is sweeter than honey?
And what is stronger than a lion?"

Samson replied:

"Oh, if you had not plowed with my heifer
You would not have dug up my riddle."

The spirit of the Lord then gripped him. He went down to Ashkelon and slew thirty men, stripped them, and gave their clothes to the thirty who had solved the riddle. But Samson was so enraged that he went home to his father. His wife meanwhile was set up with the fellow who had been his best man at the wedding.

Further Escapades of Samson

The Old Testament writers did not always distinguish foxes from jackals, often using the same Hebrew word *(shu'al)* for both. However, one can usually tell from the context whether foxes or jackals are meant. In this story the three hundred animals that Samson caught were undoubtedly jackals. To have caught three hundred foxes he would have had to range over the whole of Palestine, for the fox is a solitary beast. Even to capture three hundred jackals would be something of a feat, but not inconceivable because the jackal at least lives in packs.

(Judges 15:1-19)

SOMETIME later, during the wheat harvest, Samson went to visit his wife, taking a little goatlet as a present and saying to himself, "I shall see my wife in her bedroom." But her father would not let him go in.

"I thought you hated her," he said, "and had repudiated

her. So I gave her to your best man. But look, is not her younger sister prettier than she is? Take her instead."

"Now I cannot be blamed for anything I do to you Philistines," he roared. And he went off and trapped three hundred jackals, tied their tails together in pairs, and put a torch between each pair. Then he set the torches alight and sent the jackals plunging into the Philistine standing wheat, setting on fire not only the sheaves but the ripening grain, the vineyards, and the olive groves.

"Who did this?" the Philistines demanded.

"Samson," they were told, "the son-in-law of the Timnite, all because he gave Samson's wife to his best man."

They came then and burnt down the house of the girl's father, with her and her father in it.

"If this is how you behave," Samson vowed, "nothing will stop me till I have paid you back in full."

Indeed, he then "smote them hip and thigh with great slaughter,"* retiring afterward to a cave in the cliffside at Etam.

The Philistines responded by advancing into Judah. They set up their camp and overran Lehi.

"Why have you come against us?" the men of Judah asked them.

"To chain up Samson," they replied, "and do to him what he has done to us."

Thereupon three thousand men of Judah descended on the cave in the cliff of Etam.

"Do you not understand," they demanded of Samson, "that the Philistines control us? And now what have you done to us?"

"I merely did to them what they did to me," he retorted.

"Well, we have come to bind you and hand you over to the Philistines," the men of Judah told him.

"All right," Samson replied, "you may hand me over if you swear not to kill me yourselves."

"No, we will not," they swore. "We will simply bind you and hand you over to the Philistines. We are certainly not going to kill you."

So they bound him with two new ropes and hoisted him up from the cliff.

When they got to Lehi, the Philistines came running toward him jubilantly shouting, and at that moment the full strength of the Lord's spirit came upon Samson. The ropes

*Authorized Version's famous phrase.

around his arms withered like smoldering flax and the bindings snapped from his wrists. He reached out and grabbed the fresh jawbone of an ass he found lying on the road and with it proceeded to kill a thousand men, shouting:

"Heaps upon heaps of them, haha!
With the jawbone of an ass!
Yes, with a donkey's jawbone
I've laid a thousand low."

When he had done shouting, he flung the jawbone away and called the place Ramathlehi ("Jawbone Hill"). But he was extremely thirsty, so he called out to the Lord, "That was a fine triumph you let your servant have, but am I now to die of thirst and fall again into the hands of the uncircumcised?"

So God opened a hollow in the ground and water gushed out. As Samson drank, his spirits revived. To this day the spot in Lehi is called Enhakkore ("Fount of the Jawbone Shouter").

Samson's Second Disastrous Marriage

The biblical text does not say that Samson was married to Delilah. Probably he was not.

(Judges 16:1-21)

ONE day Samson visited Gaza and went with a prostitute he saw, and as soon as word got around that Samson was there, the Gazites set an ambush for him at the city gate and waited all night, intending to kill him in the morning light.

Samson lay abed till midnight, roused himself, then went and took hold of the two doors of the city gate, wrenched them loose from their posts, and walked off with them on his shoulders—bar and all—carrying them to the top of the hill opposite Hebron.

Sometime afterward, he fell in love with a woman from the valley of Sorek, whose name was Delilah. The chiefs of the Philistines approached her and said, "Wheedle out of him the secret of his enormous strength and how we can overpower him and chain him up tamed. Each of us will reward you with eleven hundred silver shekels."

So Delilah said to Samson, "Please tell me the secret of your great strength and if there is anything that can bind you up helpless."

Samson replied, "If I were to be tied with seven dampened thongs that have never been used, I should be as weak as any other man."

Accordingly, the Philistine chiefs brought her seven dampened thongs that had never been used, and she bound him with them. (There were men lying in wait in the room), and when she called to to him, "Oh, Samson, the Philistines are on you," he simply snapped the thongs like a piece of twine hit by a flame. So his strength was still unknown.

"You have made a fool of me," Delilah protested to Samson, "and told me lies. But tell me now what can bind you?"

"If I am tied up tightly with new ropes that have never been used, I shall be as weak as any other man."

So Delilah got new ropes and bound him with them, then she called out, "The Philistines are on you, Samson" (men again lying in wait in the room), and he broke them off his arms like thread.

"You are still making fun of me," Delilah complained, "and telling me lies. Tell me really what will bind you?"

"If you weave seven strands of my hair into your loom," he said, "and fasten them with a nail into the wall, I shall be as weak as any other man."

So Delilah wove seven strands of his hair into her loom, fastened them with a nail to the wall, and again called out, "Samson, the Philistines are on you," and he leapt out of his sleep, taking loom, nail, hair and all. So his strength was still unknown.

"How can you say you love me," she whined. "Your heart is not with me. Three times you have made a fool of me and still have not told me the secret of your great strength."

Day after day she kept at him until she broke his spirit and vexed him to death. Finally he opened his heart to her and said, "No razor has ever touched my head. I was dedicated to God as a Nazarite from my mother's womb. If my head be shaved, my strength will go and I shall become as weak as any other man."

When Delilah saw that he had confided in her utterly she

sent for the Philistine chiefs with the message: "Come once more. This time he has opened his heart to me."

They came with money in their hands.

Delilah lulled him to sleep with his head on her lap and called the barber, who shaved off the seven locks of his head. At once his strength began to ebb away.

This time when she called out, "The Philistines are on you, Samson," he awoke thinking that he would leap up and shake himself free, not knowing that the Lord had deserted him. The Philistines took him and put out his eyes. Then they brought him in bronze chains to Gaza and set him to grind in the prison house.

The End of Samson

(Judges 16:22-31)

NO sooner had the hair of his head been shorn than it started to grow again. Then one day the chiefs of the Philistines assembled for a special sacrifice to Dagon their god, celebrating with a great feast the fact that he had put Samson, their enemy, into their power.

When they were in their cups they began to shout, "Bring out Samson and let us have some sport with him." So the blinded Samson, now an object of fun, was led out of the prison and made to stand between two pillars.

The very sight of him sent the people chanting:

"Our god has put our enemy in our hands:
the scourge of our country
and the murderer of so many."

Then Samson said to the boy who was leading him by the hand: "Direct my hands toward the two pillars on which this building stands. I want to lean on them and rest a little."

This the boy did. Now, the temple was crammed with men and women, including the Philistine chiefs. Even on the terraces there were some three thousand gaping down at Samson and making fun of him.

Then Samson cried out to the Lord, "My Lord Yahweh, remember me now and give me back my old strength one last time for one great avenging act to pay back the Philistines for my two eyes."

He grasped the two center pillars on which the stability of the building depended, and with his right arm around one and his left around the other, he breathed this prayer, "Let me give up my life with the Philistines," as he braced himself in one mighty heave.

The temple came crashing down on the Philistine chiefs and the mass of people in it. So Samson killed more at his death than he ever did in his life.

His cousins and his father's family came and carried him away. They buried him between Zorah and Eshtaol in his father's sepulcher. He had judged Israel for twenty years.

Outrage at Gibeah

The next episode is the second to last in the Book of Judges and is put there to show how anarchic and corrupt Israel had become before the coming of the kings, and how the establishment of a monarchy—though this went against the grain of both Yahweh and the Israelites—was absolutely necessary. The immorality of the people of Gibeah even echoes that of Sodom in the story of Lot. What is astonishing in our eyes is that neither Yahweh nor the sacred writers appear to rebuke the husband, whose staggering insensitivity and chauvinism leads to his wife's being raped to death.

The town of Gibeah, five miles north of Jerusalem, belonged to the tribe of Benjamin and was an important center.

(Judges 19:1-30)

DURING those days when there was no king in Israel, a certain Levite who lived in one of the far hills of Ephraim took a concubine who was from Bethlehem in Judah; but this concubine, in a fit of annoyance, left him and ran off to her father's house, where she stayed a whole four months.

Her husband then went after her, hoping to coax her back to him. He arrived with his young servant and a couple of asses, and she let him into her father's house. Her father was delighted to meet him, made him welcome, and pressed him to stay. So he stayed three days with his father-in-law, eating and drinking and spending the night there.

On the fourth day, his party rose early and were just preparing to leave when the girl's father said to his son-in-law, "Have something nourishing first to give you stamina. You can leave afterward."

So the two men sat down to eat and drink. Eventually the girl's father said to the man, "Why not stay another day and enjoy yourself?"

The man got up to go, but the girl's father was so insistent that he did stay another night.

The next morning—the fifth day—up early again, he was ready to leave when the girl's father once more pressed him: "Have something nourishing first and leave in the afternoon."

Once again the two men settled down to eat and drink. When it was time to go and the man with his concubine and his boy were getting ready, the girl's father said to him, "Look, it is already nearly dusk. Do stay the night. The day is almost done. Stay and relax. Then tomorrow you can make an early start for home."

This time, however, the man declined to spend another night there and insisted on leaving. So with his concubine and the two saddled asses they traveled till they were quite near Jebus (also called Jerusalem), and since they were so close and the day far spent, the servant boy said to his master, "Sir, I think we should turn off here and spend the night in this Jebusite town."

"No," said his master, "we do not want to be in a city of strangers where there are no Israelites. We shall press on to Gibeah for the night, or possibly Ramah."

They kept going and by the time they were abreast of Gibeah—a Benjaminite town—the sun was setting. So they turned aside into Gibeah to look for lodging for the night, but finding no one to put them up, they simply squatted in the town square.

Presently an old man came by at dusk, returning home from work in the fields. He was surprised to see the travelers camped out in the square and he asked the man, "Where are you going and where are you from?" (He himself was from the hill country of Ephraim, though he lived among the Benjaminite people of Gibeah.)

"We have journeyed from Bethlehem in Judah up in the far hills of Ephraim," the man explained, "where I come from. And from Bethlehem we are now headed for home, but no one has offered to put us up for the night, even though we have our own straw and fodder for the asses, as well as bread and wine for my wife and me and for this young man, my servant. We lack nothing."

"Never mind!" the old man said. "Let me be the provider for all you want. Only do not spend the night in the public square."

He led them to his house and gave the asses their fodder, and when the travelers had washed the dust from their feet they all sat down to eat and drink.

While they were enjoying their meal, a gang of ruffians and perverts from the town began to cluster around the house, thundering on the front door and shouting to the old man, the owner: "Bring out your new guest. We want to rape him."

The master of the house went out to them and pleaded, "My brothers, you must not think of doing such a wicked thing, especially as this man is a guest in my home. Look, here is my virgin daughter and the man's concubine. Let me bring them out to you; you can debauch them any way you want to, but do nothing so appalling to this man."

When the toughs refused to listen to him, the Levite himself grabbed hold of his concubine and pushed her out to them. All that night they raped and abused her, right until the morning. Not till daybreak did they let her go.

And at daybreak she made her way to the door of the house where her husband was and collapsed, lying there till it was light. When her husband rose that morning and opened the door to resume his journey, there she was, his concubine, lying outside the front door with a hand clawing the threshold.

"Get up," he said, "We must go."

There was no answer. She was dead.

Then he tossed her across one of the asses and made for home. As soon as he had entered his house, he took a knife, grasped his concubine's body, and hacked it limb from limb into twelve pieces. These he sent piecemeal with the following message to each of the tribes of Israel: "Ever since the Israelites left the land of Egypt to this very day, has anyone seen such a crime as this? Think about it, discuss it, and give your verdict."

All who heard the story cried out, "Nothing so horrible has been done or seen ever since the Israelites left Egypt."

Ruth

Although the story of Ruth is set in the time of the Judges—a time uniformly bloody and crude—it was probably written several centuries later in an attempt to lend some humanity to that barbaric age.

For both Jews and Gentiles the story also subtly makes the point that the Messiah is not to be limited to the Chosen People, seeing that Ruth, a non-Hebrew, is a direct ancestress of King David and therefore of Christ.

An Israelite called Elimelech from the town of Bethlehem in Judah, west of the Dead Sea, has gone because of famine in Israel with his wife, Naomi, to live in the land of Moab, east of the Dead Sea. Their two sons, Mahlon and Chilion, marry Moabite girls, Ruth and Orpah; but the sons die young, leaving Ruth and Orpah widows.

Naomi too is now a widow and is concerned that she has no further sons to whom the duty would fall (according to Levitic law) of marrying their deceased brothers' wives and thus perpetuating their names. But now that there is no longer famine in Israel, Naomi sees no point in remaining in Moab and begins the journey back to her own town of Bethlehem, accompanied by her daughters-in-law Ruth and Orpah. On the way, however, she begins to have doubts about the advisability of letting the two young women deprive themselves of the chance of finding Moabite husbands in Moab.

(Ruth 1:7-22, 2:1-23, 3:1-18, 4:1-17)

WHEN Naomi and her two daughters-in-law had left the place where they had been living and were on the road into Judah, she said to them, "Go. Go back each of you to your mother's house. And the Lord be as kind to you as you have been to your dead husbands and to me. May he let each of you find happiness in a new husband and a new home."

She kissed them and they broke down and sobbed.

"No," they said to her, "we want to go back with you to your people."

"Please, my dear daughters," she begged, "turn back. Why would you want to go with me? Have I more sons in my womb to give you as husbands? Turn back and be on your way. I am too old to take a husband. Even if by some impossibility I had a husband to sleep with this very night and conceived sons, would you wait for them to grow up and so miss the chance of other husbands? Of course not! I am only sorry, my dear daughters, that Yahweh has brought me to such a pass that I can be no help to you."

Once again they broke down crying. Orpah kissed her mother-in-law goodbye while Ruth stayed by her side.

"See," said Naomi to Ruth, "your sister-in-law is returning to her people and her gods. You must follow her and go back."

"Do not ask me to leave you," Ruth begged. "I want to go wherever you go, live wherever you live: your people to be my people, and your God my God. Where you die, I shall die and there be buried. May the Lord do the worst possible to me if I ever let anything but death part you from me."

When Naomi saw that Ruth was determined to stay with her, she pressed her no more. The two of them went on and came to Bethlehem, where the whole town excitedly received them.

"Can this really be Naomi?" they all exclaimed.

"Do not call me Naomi," she replied, "call me Mara ["bitterness"] because the Almighty has visited me with bitterness. I left here full and Yahweh has brought me home empty. So why call me Naomi ["Amiable"] when the Lord has declared against me and the Almighty has afflicted me?"

Thus did Naomi return with Ruth the Moabite her daughter-in-law from the land of Moab. It was at the start of the barley harvest when they arrived in Bethlehem.

Now, Naomi had a relative, a kinsman of her husband Elimelech, a man of consequence and wealth, whose name was Boaz. Ruth the Moabite said to Naomi, "Let me go into the fields and glean some grain—if the owner will allow me to do so."

"Go, my daughter," Naomi replied.

So Ruth went out into the fields and gleaned behind the reapers. Now it so happened that the field she entered belonged to Elimelech's relative Boaz, who had just come from Bethlehem.

"The Lord be with you," he said to the reapers.

"And bless you too, sir," they answered.

"Who is that young woman?" he asked the foreman of the reapers.

"She is the Moabite girl who came with Naomi from Moab," the foreman replied. "She asked permission to glean and gather grain among the sheaves behind the reapers. She has been here gathering since morning without once taking a break."

Boaz came and addressed Ruth. "Listen, my daughter, do not go to glean in any other field except this. Stay around my women workers. See which field they are harvesting and follow them. I have warned my young men to leave you alone. When you are thirsty, go and help yourself to water from one of the vessels the reapers have filled."

Throwing herself on the ground before him, Ruth said, "You are too kind even to notice me, seeing that I am only a stranger."

"I have been told how much you have done for your mother-in-law since your husband died," Boaz replied. "How you left your father and mother and your native land to come here to a people you never knew before. May the Lord amply reward you for all you have done: the Lord God of Israel under whose wings you have come to rest."

"You are so kind to me, sir," she said. "You have comforted me and been friendly toward me, even though I am not one of your young women harvesters."

Then Boaz said to her, "Now when lunchtime comes, eat with us. Dip your bread in our sauces." So she sat with the reapers and he handed her roasted grain. After she had eaten her fill she gathered what was left over, then got up to glean again. Boaz meanwhile had instructed his harvesters to let her glean right among the sheaves themselves without stopping her. "And drop a few handfuls on purpose," he told them, "and let her pick them up without comment."

So Ruth gleaned in the field until that evening, and when she had threshed what she had gathered, it came to a whole bushel of barley. She carried this into town and showed her mother-in-law, together with the leftovers from the midday meal; and when her mother-in-law saw how much she had gleaned, she exclaimed, "Wherever did you glean today? Where in the world could you have worked? Blessed be he who has taken note of you!"

Ruth then told her mother-in-law where she had worked. "The man's name where I did my gleaning today is Boaz."

"Oh, may the Lord bless him," Naomi exclaimed: "the Lord who never stops being kind to the living and the dead!" Then she added, "You see, that man is a relative of ours, one of our closest."

"He even told me," Ruth went on, "to stay with his harvesters till the very end of the harvest."

"Good," said Naomi, "it's much better for you, my daughter, to stay with his young women workers than to risk being molested in some other field."

Ruth therefore stayed close to the young women reapers of Boaz and gleaned until the end of the barley and then of the wheat harvest, living with her mother-in-law.

One day Naomi said to Ruth, "Dear child, is it not time I got you happily settled? And Boaz, among whose women you worked, is our relative, is he not? And Boaz is going to be at the threshing floor tonight winnowing barley. Well then, bathe yourself, put on some perfume, deck yourself out, and get down to the threshing floor. Take care not to let him know you are there till he has finished eating and drinking. When he retires, note where he lies down and later go on in. Draw the cover at his feet over you and lie down there. He will tell you what to do."

"I shall do everything you say," Ruth replied.

She went to the threshing floor and carried out her mother-in-law's plan.

When Boaz had eaten and drunk and, in the best of humors, had settled himself for sleep at the foot of a heap of grain, Ruth stole in, drew the covering at his feet over herself, and lay down.

At about midnight he turned and awoke with a start to find a woman lying at his feet.

"Who are you?" he demanded.

"Ruth, and at your service, sir," she answered. "Stretch the corner of your cloak over me [i.e., claim me as wife], for you are my next of kin."

"God bless you, my child," Boaz exclaimed. "This shows you to be even more loyal to Naomi than before, because you could have gone after a young man, be he rich or poor. Rest assured that I will take care of everything. My townspeople know what a fine woman you are. However, though it is true that I am your close relative, there is someone even closer. Stay where you are for tonight, then tomorrow if he claims his right to you, well and good, but if he is not prepared to claim you, I by the Lord Yahweh will. So lie down now till morning."

Ruth lay at his feet until the morning; rising before it was light, as he had cautioned, so that nobody would know that a woman had been there on the threshing floor.

"Hold out the shawl you have on," he said. She did so and he poured six measures of barley into it and lifted it on to her.

When she returned to the city her mother-in-law asked her as soon as she got home: "Well, my dear, how did it go?" Ruth gave her a full account of Boaz's response. "What is more," she concluded, "he gave me this barley, six measures of it, so that I would not come back to you my mother-in-law empty-handed."

Then Naomi said to her, "Be patient, my child, until we see how matters develop. Boaz will not rest till he has followed the whole thing through this very day."

Meanwhile Boaz settled himself by the city gate until that same relative he had spoken of came by. He called out to him by name, "Stop a moment and come and sit beside me."

The man turned aside and sat down.

Then Boaz called ten city elders and asked them to sit down there too. Which they did.

"Now then," he said, addressing the close relative, "Naomi has returned from Moab and is selling a parcel of land which belonged to our cousin Elimelech. I wanted to let you know this so that—in the presence of these citizens and elders—you can bid for it, or if you do not wish to bid for it, to tell me so because, after you, I have the next claim."

"I want to put in my bid," the man said.

"Very well then," Boaz continued, "the day you acquire the field from Naomi you also acquire Ruth, the young Moabite woman and widow of the deceased, so as to raise a family by her and carry on his line and estate."

"Oh," said the man, "in that case I cannot exercise my claim because that would conflict with my own heritage. Let my title pass to you . . . No, I certainly cannot make my bid."

The usual procedure in Israel at that time in matters concerning the redemption or changing hands of property was for a man to pull off his sandal and hand it to the other party. This publicly sealed a contract. So now, drawing off his sandal, the relative said to Boaz, "The land is yours to buy." Whereat Boaz turned to the elders and citizens.

"You are witnesses," he said, "that I have this day bought off Naomi all the holdings of Elimelech, Chilion, and Mahlon. Furthermore, that I have acquired as my wife Ruth, the

Moabite widow of Mahlon, to continue his line and his estate so that his name will not be erased from posterity."

"Aye, aye," responded the citizens and elders at the gate. "We are witnesses. May the Lord make this wife of yours who has come into your house as fruitful as Rachel and Leah—those two who founded the nation of Israel; and may you flourish in Ephratah and win renown in Bethlehem. Moreover, may the offspring which the Lord grants you from this young woman make your house as illustrious as the house of Perez, whom Thamar bore to Judah."

Thus did Boaz take Ruth as his wife. The union was consummated and Ruth conceived. She gave birth to a son.

"Praised be the Lord!" the women around Naomi exclaimed. "He has not failed this day to give you an heir. Let that heir be famous in Israel. He will be the joy of your life and prop of your old age; for the daughter-in-law who bore him loves you and is worth more than seven sons."

Naomi took the baby and pressed him to her bosom. She became his nurse. All the women of the neighborhood gave him a name, exclaiming, "A son has been born for Naomi!" and they called him Obed ["Worshiper"]. He was to be the father of Jesse and the grandfather of David.

The Birth of Samuel

The time is somewhere between 1080 and 1040 B.C. (roughly a hundred years after the Trojan War) and the scene is Shiloh, situated among the hills of Ephraim some twelve miles west of the Jordan.

Shiloh is where the Tabernacle has been set up ever since the time of Joshua (c. 1170 B.C.). It has become the center of yearly pilgrimage for devout Jews from all over Palestine.

The story is about Hannah, the wife of an Ephraimite called Elkanah, whose other wife is called Peninnah. Peninnah has children, Hannah none.

The high priest at the sanctuary of Shiloh has the name of Eli.

(I Samuel 1:3-28)

THIS man Elkanah used to go from his town every year to sacrifice to Yahweh Sabaoth [the "Lord God of Hosts"] at Shiloh, where Hophni and Phineas, the two sons of Eli, were priests of the Lord.

At the time of sacrifice he would hand Hannah—because she was the one he loved—a single portion as big as all the portions he gave to Peninnah and her sons and daughters, although the Lord had seen fit to keep Hannah barren: a fact with which her rival used to taunt her and make her so angry that she would cry out bitterly that Yahweh had sealed up her womb.

Year after year when they went up to the house of the Lord it would be the same: Elkanah handing out his hefty portions, Peninnah taunting, and Hannah bursting into tears and refusing to eat.

"Hannah, what are you crying for?" her husband would ask. "And why are you not eating? Why be so upset [at not having children]? You have me, and am I not better than ten sons?"

One day after they had eaten, Hannah slipped away unnoticed to the Tabernacle and threw herself on God's mercy. Eli the priest was sitting on a stool by the entrance of the Lord's temple.

From the depths of her distraught soul, sobbing, she called to Yahweh as she made the following vow:

"O Lord God of Hosts,
If you will look down on your poor servant in her sorrow,
If you will remember me and not ignore me,
If you will just give your poor servant a son,
Then I promise to give him back to you for the rest of his life.
He shall not touch wine or any strong drink
And no razor shall come near his head."

As her prayers continued, Eli watched her mouth, for though the lips quivered he could hear no voice because she was speaking in her heart, and he thought that she was drunk.

"How long have you been drunk?" he said. "Get rid of your wine and leave the Lord's presence."

"Oh no, sir," Hannah replied, "I have not drunk wine or

anything strong. I am just a very unhappy woman pouring out her soul to God. Please do not think me some worthless sot. I have stayed here so long praying only because of the utter misery of my state."

"Then go in peace," Eli said to her, "and may the God of Israel abundantly answer your prayer.'

"Oh, if only that could be!" she said.

Then she left and went to their lodging, ate and drank heartily with her husband, and was no longer woebegone.

Early the next morning, after they had worshiped the Lord, they all set out for home and arrived at their house in Ramah. Elkanah made love to his wife and Yahweh remembered her prayer. For in due course Hannah gave birth to a baby boy. She called him Samuel [which means "asked of God"] "because," she said, "I asked the Lord for him."

The following year, Elkanah went with the rest of the family on the yearly pilgrimage to the Tabernacle, but without Hannah because she had said to him, "Let me wait till I have weaned the baby, then I shall go with him to make his first appearance before the Lord and present him—to remain there forever."

"Do whatever you think best," Elkanah replied to his wife. "So stay until you have weaned him. May Yahweh's will be done."

So Hannah stayed behind to nurse her son. Then when the time came and she had weaned him, she took him with her to Shiloh, where her husband had brought a three-year-old bull to sacrifice to the Lord, as well as half a bushel of flour and a skin of wine.

After they had worshiped the Lord and slaughtered the bull, Hannah took the little boy to Eli.

"Do you remember me, sir?" she said. "As surely as you live, I am the woman who stood by you here praying to Yahweh. And this boy is what I prayed for, and Yahweh answered my prayer. So now I am giving him back to Yahweh. Yes, he is dedicated to the Lord for as long as he lives."

Then she left him there and went to worship.

God Calls Samuel

The child Samuel, left behind by his parents, is brought up by Eli as a little priest, helping with matters concerning the worship of Yahweh: lighting the Tabernacle lamps, perhaps laying out the vestments, arranging kindling wood, and generally waiting on the aging Eli.

Once a year Samuel's parents journey to Shiloh to see him and to offer the seasonal sacrifice. His mother brings him a little tunic every year—just like that worn by the priests—which she has specially made for him. It is a small linen ephod or ornamented alb.

Meanwhile, God rewards Elkanah and Hannah for their gift of Samuel to him by letting Hannah bear three more sons and two daughters.

But there is a thorn in the side of old Eli: his two sons, Hophni and Phinehas, although priests, are cheating at the sacrifices and commandeering more than their share. They also seduce the young women who come to help outside the sanctuary. Eli deplores this, but seems to be powerless to stop it. Yahweh is not pleased and has decided to do away with the whole family.

(1 Samuel 3:1-20)

IN the days when the boy Samuel ministered to the Lord under Eli's tutelage, it was a rare thing for Yahweh to speak, nor did he appear. But one day when Eli (whose eyes had become so feeble that he could hardly see) was lying asleep in his usual place, and God's lamp had not yet been extinguished, and while Samuel lay asleep in the temple where the ark of God was kept, at such a time, Yahweh called, "Samuel! Samuel!"

"Coming," responded Samuel, springing up and running to Eli. "Here I am! You called me?"

"I did not call you," Eli replied. "Go back to bed."

So Samuel went back and lay down.

Again Yahweh called, "Samuel! Samuel!"

The boy hurried to him again. "Yes? You need me?"

"I never called." Eli told him. "Go back to bed." Samuel did not really know Yahweh yet or Yahweh's law.

When Yahweh called "Samuel!" the third time, and Samuel had got up and gone to Eli, saying, "Here I am! You called for something?" Eli realized that Yahweh was calling the boy, and he said to him, "Go back to bed, but if anybody calls you again, say: "Speak, Lord, for your servant hears you."

So Samuel went back and lay down in his usual place. And Yahweh came. He stood there calling as he had done before. And this time Samuel answered, "Speak, Lord, for your servant hears you."

Then Yahweh said to Samuel, "I am going to do something that will make both your ears ring. I am choosing a day to act against the family of Eli in the way I said I would, giving no quarter. I want him to know that I am passing a final judgment on his house because he did nothing to stop his sons' blasphemous behavior toward God. I have vowed that not even victims and offerings shall make up for the guilt of his family."

Samuel stayed in bed till morning. Rising early he opened the doors of the Lord's house, but was afraid to tell his vision to Eli. But Eli called him. "Samuel, my son," he said, "what did the Lord say to you? Don't hide it from me . . . the entire message, please. Hold nothing back . . . or may God punish you!"

So Samuel told him every word, concealing nothing.

Eli's only answer was: "The Lord is Yahweh, let him do to me whatsoever he wills."

Samuel grew, and the Lord was with him. Not a syllable from Yahweh's lips fell to the ground unheeded. All Israel, from Dan to Beersheba, knew that Samuel was a faithful prophet of Yahweh.

PART IV

THE DAVIDIC KINGDOM

(c. 1000 TO 900 B.C.)

Stories from the books of Samuel 1 & 2 and 1 Kings

Introduction

The books of Samuel 1 & 2 are called Kings 1 & 2 in the Roman Catholic Bible, in which Kings 1 & 2 become the Catholic 3 & 4.

Historically, the books of Samuel are fairly trustworthy; they also enshrine some of the finest writing from antiquity, which is hardly matched by anything from Egypt or Mesopotamia. "Indeed, one searches in vain . . ." writes Dr. J. G. Williams, "for anything like the psychological insight, vivid characterization, and candid honesty of these books. Even Thucydides and Herodotus scarcely measure up to the literary brilliance of this work."

As to the two books of Kings, once again the authorship is a composite work drawing from several sources and traditions. As literature they cannot compare with Samuel, nevertheless they contain several masterly pieces.

Samuel Chooses a King

Yahweh's promised punishment of the house of Eli falls with terrifying thoroughness in a massive defeat of the Israelites by the Philistines at Aphek. His delinquent sons Hophni and Phineas are slain, his daughter-in-law dies in childbirth, the Ark of the Covenant is captured and, to cap it all, the old man himself falls off his stool and breaks his neck.

Meanwhile, Samuel, now a young man, preaches repentance to the Israelites and becomes the fifteenth Judge. Things go better with Israel for the next fifty years, but the people, envious of the monarchical system of their pagan neighbors, begin to clamor for a king. Samuel himself, now an old man, has come to realize that Israel's perennial enemy, the Philistines, must not be merely checked but erased and that he is not the man to do it. Overcoming his distaste for kingship, and in a manner so artless that it seems like chance, he comes upon a fine young man who will look every inch a king.

(1 Samuel 9:1-27, 10:1)

THERE was a man called Kish, a Benjaminite: the son of Abiel, grandson of Zeror, great-grandson of Becorah, and great-great-grandson of Aphiah. He was a man of influence and he had a son called Saul—a handsome young man whom no one in Israel outdid in good looks. In fact, he was head and shoulders above everyone else.

It happened that some asses belonging to Kish, Saul's father, were lost, and Kish said to Saul his son, "Take one of the servants with you and go and look for the asses."

So taking one of his father's servants with him, Saul went in search of Kish his father's asses. They combed the hills of Ephraim; they combed the countryside of Shalishah, and did not find them. They combed the land of Shaalim, and there was nothing there. They combed the territory of Jabin and did not find them.

Reaching Zuph, Saul said to the servant who was with him, "Come, let's go back, or my father will stop worrying about the asses and start worrying about us!"

"Oh," said the servant, "there is a man of God in this town, a famous man, and everything he predicts comes true without exception. Why don't we go and see him? Perhaps he will help us in our search."

"Yes, let's go," said Saul to his servant. "But what shall we give him? We've finished the bread in our knapsacks, so we can't make a present of that to the man of God. What else do we have?"

"Well," rejoined Saul's servant, "I find I have a quarter of a silver shekel. Let's give him that and he may enlighten us."

"I agree," said Saul to his servant. "Come, let's go."

So they set off for the town where the man of God was. In those days when someone wanted to find out something from God, he would say, "We'll go and consult the seer." Today, we would use the word prophet instead of seer.

As they were climbing up toward the town they met some girls coming out to fetch water, and they asked them, "Is the seer here?"

"He is," they replied, "just ahead of you! He arrived in the city only today for a sacrifice the people are making on one of the hills. As soon as you enter the town you'll find him preparing to begin his climb up to the hill to eat. The people won't start the meal till he comes, for he has to bless the sacrifice before the guests eat. So go up right away and you'll find him now."

They went up into the town and hardly had they passed the gate when there was Samuel coming out in their direction on his way to the hill.

Now, the day before Saul's arrival the Lord had foretold to Samuel: "At this time tomorrow I shall send you a man from the tribe of Benjamin, and you are to anoint him prince over my people Israel. He will liberate my people from the grasp of the Philistines. For I have seen the oppression of my people, and their pleas have reached me."

The moment Samuel saw Saul, the Lord said to him, "There is the man I told you about, the one who is to rule my people."

Saul came up to Samuel halfway through the gate. "Tell me," he said, "where is the home of the seer?"

"I am the seer," Samuel answered. "Go on ahead of me up the hill and eat with me today. Afterward, in the morning, I shall send you on your way when I have talked to you about everything that is in your heart. As for the asses lost three days ago, forget them. They have been found. In any case, who but you and all your father's line is destined to possess the whole wealth of Israel?"

"Sir," replied Saul, "I am only a Benjaminite, from the smallest tribe in Israel, and from the humblest clan in the tribe of Benjamin. How can you say what you've just said?"

Samuel merely led Saul and his servant into the dining hall and placed them at the head of the guests, who numbered about thirty. And Samuel said to the chef, "Bring on the portion I gave you to set aside." At which the chef carved the sirloin and set it before Saul.

"Eat and enjoy," Samuel said. "It was selected especially for you when I invited the others."

So Saul dined with Samuel that day, and after they had descended the hill and gone back into town, a bed was made for Saul on the roof and there he slept.

At daybreak Samuel called up to Saul on the roof: "Rise. I am sending you on your way." So Saul arose and the two of them, he and Samuel, went outside.

Samuel Anoints Saul King

Anointing with olive oil was a practice so ancient that it went back at least as far as the third millennium B.C. (Early Bronze Age). We now know from excavations at Teleilat Ghassul near the northern tip of the Dead Sea that the olive tree was in cultivation even in the fourth millennium B.C. Anointing, which was a symbol of gladness and celebration, as well as of beauty and the divine bounty, was nothing less than a sacramental act signifying an outward confirmation of inward grace and status.

(1 Samuel 9:27, 10:1-16)

AS they were progressing toward the outskirts of the town, Samuel said to Saul, "Tell the servant to go on ahead. You yourself stand still for a moment because I want to inform you of God's purpose."

After which Samuel took a small flask of olive oil and poured it on Saul's head and kissed him, saying: "By this does Yahweh anoint you prince-elect of his people Israel. It is you who will rally the Lord's people and you who will free them from the enemies that hedge them around. The sign by which you will know that God has anointed you prince of his realm will be this:

"When you leave me today you will meet two men near Rachel's tomb on the borders of Benjamin, and they will say to you, 'The asses you went searching for have been found, and your father is no longer concerned about them but about you. He is wondering: "Whatever can I do about my son?" '

"Leaving that place, you will come to the Oak of Tabor, where you will meet three men on their way up to God's shrine at Bethel. One will be carrying three kids, one three loaves of bread, and one a pitcher of wine. They will greet you and offer you two of the loaves, which you are to accept.

"After that, you will come to Gibeath-elohim ["the Hill of God"] where there is a Philistine garrison. As you come into the town you will meet a band of ecstatics descending the hill, playing harps, tambourines, flutes and lyres, and prophesying as they go. The spirit of the Lord will surge into you and you will utter ecstacies along with them, and you will change into a new man. When these signs have befallen you, do whatever comes to hand, for God is with you. You are to go down before me into Gilgal, where I shall join you to make burnt offerings and sacrifices. You must wait seven days for me to come to you. Then I shall show you what you are to do."

As soon as Saul had turned his back on Samuel, God began to infuse in him a whole new heart, for during that day all Samuel's predictions befell him. On reaching Gibeah, there coming toward him was the band of ecstatics. Immediately God's spirit surged into him and he began to utter prophecies in the midst of them. When those who had known him before saw him uttering along with the prophets, they exclaimed, "What has come over Kish's son? Is Saul among the prophets too?" At which someone quipped, "And with such a father!" This is the origin of the catchphrase: "Is Saul among the prophets too?"

When Saul's ecstasy was over and he had gone up the hill, his uncle asked him and his boy, "Where on earth have you been?"

"Looking for donkeys," Saul replied. "But we couldn't find them, so we went to Samuel."

"And what did Samuel tell you?" his uncle asked.

"Why, that the donkeys had been found," Saul said to his uncle. But he spoke not a word about becoming a king.

NOTE

Ecstatics of various kinds, from the trance of the clairvoyant Pythoness of the oracle at Delphi, to Vergil's Sibyl at Cumae near Naples (who is considered to have prophesied Christ's nativity), not to mention the soothsayers and astrologers of the Egyptians—all shared what we would now call extrasensory perception, parapsychology, mediumship, with varying degrees of heightened consciousness including even possession. Who exactly Saul's ecstatics were the Bible does not tell us, but they were by no means rare.

Saul Begins to Blunder

There is a gap in the Hebrew text just where it is about to say how long Saul had reigned before his son Jonathan began to fight for Israel. Most likely it was some twenty-two years, and Jonathan would be a lad of nineteen or twenty.

Meanwhile the Philistines, far from having been broken, have barely been kept in check. From their strongholds in the hills they continue to harry and pillage the surrounding villages. Moreover, they have kept to themselves the arts of ironwork, which gives them a crucial advantage.

And now the headstrong Saul commits an irretrievable blunder. Hard-pressed by the Philistines and seeing his men desert, he waits for Samuel, who is to offer an important sacrifice of supplication to the Lord. But Samuel delays and the desperate Saul offers the sacrifice on his own. The burnt offering is still hot on the altar when the irate old Samuel arrives. He berates Saul for usurping the prerogatives of the priesthood. "You have disobeyed Yahweh," he tells him. "Now God will have to find somebody else to do his will and the kingship will be taken from you."

Samuel departs from Saul's camp leaving the (presumably) shocked and disconsolate king with only six hundred ill-equipped men and his son Jonathan on the hills of Jeba overlooking the Philistine host.

Jonathan, all on his own, executes a crushing defeat of the Philistines at Michmash Pass, but his father is piqued: ostensibly because Jonathan acted without orders, but probably because of his son's popularity among the troops. Saul now begins to act erratically and illogically.

(1 Samuel 14:24-45)

THE battle raged beyond Bethaven, and Saul's army, now grown to about ten thousand, remained in one piece until the fighting began to be scattered among the towns and hills of Ephraim.

This was when Saul made his great blunder. He imposed a fast on his troops under oath. "I am putting a curse on any man who eats before evening," he declared. "That is, until I have fully avenged myself on my enemies."

So none of his soldiers ate a thing, although the land was

full of food. However, when the men came upon an apiary in a mountain clearing (a veritable forest of hives), they excitedly entered it, but not one of them dared put any of the honey to his mouth for fear of the ban.

Jonathan had not heard of his father's injunction to the army and, poking a stick into the honeycomb, he raised the stick to his mouth with glistening eyes. Then one of his soldiers said, "You know your father has put the army under oath! There's a ban on anyone touching food today."

"My father!" retorted Jonathan, "what a plague he has landed us all into! Just look how bright my eyes are with that little taste of honey! If only our soldiers had made a meal of all the food they found in the enemy booty today, how much greater would their slaughter of the Philistines have been!"

Indeed, the soldiers were utterly exhausted after their defeat of the Philistines at Michmash by the end of the day, and they began to plunder sheep, cows, and calves and to butcher them on the spot, then eat the meat before it had been drained of blood [i.e., koshered].

When it was reported to Saul that his troops were committing the sin against Yahweh of eating meat with the blood in it, he exclaimed, "They are doing wrong. Roll me a boulder. Now broadcast the following order to the troops, 'Let every man bring me his ox or his sheep to slaughter here, and stop sinning against Yahweh by eating meat with blood in it.' "

So every soldier brought whatever he had commandeered and butchered it there on Saul's boulder, which in fact became an altar to Yahweh: the first that Saul ever built.

After this, Saul said, "Let's go after the Philistines tonight and annihilate the lot of them by the morning."

"By all means," his troops replied. "Do whatever you think best."

However, the priest advised, "Let us ask God." So Saul consulted the Lord. "Am I to go after the Philistines? And will you put them in Israel's hands?" But he got no reply that day. So he summoned all his officers and said, "I want you here to look into this matter and find out on whose account a wrong was done today. As the Lord lives and gives victory to Israel, I swear that even if that person proves to be my own son Jonathan, he must die."

Not one of the soldiers spoke up. So he said to the whole company, "All of you stand over there, and my son Jonathan and I will stand opposite."

"Whatever you say!" the soldiers replied.

Then Saul prayed: "O Yahweh, God of Israel, why have you not answered your servant today? If some guilt attaches to me or my son Jonathan, then O Lord God of Israel, turn up the token Urim. But if the fault lies with Israel your people, turn up Thummim."

The token indicated Saul and Jonathan, and the soldiers were free.

"Now cast between me and my son Jonathan," Saul ordered. "Whichever of us it is, he must die."

"Oh no!" shouted the soldiers, "don't let that happen."

But Saul was adamant, and the lots were cast between him and Jonathan. Jonathan was taken.

"Tell me what you have done," Saul asked him, and Jonathan told him.

"I merely tasted a drop of honey on the tip of the stick in my hand. And for that I have to die?"

"By God, yes, and today," Saul replied.

But the soldiers cried out, "What! Today's hero who brought such triumph to Israel die? By the Lord, no! Not a hair of his head shall fall to the ground. God was with him in everything he did this day."

So the army saved Jonathan and he did not die.

Then Saul gave up his pursuit of the Philistines, and they returned to their own domain.

NOTES

1. According to the Mosaic dietary laws all meat had to be drained of blood before it was cooked and eaten. The original reason for this was probably hygienic and a necessity in the sweltering climate of the desert. Flesh treated in this way was considered "kasher" (kosher), i.e., proper.

2. The passage of Samuel 14: 25-26 has been more mangled by translators than it deserves. Admittedly there has been some corruption in the Hebrew text, but the Greek of the Septuagint reads perfectly straightforwardly. The Anchor Bible, relying mainly on the Hebrew, has:

> "Now there was a honeycomb on the ground, and when the army came upon [it], its bees had left . . ."

The Living Bible puts it this way:

> ". . . they found a honeycomb on the ground in the forest."

The result in either case makes no sense. Honeycombs do not lie on the ground—even less on the ground of a forest. Besides, it is ridiculous to suppose that an army of several thousand men is going to get excited over a single honeycomb. The Greek makes everything clear. The word μελισσων, *melissōn,* which has been wrongly translated as "honeycomb," means a bee house or apiary. (There are several words for honeycomb in Greek.) Here is the Septuagint translated word for word:

> The whole territory was rich in food, and there was a forest of hives on the face of the meadow, and the men entered into the apiary, going forward chattering.

There is nothing about the bees having left. Indeed, if they had, the hives would already have been plundered by wasps, ants, and mice. Jonathan (in the Septuagint) does not just grab a chunk of honeycomb but gingerly pokes his stick into it.

3. Urim and Thummim appear to have been dice-like precious stones lodged in the high priest's ephod and used for divination.

Saul's Third Blunder

Saul has been victorious on all fronts. He has driven back the Moabites to their strongholds east of the Dead Sea, and the Ammonites to the deserts across the Jordan. To the south he has dealt with the Edomites, and in the north with the kings of Zobah. Now he is to turn his hand against the warlike and marauding nomads of the southern deserts, the Amalekites: a race that has harassed the Israelites ever since they left Egypt and endured forty years in the wilderness.

In the following story our sympathies are probably much more with Saul (even though he does show greed) than they are with the interfering, bloodthirsty old prophet, Samuel, abetted by a Yahweh cast in a similar mold. However, one must keep in mind that all these characters are symbols. The Amalekites, whom Saul now conquers, have represented the traditional "bad guys" ever since the time of Moses. Yahweh himself is a symbol of the intransigent fight of good against evil, even though we know that the Amalekites are no more evil according to their own lights than the Israelites. One must remember that the concept of deity is still primitive and evolving.

(1 Samuel 15:1-35)

SAMUEL said to Saul, "I was the one Yahweh sent to anoint you king of Israel. So listen carefully to what I have to say. The Lord of Hosts has declared this: 'I have kept a record of all the hostile things that Amalek did to Israel in its journeying out of Egypt. So go now and strike down Amalek. I want them and everything that belongs to them obliterated. Show no mercy. Kill man, woman, child, even suckling at the breast, cattle, sheep, camels, and asses.' "

Saul summoned his army and mobilized it at Telaim: two hundred thousand infantry and ten thousand troops from Judah. Approaching the Amalek capital, he lay low in the Wadi ["riverbed"] and sent a message of warning to the Kenites: "Get yourselves far from Amalek, otherwise I'll wipe you out as well. You were kind to us Israelites when we came out of Egypt." The Kenites accordingly removed themselves from the Amalekites.

Saul proceeded to overwhelm the Amalekites from the Wadi on as far as Shur on the borders of Egypt. Agag, the king of Amalek, he took alive, but he put to death the rest of the people. Saul and the army spared not only Agag but the best of the flocks and herds—the plump and the young—as well as provisions, vineyards, and whatever was of the best, refusing to destroy these. But that which was poor and good for nothing—this they destroyed.

Yahweh forthwith had a word with Samuel: "I am sorry I ever made Saul king. He has turned from me and does not carry out my commands."

Samuel was very much distressed and all through the night cried out to Yahweh. Early next morning he went to meet Saul, but Saul had gone to Carmel to erect himself a triumphal arch, and then turned his steps toward Gilgal.

Samuel caught up with him just as Saul was making burnt offerings to Yahweh of some of the best of the booty he had taken from Amalek. As Samuel drew near, Saul greeted him with: "The Lord's blessings on you! I have done everything that Yahweh commanded."

"Oh," replied Samuel, "then what is that bleating that fills my ears, and that lowing I hear?"

"Only the animals I got from Amalek," Saul answered. "The troops spared the best of the sheep and the cattle to sacrifice to your God Yahweh. The rest I destroyed."

"Stop!" interjected Saul, "and allow me to tell you what Yahweh said to me last night."

"Tell me."

"Well then, is it not true that small though you were in your own eyes you were made head of the tribes of Israel? The Lord anointed you king of Israel, sent you on a mission, and told you: 'Go and obliterate those sinful Amalekites and fight them until not one is left.' Why then did you not listen to Yahweh? Why have you grabbed the loot and done exactly what Yahweh told you not to?"

"But I did listen to Yahweh," Saul remonstrated, "and I did carry out the mission on which he sent me. I captured Agag king of Amalek and slaughtered all the Amalekites. Only, the soldiers took some sheep and oxen from the best of the spoil to make a sacrifice to the Lord our God at Gilgal."

Samuel's answer was:

"Does the Lord want burnt offerings and victims
Or rather that his word be obeyed?
Obedience is better than sacrifice,
And devotion than the fat of rams.
Headstrong will is like the sin of magic
And recalcitrance like the crime of idols.
You have rejected the word of Yahweh
So now Yahweh rejects you as king of Israel."

"Alas, I have sinned," Saul confessed. "I have gone against the Lord's commands and against your orders. Through fear I listened to the soldiers. But now, I beg you, take my sin away. Return with me and I shall cast myself down before Yahweh."

"I will not go back with you," Samuel answered, "because you have rejected the word of Yahweh, and now Yahweh rejects you as king of Israel."

As Samuel turned to go, Saul caught hold of the hem of his robe, which tore in his hands. Whereat Samuel exclaimed, "Thus does Yahweh tear the kingship of Israel from you this day and give it to the next man! . . . Yes, the Everlasting One of Israel does not lie, nor does he change his mind, for he is not like fickle man."

Saul pleaded, "Although I have sinned, honor me still before the elders of my people and before Israel. Go back with me and let me prostrate myself in front of Yahweh your God."

So Samuel turned and followed Saul back, and Saul prostrated himself before the Lord. Then Samuel ordered, "Bring Agag out to me, king of Amalek."

Agag came to him, fat, chained, and trembling as he uttered, "So it is you. O bitter Death!"

Samuel answered, "Just as your sword has rendered women childless, so now shall your mother be a childless woman."

Then Samuel hewed Agag to pieces before Yahweh in Gilgal. After which he left for Ramah, while Saul went to his house in Gibeah. Samuel till the day of his death never saw Saul again, though he often mourned him. Yahweh, for his part, regretted that he had ever made Saul king of Israel.

Samuel Surreptitiously Anoints David

The southernmost tribe of Israel, Judah, now enters the picture. With a culture less affected than the northern tribes by the leavening and more liberal traditions of the surrounding Canaanites, Judah would be a more fertile ground for producing a thoroughly Yahvistic successor to Saul—or so the Yahvistic old prophet Samuel probably thought. And although Saul, in spite of his blunders, was not doing too badly, Samuel now goes south on his quest for a substitute. With his penchant for picking good-looking young men, he sorts through the eight sons of Jesse: the grandson of Boaz and Ruth (see page 164) and a man of substance and standing.

Bethlehem, a village nestling among the highlands of Judah some six miles from Jerusalem, was one of the region's richest places.

(1 Samuel 16:1-23)

YAHWEH now said to Samuel, "How long will you go on mourning for Saul, even though I have repudiated him as king? Fill your horn with oil and go. I am sending you to Jesse in Bethlehem, for I have found a king among his sons."

"But how can I go?" Samuel responded. "Saul will hear of it and kill me."

"Just take a calf from the herd along with you and announce that you have come to sacrifice to the Lord. Then I shall tell you what to do. You are to anoint the man I point out to you."

Samuel did what the Lord told him and when he arrived at Bethlehem, the elders of the town came out nervously to meet him. "Seer, is your visit peaceful?" they asked him.

"Yes, peaceful," he said. "I am here to sacrifice to Yahweh. So come and be purified and celebrate with me today."

Then he purified Jesse and his sons and called them to the sacrifice. When they came and his eyes fell on Eliab, he thought, "This surely is the one the Lord is going to anoint!"

But Yahweh told him, "Don't judge by good looks and stature. I have not chosen this one. God sees not as man sees. Man looks into the face. God looks into the heart."

Jesse then called on Abinadab to present himself to Samuel. "The Lord has not chosen this one either," Samuel said. So Jesse brought forward Shammah. "No, nor this one," Samuel repeated.

When Jesse had gone through all seven sons before Samuel, the seer said, "Yahweh has chosen none of these. Are they all the boys you have?"

"Well, there is the youngest," he answered. "He is out shepherding."

"Have him fetched," Samuel said to Jesse. "We won't sit down to eat until he comes."

Jesse sent for him and had him brought. He was a fine-looking boy, ruddy, attractive, with beautiful features.

"He is the one," Yahweh said to Samuel. "He is David. Anoint him at once."

Samuel took his horn of oil there and then and in the midst of his brothers anointed him. From that moment onward the Lord's spirit possessed David and abided with him. Samuel, for his part, got up and went to Ramah.

Meanwhile, the spirit of the Lord had deserted Saul, and a spirit of gloom from the Lord took to haunting him. His attendants said to him, "There is no doubt that a deep gloom from God is hanging over you. Let your majesty give us your servants the order and we will look for someone who plays well on the harp, who can play to you when this gloom descends on you and so soothe you and heal you."

Saul at once said to his attendants, "Yes, find me somebody who plays well and bring him to me."

At which one of the courtiers spoke up and said, "I happen to know that Jesse of Bethlehem has a son who plays the harp. He is strong, brave, discreet, handsome, and the Lord is with him."

So Saul dispatched messengers to Jesse, saying: "Send me David your son, the one out with the flocks."

Jesse loaded a donkey with provisions, a skin of wine, and a kid, and sent these in David's care to Saul. When David came to Saul and stood before him, Saul lost his heart to him. He made him his armor bearer and sent word to Jesse: "Please let David stay in my service. I like him exceedingly."

Thereafter, whenever the spirit of gloom came upon Saul from God, David would take up his harp and play; and Saul would be soothed and healed, and the gloom would leave him.

David and Goliath

In the story of David and Goliath the Biblical record derives from two different and sometimes contradictory traditions. I follow the Anchor Bible in combining them into one single and consistent account.

As to Goliath's great height, there are also two versions. The Hebrew says that he was "four cubits and a span," a cubit being the length from armpit to tip of middle finger, and a span the width of a man's hand (spread) from thumb tip to little finger. This would make Goliath six feet nine inches, which might not seem excessive to us but in those days a mere five feet nine was considered tall. The other version, given in the Septuagint and the Vulgate, makes him six cubits and a span, and thus over nine feet. I have kept to that.

Champion combat was often resorted to in the ancient world, thus both gratifying the people's delight in spectacle and resolving a conflict. One thinks of Achilles challenging Hector outside the walls of Troy, and Aenaes' duel with the Latin chieftain Turnus outside what was to become Rome.

(1 Samuel 17:1-11, 32-54)

THE Philistines had gathered their forces for battle, mustering at Socoh in Judah and camped between Socoh and Azekah on the borders of Ephes-dammin.

Saul therefore set up camp in the Valley of the Terebinths and drew up Israel's army to face the Philistines, who were positioned immediately opposite the Israelites, with a valley in between.

Then out of the ranks of the Philistines there strutted a powerful infantryman from Gath named Goliath, whose height was six cubits and a span. He wore a helmet on his head, was clothed in scaled coat of mail weighing five thousand bronze shekels [about two hundred pounds], and the greaves around his legs were of bronze. A bronze shield was slung between his shoulder blades, and the shaft of his spear was like a weaver's beam: the head alone of the spear weighed six hundred iron shekels [about twenty-five pounds]. His shield bearer walked in front of him.

Goliath stood shouting across to the Israelite ranks: "What

is the point of marching out in battle order? I am a Philistine, am I not? And you are servants of Saul? So, pick a man among you to come down and fight me hand to hand. If he wins this fight and kills me, we shall become your slaves. But if I win and kill him, you will have to serve us as slaves."

Then the Philistine went on, "Look, I am challenging the drawn ranks of Israel this day. Give me a man who will fight it out with me in single combat."

Hearing which harangue, Saul and the Israelites were full of dismay and very frightened. But David stepped up and said to Saul, "There is no need for your heart to sink. I your servant shall go and fight this Philistine."

"No, you cannot go and fight the Philistine," Saul answered. "You are only a boy, and this man has been trained as a soldier from his youth."

"Sir," persisted David, "I your servant used to look after my father's sheep, and whenever a lion or bear went and carried off one of the flock, I gave chase and clubbed it down and snatched the sheep from its jaws. If one of them sprang at me, I would catch it by the throat and throttle it. Yes sir, I have killed both lion and bear, and this uncircumcised Philistine will be no different. May I not go and strike him down and erase this insult to Israel? Who is this uncircumcised ruffian that dares to challenge the army of the living God? The Lord who saved me from the clutches of lion and bear will save me from this Philistine."

"Very well then, go," Saul said to David. "And the Lord be with you!"

Then Saul dressed David in his own armor, his coat of mail, with a bronze helmet for his head and his own sword buckled to his side. But after trying to walk a step or two, David exclaimed to Saul, "I can't move in all this. I'm not used to it." So the armor was removed.

Then, with a stick in hand, he picked out five smooth pebbles from the wadi and lodged them in the shepherd's pouch he had with him, and he marched out to meet the Philistine champion, who advanced against him with his shield bearer walking ahead.

The moment Goliath caught sight of David he dismissed him—a fresh-looking stripling with a pretty face—and he jeered, "Am I a dog to be come at with sticks and stones?"

"No," replied David, "something worse than a dog!"

At which the Philistine called down curses on David from

his gods. "Come to me," he bawled, "and I'll give your meat to the vultures and the jackals!"

David shouted back: "You come against me with sword, spear, and buckler, and I come against you with the name of Yahweh Lord of the armies of heaven and of Israel, which you have insulted this day. This day, on which Yahweh will hand you over to me and I will remove your head from you and give your carcass and the corpses of you Philistines to the birds of the air and the beasts of the wild. Then the whole earth will ring with the news that Israel has a God indeed, and this mass of people here will know that it is not by sword or spear that Yahweh gives the victory. No, the battle is the Lord's and it is he that will put you in our hands."

The Philistine came looming toward David for the attack, and David as he ran out to meet him reached into his pouch for a stone, which he fixed into his sling and whirled at the Philistine, striking him in the forehead. The stone sank into the giant's forehead as he tottered face downward to the ground. David ran up and stood over him, then dragged Goliath's sword from its scabbard, and dispatched him, severing his head.

When the Philistines saw that their champion was dead, they turned and ran. The men of Israel surged forward shouting, and they pursued them as far as the entrance to Gath and the gates of Ekron. All along the Shaarim road the Philistine dead and wounded were strewn, almost to Gath and Ekron. And when they had finished pursuing the Philistines, the Israelites turned back and looted their camp. David took Goliath's head and brought it to Jerusalem, but he kept the Philistine's armor in his own tent.

Saul's Growing Paranoia

Chapter 18 of the first Book of Samuel describes the meeting of David and Saul's son Jonathan, who takes to David immediately and begins to love him as his own self. The two young men, both brave and strong, form a friendship for each other which has become a byword of male comradeship. As the King James Bible puts it: "The soul of Jonathan was knit with the soul of David, and Jonathan loved him as his own soul."

Meanwhile, Saul grows more and more suspicious and moody. He puts David in charge of the army and sends him on dangerous missions, but the more David comes back a triumphant hero, the more Saul becomes inflamed with jealousy. He hears the women singing: "Saul has slain his thousands, but David his tens of thousands," and the next day he rampages through the palace like a man possessed. David tries to soothe him with the harp, as he has so often done before, but the king in a sudden seizure hurls the spear he has been nursing at the young man, narrowly missing him as David dodges.

David is banished from court, but a little later warily reinstated. Saul gives his elder daughter, Merab (who had been promised to David as a reward for slaying Goliath), to another man.

(1 Samuel 18:20-27)

SAUL'S other daughter, however, Michal, had fallen in love with David, and when Saul heard of it he saw his opportunity. "If I give her to him," he thought, "she can be used as a tool to deliver him into the hands of the Philistines."

So he instructed his courtiers to encourage David privately and to tell him, "You're in the king's favor and his whole court loves you. Don't hold back from letting yourself be a son-in-law to the king."

When Saul's henchmen whispered this in David's ear, David replied, "Do you think it a trifle to offer oneself as son-in-law to the king? I am a poor man and quite undistinguished."

Saul's courtiers came back and reported what David had said. "Well then, tell him this," Saul responded: "the only dowry the king requires is a hundred Philistine foreskins, as vengeance on his royal foes." Saul was, of course, expecting David to fall into the hands of the Philistines.

When Saul's toadies reported this to David, David saw that being the king's son-in-law was a great opportunity. So he went out with his men and slew a hundred Philistines and laid out their foreskins before the king, thus claiming his son-in-lawship. The king accordingly gave him his daughter Michal for his bride.

Saul Throws a Second Spear at David

(1 Samuel 18:28-30, 19:1-18)

WHEN Saul saw that the Lord was with David and that his daughter Michal (and the whole of Israel) loved him, he distrusted him all the more. He talked to his son Jonathan about killing David, and to his close associates too, but Jonathan loved David deeply and he warned him: "Be careful tomorrow morning. Lie low in a secret spot while I approach my father in the field where you will be and speak to him about you. Then I'll come and tell you whatever I can find out."

Accordingly, Jonathan said nice things about David to his father. "The king mustn't hurt his servant David," he urged. "He has done nothing to hurt you. In fact, his behavior has been faultless. And he has risked his own life to slay the Philistine, and he won a triumph for Israel. You were happy when you heard it. So why now commit a crime and spill innocent blood by killing David? There is no cause."

Saul listened to Jonathan. "As Yahweh lives," he swore, "David won't be killed."

Jonathan called David and told him this, then led him out to Saul; and David went back to serving Saul as before.

War broke out once more and David marched against the Philistines, scoring a great victory with much slaughter. Whereat they fled. But once again, as Saul was sitting in his house, nursing his spear, and David was playing on the harp, the spirit of gloom from God swept upon Saul and he aimed his spear at David to pin him to the wall, but David jumped aside and fled as the spear stuck fast in the wall.

That same night Saul dispatched guards to David's house to watch it, with the idea of killing him in the morning. But Michal his wife informed him and said, "If you don't escape tonight, tomorrow you'll be dead."

She let him down through a window and when he had got safely away, Michal took a statue, laid it on the bed, arranged a mass of goat's hair at its head, and covered it with a blanket.

When Saul's guards came to arrest David, she told them he was sick. Saul then sent other officers with the command: "Bring him to me, bed and all, to kill."

When the officers arrived, what did they uncover but a statue in the bed with a mass of goat's hair at its head!

Saul said to Michal, "Why have you betrayed me? You have let my enemy get away unscathed."

"Because," Michal told him, "he threatened to kill me if I didn't."

The Slaughter of the Priests of Nob

As Saul's determination to do away with David grows, so do the love and fealty to each other of David and Jonathan. After a meeting with Jonathan at Gibeah, David heads south and at the little town of Nob, northeast of Jerusalem, he persuades the priest of the Tabernacle, Ahimelech, to let him and his famished men eat the consecrated bread of the temple. Ahimelech also hands him the sword of Goliath, which had been reverently wrapped in a cloth and put aside.

After a dangerous encounter at the court of King Achish the Philistine, where he escapes only by pretending to be mad (spitting and drooling), David sets up in the Cave of Adullam in the Judean highlands some fifteen miles from Bethlehem, where members of his tribe join him with four hundred young desperadoes. He has also moved his parents for safety to Mispah and put them under the protection of the Moabite king.

Meanwhile, the impassioned Saul keeps up the pursuit.

(1 Samuel 22:6-19)

WHEN Saul heard that David and his band had been seen, he was sitting under a tamarisk tree high in Gibeah, with his spear in his hand and all his court about him.

"Listen, you Benjaminites," he declared, "is the son of Jesse going to give you fields and vineyards? Is he going to promote any of you to be sergeants and captains? Then why are you part of his conspiracy? Not one of you tells me how my own son is in league with the son of Jesse. Not one of you has enough feeling for me to tell me that my own son is this very day supporting a highway brigand against me."

Then Doeg the Edomite, who was in charge of Saul's servants, spoke up and said, "I saw the son of Jesse when he came to Nob to see the priest Ahimelech, son of Ahitub, who consulted God for him and gave him food and the sword of Goliath the Philistine."

Forthwith the king sent for Ahimelech son of Ahitub, as well as all his family and the entire priesthood of Nob.

"Listen, you son of Ahitub," he shouted.

"Yes, my lord," quavered he.

"Why have you plotted against me, you and the son of Jesse? You gave him food and a sword and you consulted God for him. You encouraged him to rebel against me and turn himself into a highway robber—which he is to this day."

"But sir," expostulated Ahimelech, "I thought that of all your subjects nobody was so loyal as David: the king's own son-in-law and captain of his bodyguard—highly esteemed in your house. Nor was this the first time that I consulted God for him. By no means! So the king must not pin any suspicion on me his servant or on any of my family. Your servant knows nothing of this matter, great or small."

"Nonetheless Ahimelech," Saul retorted, "you are going to die: you and your whole family."

And the king shouted an order to his guards who were standing by: "Round up these priests of Yahweh and kill them. They are hand in glove with David. They knew he was a runaway and did not tell me."

The king's officers, however, refused to lift a finger against the priests of Yahweh; so the king turned to Doeg: "You go and strike down these priests," he ordered.

At which Doeg the Edomite rounded on the priests and murdered them, eighty-five in all—all wearing the priestly ephod. Then Saul struck at Nob, the city of priests, and put to the edge of the sword every man, woman, child, and babe, every ox, ass, and sheep.

NOTE

There is a problem about the tree under which Saul was sitting when he addressed his court. The Hebrew text says *eshel*, translated as "tamarisk," but the tamarisk is hardly more than a tall bush. The word used in the Septuagint is ἀρουρα (*aroura*), which usually means arable land or a field. St. Jerome translates it as "a wood." But in none of my lexicons is it given as a tree of any kind.

David and Abigail

Saul's pursuit of David, after a brief reconciliation, is soon to be renewed, but meantime the biblical writers give us the story of how David meets the beautiful and intelligent Abigail, who is to be not only a compensation for his having lost his royal wife, Michal (whom Saul has forced to marry someone else), but an important auxiliary on his path to the kingship.

Now David has taken his small troop to the wilderness of Maon, which stretches fifteen miles or so west of the southern end of the Dead Sea and is just south of the pleasant hill village of Carmel with its gardens and vineyards.

(1 Samuel 25:2-43)

THERE was a man of Maon with property in Carmel. He was a rich man, very rich, with three thousand sheep and one thousand goats, and he was shearing his sheep in Carmel.

The man's name was Nabal ["fool"], and his wife's name was Abigail. She was an intelligent and beautiful woman, but he was an ill-mannered boor.

When David heard in the desert that Nabal was shearing his sheep, he sent ten young men to Carmel with the following instructions: "When you come to Nabal, salute him in my name and say, 'Peace to you! Peace to your house! Peace to everything that is yours! I heard that you were sheep shearing. Now, some of your shepherds were with us in the wilderness and we did not molest them. In fact, they didn't lose a single one of their flocks all the days they were with us in the Carmel hills. Ask your own young men and they will confirm this. So please treat my young men kindly, for we've come on a happy day, and give us and your son David whatever you can spare.' "

David's men accordingly came, gave Nabal David's message, and waited. Nabal's reply was: "Who is this David, this son of Jesse? There are too many slaves these days running away from their masters. Am I expected to take my bread, my wine, my meat—specially slaughtered for my shearers—and hand them out to people who come from I don't know where?"

So David's men turned for home and when they had got back reported everything to him. "Strap on your swords," he ordered, and everyone strapped on his sword as David strapped on his. Four hundred set off behind him, and two hundred stayed with the gear.

Meanwhile, Abigail, Nabal's wife, had been told by one of the servants: "You know, David sent bearings of greeting out of the wilderness to our master and he was rude to them! Yet these men were extremely good to us and gave us no trouble at all. In fact, we didn't lose a thing the whole time we were with them out in the fields. They were like a protecting wall to us night and day the entire time we were with them tending our sheep. May I advise you, madam, to be well warned, because your husband and house are in danger. As for him, he is such an oaf that no one can talk to him."

Abigail quickly collected two hundred loaves, two skins of wine, five sheep ready dressed, a bushel of roasted grain, a hundred clusters of raisins, and two hundred fig cakes, and she had these loaded onto asses.

"Go on ahead of me," she told her servants, "I'll be right behind you." To her husband, Nabal, she said not a word.

As it happened, she was riding her ass down toward the foot of the mountain just as David and his men were beginning to come up. And they met. (David had been fuming, "What a lot of use it's been protecting this fellow's possessions in the wilderness and not losing a blessed thing of his! He has repaid kindness with rudeness. God can do so-and-so to David, and add some, if I've left one wall-pissing manjack of them alive by morning!")

The moment Abigail caught sight of David she dismounted from her ass and threw herself before him on the ground, right at his feet.

"My lord," she cried, "let me take the blame for it all. Let your maidservant explain. I beg you hear what your maidservant has to tell you. Please, my lord, ignore that pestilent man [my husband]. He is a fool, as his name says. For my part, I never saw the young men you sent, so now let this offering your maidservant has brought my lord be distributed to the company who follow my lord. Forgive your maidservant's boldness, but Yahweh is certainly going to establish your house because you fight on his side. So in all your days evil must never be found in you. And if at any time someone harries you and wants your life, your life will be safely wrapped up among the living in Yahweh's keeping, but the lives of your enemies will be whirled about and slung out into oblivion. And when Yahweh has fulfilled all that he has in store for you, my lord, and made you king of Israel, you must have no remorse or scruples because of having once shed innocent blood in an act of vengeance. And [lastly] when Yahweh has been generous to you, my lord, please remember me your handmaid."

David replied to Abigail, "Praised be the Lord God of Israel for sending you to meet me! And praised be your good sense! And praised be you yourself for having kept me this day from being guilty of blood and avenging myself by my own hand! Otherwise, as Yahweh God of Israel lives and has withheld me from harming you, I swear that if you hadn't come so quickly to meet me, not a single fellow of them would I have left to Nabal by the light of morning."

David then took from her the offering she had brought him and said, "Go home now in peace. I accept all that you have said and I grant your request."

Nabal was throwing a party when Abigail got back to him: a banquet fit for a king. He was bubbling with good cheer and was very drunk, so she said not a word about anything till it was daylight. Then in the morning when Nabal's wine had left him, his wife told him everything and his heart died within him and he became like a stone. Ten days later the Lord struck him down dead.

When David heard the news he exclaimed, "I thank the Lord for vindicating me from Nabal's insult and saving me from doing wrong. He has turned Nabal's evil back on his own head."

Then David sent overtures to Abigail that he would take her as his wife. His messengers came to Abigail, announcing, "David sends us to say that he wants to take you as his wife."

She arose and bowed herself low to the ground. "I am ready to be my lord's slave," she declared, "and wash your servants' feet. And now, my lord, by the living God and your own life, since Yahweh has kept you from the guilt of blood and from taking the law into your own hands, let your enemies and anybody who wants to harm you end up like Nabal."

She quickly made herself ready, mounted her ass, and with five young serving women to attend her followed David's messengers and became his wife.

(David also took Ahinoam from [the village of] Jezreel. So both these women became his wives.)

The Witch of Endor

Although David spares Saul's life a second time (having come upon him asleep unguarded in his tent) and receives the same protestations of renewed love that he received before, he has the good sense to realize that he is far from safe as long as Saul is alive, and he takes himself and his little army of six hundred to join the Philistine king, Achish, as a mercenary leader. Achish gives him the town of Ziklag (at the southern edges of Judah and some twelve miles from the sea) as his headquarters.

Samuel meanwhile has died, and Saul, feeling himself very much alone, views with dread a renewed mustering of the Philistines. He probably knows that David has gone over to the Philistines, but he does not know that King Achish has exonerated David from fighting against his own people.

The "Witch of Endor" was in fact a medium possessing the power of calling up the souls of the dead. Though dealing with mediums was expressly forbidden by Levitic law (a prohibition endorsed by Saul himself), the desperate king now seeks one out—even disguising himself and taking the risk of passing through the enemy lines to get to Endor, which was only two miles from the Philistine camp. His own camp was on a mountain in northern Israel, about seven miles west of the Jordan.

(1 Samuel 28:4-25)

THE Philistines had mustered and were encamped at Shunem; so Saul mobilized Israel and set up camp on Mount Giboa. When he looked down on the Philistine army his heart quailed within him. He consulted Yahweh, but Yahweh would not answer him by either dreams, lots, or oracle. Saul therefore said to his ministers, "Find me a woman who has the gift of mediumship, and I shall go and ask her what I should do."

They told him, "There is a woman with the divining spirit at Endor." So Saul disguised himself in different garb and set out with two companions, reaching the woman at nightfall. He said to her, "Bring up a spirit for me: bring the man I tell you."

The woman replied, "Surely you know what Saul has

done: how he has rooted out mediums and necromancers from the land? Are you trying to trap me and get me killed?"

"As the Lord lives," Saul swore to her, "I promise that nothing will happen to you."

"Then who is it you want me to bring up for you?" the woman asked.

"Bring up Samuel for me," he said.

The moment her eyes fell on Samuel, she shrieked, "You have tricked me. You are Saul."

"Don't be afraid," the king reassured her. "What do you see?"

"I see a specter," she said, "coming up from the earth."

"What does it look like?" he asked.

"It's an old man coming up. He is wrapped in a cloak."

Then Saul knew that it was Samuel and he prostrated himself on the ground in reverence.

"Why have you disturbed me and brought me up?" Samuel asked.

"Because I am in dire trouble," Saul answered. "The Philistines are at war with me, but God has abandoned me and no longer answers me by either oracle or dreams. That is why I have called on you to ask what I must do."

"Why ask me," Samuel retorted, "seeing that Yahweh has abandoned you and is with your rival? The Lord has dealt with you exactly as he said he would and as I told you. He is going to wrest your kingdom from you and give it to David your rival: all because you disobeyed Yahweh and did not respect his great anger against Amalek. That is why he has treated you like this today. Moreover, Yahweh will let you and the whole Israelite army fall into the hands of the Philistines. And tomorrow you and your sons will be with me."

At this, Saul collapsed upon the floor. He was terrified by Samuel's prediction. Indeed, all strength had left him, for he had not eaten for a day and a night.

The woman came up to Saul, seeing how shattered he was, and said, "Listen, I your humble servant have obeyed you and put my life in your hands. I did what you asked me to. Now then, sir, you pay attention to me. I am going to serve you a little something, and you must eat it and gain strength to go on your way."

It happened that the woman had been fattening a calf for the house, and she went out and slaughtered it. She kneaded some meal into dough and baked unleaven bread. But Saul would not eat. However, when his servants and the woman urged him, he listened at last, got up from the floor, and sat down on a bed.

She served Saul and his servants, and when they had eaten they departed, walking through the night.

The Death of Saul and Jonathan

While Saul is nerving himself for the coming battle with the Philistines, David learns that his headquarters at Ziklag has been raided and sacked by the Amalekites and both his wives, Abigail and Ahinoam, captured.

In a forced march and brilliant maneuver he catches up with the plunderers and slaughters them all, except for four hundred young men who get away on camels, and recovers his wives and the wives and daughters of his soldiers: a singular success compared to the isolation and spirit of doom of the pathetic Saul.

(1 Samuel 31:1-10)

MEANWHILE the Philistines attacked Israel and as the Israelite troops fled before them they were butchered on the slopes of Mount Gilboa. The Philistines caught up with Saul and his sons. They cut down Jonathan, Abimadab, and Malchishua, his sons.

The battle raged around Saul. Then the archers marked him and he was grievously wounded in the belly.

"Draw your sword and run me through," he pleaded with his armor bearer. "I don't want to become a plaything of these uncircumcised heathens."

But his armor bearer was too afraid to do it. So Saul took the sword himself and fell upon it. Then his armor bearer, seeing that he was dead, also fell on his sword and died with him. So Saul, his three sons, and his armor bearer all died together that day.

When the Israelites who lived on the other side of the valley beyond the Jordan saw that their army had been routed and that Saul and his sons were dead, they abandoned their cities and fled, and the Philistines came and dwelt in them.

The following day when the Philistines came to strip the slain, they found Saul and his three sons lying dead on Mount Gilboa. They cut off the king's head and and stripped him of his armor. Then they broadcast the joyful news all through their territories and temples. They exhibited Saul's armor in the shrine of Astarte; his body they nailed to the walls of Bethshan.

David Laments Saul and Jonathan

Though Saul was now dead, and also Jonathan, the heir apparent, David by no means became automatically king of all Israel. Abner, Saul's uncle, set up Saul's remaining son, Ishbosheth, as puppet king of all the northern tribes, but was not strong enough (after the devastating defeat at Gilboa) to prevent David's being proclaimed king of Judah at Hebron. Hebron was a well-fortified hill town, with a long Canaanite history, twenty miles south of Jerusalem. David now makes Hebron his capital and is to reign there for seven years, i.e., from 1013 to 1006 B.C.

But all this takes place only after the following episode, in which a suitably bedraggled escapee from the slaughter at Gilboa arrives and delivers a quite different account of Saul's death from that given in 1 Samuel 31. Since both accounts cannot be true, the easiest explanation is to assume that the man, who expects to be well rewarded for his news, is lying.

(2 Samuel 1:1-27)

AFTER the death of Saul, when David had been back at Ziklag for two days on his return from crushing the Amalekites, there appeared on the third day a man from Saul's camp with his clothes in tatters and dust on his head. He threw himself on the ground at David's feet.

"Where do you come from?" David asked him.

"I escaped from the Israelite lines," he said.

"How was it there?" David asked. "Tell me."

"The troops fled from the battlefield," he replied. "Many fell and many are dead. Saul and his son Jonathan are both dead."

"How do you know that Saul and his son Jonathan are dead?" David asked the young soldier.

"Because I was there on Mount Gilboa," the youth replied. "Just as Saul, with the chariots and horses closing in on him, was leaning on his spear, he turned and saw me and called me to him.

" 'At the ready, sir!' I said.

" 'Who are you?' he asked me.

" 'An Amalekite,' sir."

" 'Stand over me and kill me,' he said. 'A terrible darkness swamps me, but I cannot die.'

"So I stood over him and dispatched him. I knew he couldn't live, wounded as he was. Then I took the diadem from his head and the bracelet from his arm, and have brought them here to you, sir."

David clutched his clothes and rent them, as did all the men who were with him. They mourned and wept and fasted till sundown for Saul and his son Jonathan, and for all the Lord's people and men of Israel who had fallen by the sword.

Later David asked the young man who had brought the news: "Where are you from?"

"I am the son of a foreigner, an Amalekite," he said.

"How is it that you didn't hesitate to lift your hand against the Lord's anointed?" David asked.

Then, turning to one of his guards, he ordered, "Go and fall on him."

The guard struck him down and he died as David pronounced, "Your blood is on your own head. You condemned yourself out of your own mouth when you said, 'Yes, I killed the Lord's anointed.' "

David sang this lament for Saul and his son Jonathan, and he commanded it to be taught to the young children of Judah. It is recorded in the book of Jashar.

The prime of Israel is slain in the hills.
How have the valiant fallen!
Tell it not in Gath.
Publish it not in the streets of Ashkelon,
Or the daughters of the Philistines will rejoice,
The daughters of the uncircumcised exult.
O you mountains of Gilboa,
Let there be no dew on you,
Let there be no rain
And no harvesting from your furrows.

The shield of the mighty is vilely cast away,
The shield of Saul, the anointed shield,
Is cast away to gather rust.

From the blood of the slain,
From the fat of the brave,
The bow of Jonathan never did flinch,
And the sword of Saul
Never did return to him empty.

Oh, Saul and Jonathan,
How lovely and comely in life you were,
And in death not divided.
Swifter than eagles you were,
Stronger than lions.

You daughters of Israel, shed tears over Saul.
He clothed you in scarlet,
He wove jewels of gold into your gowns.

How the heroes have succumbed in battle!
Jonathan, slain in the hills!
My brother Jonathan, how I grieve for you!
Beautiful I thought you,
Wonderful your love for me
Surpassing the love of women.

The valiant are fallen.
The weapons of war annulled.

NOTE

The book of Jashar was an anthology of ancient poetry and songs, cited three times in the Old Testament but now lost (probably because it enshrined a mainly oral tradition).

David Dances Naked Before the Ark

After seven years of a divided kingdom, with David reigning in Judah and Saul's son Ishbosheth reigning as a puppet king in Israel (the northern provinces), the latter is assassinated and David at the age of thirty-seven becomes king of all twelve tribes of Israel.

In an astute move to consolidate the union of north and south, David conquers the Jebusites (an ancient Canaanite tribe) and makes their city, Jerusalem (conveniently placed halfway between the two sections of Jewry), his capital; which he now proceeds to make worthy of the distinction. He is befriended by the king of Tyre, a rich and sophisticated Phoenician city on the coast, who lends him carpenters and masons and provides him with cedar wood to make himself a palace on Mount Zion—the heart of Jerusalem. Jerusalem becomes the "City of David" (as is Bethlehem).

After two more crushing defeats of the Philistines, which finally end a hundred years of mutual struggle, David is ready to make a move of paramount religious and symbolical importance: the retrieval of the Ark of the Covenant, which ever since the rule of Samuel and the reign of Saul has been hidden in a house at Kirjathjearim (or Baaljudah).

(2 Samuel 6:16-23)

WITH an elite cortege of thirty thousand troops from all Israel and with his army from Judah, David went to Baaljudah to bring home the Ark of the Lord: Yahweh's throne between two cherubim.

It so happened that as as the Ark came into the City of David, Michal, Saul's daughter, was watching from a window and when she saw David the king prancing and strumming, she despised him in her heart.

They carried the Lord's Ark and set it up inside the tent that David had erected for it. Then David sacrificed burnt offerings to the Lord and when he had finished these holocausts and peace offerings, he blessed the people in the name of Yahweh and distrubuted among the entire concourse of Israelites, both men and women, a roll of bread each, a date cake, and a cake of raisins. After which everybody went home.

When David got back to his own house ready to greet his household, Michal, Saul's daughter, came out to meet him. "What a fine spectacle the King of Israel made of himself today!" she exclaimed, "exposing himself in front of all the little servant girls, as naked as any common dancer!"

"I danced for Yahweh," David retorted. "And I thank Yahweh for choosing me rather than your father or anyone else from his family to be king over the Lord's people of Israel. I'll gambol in front of the Lord and play the fool more than this and make myself cheap in his eyes. And as for the little servant girls, let them be impressed."

As a consequence, Michal daughter of Saul was childless till the day of her death.

NOTES

1. Michal had been torn from her husband and returned to David.
2. The cedar is not what is called a cedar in America, which is really a cypress. The cedar is a tall conifer of enormous girth, with hard, dark, sweet-smelling wood. It came mainly from the hills of Lebanon. Even in David's day the cedar forests had been seriously depleted.

David's Sin With Bathsheba

David had many wives and concubines in the manner of the times, when the number and quality of a king's harem reflected his power and prestige. Moreover, throughout the Old Testament, heterosexual prowess was given a very full rein. While king at Hebron he had fathered six sons by his six wives and concubines. Now at Jerusalem he has taken further consorts and spawned another eleven children—sons and daughters. In the following story, therefore, it is not so much that the physical coupling of a lustful, middle-aged man with a beautiful young woman is held up as wrong, even if illicit; nor even that he took something that belonged to another (though that is not excluded); no, what Nathan the prophet makes clear to the king is that the heinousness of his sin consists in the fact that a rich and powerful man takes something from a poor and powerless one. It is the abuse of power in high places, where justice is supposed to be protected, which constitutes the essence of David's sin. That, and of course the murder of the woman's husband.

From the context it seems that David rose from sleep on his roof after a late siesta—which might be between five and six—a time when the afternoon sun even in the spring could be uncomfortably hot. Bathsheba too was probably rising from her siesta: a likely time to take a bath and prepare herself for the evening.

There is a pathetic irony about Uriah's probity and devotion to duty. His name means "the Lord is Light," and he was obviously an upstanding and brave young officer whose very staunchness proved his downfall. When David discovers that he himself has made Bathsheba pregnant, he tries twice to solve the problem by getting Uriah to go home and make love to his wife so that the baby can be passed off as his. The second time he even gets Uriah drunk, but the upright young man refuses on both occasions to go home and make love to his wife because he is a soldier on campaign duty and by Levitic injunction soldiers on campaign were supposed not to sleep with their wives: a taboo which it is doubtful that David took very seriously himself. Uriah might still have saved himself if he had been less honest and allowed himself to pry into the letter he carried to Joab containing his own death warrant.

(2 Samuel 11:1-27 & 12:1-25)

IT was that time of the year once more when monarchs march out on campaign, and David dispatched Joab with his retinue and the Israelite army to attack the Ammonites and besiege their city of Rabbah, while he himself remained in Jerusalem.

One late afternoon David rose from his couch and was strolling on the palace roof when his eyes fell on a woman—a singularly beautiful woman—bathing. He made inquiries as to who she was and was told that she was Bathsheba, daughter of Eliam and wife of Uriah the Hittite. So David sent his go-betweens to get her and she came and he slept with her. The timing was just after her menstrual period and she returned home pregnant. So she sent a message to David, saying: "I am pregnant."

David got in touch with Joab. "Send me Uriah the Hittite," he said. So Joab sent Uriah to him, and when Uriah came, David asked him if all was well with Joab and if the troops were well and the war going well.

"Everything is fine," Uriah replied.

Then David told him, "Go on back home and enjoy your wife." And when Uriah left the king's presence David sent him a present of delicacies from the royal table, but Uriah never went home; he spent the night in the king's household.

When David was told that Uriah had not gone home, he sent for him and said, "Haven't you just come back from the front? How could you possibly not go home?"

"Sir, the Ark and all Israel and Judah are out under tents," Uriah answered. "Joab my commander and the rest of your majesty's servants are encamped on the battlefield. How can I possibly go to my own house and eat and drink and sleep with my wife? No, sir, not by your life and health! I won't do such a thing."

"Very well, stay here for today," David said to him, "and tomorrow I'll send you on your way."

So Uriah stayed in Jerusalem that day, and David invited him on the next to dine again. And he made him drunk. Uriah, however, went and slept on a couch that night in the royal household and never went home.

So next morning David wrote a letter to Joab and sent it to him by Uriah's hand. This is what he wrote in the letter: "Place Uriah in the thick of the fighting, then desert him. I want him cut down dead."

Joab accordingly stationed Uriah in the hottest spot of the besieging party, and when the besieged made a bold sortie out of the city against Joab's forces, several of David's men fell and among those who lost their lives was Uriah.

Joab sent an account of the action to David, instructing the courier: "When you have concluded your report of the battle to the king, if his anger flares up, add this: 'Your officer Uriah the Hittite was killed too.' "

When Joab's courier came before the king in Jerusalem he reported everything to David as Joab had instructed him. "They overwhelmed us," he said to David. "They made a sortie out into the open. We charged them and drove them back to the city gate, but a shower of arrows hit us from the battlements and some eighteen of your majesty's soldiers lost their lives."

At this conclusion of the courier's report of the battle, David's anger flared up against Joab. "Why ever did he attack so close to the city? Didn't he know that he'd be shot at from the battlements? How else was Abimelech son of Jerubaal killed? Didn't a woman fling down a millstone on him from the walls when he was killed at Thebez? Why ever did he go so close to the battlements?"

"In addition, sir," the courier said to the king, "your officer Uriah the Hittite is dead."

"Oh!" said David to the courier. "In that case tell Joab this: 'Don't be disheartened by the setback. The sword devours sometimes one, sometimes another. Put fire into your soldiers and raze the city.' That'll encourage him."

When Uriah's wife heard that her husband was dead she mourned for her lord, but as soon as the time of mourning was over, David sent for her and had her brought into the palace. She became his wife and bore him a son.

But Yahweh was not well pleased with what David had done. He sent Nathan the prophet to him. Nathan came and put the following case to David: "There were two men in a certain city, one rich and one poor. The rich man possessed a great many sheep and cattle, but the poor man had nothing at all except one little ewe lamb which he brought up and reared in his home with his own children. It ate from his plate, drank from his cup, slept in his arms like a baby daughter.

"One day a guest visited the rich man and instead of taking one of his own sheep or cattle to make a banquet for the guest, he seized the poor man's ewe lamb and butchered it for the visitor."

This sent David seething against the rich man. "By the living God," he declared to Nathan, "the man who did this is a devil in hell. He must be made to pay sevenfold for the ewe lamb and for his pitiless conduct."

"You are the man," Nathan said to David. "Yahweh tells you this: '*I* anointed you king of Israel. *I* saved you from the clutches of Saul. *I* gave you your master's daughter and his wives to your embrace. *I* bestowed on you the kingdoms of Israel and Judah. And if all this were not enough, I would double it. How could you treat Yahweh with such contempt? How could you do something so abhorrent to him? Uriah the Hittite you slashed down by the sword to make his wife your own . . . yes, while you were having him murdered by an Ammonite's sword. Very well, a sword shall cleave to your house. You held me in contempt when you usurped the wife of Uriah the Hittite for your own. So now I am going to raise trouble for you out of your own house. I'll take your wives and give them, right before your eyes, to somebody else, who will have intercourse with them in broad daylight. *You* may have acted in secret, but I am going to act in the full blaze of the sun.' "

"I have sinned against the Lord," David confessed to Nathan.

"Yes," replied Nathan, "but the Lord has commuted your sin. You are not going to die. Instead, since you made so little of Yahweh by this breach, the son born to you will die."

Nathan returned home and Yahweh struck the child which Uriah's wife had borne to David and it sickened. David pleaded with Yahweh for the boy. He fasted. He kept to himself. He lay on the floor. The senior members of his staff came to him and tried to get him up from the floor, but he would not; nor would he touch a morsel of food with them.

On the seventh day the child died, but his servants were too afraid to tell him that the child was dead. "He wouldn't hear us when the child was still alive," they said to themselves. "How can we tell him the child is dead? He'll do something reckless."

David, however, saw his servants whispering together and he knew that the child had died.

"Is the boy dead?" he asked them.

"Yes, he's dead," they replied.

At which David got up from the floor, took a bath, anointed himself, changed, and betook himself to the Lord's chapel to pray. Returning to the palace, he called for food and ate.

"How is it," his attendants asked him, "that while the child was alive you fasted and cried and went sleepless, and now that the child is dead you get up and eat?"

"So long as the child was alive," he answered, "I fasted and poured out tears for him because I thought: 'Who knows? perhaps Yahweh will take pity on me and let the boy live.' But now the boy is dead, what is the point of fasting? Would that bring him back? I'd only go and join him, he wouldn't rejoin me!"

David comforted Bathsheba his wife. He went into her and slept with her and she conceived and bore a son. She called him Solomon ["the Replacement"]. Yahweh loved him and sent a message through Nathan the prophet to say that his name was to be Jedidiah ["Beloved of Yahweh"].

NOTES

1. Verse 4 of chapter II sets a problem: Bathsheba's intercourse with David. I have translated it: "the timing was just after her menstrual period." The Hebrew text has (literally): "and she was purifying herself." The Greek gives it as: "she was purifying herself from her uncleanness"; and the Latin of St. Jerome: "immediately she was purified from her uncleanness." There seems to be no doubt that all these phrases mean the same thing: that she had recently menstruated and that the seven days of ritual impurity prescribed by Levitic law were just past. But if she had just menstruated, how could she have become pregnant when normally ovulation takes place twelve to sixteen days *before* menstruation? I have no answer. The Anchor Bible cites a reference to pre-Islamic tribesmen who believed that the optimum time for a woman to conceive was just after "she is cleansed from her impurity." Is it possible that celibate priests putting this whole account together were confused about womanly processes?

2. When David tells Uriah: "Go on back home and enjoy your wife," the biblical phrase is "wash your feet:" i.e., relax, and in this context (given the recurrent equation of the feet with genitals) a euphemism for intercourse.

The Rape of Tamar

One of the drawbacks of polygamy, especially for a dynasty, is that it produces a plethora of sons who are only halfbrothers, generally ambitious and apt to being pushed toward the throne by jealous mothers. In the following story, Absalom is an illustration of the kind of thing that can happen.

Absalom was the son of David by the princess daughter of Talmai, king of a small domain in northern Israel. He was stunningly handsome—"flawless from the soles of his feet to the crown of his head" (2 Samuel 14:25)—and proud of his long hair, which weighed two and a half pounds when he shaved it off once a year. Beautiful though this young man was and doted on by his father, he was also single-minded, jealous of his older halfbrother Amnon, vindictive, and ruthless. As with all his sons, David seems to have been morally incapable of disciplining him.

The king now, with Joab, his general, has just returned to Jerusalem after taking the Ammonite city of Rabbah, carrying off a vast amount of loot including the king of Rabbah's crown, which "weighed a talent of solid gold, set with precious stones" (2 Samuel 12:30), and which he puts on his own head.

(2 Samuel 13:1-38)

SOME time afterward, David's son Amnon fell in love with Tamar, the full sister of David's son Absalom. She was exceedingly beautiful. Amnon was so tormented by his passion for his halfsister Tamar that it made him sick, for she was a virgin and there seemed nothing he could do about it. Then his friend Jonadab, son of David's brother Shimeah and a crafty one, said: "Look at you, Amnon, son of a king and wasting away morning after morning. What's the reason for it? Tell me."

"It's Tamar," Amnon confided, "sister of my brother Absalom. I'm in love with her."

"I'll tell you what," said Jonadab: "stretch out on your bed and play sick. When your father comes to visit you say to him, 'Please may my sister come and take care of me. I'd like to watch her cook something for me right in front of my eyes and I'll eat out of her hands.' "

So Amnon stretched out and played sick, and when the king came to see him he said, "Please may my sister come and cook a couple of nourishing dumplings right in front of my eyes, and I'll eat out of her hands."

Whereupon David sent word to Tamar at home: "Go to your brother Amnon's house and fix him something to eat." So Tamar went to her brother Amnon's house and there where he was lying down she kneaded some dough into dumplings in front of him, then boiled them. But when she brought the pan to serve him he refused to eat.

"I want everyone out of here," he ordered, and when everybody had left he said to Tamar, "Bring the food over here into the bedroom. I'd like you to feed me yourself."

So Tamar carried the dumplings she had made into her brother's bedroom, but as she offered him a morsel he grabbed her.

"Darling sister," he panted, "come to bed with me!"

"Oh Amnon," she cried, "don't force me! Such a thing is not done in Israel. Don't be so silly. I'd be in disgrace, and you'd be the greatest fool in Israel. Speak to the king and he'll let you marry me."

Amnon would not listen to her. He overpowered her and forced intercourse. Then a feeling of repulsion swept over him and he began to hate her even more than he had loved her.

"Get up!" he shouted. "Get out of here!"

"Don't do this to me, my brother," she pleaded. "To send me away now is even worse than what you've just done."

He was adamant. He called his servant and commanded, "Put this woman out and bolt the door behind her."

So the servant hustled her out and bolted the door behind her. She was wearing the long-sleeved costume that daughters of the king who were virgins wore. This she began to tear at her rich clothes and sprinkle dirt on her head, holding up her hands to her face and crying as she went.

Her brother Absalom said to her, "So brother Amnon has raped you, has he? There! there! Sister, don't take it so badly. At least he is your brother."

From then onward Tamar lived like a woman in mourning in the house of Absalom her brother.

* * *

Two years went by and Absalom was having a sheep shearing at Baalhazor in Ephraim, to which he invited all the king's sons. He came to the king and said, "I your servant am having a sheep-shearing party, do come with your court."

"No, my boy," the king replied, "we'd be far too many for you if we all came."

Absalom begged him, but he would not go. Then when the king was bidding him farewell, Absalom said, "At least let my brother Amnon come."

"Why do you want *him*?" asked the king.

After much pressing from Absalom he allowed Amnon and all the other royal sons to go with him.

Absalom had prepared a banquet fit for a king. He had also given his servants these instructions: "Watch for when Amnon gets drunk and I give the signal. Strike him down and kill him. Don't be afraid. This is an order. So be prompt and thorough."

Absalom's servants did to Amnon exactly as Absalom had instructed them. All the king's sons leapt up, jumped on to their mules, and fled. But while they were still on their way, a report reached David that Absalom had killed all the king's sons, every single one of them.

The king reared up, tore his clothes, and threw himself on the floor. Those standing around, his attendants, tore their clothes too. Then Jonadab, son of David's brother Shimeah, said: "My lord king, you must not imagine that all your sons have been killed; only Amnon is dead: killed because of Absalom's rage ever since Amnon raped his sister Tamar. So my lord the king need not take to heart the report that all the king's sons are dead. Only Amnon is dead."

Absalom meanwhile had fled. Then a young sentry on the watch scanning the horizon saw a crowd of people hurrying down the hillside on the Horonaim road and he hastened to the king. "Sir, I've seen them, the men," he reported, "coming this way on the mountain road."

"You see," Jonadab remarked to the king, "the king's sons are all back, just as I your servant told you."

Hardly had he finished speaking when the king's sons appeared, sobbing and moaning. At which the king and all his attendants broke down with them.

David continued to mourn for his son day after day. And Absalom took refuge with [his grandfather] King Talmai of Geshur (the son of Ammihud).

The Revolt of Absalom

For three years after the rape of Tamar, Absalom stayed in exile at the court of his grandfather Talmai, king of Geshur, because David refused to have him back. Finally, through the machinations of Joab, the king allowed him to return to Jerusalem but refused to see him.

Another two years pass before Absalom is accepted into the royal presence. Father and son kiss and reconcile, but Absalom (no doubt noticing how David has aged and also feeling himself insecure) lays down the groundwork for taking over the throne of Israel. Not only does he begin to assume the trappings of kingship, with a fine chariot and horses and an escort of fifty outrunners, but he mixes affably with the people and, with his good looks and popularity, cleverly makes them impatient for his accession to the throne. Indeed, he "stole the hearts of the men of Israel" (2 Samuel 15:6) and goes so far as to have himself declared king at Hebron.

David, no longer safe in his own capital, gathers his staff and the elite core of his troops and prepares to depart from Jerusalem, leaving behind ten of his concubines to look after the palace.

(2 Samuel 15:23-37 & 16:1-23)

THE countryside was loud with lament as all David's troops passed before the king and crossed the Wadi Kidron on the road through the Mount of Olives toward the desert. And then the king himself passed over. There too were the priests Zadok and Abiathar, with the Levites carrying the Lord's Ark of the Covenant. They rested the Ark while the entire army passed out of the city.

Then the king said to Zadok, "Take God's Ark back to Jerusalem. If Yahweh is not displeased with me, he will bring me home again and let me see the Ark once more in its tabernacle. But if he says to me, 'I am not pleased with you,' very well, here I am, let him do with me whatsoever he wills."

He turned to Zadok the priest and said, "Now you and Abiathar go back quietly to the city with your son Ahimaaz and Abiathar's son Jonathan while I wait in the prairies of the desert for news of you."

Zadok and Abiathar accordingly carried the Ark back to Jerusalem and deposited it there while David climbed the ascent of Mount of Olives, sobbing as he went. He walked barefoot and bareheaded. And so did the whole company as they made the ascent; they sobbed too.

David was told that Ahithophel [his most trusted adviser] had defected to Absalom and he remarked, "I hope Yahweh will make Ahithophel give him bad advice!"

When David was nearing the top of the mountain where God's shrine is, who should come to meet him but Hushai (David's staunch friend from the town of Archi). His clothes were torn, and there was earth on his head.

"If you come along with me," David said to him, "you'll only be a burden, but if you return to Jerusalem you can pretend to Absalom: 'Look, King, I am at your disposal just as I was at your father's,' and so you can undermine Ahithophel's advice. The two priests Zadok and Abiathar will be with you there, and you can pass on to them whatever you hear at the palace. Their two sons are with them too: Zadok's son Ahimaaz and Abiather's son Jonathan. Through them you can relay to me anything you hear."

So Hushai, a true friend to David, returned to the city just as Absalom was entering Jerusalem.

Hardly had David crossed the top of the hill when he ran into Zeba, the servant of Mephisboseth [Jonathan's son and grandson of Saul], coming to meet him with two asses laden with two hundred loaves of bread, a hundred bunches of raisins, a hundred baskets of summer fruits, and a skinful of wine.

"What are these for?" the king asked Zeba.

"The asses, sire, are mounts for the royal household," Zeba replied. "The bread and summer fruits are for your young soldiers to eat, and the wine is a draft for anyone who feels faint in the desert."

"But where is Mephisboseth, your master's son?" the king asked.

"He stayed behind in Jerusalem, sire," Zeba answered. "He said, 'Now Israel will restore to me my grandfather's kingdom.' "

"In that case," the king told Zeba, "everything belonging to Mephisboseth is now yours."

"Oh, I hope I can please your majesty!" burst out Zeba, abasing himself.

When King David got as far as Bahurim, a man by the name of Shimei (son of Hera and a relative of Saul's) suddenly appeared, cursing as he came and throwing stones at David and his retinue—even at the army and the various war heroes. As he cursed he shouted, "Get out of here! Get out of here! you blood-spattered murderer! you devil in hell! The Lord is paying you back for all the blood you spilt of the house of Saul. You stole his kingdom and now the Lord has handed it over to Absalom your son. Calamity is closing in on you because you are a blood-spattered man."

Whereupon, Abishai son of Zeruiah exclaimed to the king, "Why let this dead dog curse my lord the king? I'll go and lop his head off."

"What does it matter, you son of Zeruiah?" the king retorted. "Leave him alone and let him curse. It's because Yahweh has told him, 'Curse David,' so who is going to stop him? Why, my own son, the fruit of my loins," continued the king, turning to Abishai and his attendants, "is trying to kill me, so how much more should this Benjaminite be free to curse! Who knows, Yahweh may take pity on my troubles and out of these curses bring me blessings today."

So David and his men walked along the road, with Shimei cursing him on the opposite slope, throwing stones and flinging earth. The king and his entourage arrived at the banks of the Jordan exhausted, and there they refreshed themselves.

Meanwhile, Absalom and all his retinue entered Jerusalem accompanied by Ahithophel. Then David's friend Hushai (the man from Archi) arrived, exclaiming, "Long live the king!" as he came into Absalom's presence.

"Is this how you show loyalty to your friend?" Absalom asked him. "Why didn't you go with David?"

"Because, sire," replied Hushai, "I serve him whom Yahweh and the people and all Israel have chosen. His I am and with him I'll stay. Besides, whom should I serve if not David's son? As I have served your father, so shall I now serve you."

Absalom then asked Ahithophel's advice: "What shall I do next?"

"Go and sleep with your father's concubines—the ones he has left behind to keep the palace—" was Ahithophel's reply. "That will show all Israel how you have disgraced your father. It will also encourage your supporters."

So a tent was put up for Absalom on the palace roof and, before the gaze of all Israel, Absalom went in to sleep with his father's concubines.

(In those days Ahithophel's counsel was followed as if it were the word of God, both by David and now by Absalom.)

The Death of Absalom

Instead of taking the good advice of the wary old retainer Ahithophel and attacking David in the wilderness before he has time to gain strength, Absalom falls into the trap laid by the double agent Hushai and listens to his specious argument that it would be better to wait till he has built up overwhelming forces. This Absalom proceeds to do (while the discountenanced Ahithophel goes off and hangs himself), but when he finally moves against his father in the wooded country of Ephraim across the Jordan, David has behind him a well-rested and reorganized army. His commanders will not let the king himself fight, but he reviews the troops as they pass out of the city gates at Mahanaim.

(2 Samuel 18:5-33 & 19:1-8)

THE king enjoined [his commanders] Joab, Abishai, and Ittai: "For my sake, take good care of young Absalom." All the troops heard him give this instruction to his generals.

Then the army took the field against Israel and the battle was fought in the forest of Ephraim. The forces of Israel were routed by David's troops and the slaughter that day was tremendous—no less than twenty thousand fell. The fighting blazed over the whole countryside, and more were lost in the forest than were killed by the sword.

Absalom, running into David's men, galloped away on his mule, but the mule plunged under an enormous, branchy oak tree and Absalom's hair was caught in the branches and he was left dangling between earth and sky as the mule fled onward.

A soldier who saw this reported it to Joab: "I have just seen Absalom hanging from a tree," he said.

"What! you saw him," returned Joab, "and you didn't cut him down? I would have rewarded you with ten pieces of silver and an officer's belt."

"Sir," said the man to Joab, "not for a thousand pieces of silver would I lay a finger on the king's son. In our very hearing the king charged you and Abishai and Ittai to 'take good care of young Absalom.' To do otherwise is as much as my life's worth, for it wouldn't be kept from the king and you wouldn't stand by me."

"Well, I'm not going to argue with you," retorted Joab,

and seizing three lances he plunged them into Absalom's heart as he panted for life, dangling still from the tree. Ten young soldiers then ran up (armor bearers of Joab) and finished him off.

Then Joab with a bugle call checked the army from pursuing Israel and turned it back. They took down Absalom and threw him into a deep pit in the forest, piling it high with a cairn of stones. Absalom during his lifetime had erected a monument to himself in the Valley of the King, saying, "I have no son by whom I may be remembered," and he named the monument after himself. To this day it is called the "Monument of Absalom."

Then Ahimaaz son of Zadok said, "Let me run to the king with the news that Yahweh has freed him from the power of his enemies."

"No," said Joab, "not today. It would not be good news to the king that his son is dead. You can take the news another day."

Joab, however, told a man from Cush, "Go and tell the king what you have seen."

The Cushite bowed and went off. At which Ahimaaz son of Zadok again said to Joab, "Whatever the news, why can't I go too and run after the Cushite?"

"Why do you want to run off, my son?" asked Joab. "It won't be good news."

"Whatever the news," pleaded Ahimaaz, "let me run off too."

"All right, then, run!" said Joab.

Ahimaaz, sprinting through a shortcut, passed the Cushite.

David was sitting between the city gates when the watchman posted on the walls looked out and saw a sole man running their way, and he shouted the news down to the king.

"If he is by himself, he brings tidings," the king said.

As the runner drew nearer, the watchman caught sight of another man running. "Here comes another lone runner," he called down to the king.

"Then he brings news too," the king replied.

"The first runner now looks to me like Ahimaaz son of Zadok," announced the watchman.

"A good man!" commented the king. "And his news will be good."

Ahimaaz arrived and threw himself before the king. "Praised be the Lord your God," he exclaimed, "who has destroyed those who wanted to raise a hand against your majesty!"

"And young Absalom? Is he all right?" returned the king.

Ahimaaz hedged: "Well, there was a lot going on when Joab sent me, your servant, off. I don't exactly know what happened."

"All right, stand at ease over there," the king told him.

Hardly had he taken up his position when the Cushite appeared.

"Good news for my lord the king!" he announced. "Yahweh today has freed you from the hands of your rebels."

"But is young Absalom safe?" the king asked.

"May all your majesty's enemies and every rebel meet the fate of that young man!" the Cushite blurted.

The king began to shake. He went up into the room above the gatehouse, sobbing as he went: "Absalom, my son! Oh, my son, my son Absalom! Why couldn't I have died instead of you? Oh, Absalom my son! my son Absalom!"

When Joab heard how the king was weeping and lamenting for his son, the triumph of the day turned into a day of grief for the whole army. The news soon spread that the king was brokenhearted for his son. The troops slunk into the city that day like an army in disgrace which had fled the field. The king hid his face, continuously wailing, "Oh my son Absalom! Absalom my son!"

Whereupon Joab entered the king's quarters and said to him, "Today you have embarrassed all your subjects who this day have saved your life, as well as the lives of your sons and daughters, and the lives of your wives and concubines. You seem to love those that hate you and hate those that love you. In fact, you have made it quite clear today that your ministers and subjects mean nothing to you, because if Absalom were alive right now you'd be happy and we'd all be dead. So get up and go out there and congratulate your troops, because I swear by Yahweh that if you don't, not a single man of them will still be with you by morning. You'll be in a plight worse than anything that has ever happened to you since childhood."

So the king bestirred himself and presided at the city gates, and once the army heard that the king was enthroned there, they gathered before him.

NOTE

The mule—offspring of a mare and a jackass—was a royal animal: partly because the breeding of hybrids was forbidden by Mosaic law and mules therefore had to be imported, and partly because of the mule's superior strength and endurance.

The Wisdom of Solomon

David never slept again with the ten concubines whom Absalom had publicly seduced. Indeed, as an old man toward the end of a reign of more than forty years, he never slept with anyone—though a beautiful young woman called Abishag was hired to lie in bed with him and keep him warm.

Meanwhile Bathsheba has seen to it that her son Solomon is to succeed his father, who does not live very much longer after handing over the kingdom. David is buried with pomp in the heart of Jerusalem on Mount Zion; and now the new king—a young man hardly twenty years old—settles down to a reign which is to succeed years of strife and war with years of peace and glory.

But first there has to be a bloodbath. Using the soldier Benaiah as his hatchet man, he eliminates his half brother Adonijah on the pretext that he was seditiously plotting a marriage with Abishag, the beautiful young Shunammite who looked after David. Next, the priest Abiathar is defrocked from the high priesthood and banished. The loyal Zadok becomes high priest. Then the warmongering general, Joab, is punished for his many murders and dispatched by Benaiah's sword as he clings to the horns of the altar. Finally, Shimei the ranter, having overstepped the limits imposed on him by Solomon, falls to the same sword.

Secure on his throne, Solomon now adds to his prestige by marrying a daughter of Pharaoh, the king of Egypt, and he will build her a palace.

(1 Kings 3:3-28)

SOLOMON loved the Lord and walked in the precepts of his father, except that he still sacrificed and burned incense on hilltop altars [a practice Yahweh frowned on as being a pagan custom].

One of the most important hilltop shrines was at Gibeon, and there Solomon went to offer a sacrifice of a thousand burnt offerings. That night the Lord appeared to Solomon in a dream and said, "What of all things would you most like me to give you?"

Solomon replied, "Lord, you have been wonderfully kind

to your servant David my father. He walked with you in truth and justice and an upright heart. You treated him with utmost generosity and gave him a son to sit on his throne. But my Lord God, now that you have made me king to succeed my father, I am a mere child and don't know whether I am coming or going. Besides, I your lowly servant am the center of your chosen people: that multitudinous nation uncountable in its numbers. So give me, please, an understanding heart, able to be just and to discern between good and evil. Because otherwise, how could anybody face the task of doing rightly by this people, your own teeming people?"

The Lord was pleased that Solomon had asked for such a thing and he said, "Because you have asked for this and not for a long life and riches, and because you have asked for wisdom and an understanding heart, I am going to give you exactly what you asked for: a heart so wise and understanding that none has been like it before, and none shall be like it again. What is more, I am going to give you what you didn't ask for: riches and fame beyond anything attained by any king before. Moreover, if you walk in my ways and keep my commandments as your father did, I shall grant you a long life."

Solomon woke up and saw that it was all a dream. Nevertheless, when he returned to Jerusalem he stood before the Lord's Ark of the Covenant, offering sacrifices and burnt offerings. Then he invited all his ministers to a great banquet.

Sometime afterward two prostitutes brought a case before the king. One of them pleaded, "This woman and I live in the same house and we both delivered our babies in the same bedroom, she delivering hers three days after I did. We were together and there was no one else in the house—just us two. This woman's baby died in the night, because she smothered him in her sleep. So she got up in the middle of the night and took my baby from my side as I slept and put it to her bosom, slipping her dead baby into mine. In the morning when I woke up to nurse my baby, it was dead. But when I looked more closely at him in the light of day, I saw that it was not the baby I had given birth to."

"Oh no!" cried out the other woman. "Your baby is the dead one and mine the living."

"Liar!" shouted the first. "The truth is quite the reverse: my baby is is alive and yours is dead."

"Not at all," screamed the latter. 'My baby lives and yours is dead." And they went on wrangling in front of the king.

"So," said the king, "one of you asserts, 'My son is the live baby and yours the dead one,' while the other says 'No, your son is the dead baby and mine the live one.' Very well, bring me a sword."

When they had brought the king a sword, he ordered, "Split the baby in two and give a half to each mother."

At which the woman whose baby really was the live one cried out in anguish, "Oh no, my lord, give her the live child and don't kill him!" while the other merely said, "All right, let it be neither yours nor mine, we'll split him."

Whereupon the king said, "Give the live baby to the woman who wants him to live, for she is his mother."

Word of the king's judgment spread through Israel and everyone was in awe of the king, seeing how the radiance of God's wisdom was in him to do justice.

Solomon in All His Glory

Solomon was Bathsheba's second son by David and ruled over a united Israel and Judah for forty years: from 973 to 933 B.C. In every way his reign represented the high-water mark of early Israelite history. Politically secure, he was able to encourage within his empire vigorous trade routes that linked Africa and Arabia with all Asia Minor. His fleet patrolled the seas from the Gulf of Aqaba in the Red Sea to the shores of distant Ophir. His harem, according to the Bible, comprised seven hundred wives: women from all over the Near East. His wisdom and the manner of his life made him the wonder of the world, and yet the writers of the Old Testament were undecided about him. They viewed with suspicion the international thrust of his foreign policy, and they were not ready for his tolerance of a pluralist society in which non-Jewish religions and practices were allowed to flourish.

(1 Kings 4:7, 20-34)

SOLOMON appointed twelve officials to supervise in turn, one month each, the raising of revenues throughout Israel: revenues for the king's household.

Under Solomon, Judah and Israel were as populous as the sands of the seashore. There was abundant food and drink and an air of celebration. Solomon held sway over all the kingdoms from the river Euphrates to the coastlands of the Philistines—right to the borders of Egypt. From these kingdoms he received tribute and revenues throughout his lifetime.

The daily provision for Solomon's palace was a hundred and ninety-five bushels of fine flour, three hundred and ninety bushels of meal, ten oxen specially fattened, twenty oxen pasture-fed, and one hundred rams—not to mention stags, gazelles, roebucks, and plump fowl. His dominion ranged over all the kingdoms west of the Euphrates, from Tiphsah to Gaza; and there was peace on all sides. Indeed, throughout the reign of Solomon, from Dan to Beersheba, Judah and Israel lived without fear: every man under his own vine, under his own fig tree.

In Solomon's stables were forty thousand horses, and he employed twelve thousand charioteers. The king's officials mentioned above not only made sure in their turn that the revenues covered the upkeep of all this, but the king's table as well; and this included providing barley and straw for the royal horses and camels wherever they and the king might be.

God endowed Solomon with singular wisdom and understanding, and a breadth of spirit as wide as the sands of the sea. Indeed, his wisdom dwarfed that of all the easterners, including that of the Egyptians. He was the wisest man alive: wiser than Eathan the Ezrahite, and Heman, Calcol, and Darda—the sons of Mahol. His renown was spread through the surrounding nations. He was the author of three thousand proverbs; his poems numbered one thousand and five. He could discourse on trees, from the great cedar of Lebanon to the little hyssop that springs from the wall. He could speak about mammals and birds, reptiles and fishes. People came from everywhere to hear Solomon; even kings came, drawn by tales of his learning.

NOTES

1. The conversion of weights and measurements (and also money) from biblical times into contemporary amounts can only be an approximation. I have usually been guided by the figures given in The Living Bible.

2. It is not certain who Eathan the Ezrahite was. As to Heman, there were three: a grandson of Jacob and Zerah, a grandson of Samuel, and of this one, who with his brothers Calcol and Darda was a son of Mahol, nothing seems to be known.

The Building of the Temple (969-962 B.C.)

Whatever the achievements of Solomon, it is obvious that in the eyes of the biblical writers his greatest achievement was the building of the Temple. That which David had planned and dreamed of, Solomon in a reign of unprecedented peace and prosperity accomplished. But the obstacles to his great and ambitious scheme were daunting. At the best of times the Israelites were far from being a culturally sophisticated people, and now after years of almost incessant war, there can hardly have been the knowledge, the materials, and the craftsmen necessary for so mighty an undertaking. Solomon had recourse to one he made his friend: Hiram, the new king of Tyre, who had just ascended the throne in 969 B.C. Tyre, the richest and most important of the Phoenician cities on the Palestinian coast, enjoyed all those assets that the Israelites lacked: skilled artisans, raw materials, architectural experience. So now, some four years after Solomon has become king, he sends a message to Hiram suggesting a deal in which Solomon is to pay in kind (wheat and oil) for timber and skilled labor. The Temple is to be built on Mount Moriah, east of Mount Zion (the two hills of Jerusalem).

(1 Kings 5:7-18, 6:7-29, 37-38, 7:13-22, 48-51)

HIRAM was well pleased with Solomon's message. "Praised be Yahweh this day," he uttered, "for giving David so percipient a son to rule over that populous nation!" Hiram then sent the following reply to Solomon: "I have noted your requirements for cedar and pine beams, and I shall do as you ask. My workmen will bring the logs down from Lebanon to the sea, where I shall float them by raft and land them wherever you tell me. In return, you can furnish me with provender for my household."

Accordingly, Hiram provided Solomon with all the cedar and pine he wanted, and Solomon made him an annual payment of a hundred and twenty-five thousand bushels of wheat for his household and ninety-six gallons of virgin olive oil.

This is an example of the intelligence which the Lord promised Solomon: this peaceable and profitable pact between Hiram and Solomon.

King Solomon levied a work force from all over Israel: a levy of thirty thousand men. He sent them out in rotation, ten thousand at a time, so that for every month in Lebanon, they spent two months at home. The supervisor of all this drafted labor was Adoniram. Besides these men, Solomon recruited seventy thousand carriers and eight thousand stonecutters for the mountain quarries, and three thousand, three hundred foremen.

For the foundations of the Temple the king ordered the stonecutters to quarry and dress huge (and costly) blocks. Both Solomon's and Hiram's masons quarried the stone, while the shaping of the stones and timber for the building was undertaken by artisans from Gebal. The actual construction was done with ready-dressed stone so that all during the building of the Temple there was not a sound of hammer and ax or the clink of tools.

While Solomon was building the Temple, the Lord sent him the following message: "If you will walk in my ways and keep to all my wishes and injunctions, I shall honor the pledge I made to David your father, to live among the people of Israel and never desert them."

At last Solomon finished building the Temple. The inside walls were paneled with cedar and the floors laid in planks of pine. The inner thirty-foot chamber at the rear of the sanctuary—the Holy of Holies—was also paneled with cedar from floor to ceiling. The Temple itself, excluding the Holy of Holies, was sixty feet long, and the cedar paneling that covered every part of the walls was intricately carved with designs of fruit and open-petaled flowers. The inner sanctuary, which housed the Lord's Ark of the Covenant, was thirty feet long, thirty feet wide, and thirty high: its entire surface was covered in pure gold. The altar was of cedar wood encased in gold.

The rest of the Temple interior was overlaid with gold, the plates being fastened with nails of gold. Indeed there was nothing in the whole Temple, including the cedar altar, that was not overlaid with gold.

Flanking the inner sanctuary, Solomon set up two cherubim carved in olive wood, each fifteen feet high. The tips of their outspread wings, each seven and a half feet long, reached from wall to wall, the shoulders of the wings meeting in the middle. These cherubim were encased in gold.

Solomon also had all the walls of the Temple embossed with elaborate carvings of figures and angels, palm trees, and flowers in full bloom. The floors of both the inner and outer Temple were overlaid with gold, and the walls of the inner sanctuary were of polished marble in three contrasting rows topped by a border of cedar wood.

King Solomon had a man called Hiram brought in from Tyre: a skilled craftsman in bronze, a fine artist. He was the son of a widow from the tribe of Naphtali whose father was Tyrian. Hiram took charge of Solomon's whole enterprise. He cast two bronze pillars, each twenty-seven feet high and eighteen feet around. The capitals of the pillars were also cast in bronze, each seven and a half feet high and six feet wide. A mesh of delicately linked latticework covered each capital in a sevenfold repeated design of four hundred pomegranates in double rows topped by flowering lilies.

These two pillars Hiram set up in the porch of the Temple and he gave them names. The one on the righthand side was called Jachin ["Firm One"] and the one on the left, Boaz ["Stolid"].

All the vessels used in the House of the Lord were fashioned by Solomon out of solid gold. This included the encased altar and the table on which were set the consecrated loaves, as well as the candelabra which flanked the sanctuary: five on the right and five on the left, all of gold. Then there were the golden lilies, the gold lamps over them, and the golden snuffers. Everything—bowls, flesh hooks, basins, spoons, censers, even the door hinges of both the inner and outer sanctuary—was of solid gold.

When Solomon had completed the entire work of the Lord's Temple, he brought together all the silver and gold vessels which David his father had set aside, and lodged them in the treasury of the Lord's House.

NOTES

1. In the time of Solomon the city of Tyre was situated on a small island and was considered impregnable until Alexander the Great late in the fourth century B.C. connected it by a causeway to the mainland. The small Island of Hercules which was an appendage of Tyre is now submerged. It was from Tyre that Phoenician colonists under Queen Elissa (Vergil's Dido) founded Carthage in 814 B.C.

2. Hiram was so famous to the biblical writers in connection with the building of the Temple that they anachronistically placed him on the throne of Tyre in David's time (2 Samuel 5:11, 1 Chronicles 14:1, 22:4).

Solomon Visited by the Queen of Sheba

Once the Temple is completed (an enterprise taking seven years), Solomon turns his attention to his own palace, which is no less magnificent. He also builds a palace for his Egyptian queen. Meanwhile, from a shipyard at Ezion-geber on the Red Sea, he assembles a navy whose crews are trained by experienced sailors lent by King Hiram of Tyre. Solomon's ships traded back and forth from (probably) Yemen in southern Arabia, bringing back the fabled gold of Ophir.

There is a tradition that the Queen of Sheba came from Ethiopia, and this is not impossible because from time to time southwestern Arabia (whence the queen stemmed) had close ties with Ethiopia. The Ethiopians even gave her a name, Balkis, maintaining that Solomon had a son by her named Manelik, who became the forebear of the emperors of Ethiopia right down to the late Emperor Haile Salassie.

(1 Kings 10:14-29 & 1-13)

THE weight of gold that was brought to Solomon each year came to six hundred and sixty-five talents [about twenty-five million dollars]. Besides which, tributes and taxes flowed in from the merchants, the kings of Arabia, and the various governors.

Solomon had two hundred suits of armor fashioned out of beaten gold (six hundred shekels of gold going into each [about ten thousand dollars' worth]), as well as three hundred shields of the same, with three pounds of solid gold to each shield. These he housed in his palace in the Hall of the Forest of Lebanon.

The king also made a great throne of ivory inlaid with pure gold. There were six steps up to the throne, which had a rounded back with an armrest on either side flanked by a standing lion on each step, making twelve lions in all. Nowhere in the world was there a throne like it.

All King Solomon's drinking goblets were of solid gold, as was his dinner service in the Hall of the Forest of Lebanon. Nothing was of silver, which in the days of Solomon was of little account.

Every three years the king's fleet, with ships from King Hiram, arrived at Tharshish loaded down with gold and silver, tusks of ivory, apes, and peacocks. Little wonder that King Solomon excelled every king on earth in riches and wisdom! The whole world wanted to come and sit at his feet and hear the wisdom that God had lodged in his heart. Year after year they brought him presents of silver and gold, garments and armor, spices, horses, and mules.

Solomon built up a stable of chariots and horses, with one thousand, four hundred chariots and twelve thousand cavalrymen who lived in special chariot cities or with the king in Jerusalem—where the king made silver as common as pebbles, and cedar wood as common as the rank sycamores of the plains.

Solomon's horses were procured for him out of Egypt and southern Turkey, where his agents bought them at wholesale prices. A four-horse chariot from Egypt would cost six hundred silver shekels [about six hundred dollars], and a horse some hundred and fifty [two hundred fifty dollars]. This was the going rate among the Hittite and Syrian monarchs.

When the Queen of Sheba heard of Solomon's fame and all Yahweh's blessings on him, she came to try him with hard questions. She arrived in Jerusalem with a caravan heavy with riches: camels loaded with spices and an immense quantity of gold and precious stones. She presented herself to Solomon and plied him with all the questions in her heart. Solomon answered her every problem. Not a thing was hid from the king; not an answer lingered.

When the Queen of Sheba perceived the wisdom of Solomon and the palace he had built himself, and his sumptuous table, and the number of his servants and ministers in all their liveries, and his own wardrobe, and his cupbearers, and the profuse sacrifices he heaped up in the Lord's House—she was beside herself.

"So it's all true," she cried out to the king, "everything I heard in my own country! Your words, your wisdom! I didn't believe what they told me till I came and saw it for myself. The fact is, I wasn't told half the truth. Your wisdom and all your works far excel the rumor of your fame. . . . Oh, you lucky wives! You lucky servants and ministers who can stand continually in his presence and enjoy the blessedness of his converse! Praised be the Lord Yahweh for his delight in him and for setting him on the throne of Israel.

How the Lord must love Israel to give her such a king to rule and judge!"

She proceeded to present Solomon with a hundred and twenty talents of gold [about five million dollars], along with precious stones and a vast store of spices. In fact, this gift of spices from the Queen of Sheba to Solomon was the largest he ever received.

In return Solomon gave the Queen of Sheba (in addition to his outpourings of royal bounty) whatsoever she fancied or asked for . . . Then she and her train returned to their own country.

NOTES

1. Where did Solomon acquire so much gold? Some came by way of tribute, some as booty, but the bulk must have been especially mined. Nobody knows from where because the various sites mentioned in the Bible have all still to be located. Southern Arabia is a possibility. (Ryder Haggard's *King Solomon's Mines* is a good read.)

2. As already noted, the location of Tharshish (or Tarshish) is only conjectural, as is Ophir.

3. In 1 Kings 10:5, I prefer the Septuagint reading of εξ'ἐδυτης ἐγευετο ("she became out of herself") to the Hebrew and to Jerome's Latin: "*non habebat ultra spiritum*" ("she had no spirit left in her,") which the Jerusalem Bible translates both literally and aptly as: "it left her breathless."

4. For the sake of logic I have transposed verses 1 Kings 10:1-13 and 1 Kings 10:14-29.

Solomon's Sin

The measure to which our concept of divine justice has evolved since these times (c. 950 B.C.) can perhaps be gauged by the reflection that what made Yahweh displeased with Solomon is precisely that which we would praise him for today. Solomon reigned over a heterogenous amalgam of mixed races and mixed religions: a pluralistic society if ever there was one. He leant over backward to ensure that all should enjoy religious liberty. Not only that, but he was at pains to show that he cared for the welfare of all his subjects, not merely of the Judeans and Israelites. The reason for his enormous harem of seven hundred wives and three hundred concubines could not have been simple lust, but a means of demonstrating that he wished to honor the races from which these women were selected. Naturally he would also wish to provide them with the means of practicing their own religions, so he built them shrines to their gods. Of course, from the biblical point of view no consideration was as important as keeping the Israelites free from idolatry.

(1 Kings 11:1-13, 41-43)

KING Solomon was a lover of women. Besides the daughter of Pharaoh, he made liaisons with a number of foreign women: girls from Moab and Ammon, from Edom and Sidon, and Hittites too. These were the people about which Yahweh clearly enjoined the Israelites: "You must not marry into them or let them marry into you, because they are sure to turn away your hearts to follow their own gods."

Nonetheless, Solomon linked himself to them with passion. He had seven hundred wives and three hundred concubines, and they did indeed turn away his heart so that in his old age his heart was no longer in tune with God the way his father David's heart had been. He flirted with Ashtoreth, the goddess of the Sidonians, and went after Moloch, the thoroughly vile god of the Ammonites. There is no doubt that this distressed Yahweh and that Solomon was not following in his father's footsteps.

He set up a shrine on the Mount of Olives for Chemosh, the perverted god of Moab, and for Moloch, the unspeakable god of the Ammonites. And he followed this pattern with all his foreign women, letting them burn their incense and offer sacrifices to their various gods.

Yahweh naturally was angry with Solomon for this turning away from the Lord God of Israel, especially since he had twice come to warn him not to go after strange gods. But Solomon took no notice. So now Yahweh said to him, "Because you have done these things and not kept our agreement or obeyed my laws, I am going to wrest the kingdom from you and give it to one of your subjects. However, for David your father's sake I won't do this in your lifetime, but I'll wrench it away from your son—though not the whole kingdom. I shall let your son retain one tribe . . . again for the sake of your father David and for Jerusalem, my chosen city."

* * *

The rest of Solomon's doings and sayings are all recorded in "The Acts of Solomon." Solomon reigned in Jerusalem over all Israel for forty years, and when he died and slept with his fathers, he was buried in the City of David his father, and his son Rehoboam reigned in his stead.

PART V

THE DIVIDED KINGDOM: ISRAEL AND JUDAH

(c. 933 TO 800 B.C.)

Stories from the books of 1 & 2 Kings

Introduction

The year 933 B.C., when Solomon died and his son Rehoboam succeeded to the throne, marked the end of the united kingdom of Israel. From then onward there were two kingdoms: Israel, comprising the north and west of Palestine, and Judah (with Jerusalem and the Temple as its focus) the south. The valuation of the various kings' reigns in the judgment of the biblical writers depended on the extent to which they encouraged worship in the Temple at Jerusalem. Under such a criterion all the northern kings naturally fall short because they had their own shrines and "high places."

Much of the next decades was spent in a smoldering rivalry between Judah and Israel, with Judah getting the worst of it, though Judah enjoyed the mixed blessing of the Davidic dynasty for three and a half centuries, whereas Israel lasted just over two with a succession of unrelated monarchs, of whom the most successful in bringing a measure of peace, prosperity, and international respect throughout Israel was Omri, its sixth king. It was he who founded a new capital for the Northern Kingdom at Samaria and who cemented a most useful alliance with the Phoenicians by marrying his son Ahab to the daughter of Ethbaal king of Sidon, Jezebel. And it was Jezebel who earned the hatred of the biblical writers by fostering the cult of Phoenician deities throughout Israel.

Meanwhile, the small principality of Damascus, some sixty miles east of the coast, blossomed into the powerful Aramean kingdom of Syria, which under its king Benhadad II and his successors was to be a thorn in the flesh of Israel for the next century and a half.

Rehoboam and Jeroboam: The First Two Kings of the Divided Monarchy

The following account describes how Solomon's kingdom broke into two: precipitated by the foolish haughtiness of his successor, Rehoboam (his son by the Ammonite princess Naamah). Rehoboam was to be the last king of a united Israelite realm. Solomon's expanded court and empire had indeed brought glory to Israel but at a price: administrative costs had leapt, there was conscription of labor and increased taxation. As to Jeroboam, who became the first king of the Northern Kingdom, he had already rebelled against Solomon and fled in exile to Egypt. Now he returns, with apparently good intentions.

(1 Kings 1:14, 16, 18-19, 25-33, 14:1-12, 17-20)

AND now Rehoboam betook himself to Shechem, where all Israel was gathered to crown him king.

Meanwhile, as soon as Jeroboam (son of Nebat), who was still in Egypt, where he had fled from the presence of King Solomon, heard of Solomon's death, he returned and led a delegation of the people to Rehoboam.

"Your father laid a heavy burden on us," they declared, "so we ask you to lighten some of the load your father put on us, then we shall be your loyal subjects."

"Come back in three days," he told them, and the people departed.

King Rehoboam now consulted the old ministers who had served his father Solomon. "What answer do you advise me to give the people?" he asked.

"If you are kind to them," they replied, "and yield a little and grant their petition, they will be your loyal subjects forever."

Rehoboam, however, rejected the advice of the old ministers and went off to consult the young men who had been his schoolmates. He asked them, "How would you advise me to reply to this people's demand that I lighten the burden which my father laid on them?"

The young men who had been brought up with him replied, "This is what you must say to these people who are grumbling about the burden your father made them bear and now want you to make it lighter. Tell them:

" 'My little finger is thicker than my father's loins. If my father's yoke was heavy, I'll make mine twice as heavy. My father whipped you with ordinary whips. I shall whip you with scorpions.' "

Accordingly, when Jeroboam and his delegation returned to Rehoboam on the third day as ordered, the king, following the advice not of the old men but of the young ones, answered them harshly: "If my father's yoke was heavy, I'll make mine twice as heavy. My father whipped you with ordinary whips. I shall whip you with scorpions."

When the people heard this high-handed answer from the king, they denounced him, and when Rehoboam sent Hadoram to collect their taxes they promptly stoned him to death. Rehoboam still reigned over the Hebrew cities of Judah, but the rest of Israel ever since has refused to be ruled by the house of David.

Jeroboam meanwhile rebuilt the city of Shechem among the hills of Ephraim and he lived there. Later he built up Penuel, thinking to himself, "If the populace go to the Lord's Temple in Jerusalem, there is danger of the kingdom's falling back to the house of David, because the people will become reattached to Rehoboam since he is the lawful king of Judah. Then they will kill me."

Consequently, Jeroboam took counsel and made two golden calves, announcing to the people: "It is too difficult for you to travel to Jerusalem to worship, so, look, Israel, here are images you can use as symbols of your delivery from the captivity of Egypt."

He set up one calf in Bethel and the other in Dan. This, however, became an occasion of sin because the people began to worship them, traveling even as far as the calf in Dan. He also made altars on the hilltops and ordained priests from the lowest orders: people not even of the house of Levi.

Jeroboam also made a festival like the annual Festival of Tabernacles at Jerusalem on the fifteenth day of the eighth month [i.e., the 1st of November], and he went to Bethel to sacrifice on the altar before the calves he had set up, and he burned incense there before them. There too he established the hill shrines which he had made.

About this time Jeroboam's son Abijah fell sick and Jeroboam said to his wife, "Will you please go and see the prophet Ahijah in Silo—the man who told me I would be king of this people. But dress in disguise so he won't know that you are Jeroboam's wife. And take him a present of ten loaves, some little cakes for his children, some grapes and a pot of honey, and ask him to tell you if the boy is going to recover."

Jeroboam's wife did as he told her. She got herself ready and set out for Silo and duly arrived at Ahijah's house. But he was an old man now: his eyes too dim to see her. The Lord, however, had said to Ahijah, "Listen, the wife of Jeroboam, pretending to be someone else, is coming to consult you about her son, who is sick. I'll tell you what to say to her."

So when Ahijah heard her footsteps approaching his front door, he called out, "Come in, wife of Jeroboam, why are you pretending to be somebody else? I am afraid I have sad news for you. This is the report that you must take back to Jeroboam from Yahweh God of Israel: 'I raised you up from the common ranks and made you king of my people Israel. I wrested the kingdom away from the house of David and gave it to you, but you have not kept my commandments like my servant David, who devoted his whole heart to doing only that which pleased me. And you, you have done more evil than all who came before you. You have set up strange gods and enraged me with your golden calves. So since you have turned your back on me, I am going to bring ruin to the house of Jeroboam. I am going to wipe out every male of Jeroboam's house, be he fettered or free, throughout the land of Israel. I am going to flush out his family like manure from a stable. And those of Jeroboam's people that die in the city are to be guzzled by dogs; and those that die in the field are to be the food of birds.'

"Yahweh has vowed this, so get up and go home. But the moment your feet enter the town, your boy will die."

So Jeroboam's wife got up and left and returned to Tirzah, but just as she walked through her door the child expired. They buried him and all Israel mourned, just as Yahweh had foretold through his prophet Ahijah.

The rest of Jeroboam's deeds, his wars and the events of his reign, are of course all recorded in "The Annals of the Kings of Israel." His reign lasted twenty-two years before he was gathered to his fathers. He was succeeded on the throne by his son Nadab.

NOTES

1. "Scorpions" was the name for scourges tipped with metal.
2. "My little finger is thicker than my father's loins" is an obviously insulting euphemism for "my father's phallus."

The Coming of Elijah

Some fifty-eight years have gone by since the death of Solomon and the breakup of a united kingdom of the Israelites. Ahab, son of Omri, now reigns over Israel as its seventh king. His queen is Jezebel, a Phoenician princess from Tyre, and their daughter Athaliah is later to marry Jehoram, King of Judah, and on his death hold the throne herself for six years until she is murdered. However, the attention of the following stories is not focused on that, but on the theological power struggle raging between the Yahvists and the adherents of the foreign queen Jezebel, who has imported the worship of the Phoenician god Baal into Israel: a worship that is now spreading from its center in Samaria to all the provinces.

The word *baal* meant "lord" or "master" and was not new to the Hebrews. As such it was even used as a title for Yahweh himself right up to the time of David. Baal, however, was also the name of an ancient Canaanite deity: a universal nature god like the Greek Zeus: commander of rains, clouds, and thunder. As such the concept of Baal was not in itself incompatible with the concept of Yahweh, but since Baal also represented the raw potency of nature and his worship stressed the place of fertility, sex, and eroticism in human life, the Hebrew prophets beginning with Elijah fought to prevent not merely the full identification of Yahweh with Baal but to demolish Baal altogether.

However, in this first story, we see Elijah not so much the fiery champion of the prophetic party (though he does forecast a drought which is to come as punishment for Jezebel's "misdeeds") as the humane miracle worker.

(1 Kings 17:1-24)

AND Elijah the prophet from Tishbe in the region of Gilead said to Ahab the king: "As surely as Yahweh God of Israel lives, and before whom I stand, there is to be no dew or rain for several years until I say so."

The following command then came to him from the Lord: "Leave this place and go eastward. Seclude yourself by the torrent of Cherith just where it joins the Jordan. You can drink from the torrent and I have commanded the ravens to feed you."

So Elijah went and did as the Lord said. He lived beside the torrent just where it joins the Jordan, and the ravens brought him bread and meat every morning, and bread and meat again in the evening. He drank from the torrent.

After a time, however, the torrent dried up because no rain had fallen anywhere in the land. Whereupon this command came to him from Yahweh: "Rouse yourself and go to Zarephath, near the city of Sidon. You are to put up in the house of a certain widow whom I have ordered to feed you."

So Elijah roused himself and went to Zarephath, and just as he came to the town gate, whom should he see but the widow gathering sticks? He called to her and said, "Can you fetch me a cup of water to drink, please," and as she went to get the water he called after her, "Oh, and bring me a bite of bread as well!"

"I'm sorry," the widow called back, "but I swear to God that I haven't a crumb of bread. All I have is a handful of flour in a crock and a small cruet of oil. I'm actually collecting a couple of bundles of sticks to cook up a meal for my son and me to eat and then die."

"Bear up!" Elijah called to her. "Go and do what you said, but first bake me a little loaf out of your flour and bring it out here, then cook something for yourself and your son. Yahweh God of Israel promises that your crock of flour and your cruet of oil will last until he sends rain down on the earth."

The widow went and did as Elijah said. Then he ate, and she and her son ate, but from that day onward neither the crock of flour nor the cruet of oil ever grew less—just as the Lord had promised through Elijah.

Some time later, however, in this widow's home, her son fell grievously ill; so ill that he died, and the widow cried out, "What have you done to me, you man of God? Have you come to punish me for my sins and kill my son?"

Elijah replied, "Hand your son to me," and he took him from her breast and carried him to his bedroom, where he laid him on his own bed.

"O Yahweh my Lord God," Elijah prayed, "why have

you struck at this widow with whom I am staying and killed her son?"

Then three times he lay stretched out over the boy, calling on the Lord, "O Yahweh my God, please, make the soul of this boy go back into him."

Yahweh heard Elijah's prayer. The soul of the boy went back into him and once more he lived. Elijah carried him out of the bedroom downstairs and gave him to his mother.

"Oh, you really are a man of God!" she cried out. "Only truth issues from your lips from the Lord."

Elijah and the Prophets of Baal

This story is often considered one of the masterpieces of biblical narrative. It was probably written in Judah about two hundred years after the time of Elijah. Ahab the son of Omri had ascended the throne of Israel in 875 B.C. and centered his government in the new city of Samaria (built by his father), which became the capital of the kingdom of Israel and gave its name to the whole province.

Though a resourceful ruler who made his country respected even by the warlike Assyrians who threatened its borders, Ahab could never be forgiven by the biblical writers for supporting his dominating queen, Jezebel, in spreading her cult of the Phoenician deities Baal and Ashtoreth (Baal's female equivalent). In all such matters, however, one must remember that religion itself is seldom as much the reason for policy as are money, trade, power, and politics. In this case it was an enormous asset to Ahab to have a wife who linked him to the powerful and prosperous Phoenicians.

(1 Kings 18:1-46)

A long time went by and some three years later the word of Yahweh came to Elijah: "Go and present yourself to King Ahab because I am about to send down rain on the earth again." So Elijah set off to present himself to Ahab.

Now since the famine in Samaria was worse than ever, Ahab had summoned his palace manager, Obadiah. (This Obadiah was a truly God-fearing man who, once when Queen

Jezebel was butchering the prophets of Yahweh, rounded up a hundred of them and hid them fifty by fifty in a cave, where he provided them with food and water.) Then said Ahab to Obadiah, "Look, we must scour the countryside for springs and brooks to see if we can possibly find enough water and grass to keep our horses and mules alive; otherwise we are going to lose the lot."

They divided the land between them so as to cover the whole terrain. Ahab went one way by himself, and Obadiah another, also by himself. While Obadiah was traveling along, whom should he run into but Elijah, coming to see Ahab? He recognized him at once and fell down before him, exclaiming, "Is it really my lord Elijah?"

"It is indeed," Elijah replied. "Go and tell your master that Elijah is here."

To which Obadiah replied, "What have I done wrong to be handed over to Ahab to be killed? For I swear to God that there isn't a nation or kingdom which my master hasn't combed through to find you. Every nation and kingdom where you were not found he made them swear that you were not there. And now you blithely say, 'Go and tell your master that Elijah is here,' when the moment I've left you the spirit of the Lord will waft you off to some other place heaven knows where, then when I announce to Ahab that you've been found and he can't find you, he'll kill me: me, who have been a God-fearing man since my youth. . . . Has nobody told you, sir, what I did when Jezebel was slaughtering the Lord's prophets and how I hid a hundred of them in two lots of fifty and fed them food and water? And now you say, 'Go and tell your master that Elijah is here'! He'll kill me."

Elijah answered, "I swear to you before the face of Yahweh Lord of Hosts that I will this very day present myself to Ahab."

Accordingly, as soon as Obadiah had found Ahab and told him, Ahab went to meet Elijah. The first thing he said to him when he saw him was: "So it's you, is it? The curse of Israel!"

"Not I," returned Elijah. "It's you and your whole family that are the curse of Israel because you have forsaken the Lord's commandments and gone after Baal. Summon all Israel to meet me on Mount Carmel, as well as the four hundred and fifty prophets of Baal who eat at Jezebel's table."

So Ahab summoned all Israel and assembled them with

the prophets on Mount Carmel. Elijah, stepping forward before the whole concourse, declaimed, "How long are you people going to go on tottering on alternate legs? If Yahweh be God, follow Yahweh; but if Baal be God, then follow Baal."

The people were dumb.

Then Elijah said to them, "Here I am, a single prophet of Yahweh all by myself, and here are the four hundred and fifty prophets of Baal. Let two bullocks be alloted us. Let them choose one and cut it up and put it on the wood, but not light the fire under it. I shall prepare the other bullock and also lay it on the wood without a fire underneath. Then let them call on the name of their gods, and I shall call on the name of my God Yahweh. And the God that answers by fire, he is the true God."

The people were delighted with this proposal, and Elijah said to the prophets of Baal, "You choose your bullock and dress it first, because there are a lot of you. Then call on your gods, but don't light the fire underneath."

So they chose their bullock, prepared it, and began to call on the name of Baal. They called from morn till noon. "Great Baal, listen!" they pleaded. But there was no answer, not a sound, though they pranced around their altar. When midday came, Elijah started to jeer at them, "Shout louder. He's a god, after all, and may be out gossiping, or on business, or on a trip somewhere; or perhaps he's asleep and needs to be woken up."

So they bawled their heads off and cut themselves with knives and daggers—as is their wont—till the blood streamed. They went on raving well into the afternoon until it was time for the evening sacrifice, but there was no voice, no answer. Then said Elijah to the people, "Come, gather nearer." When they had drawn closer, he proceeded to repair Yahweh's altar which had been dismantled. He took twelve stones representing the twelve tribes of Jacob (to whom God had said: "Israel is to be your name") and used them to build an altar to the Lord, digging a trench around it the width of two spades for water. Then he piled the firewood neatly on it, cut up the bullock, and laid it over the wood.

"Now," he said, "pour four full buckets of water all over the offering and over the wood . . ." Then: "Do it again." And when they had done it a second time: "And yet again," he ordered. After the third time the whole altar was dripping with water and the trench brimming.

It was now time for the evening sacrifice, and the prophet

Elijah, stepping toward the altar, prayed aloud: "O Lord God of Abraham, Isaac, and Jacob, manifest today that you are the God of Israel and that I your servant have done all this at your command. Hear me, O Lord, hear me, and let these people know that you are their true Lord and God, so have their hearts turned back to you."

All of a sudden the Lord's lightning flashed down from heaven, setting the carcass, the wood, the very stones and dust sizzling as it licked up every drop of water in the trough.

At the sight of this the people fell on their faces, yelling, "Yahweh is God! Yahweh is God!"

Then Elijah ordered, "Seize the prophets of Baal. Don't let one of them get away."

They were all captured and Elijah took them down to the brook of Kishon and killed them there.

"Now," said Elijah to Ahab, "you can go and eat and drink because I hear the sound of a mighty rain."

Ahab got ready to eat and drink, while Elijah climbed to the top of Mount Carmel, where he threw himself on his knees and with his head bowed between his knees said to his servant, "Climb up higher and scan the sea." When he did so, he gazed out, but reported, "I see nothing."

Seven times Elijah made him return to the lookout, and at last, on the seventh time, the lad called, "There's a little cloud like a man's hand coming up over the sea."

"Quick," Elijah called back. "Get yourself to Ahab and tell him to harness his chariot and go before the rain stops him."

While they were all bustling this way and that, the sky grew black with clouds, and a great wind began to drive down the rain. Ahab mounted his chariot and fled towards Jezreel, while Elijah in a surge of divine spirit hitched up his clothes and sprinted ahead of Ahab all the way to the gates of Jezreel.

NOTE

1. In 1 Kings 18:19 there is some confusion about the number of the prophets of Baal. Some texts have: "four hundred and fifty prophets of Baal, and four hundred prophets of Asherah who eat at Jezebel's table." This proliferation of prophets suggests a conflation of two separate accounts.

The Mantle of Elijah Falls on Elisha

(1 Kings 19:1-21)

WHEN Ahab told his wife Jezebel everything that Elijah had done and how he had put to the sword all her prophets, Jezebel sent this message to Elijah: "As sure as you are Elijah and I am Jezebel, I swear to the gods, they can do their very worst to me if by this time tomorrow I haven't snuffed out your life like one of the rest."

So Elijah fleeing in a blind panic found himself arrived at Beersheba in Judah, where he left his servant lad and walked off a whole day's journey into the desert. He went and sat under a juniper bush, sighing that he wanted his life to end. "I've had enough, Lord," he prayed. "Take my life away. I'm no better than my fathers."

He had flung himself down and gone to sleep in the shade of the bush when to his surprise something or someone nudged him, saying, "Get up and eat." He looked up and there at his head was a freshly baked loaf on coals and a pitcher of water. He ate and drank, then fell asleep again. And it came again—an angel of the Lord, who touched him and said, "Get up and eat, for you have a long way to go."

So he got up again and after eating and drinking walked on the strength of that food for forty days and forty nights as far as the mountain of God, Horeb. There he holed up in a cave, and there God's word reached him, demanding: "Elijah, what are you doing here?"

To which he answered, "Without stint I have striven for the Lord God of Hosts all because the children of Israel have broken their pact with you, have torn down your altars, and put your prophets to the sword, till nobody is left but me, just me all by myself, and now they want to take my life as well."

"Come out of the cave," Yahweh said, "and stand and wait for me on the mountainside."

Then Yahweh himself passed by, and a great, strong wind came, blasting the mountain and shattering the rocks in the Lord's path. But Yahweh was not in the wind. And after the wind came an earthquake. But Yahweh was not in the earthquake. And after the earthquake, fire, but Yahweh was not in the fire. And after the fire, a still small voice: Yahweh himself.

Elijah, hearing it, threw his mantle around his head and came out of the cave and stood at the entrance.

"Elijah, why are you here?" the voice once again said to him. And once again he answered, "Without stint I have striven for the Lord God of Hosts, all because the children of Israel have broken their pact with you, have torn down your altars and put your prophets to the sword, till nobody is left but me, all by myself, and now they want to take my life away as well."

"Go," the Lord replied. "Take the desert road again and go to Damascus. There anoint Hazael as king of Syria, and anoint Jehu the son of Nimshi as king of Israel. Then anoint Elisha the son of Shaphat from Abelmeholah as my prophet in your stead. Whoever escapes the sword of Hazael shall fall to the sword of Jehu, and whoever escapes the sword of Jehu shall be slain by Elisha. But there are still seven thousand loyal souls left to me in Israel: not every knee has bowed to Baal, not every mouth has kissed him."

Elijah set off and he found Elisha the son of Shaphat behind the plow, the last in a team of twelve pairs of oxen plowing. Elijah came up to him and threw his mantle over him. Elisha left his oxen and ran after Elijah.

"Please," he said, "first let me go and kiss my father and mother goodbye. Then I will follow you."

"Go," Elijah replied, "but come back. I have done my part."

Elisha returned to the oxen, slaughtered his pair, made a fire out of the plow and cooked the meat for all the plowmen, who ate heartily. After which he got up and walked behind Elijah, whom now he served.

Naboth's Vineyard

The following incident takes place after Ahab has returned from a second successful campaign against the Syrians under Benhadad II. Elijah's rebuke of Ahab for his maltreatment of Naboth is parallel to that of Nathan when he lashed out at David for his treatment of Uriah, but it is even more devastating. The Yahvist or prophetic party, which generally supported the monarchs in their foreign policy if it was warlike enough, now get the chance of giving utterance to their gut feelings about their kings.

(1 Kings 21:1-29)

NABOTH, a man from Jezreel, had a vineyard near the palace of Ahab king of Samaria. And Ahab said to Naboth, "Let me have your vineyard for a kitchen garden because it's so conveniently close to my palace. I'll trade you a finer vineyard or, if you prefer, give you its value in money."

"God forbid that I should ever give up a piece of land that has been in the family for generations," Naboth replied.

Ahab returned home crestfallen and annoyed at Naboth's refusal to let him have this piece of property that had been in the family so long. He lay down on his bed, turned his face to the wall, and would not eat.

His wife Jezebel came to him and asked, "What has so upset you that you won't eat?"

"It's this," he said: "when I approached Naboth the Jezreelite and asked him to let me have his vineyard in exchange for money or, if he preferred, a much better vineyard, he simply replied, 'No, I don't want to give you my vineyard.' "

"Aren't you the king of Israel with absolute power?" Ahab's wife taunted. "Never mind, get up and have a good dinner. Don't give Naboth's vineyard a thought. I'll get it for you."

She then wrote letters in Ahab's name, sealed with his seal, and dispatched them to the elders and chief citizens of Naboth's town. In the letters she said: "Proclaim a fast, and have Naboth put on trial before the civic leaders. Bribe two witnesses, two thoroughgoing scoundrels, to bear false testimony against him and accuse him of blasphemy against God and treason against the king. Then have him dragged out and stoned to death."

The city leaders, both the elders and the nobles of the town where Naboth lived, did as Jezebel commanded them in her letters. They brought in two scoundrels and had them accuse him. And like the demons they were, they charged Naboth before the assembly of blasphemy and treason. Naboth was accordingly dragged outside the city and stoned to death.

The news that Naboth had been stoned was reported to

Jezebel, and as soon as she heard that Naboth was dead she said to Ahab, "Quick, go and take possession of Naboth the Jezreelite's vineyard. The man who refused to sell it to you is no longer living. I tell you, he's dead."

When Ahab heard this, that Naboth was truly dead, he set off for Naboth's vineyard to take possession of it. Meanwhile, the Lord had said to Elijah the Tishbite: "I want you to tell Ahab this: 'Yahweh declares that you have not only stolen but murdered.' After which, say: 'The Lord adds this: In the very spot where dogs licked up the blood of Naboth, dogs will lick your blood too.' "

"Have you found me, O my enemy?" Ahab exclaimed to Elijah [as soon as they met].

"Yes, I have found you," he answered, "and because you have sold yourself to evil in God's sight, the Lord says: 'I am going to bring down evil upon you. I am going to cut down your descendants in Israel to the last man, yes, every male of you no matter where he hides. I'll do to yours what I did to the house of Jeroboam son of Nebat, and to the house of Baasha son of Ahijah, because of the anger that you've caused me by leading all Israel into sin.' "

Then, of Jezebel Yahweh said, "The dogs will devour her beneath the ramparts of Jezreel. And as to Ahab, the dogs will eat him up too if he dies in the city, but if he dies in the country, he will be fodder for birds."

There was no one in God's sight so sold to evil as Ahab, set on to it by Jezebel his wife. His especial abomination was to have worshiped idols the way the Amorites did—those people which the Lord had expelled to make room for the children of Israel.

When Ahab heard these prophecies, he went away crying and rending his clothes. He dressed his body in rags, fasted, slept in sackcloth, and walked with his head down. At which Yahweh said to Elijah the Tishbite, "Have you seen how Ahab has abased himself before me? Because he has so humbled himself for me, I will not bring down his punishment on him while he lives, but defer the ruin of his house till the days of his son."

The Curious Death of King Ahab

Despite King Ahab's successes in withstanding the encroachments of the Syrians, the biblical writers give him scant credit for a not unsuccessful reign of twenty-two years. Always sympathizing with the Yahvist or prophetic party, they tended to view the monarchy with suspicion, and this monarch's wife, Jezebel, with hatred.

In the following story, four hundred prophets are summoned by Ahab, but they are prophets of Phoenician deities, and so the biblical account naturally implies that they are false prophets. Our word "prophet" comes from the Greek and means both "one who speaks for another" and "one who speaks beforehand." Both meanings fit the use of the word in the Bible. The role of the prophet or prophetess was to channel the divine message to mankind—a message which often foretold future events. The word prophet could also mean seer or visionary, and on occasion an ecstatic. There is abundant extrabiblical evidence to show that prophetic activity was not a purely Hebrew phenomenon, but existed in biblical times throughout the Near East, not to mention Greece and Southern Italy.

Meanwhile, Ahab has brought to an end the intermittent fighting between Israel and Judah and made an alliance with Jehoshaphat (the sixth king of Judah in the Davidic line). Jehoshaphat's son, Jehoram, marries Athaliah, Ahab and Jezebel's daughter.

(1 Kings 22:1-38)

FOR three years there was no war between Syria and Israel, but during the third year Jehoshaphat king of Judah came on a visit to Ahab king of Israel (who had previously remarked to his ministers, "You know, Ramoth-gilead is ours and yet here we sit doing nothing to retake it from the clutches of the king of Syria"), and now Ahab asked him, "Will you join me in retaking Ramoth-gilead?"

"Of course," Jehoshaphat replied. "You and I are as one. My people are your people, my horses your horses." Then he added, "I beg you ask the Lord about it today."

Ahab king of Israel then summoned his prophets, some

four hundred of them, and he asked them, "Shall I or shan't I attack Ramoth-gilead?"

"Go ahead," they all said. "Yahweh will put it into your majesty's hands."

Jehoshaphat however asked, "Is there no prophet of the Lord here whom we may consult?"

"Well, there *is* one man whom we may consult about the Lord's wishes," Ahab replied to Jehoshaphat. "Micaiah son of Imlah, but I hate him because he never prophesies anything good about me, always bad."

"Oh, don't say that, King!" Jehoshaphat exclaimed while Ahab called an aide. "Quickly go and get Micaiah son of Imlah," he ordered.

Then in the ample space at the entrance of the gates of Samaria, where the kings of Israel and Judah sat enthroned each in his regalia, the four hundred prophets began to prophesy before them. One of them, Zedekiah son of Chenaanah, had fashioned two horns of iron and was proclaiming, "This is how you will charge the Syrians and destroy them." The rest of the prophets spoke in a similar vein, urging the king to march on Ramoth-gilead because the Lord was going to deliver it into their hands.

Meanwhile the messenger who had gone to fetch Micaiah said to him, "Listen, all the prophets are unanimous in predicting success for the king. You must do the same: tell him only of success."

"I swear to God," Micaiah retorted, "I'll say only what the Lord puts into my mouth."

However, when he stood before Ahab and the king asked him, "Micaiah, are we to march against Ramoth-gilead and attack it or not?" he replied, "Of course, do it: the Lord will put it into your majesty's hands."

"In God's name," scolded the king, "how many times have I told you to speak nothing but the truth to me from the Lord?"

Whereat Micaiah confessed, "I saw all Israel scattered like sheep on the hillsides, like sheep without a shepherd. And the Lord said, 'They have no leader. Let every man of them go back to his own home.' "

King Ahab of Israel turned to Jehoshaphat: "Didn't I tell you—he never prophesies anything good about me, always the worst!"

Micaiah continued, "Take heed of the scene that I saw: Yahweh seated on his throne, with the whole court of heaven standing to his right and left. And Yahweh said to them,

'Who among you will trick Ahab king of Israel into attacking Ramoth-gilead?'

"The angelic spirits murmured one thing after another, until at last a certain angel stepped forward before Yahweh and spoke: 'I shall trick him.'

" 'How?' said the Lord.

" 'I shall invent lies for the lips of all his prophets.'

" 'You trickster!' said the Lord. 'Go and do it.'

"So you see, Yahweh has put a lying spirit into the mouth of every prophet here, and the Lord has condemned you."

At that, Zedekiah son of Chenaanah struck Micaiah on the face, saying, "Are you suggesting that the spirit of the Lord has deserted me and speaks only through you?"

"You'll find out all too well," Micaiah retorted, "on the day you go hiding in closets within closets."

"Arrest Micaiah," King Ahab ordered. "Put him in the charge of the town mayor and of my son Joash. Tell them the king's orders are to clap this fellow in jail on a lowly ration of bread and water till I return in peace."

"If you return all in one piece,"* quipped Micaiah. "Which would only mean that Yahweh never said a thing through me. . . . I hope all you people are listening."

So Ahab king of Israel and Jehoshaphat king of Judah marched on Ramoth-gilead. Then said Ahab to Jehoshaphat, "I'm going into battle disguised. You can dress up as royalty."

So the king of Israel went into battle incognito. But the king of Syria had ordered his thirty-two chariot captains not to bother fighting small or great, but to focus on the king of Israel. Consequently, when these captains saw Jehoshaphat they mistook him for the king of Israel and concentrated all their attack on him till he shouted out his identity. When they realized that he was not the king of Israel they turned away.

A Syrian soldier, however, drawing his bow at random hit the king of Israel between the lungs and the stomach. "Turn and take me out of the fight," the king gasped to his charioteer. "I am gravely wounded."

Later that day as the battle raged more fiercely, the king reentered the fight against the Syrians, propped up in his chariot, the blood streaming from his wound down onto the floorboards. He died that evening, the blood still oozing from his arrow thrust all over the well of the chariot.

*Although this play on words is not found in the Hebrew or Greek texts, it is very much in the spirit of Micaiah's reply.

Toward sunset the herald's cry rang through the army: "Every man back to his own country. Every man back to his city: the king is dead!"

They carried him into Samaria and buried him there. While they were washing down his chariot in the pool at Samaria, pigs and dogs came licking up the blood, and prostitutes mopped it up—all as predicted by the word of Yahweh.

The rest of Ahab's story, all his exploits, the house of ivory that he built, the cities he erected, they are all recorded in "The Annals of the Kings of Israel." Ahab was laid to rest with his fathers, and his son Ahaziah mounted the throne in his stead.

The Strange Departure of Elijah

Elijah, sensing that he would never live long enough to win the cause of Yahvism against the thoroughly "unorthodox" royal house of Israel, has chosen a no less intransigent champion of the prophetic party than himself to carry on the work of purifying the nation: a young farmer called Elisha. For the next fifty years Elisha is to prove himself a stalwart patriot helping Israel to victories: a king critic and a miracle worker whose often crusty manner belies a humane soul.

(2 Kings 2:1-25)

THE time approached when the Lord was to take Elijah up to heaven in a whirlwind. Elijah and Elisha were just leaving Gilgal, and Elijah turned to Elisha, saying, "You stay here because Yahweh has sent me on to Bethel."

"Not on your life or the Lord's!" Elisha answered him. "I refuse to desert you."

So they went on together to Bethel, and while there the young prophets of Bethel came to Elisha and said, "Are you aware that Yahweh will take your master from you today?"

"Quiet!" he barked, "Of course I'm aware."

When Elijah said to Elisha, "You stay here because Yahweh is sending me on to Jericho," Elisha answered again, "Not on your or the Lord's life will I leave you!"

So they went on to Jericho together. And there, when the young prophets of Jericho came up to Elisha and said, "Do you know that Yahweh will take your master from you today?" he muttered, "Will you please hold your tongues? Of course I know it!"

Elijah then said to him, "Stay here, will you, because Yahweh is sending me on to the Jordan," and once more he answered, "Not on the Lord's life or yours! I *will* not leave you."

So they went on together, with fifty young prophets of the brotherhood following them. These fifty young prophets kept at a distance but within eyeshot, watching the two as they stood by the Jordan. It was then that Elijah, folding his cloak into a bundle, hit the water with it, and the river splayed out in every direction, leaving a dry bed for them to walk through.

After they had crossed over, Elijah said to Elisha, "Ask me for something you would like before I am taken from you."

Elisha replied, "I ask that your prophetic spirit in me may be doubled."

"You have asked for a hard thing," Elijah responded. "Nevertheless, if you see me being taken from you, you shall have your wish. But if you do not see me, you will not."

As they went along walking and talking together, a chariot of fire with fiery coursers suddenly loomed in between them, and Elijah was swept up in a whirlwind to heaven.

"My father, oh my father! The chariot of Israel and the charioteers!" Elisha cried out as he witnessed it. And that was the last he saw of him as in dismay he tore his own cloak in two. Then, picking up the mantle of Elijah that had fallen to the ground, he walked back and stood on the banks of the Jordan and with the fallen mantle hit the waters, but they did not divide. "Where is Elijah's God now?" he muttered as he struck the river again, and this time the waters splayed out in every direction so he could cross to the other side.

The young prophets of Jericho, who had seen it all from a distance, called out as they came to meet him, "The spirit of Elijah now rests in Elisha," and they bowed to the ground before him.

"Listen," they said, "there are fifty strapping fellows among us who can go and look for your master. The power of the Lord which wafted him away may have dropped him in the Jordan or on a mountaintop or in some ravine."

"Don't bother to go and look," Elisha told them, but they went on pressing him till he felt embarrassed and finally said, "All right, send them out," and fifty young men were dispatched. For three days they searched and found nothing. When they returned to Elisha, who had put up in Jericho, he remarked, "Didn't I tell you not to bother?"

Elisha and the Shunemite Lady

(2 Kings 4:8-37)

One day Elisha was going through Shunem and a great lady there pressed him to dine. Ever after, whenever he passed that way he turned aside to eat at her house. Later the lady said to her husband, "You know, I'm sure that our guest is a holy man of God. Why don't we make a little room for him on the roof, where we can put a bed, a table and chair, and a lamp, so whenever he visits us he can stay there?"

One day after Elisha had come in and gone to his bedroom upstairs to rest, he asked his servant boy Gehazi to call the lady of the house, this Shunemite. This he did and when she was standing there next to him, he said to Gehazi, "Will you tell Madam this: 'My dear, you've been so kind to us in every way, is there anything I can do for you? Put in a word for you to the king? Or speak to the commander-in-chief?"

"I lack for nothing among my own people," she replied.

Afterward he asked his lad Gehazi, "What can we possibly do for her?"

"Well, she has no son," he suggested, "and her husband is old."

"Go and call her back."

He did so, and as she stood by the door Elisha said to her, "About a year from now, at exactly this hour you will swaddle a newborn baby boy."

"Please, sir," she burst out, "don't tell such lies! And you a man of God!"

However, the good woman conceived and bore a son at the very time and hour that Elisha had predicted.

* * *

One day when the boy was older and had gone out to the harvesters to meet his father, he suddenly cried out, "Oh my head! my head!"

"Carry him home to his mother," his father said to a servant, who carried him back to his mother, and she cuddled him on her lap till about noon, when he died. She took him upstairs and laid him on the holy man's bed, then went out, shutting the door behind her. She called her husband and said, "Send me off with one of our boys on a donkey. I want to go as fast as possible to the holy man and hurry back."

"Why do you want to see him today?" he asked. "It isn't the new moon or the Sabbath."

"Goodbye!" she said.

Having saddled the donkey she told the boy, "Hurry! Make him go! Don't slacken for a moment unless I tell you to."

Off they went and were nearing the man of God's place on Mount Carmel when he saw her coming toward him from a distance and he turned to his lad Gehazi: "Look, the Shunemite woman! Run and meet her and ask her if everything is all right with her and her husband and her son."

"Everything is fine," she told Gehazi, but as soon as she reached the man of God on the hill she caught hold of him by the feet so that Gehazi ran up to push her away.

"No, leave her alone," Elisha ordered. "She's in a state of anguish, and the Lord has kept this from me and never told me."

"Sir, did I ever ask you for a son?" she wept. "And didn't I say, 'Don't tell me lies?' "

Elisha turned to Gehasi. "Get ready," he said. "Take my staff and hurry. Don't salute anybody you meet. If anyone salutes you, don't answer. Lay my staff on the child's face."

Here the boy's mother broke in: "I'm not leaving you—not on your life or the Lord's."

So Elisha followed behind her. Gehazi, however, had already gone, but when he laid the staff on the child's face and there was neither breath nor stir he ran back to meet Elisha and said, "The boy hasn't revived."

Elisha arrived at the house and there was the boy lying dead on his bed. So he went in, shut the door on them both, and began to pray to the Lord. Then he got up and lay over the boy, putting his mouth over the boy's mouth, his eyes over his eyes, the palms of his hands over his hands. As he lay stretched-out over him, the boy's body began to grow warm. At which the prophet got up and walked about the house a little, to and fro. Then he went upstairs again and this time when he lay on the boy, the boy sneezed seven times and opened his eyes. Elisha shouted for Gehazi. "Call her," he said. Gehazi called and she hurried into the room. "Here's your son, take him," he said. She came and fell at his feet, quite prostrate with her thanks, then picked up her boy and went out.

Naaman the Leper

(2 Kings 5:1-44)

NAAMAN, commander-in-chief of the king of Syria's army, was a great man with his master and a national hero because the Lord had made him savior of Syria. He was brave and rich, but a leper.

Bands of Syrian marauders in one of their raids into Israel had brought back a little girl as captive who was now a maid in the service of Naaman's wife, and one day she remarked to her mistress, "I wish my master had met the great Samaritan prophet because I'm sure he would have healed him of his leprosy."

When Naaman reported this remark to the king of Syria, he said to him, "You must go there. I'll send a letter of introduction with you to the king of Israel."

So Naaman departed, taking with him ten talents of silver and six thousand gold sovereigns as well as ten changes of clothes. The letter of introduction which Naaman presented to the king of Israel said: "In this letter I am introducing to you my officer Naaman, in the hopes that you will cure him of his leprosy."

When the king of Israel read the letter he rent his clothes in exasperation. "Am I god?" he shouted, "to kill and to give life, that this man should send me someone to cure of his leprosy? Take note, please, he only wants to pick a quarrel with me."

When Elisha the man of God heard that the king of Israel had rent his clothes, he sent a message saying: "Why have you rent your clothes? Let the man come to me, and I'll show him that there is a prophet here in Israel."

So Naaman arrived with his horses and his chariots, and he stood at the door of Elisha's house and Elisha merely sent a message out to him: "Go and wash seven times in the Jordan and your skin will once again be healthy and clean."

Naaman turned away in disgust: "I thought he would at least come out to me," he fumed. "I thought he would stand there and call on Yahweh and put his hands on my leprosy and heal me. Aren't the rivers Abana and Pharpar of Damascus far better than all the rivers of Israel for me to wash in and be healed?"

As he peevishly turned away to leave, his aides came to him and said, "Sire, if the prophet had told you to do some marvelous thing, surely you would have done it. How much readier should you be to do it when he says simply: " 'Go and wash and you will be cured'?"

As a result, Naaman went down to the Jordan and dipped himself in the river seven times just as the man of God had prescribed, and he was completely cured: his skin was made as clean and new as a little child's.

He and his party went back to the prophet and, standing before him, he declared, "Now I know that the God of Israel really is the only God in the whole world. Please will you accept a token of my gratitude?"

"Absolutely not," Elisha returned: "by Yahweh my God I swear it!"

When pressed, he still refused. "Just as you wish," Naaman conceded. "But will you grant me this favor: to carry away from here two mule loads of earth, because from now on I mean to offer no other sacrifice or offering except to Yahweh. And there is one thing more: will you ask the Lord to overlook the times my master the king goes to worship in the temple of Rimmon leaning on my arm and I have to bow down with him when he bows?"

"I will," Elisha replied. "Go in peace."

It was the earth's springtime when Naaman departed, but he had not gone very far when Gehazi the prophet's servant said to himself, "My master has let Naaman this Syrian go without taking any of his gifts. I swear by God I'll run after him and get something out of him."

So he hurried after Naaman, who, when he saw him running after them, jumped down from his chariot to meet him. "Is everything all right?" he asked.

"Fine!" said Gehazi, "but my master has sent me to tell you that two young prophets have just arrived from the hills of Ephraim, and will you please give them a talent in silver and two new outfits?"

"Of course! Take two talents," he said, and he pressed on him two talents' worth of silver in two bags, together with two new outfits. These he loaded onto two of his servants to carry back with Gehazi. It was dusk when Gehazi relieved them of the goods and dismissed them. Then he took the loot to his own quarters and stowed it away. When, however, he stood at last before his master and Elisha asked him, "Well, Gehazi, where have you been?"

"Oh, nowhere, sir," he answered.

"Didn't you realize," Elisha snapped, "that I was there with you in spirit when the Syrian turned back from his chariot to meet you? Well, now you have fine new clothes and money to buy olive groves and vineyards, sheep and cattle, and can have servants, both men and women. However, from now on Naaman's leprosy will cling to *you* and to your children and their children forever."

Gehazi went from his master's presence a leper—white as snow.

Jehu Driving Furiously

Jehoshaphat, the sixth king of Judah in the house of David, has died after a reign of twenty-four years. He is succeeded by his son Jehoram, who is married to Athaliah, daughter of Ahab and Jezebel (of Israel). The alliance between Judah and Israel is kept—with Judah the weaker partner—but the headstrong Athaliah shows the same anti-Yahvist tendencies as her mother and is influencing her husband (as she is soon to influence her son Ahaziah, the next king of Judah).

The prophet Elisha casts around for an ally in his struggle to promote the cause of Yahweh and alights on Jehu, a son of the late Jehoshaphat and commander-in-chief of the new king of Israel, who is also called Jehoram.

Meanwhile, Israel's old enemy, King Benhadad of Syria, is now a sick old man in his capital of Damascus, unaware that his trusted officer Hazael is planning to hasten his demise.

As to Queen Jezebel's fortunes in this story, at the moment they are riding high. She has a son on the throne of

Israel (Jehoram, brother-in-law of the Jehoram, King of Judah, now dead) and a grandson on the throne of Judah (Ahaziah). That Jezebel was a powerful and unscrupulous woman there can be no doubt, and yet the picture the biblical writers leave us of her seems a little unfair. It is true that her treatment of Nathan was disgraceful, but hardly more so than that meted out time and time again by the Israelites to their neighbors, with Yahweh himself abetting. It suited her husband, Ahab, to encourage her cult of Phoenician deities because it strengthened his hand against the Yahvist party, which was always at heart anti-monarchist. There is every evidence that she was loyal to her husband and faithful to her dependents. She met her end with courage and dignity. And yet the only legacy she has left us is the phrase "a painted Jezebel" as the image of a loose woman.

(2 Kings 8:7-15, 9:1-36, 10:1-36)

WHEN Elisha came to Damascus, his arrival was reported to Benhadad king of Syria, who was sick. The king charged Hazael to visit the prophet taking a present, and ask him if he would recover from his illness. So Hazael went to see the prophet, bearing with him forty camel loads of gifts of the best things of Damascus. He said on meeting him, "Your good son Benhadad king of Syria has sent me to ask you if he will recover."

"Go and tell him," Elisha replied, "that he will recover. The Lord, however, has shown me that he will also die."

Saying which, the prophet stared fixedly at him, and his face went all red as he burst into tears.

"Whatever is it, sir, that's making you cry?" Hazael asked.

"Because I see the abominable things you are going to do to the children of Israel," he said. "You will burn down their houses, put their young men to the sword, dash out the brains of babies, and rip open their pregnant women."

"Could I ever be such a dog and do anything so monstrous?" he protested.

"Well, Yahweh has shown me that you are to be king of Syria," Elisha responded.

The next day Hazael soaked a blanket in water and held it down over the king's face till he suffocated. Now he was king instead.

Meanwhile, the prophet Elisha had summoned one of the young prophets and said to him, "Prepare to take this flask of oil to Ramoth-gilead. When you arrive there you will meet Jehu the son of Jehoshaphat and grandson of Nimshi. Go in and rouse him from among his brother officers and take him into an inner room. There pour the flask of oil on his head as you utter, 'Thus says the Lord: I anoint you king of Israel.' Then hurry away. Don't linger."

The young prophet went to Ramoth-gilead and approached the place where all the army officers were sitting around and he said, "I have a message for you, Captain."

"For which of us?" Jehu asked.

"For you, Captain."

Jehu got up and went with him into an inner room, where the young man poured oil over his head as he uttered, "Thus says the Lord God of Israel: I anoint you king of Yaweh's people, Israel. You are to strike down the house of Ahab your master and avenge the blood of my servants the prophets who suffered at the hands of Jezebel. The entire establishment of Ahab is to be dismantled, every manjack of them in Israel—fettered or free. I mean to destroy the house of Ahab as I destroyed the house of Jeroboam son of Nebat, and the house of Baasha son of Ahijah. Dogs shall devour Jezebel in the public square of Jezreel and no one will bury her."

Uttering which, he flung open the door and fled.

When Jehu returned to his fellow officers, they asked him, "Is everything all right? What did that crazy fellow come to tell you?"

"You know very well who he is and what he came to tell me," Jehu retorted.

"No, we don't. You tell us."

"Very well. After saying all sorts of things, he announced, 'The Lord declares: I anoint you king of Israel.' "

Immediately every man of them took off his cloak and spread it on the steps before Jehu's path as they sounded the trumpet, proclaiming: "Long live King Jehu!"

So Jehu son of Jehoshaphat and grandson of Nimshi began to plot against Joram the king, who had secured himself and the Israelite forces inside Ramoth-gilead against Hazael king of Syria, but who now returned to Jezreel to nurse the wounds which the Syrians had given him in the fight against King Hazael.

Jehu said to the men with him, "Since you want me to be king, don't let anyone slip out of this town and spread the news in Jezreel." Then he mounted his chariot and drove to Jezreel, where Joram was sick and where Ahaziah king of Judah had come to visit him.

When the watchman up on the tower of Jezreel looked out and saw Jehu and his escort approaching, he called out, "I see soldiers coming." At which Joram had a horseman dispatched to go and meet them and ask, "Do you come in peace?"

So the man on horseback rode out to Jehu. "The king wants to know if you come in peace," he asked.

"What is peace to you?" Jehu replied. "Get behind me and follow."

The watchman shouted down, "The messenger got to them, but isn't coming back." So Joram sent out a second horseman who rode out and asked them, "Is it peace?"

"What's peace to you?" Jehu answered. "Line up behind me."

"He isn't coming back either," the watchman called out. "It must be Jehu son of Nimshi, he's driving so furiously."

"Make ready my chariot," Joram commanded. The chariot was harnessed and Joram king of Israel drove out with Ahaziah king of Judah, each in his own chariot, to meet Jehu. They met at Naboth the Jezreelite's vineyard, and when Joram saw Jehu he called out, "Is it peace, Jehu?"

"What peace," he called back, "when the fornications of that witch your mother Jezebel are in full flush?"

Joram reined in his horses and wheeled, shouting to Ahaziah as he fled: "It's treason, Ahaziah." But Jehu, drawing his bow with his full strength, shot Joram straight between the shoulders. The arrow pierced his heart and he tottered to his knees in the chariot.

"Pick him up and toss him into the plot of Naboth's vineyard," Jehu said to Bidkar his lieutenant, "for I remember that time you and I rode together behind Ahab, this man's father, and Yahweh laid on him this punishment: 'The blood of Naboth and the blood of his sons is vivid before me. Therefore in this very plot I shall requite an avenging.' So pick him up and pitch him into the plot of Naboth's vineyard, thus fulfilling the word of the Lord."

When Ahaziah king of Judah saw what was happening, he fled down the road to Bethhaggar with Jehu in pursuit, shouting, "Shoot him down in his chariot too." They shot him where the road begins to climb to Gur near Ibleam, and he was just able to reach Megiddo before he died. His retainers carried him by chariot to Jerusalem and buried him in the tomb of his fathers in the city of David.

When Jezebel heard that Jehu was entering Jezreel, she made up her eyes with kohl, dressed her hair, and sat at a window, gazing down. As Jehu rode through the gate she shouted, "Still enjoying your day? You king-murderer!? You Zimri!"

Jehu looked up at the window and saw her. "And what do you think you are?" he yelled back. "Come down and join me!"

Then he called to two palace eunuchs who were looking on: "Throw her down." They threw her, her blood spattering the wall as she fell, and she was trampled on by the hooves of the horses.

Jehu went into the palace and sat down to eat and drink, after which he said, "Go and see to that accursed woman. Bury her. She was, after all, the daughter of a king."

They went to bury her, but found only the skull and remnants of her feet and hands. When they came back and reported this to Jehu, he observed, "This is exactly what Yahweh said would happen through his servant Elisha the Thesbite. 'In the public square of Jezreel,' he promised, 'wild dogs shall feast on the body of Jezebel. Her carcass will be strewn like manure over the fields of Jezreel so that no passerby will tell that this was Jezebel.' "

NOTES

1. As to Naboth's sons having been stoned along with their father, there is no mention of this having happened in the account of 1 Kings 21:13.

Jehu Consolidates His Position

Jehu, with Yahweh's tacit approval, having engineered the slaughter of Ahab's seventy sons in Samaria, goes on to kill the rest of the royal family in Jezreel, together with his chief ministers, his personal friends, even his house chaplains. Then, traveling to Samaria, he runs into forty-two relatives of Ahaziah King of Judah who are on their way to Jezreel to pay their respects, not knowing that Ahab is dead. He butchers them too.

(2 Kings 10:19-30)

Jehu then gathered all the people together and said to them, "Ahab worshiped Baal a little. I am going to worship Baal a lot. So call together the prophets of Baal and all his hangers-on, and all his priests without exception, because

I am going to offer a great sacrifice to Baal and whosoever absents himself shall die." (This was a trick of Jehu's to exterminate the worshipers of Baal.) "So, proclaim a solemn festival to Baal." And they proclaimed it.

He sent notices to the very ends of Israel and the worshipers of Baal came flocking in till not one was left behind. They crowded into the temple of Baal so that the temple was crammed from end to end. He gave orders to those in charge of the robing room to lay out vestments for all the priests of Baal, and they laid them out.

Then Jehu and Jehonadab the son of Rechab entered the temple and said to the worshippers of Baal, "Make sure that there is nobody here who serves Yahweh, only those who worship Baal."

After they were all inside and ready to offer sacrifices and burnt offerings, Jehu posted eighty militiamen outside the temple with the injuction: "If any man lets anyone in there escape, he'll pay for it life for life."

As soon as Jehu had finished sacrificing his burnt offering, he gave the signal to the captains of the militia to go in and kill the lot, and let not one get away. The captains took in their men and put all the worshipers to the sword, dragging their bodies outside. Then they went into the inner sanctuary of Baal and hauled out Baal's statue and burnt it. They smashed to pieces all the other idols and they wrecked the temple, turning it into a public jakes—which it is to this day. Thus did Jehu obliterate all trace of Baal from Israel. However, he still clung to the sinful practices that Jeroboam son of Nebat had led Israel into when he set up his golden calves in Bethel and Dan. Nevertheless, Yahweh said to Jehu, "Because you have so thoroughly executed my designs and dealt with the dynasty of Ahab after my own heart, your offspring shall sit on the throne of Israel on and on till the fourth generation."

NOTES

1. Jehonadab son of Rechab became the father of the Rechabite sect: quasifanatical zealots who eschewed wine, vineyards, agriculture, and even the building of houses.

2. Despite Yahweh's approval of the bloodbath when Jehu butchers the worshipers of Baal, in Hosea 1:4, Yahweh says, "I am soon going to make the house of Jehu pay for the bloodshed at Jezreel."

3. Jeroboam son of Nebat was the first king of the Northern Kingdom (Israel), who reigned from about 922 to 901 B.C. The reason he set up the golden bull images in his kingdom at Bethel and Dan was to discourage his subjects from going to Jerusalem to

worship. The images were to serve as symbols of Yahweh, as they had done several hundred years before in the time of Moses. The practice, however, was seen by the biblical writers as dangerously close to idolatry, and Jeroboam was branded through posterity as the very personification of the evil king.

4. The city of Jezreel, where Jezebel met her end, was the favorite residence of her and her husband, Ahab. It was located in the fertile valley of Jezreel, which separates Galilee from Samaria.

5. Kohl, with which Jezebel painted her eyes, was a powder of antimony: the equivalent of mascara.

PART VI

PALESTINE DURING THE ASSYRIAN, BABYLONIAN, PERSIAN, AND GREEK DOMINATION

(c. 842 TO 4 B.C.)

Stories from the Apocrypha and the Books of Jonah, Job, Esther, Ezekiel, and Daniel

Introduction

The stories of Tobit, Judith, Maccabees, and parts of Esther and Daniel (which includes Susanna) are relegated in the King James and other Protestant bibles to the Apocryphal books or Apocrypha: i.e., books which were not included in the original Hebrew scriptures because they were written after about 150 B.C., and they were not included by the Reformers for this and doctrinal reasons. They were, however, contained in the Septuagint, the Greek translation of the Old Testament, and St. Jerome, translating from Hebrew and Greek in the latter part of the fourth century, tentatively and with some reservations included them in his Vulgate, calling them "Aprocrypha": i.e., the "hidden away" or "withdrawn" books because they had been removed by scholars from public use. The very name Vulgate, incidentally, means "for common or public use."

The Apocryphal books have remained part of the Catholic canon and were reaffirmed by the Council of Trent in 1546. In Catholic usage they are not called "Apocrypha," a term reserved for non-canonical writings. The Apocryphal books undoubtedly contain some of the best stories in the Bible, besides throwing light on the struggle of the Jews between 515 B.C. and A.D. 70 to maintain their identity and way of life in the face of religious, political, and armed oppression.

Jonah

Jonah, the fifth of the Minor Prophets, probably came from Israel rather than from Judah and, unlike the quasi-fictional persona of this story, practiced as a prophet about 780 B.C. when Nineveh, "that great city," had not yet become the capital of the Assyrian empire and was no more than a provincial town. It was not till 705 B.C. that Sennacherib, the greatest of the Assyrian monarchs (who was to reduce Judah to a mere vassal state), made it his residence.

As to the great fish that swallowed Jonah, this is always supposed to have been a whale, but most species of whale can only swallow the microscopic organisms called plankton, which they sieve through their mouths. The only whale that could swallow a man is the sperm whale—which is not found in the Mediterranean. Could it have been a large shark? Possibly, but sharks have rows of sharp teeth and not much would have been left of Jonah by the time he reached the shark's inside—even if he could have existed there for three days and three nights.

If, then, we are forced to regard the story of Jonah as fantasy or parable, the question to ask is: what does it teach? Here interpretations differ, though there seems no doubt that it points to the necessity of repentance and to the universality of divine mercy (perhaps also to the divine sense of humor).

(Jonah 1:1-17, 2:1-10, 4:1-11)

YAHWEH's word came to Jonah the son of Amittai, bidding him, "Get yourself up and go to Nineveh, that great city, and cry out against it because the stench of its wickedness rises before me."

Jonah got up but only to escape from the presence of Yahweh, intending to flee to Tarshish. At Joppa he found a ship sailing to Tarshish, so he paid for a passage and settled himself down in the hold ready to leave for Tarshish—far from the Lord's presence.

Yahweh, however, sent a great wind to churn up the sea and raise such a storm that the ship was near to being battered to pieces. The sailors in their terror cried out to their gods, flinging the cargo into the sea to lighten the ship. But Jonah had gone into the bowels of the ship and there he lay—fast asleep. The captain went down to him. "What do you mean, sluggard!" he bellowed. "Get up and call on your God. Maybe he will think twice about letting us all drown."

The sailors, meanwhile, said to one another, "What we must do is draw lots to see who among us is causing this storm."

They drew their lots and the lot fell on Jonah.

"Now tell us," they said to him, "what have you done to

cause this havoc? What is your occupation? Where are you from, where are you going, and what is your nation?"

"I am a Jew," he replied to them. "I worship Yahweh, Lord God of heaven, who made the sea and the earth."

At this, the men were all the more anxious and they asked him, "Why have you done this? [That is, flee from the presence of Yahweh, about which he had already told them.] What can we do with you," they continued, "to make the sea calm?" for the sea was a seething caldron of billows.

"Pick me up," he said, "and throw me into the ocean. Then the sea will calm down for you, because I know that this storm has hit you only because of me."

The sailors nevertheless continued to row with all their strength to get back to dry land, but they could make no progress because the waves so buffeted and fought them. They too then cried to Yahweh, "Oh Lord, we beseech you, do not let us drown just because of this man's life, and do not blame us either if we let an innocent man drown."

At which they hoisted Jonah up and pitched him into the sea. At once the raging waves were quiet. The men were full of awe before the power of Yahweh. They offered him a sacrifice and swore their vows.

Meanwhile the Lord had made sure that a great fish was ready to gulp down Jonah, and inside the belly of that fish Jonah spent the next three days and three nights.

Jonah prayed to the Lord his God from the belly of the fish:

"I cried out in my affliction to Yahweh,
  and he heard me.
I cried out from the belly of hell,
  and Yahweh listened.
Lord, you had cast me into the deep
  and into the heart of the ocean.
The swamp of your sea was around me,
  and your wild waves billowed over me.
I said to myself: I am jettisoned
  far from your sight,
How shall I see again your holy temple?

Oh, the waters overwhelmed me, right to my soul.
The depths closed in on me
  and the seas buried my head.
I was dropped to the bottoms of mountains,
I was locked in earth's bottomless prisons.
Yet you lifted me up, high above perdition,
  O Lord my God!

After which the Lord spoke to the fish, and it spewed out Jonah on to dry land.

But the word of Yahweh reached Jonah a second time: "Get up and go to Nineveh, that great city," he said, "and proclaim in it the message that I tell you." So Jonah stirred himself and went to Nineveh as Yahweh bade him. But the expanse of the city of Nineveh was so great that to traverse it took three days, and Jonah had only begun to enter it at the end of the first day as he cried out, "Just forty more days, and Nineveh will be destroyed."

The people of Nineveh believed in God and they declared a fast and put on sackcloth, from the greatest to the least; and when the king of Nineveh heard of it, he deserted his throne, discarded his royal robes, and put on sackcloth and sat in ashes. Moreover, he had it proclaimed and broadcast all over Nineveh by royal and constitutional decree that neither man nor beast, ox nor sheep, should taste a morsel or drink a drop of water. Man and beast must be covered in sackcloth . . . "And let everyone cry mightily to God, and stop doing evil and turn from violence. Who knows but that God may change his mind and let his rage abate, and we be saved?"

When God saw their new behavior and that they had turned from their evil ways, his will to punish changed to a will of compassion and he did not do it.

But this was not to Jonah's taste. He was disgusted. He prayed a prayer of protest to the Lord: "Yahweh, this is precisely what I feared you'd do when I was back at home. That was why I fled to Tarshish. I knew full well that you are a soft and clement God, slow to anger, excessively kind and ready to forgive. So Lord, just take my life away. I'm better off dead than alive."

"Do you think you have good reason to be angry?" the Lord then asked.

At which Jonah simply plodded out of the city and squatted down at a spot on its east side. There he made a little shelter and sat in its shadow, waiting to see if anything would happen to Nineveh.

The Lord God then made a gourd grow, which trailed up over Jonah's head and shielded him in its shade. This gave him some comfort and Jonah was more than glad of that gourd. God, however, arranged for a worm to attack the gourd, and next morning it was shriveled. Then when the sun was high God blew a hot and blistering wind, and the sun beat down on the head of Jonah till he broiled in the heat and yearned for his life to end. "How much better off dead!" he groaned.

"Do you think you have reason to be angry because of the gourd?" God asked Jonah.

"Of course I have reason to be angry," he replied, "angry enough to die!"

"So you were sorry for the loss of your gourd," God went on, "which you did nothing either to produce or tend. It sprang up one night and in one night perished. Ought I not, then, to be sorry for Nineveh, that great city, where a hundred and twenty thousand living souls can't tell their right hand from their left? And what about all their animals?"

NOTES

1. Joppa, where Jonah embarked, is the modern Jaffa, which has become assimilated into the Israeli city of Tel Aviv. It was once under the control of the Phoenicians. As to Tarshish, nobody knows where that was: it could be as far away as Tartessus, northwest of Gibraltar, or as near as Cyprus.

2. Nineveh in Mesopotamia, situated on the east bank of the river Tigris, achieved the height of its fame during the seventh century B.C. However, it succumbed to the allied forces of the Babylonians and Medes in 612 B.C. Though the assertion that the expanse of the city was so great that it took Jonah three days to traverse it is undoubtedly another "fish story," modern excavations have shown that the walls of Nineveh were eight miles in circumference and enclosed an area of eighteen hundred acres. Perhaps too there were considerable surrounding suburbs.

3. The Hebrew for the plant that grew up and sheltered Jonah is *qiqayon*, which St. Jerome translated as ivy, though he did also suggest that it might be the castor-oil tree. The Septuagint has it as gourd (*Cucurbita pepo*). Both the latter are self-seeding and so fast growing that one can almost see them grow. The biblical account is not so farfetched as one might think. The seedling appears overnight and in a week or two is trailing or standing its large leaves over Jonah's head, where the original roofing has been burnt up. The plant does not suddenly die "the next day," but the day after the worm appears which eats through its main stem. Only a day would be needed in the hot sun for the whole plant to wither. The biblical account is elliptical and can be stretched to cover many days.

Tobit and Tobias

The setting is eighth century B.C. Nineveh, where a large number of Israelites found themselves exiled after the destruction of the Northern Kingdom of Israel by the Assyrians. The theme of the story is God's love for the pious and compassionate, whom he will always protect and heal.

Chapter 1 of Tobias consists of a eulogy on the piety, honesty, and kindness of Tobit in Nineveh, where he has settled with Anna, his wife and Tobias, his son. We are told how he keeps himself pure from idolatry, feeds the hungry, clothes the naked, and buries the dead. And now he has just returned to his home and possessions after a period of exile, when he had to flee from the Assyrian king Sennacherib, who hated the Israelites.

(Tobias 2:1-23, 3:1-25, 4:1-23, 5:1-28)

ONE day during a festival of the Lord, a fine banquet was prepared in Tobit's house, and he said to his son, "Go and bring in some of our own tribe, ones that fear God, to celebrate with us."

The young man went and came back with the news that a murdered Israelite lay out in the gutter. Tobit leapt up from the table leaving his dinner untouched and went out and quietly brought the dead body home, meaning after sundown to bury it secretly. So he hid the corpse, then mournfully and anxiously ate his dinner, recalling the words which the Lord spoke through the lips of the prophet Amos:

I will turn your feasts into mourning
And all your songs into dirges.

After sunset Tobit carried the dead man out and buried him. Whereupon his neighbors rounded on him, saying, "Once already you were nearly killed for doing this and only narrowly escaped death, and here you are burying dead again!"

Tobit nonetheless—more devoted to God than to the king—continued to carry away murdered Israelites, hide them in his house, and at midnight bury them. And one day, exhausted with burying, he came home, threw himself down by the wall, and slept. But during his slumber some bird droppings from a swallow's nest [up in the eaves] fell into his eyes, and its hot lime blinded him.

The Lord allowed this accident to happen so as to manifest to all generations Tobit's exemplary patience—as with holy Job. For despite the fact that he had served God from infancy and kept his commandments, he made no complaint against God for letting him suffer blindness. On the contrary, his devotion to God was unshaken and every day of his life he poured out his thanks. And just as sainted Job was disparaged by the local landowners, so was Tobit's life reduced to nothing by his own parents and family. "Where is your reward," they jeered, "for all that almsgiving and burying of the dead?"

But Tobit cut them short. "Don't talk like that," he said. "We are the children of saints and the life we look forward to is the life God gives to those whose faith in him never wavers."

Anna his wife went out every day to work as a weaver, bringing home for their livelihood whatever she could get. One day she was given a young goat and brought it home. When her husband heard it bleating, he exclaimed, "I hope it isn't stolen. If it is, take it right back to its owners. You know we cannot eat or touch anything that comes by theft."

"Well, since you've reduced us to nothing," his wife retorted angrily, "we just have to live by charity." And she went on nagging.

Tobit heaved a deep sigh and with tears in his eyes he prayed: "O Lord, all your judgments are just, and all your ways merciful, full of truth and soundness. And now Lord, think of me: overlook my sins, forget my transgressions and those of my parents before me. For we Israelites have not followed your commandments, and that is why we are handed over to be pillaged, made captives, and killed. That is why we have become a legend of catastrophe among the nations where you have scattered us. So, Lord, your condemnation of us is right because we have not behaved as you would have us, and we have not walked sincerely before you. Do with me, Lord, whatever you will, and commend my spirit to be received in peace, because it is better for me to die than live."

It so happened that on the very same day, Sarah the daughter of Raguel in the Median town of Rages, was jeered at by one of her father's maids because she had been given to seven husbands, and a most persistent demon by the name of Asmodeus had killed each one of them as he attempted to consummate the marriage. When Sarah reproved the maid for her impertinence, the girl sneered back, "Husband murderer! We aren't going to see any son or daughter of yours on this earth. Or will you kill me too, just as you've killed off seven husbands?"

The gibe made Sarah run upstairs to her bedroom, where for three days she ate nothing and drank nothing, but poured out her prayers with her tears, beseeching God to remove from her this disgrace. And on the third day she concluded her praying with this wonderful eulogy of the Lord.

"Blessed be your name, O God of our fathers,
You who change from anger to mercy,
You who forgive those in trouble
  if they but call on you.
Lord, to you I turn my face,
To you I direct my eyes.
That which I beg, Lord,
Is that you unchain from me the shackles of this curse,
  or else take me away out of this world.

You know, Lord, that I never lusted after a husband,
And have kept my soul clean from every prurient wish.
I never joined those who played with sex,
Or shared in frivolous doings.
A husband I did consent to take, yes,
But because of reverence to you,
Not because of any wanton desire of mine.
And either I was unworthy of them,
Or they perhaps unworthy of me—
If you were keeping me for some other man.
Your designs are beyond our ken,
But this we know:
That all who serve you, no matter what their trial,
Will see it end in triumph
  with every agony withdrawn
And every correction tempered with your mercy.
For you take no delight in our being lost:
You who follow every tempest with a calm,
And tears and sobbing with a shower of joy.
Let your name, O God of Israel, be blessed forever!"

Both these outpourings were heard by the Most High at the same time, and he dispatched his holy angel Raphael to heal them both: both these afflicted people whose prayers had reached the Lord together.

Tobit meanwhile, imagining that his prayer was heard and that he would die, called his son Tobias and said:

"Listen, dear son, to what I am going to tell you now and make it the cornerstone of your heart.

"When God takes my soul and you have buried my body, be loyal to your mother for the rest of her life. Never forget what she went through to conceive and give you birth. When she dies, bury her by my side.

"Every day of your life keep God in the forefront of your mind. Beware of sin and never transgress the commandments of the Lord our God.

"Give alms generously, and never turn away from the poorest of the poor, or God will turn away from you.

"Show whatever sympathy lies in your path to show. Give abundantly if you have abundance, but be no less diligent in giving a little if you have much less—and willingly. By doing so you will be storing up treasure against the day of need. Because alms are a salve against sin and a salve against death. Almsgiving keeps the soul from ever going down into darkness: it works like magic in the sight of the Most High God.

"Keep yourself, dear son, from fornication, and never succumb to the crime of being unfaithful to your wife.

"Let no pride ride high in your thought or speech, for pride is the source of all perdition.

"When a workman works for you, pay him his wages at once, and never delay in defraying the salaries of your servants.

"See that you never do to another what you would hate to have done to you.

"Share your food with the starving and the needy, and give your own clothes to those in rags.

"Set out your bread and wine for the funeral of a good man, but partake of nothing at the funeral of a scoundrel.

"Go to the wise always for advice. And bless God always, asking him to direct your footsteps and have your decisions in his keeping.

"Lastly there is this, my son: when you were still a child I lent ten talents of silver to Gabelus in the Median city of Rages, and I still have his note of hand. Arrange to go and see him and get back the loan in exchange for his note of hand. Have no fear, my boy, because though we may lead a poor life, we shall be blessed with many good things if we serve God and keep from all sin and follow the good."

Tobias, answering his father, said, "Everything you've told me, Father, I shall do, but how exactly I am to retrieve this loan, I have no idea. The man doesn't know me and I don't know him. What proof can I give him? Besides, I have no inkling of how to get there."

His father replied, "The note of hand which I possess will be enough. When you show him, he will pay you. Start at once. Hire a reliable man to go with you. I want you to get the money back before I die."

When Tobias left his father's presence, whom should he run into but a magnificent young man standing there as if he were waiting to begin the journey? Unaware that he was an angel of God—indeed, Raphael—Tobias greeted him with: "Where are you from, you fine young man?"

"From the children of Israel," he replied.

When Tobias asked him, "Do you know the way to the land of the Medes?" he answered, "I know it well. I have walked it by every conceivable route. I have even lodged with our friend Gabelus who lives in the Median city of Rages in the hills of Ecbatana."

"Wait a moment, please," Tobias said excitedly. "I must run and tell my father this."

Tobias hurried to his father and told him everything. His father, beside himself with wonder, wanted the young man to come to him. And he came.

"Be happy always!" the young man said in greeting.

"How can I be happy sitting in pitch darkness," Tobit replied, "with no chink of heaven's light."

"Have courage!" the young man answered. "God will cure you soon."

Then Tobit asked, "Can you escort my son to Gabelus in the Median city of Rages? I will pay you when you return."

"Yes, I shall escort your son there," said the angel, "and bring him safely home to you."

"Tell me, please," Tobit asked, "your family and your tribe?"

"Are you hiring me to go and find *my* family," smiled the angel, "or hiring me to escort your son? However, to set your mind at rest, I am Azariah son of the great Ananiah."

"Ah, that is indeed a noble line," Tobit commented. "Please forgive me for prying into your family."

"No matter," said the angel. "I shall conduct your boy safely and safely bring him home to you again."

"God speed your journey," Tobit said, "and may his angel walk by your side."

When everything was ready and their haversacks packed for the trip, Tobias said goodbye to his father and mother, and the two of them set off together. As soon as they had gone, his mother broke down in tears and sobbed: "You have knocked away the prop of our old age and sent him from us. Oh, how I wish that money you've sent him for had never existed! We were rich in our poverty as long as we had our son."

"Don't cry," Tobit comforted her, "our son will come back safely. You will see him again. It's my belief that God's good angel goes with him, making sure that everything works out well for him, so he'll come back to us with joy."

At these words, his mother stopped her crying and was quiet.

Tobias and the Angel Travel to Rages

As to the "large fish" that comes at Tobias out of the waters of the Tigris, the Greek, Latin, and Hebrew texts all have "fish," otherwise it might be tempting at first sight to translate the word as "crocodile," except that a crocodile would not "pant on dry land before Tobias' feet," as described in the Vulgate. But if a fish, what kind of fish? The only possibilities would seem to be sturgeon or pike, though sturgeon normally inhabit lakes, not rivers. My own guess is pike: a large, voracious fish that can measure up to four feet and which has the instincts of a shark and is certainly capable of attacking a bather. Pike are to be found in rivers throughout Europe and the Middle East. They are also excellent eating, as Tobias and the angel demonstrate.

Another problem is the word Γενυς (*genus*), which normally means under-jaw or simply mouth. St. Jerome, followed by everyone else, translates it as "gills," which I suppose is possible, so I have kept it.

It is interesting that Tobias' pet dog followed him, because the Hebrews in general did not think much of dogs, considering them chiefly as scavengers. We have to remember that this story is set in the region between the rivers Euphrates and Tigris, what we would now called Mesopotamia ("Between Two Rivers"), amid a culture far more ancient, sophisticated, and advanced than either Israel's or Judah's. This was where the dog (*Canis familiaris*), whose wild ancestor was the wolf (*Canis lupus*), apparently was first domesticated.

(Tobias 6:1-22)

SO the young man marched along, his dog at his heels and the angel with him. That first night they camped on the banks of the Tigris, but when Tobias went to wash his feet in the river, a huge pike plunged up out of the water ready to snap at the young man's feet, and Tobias screamed out in terror, "Help, sir, the creature's at me!"

"Grab it by the gills," the angel shouted, "and yank it on to the bank."

The young man took hold of the fish and dragged it on to dry land, where it thrashed and panted at his feet.

"Now clean out its inside," said the angel, "but keep the heart, gall, and liver: these are going to be useful medicines later." When Tobias had done what the angel told him, he roasted the rest of the fish. What they did not eat they salted for the future until they should reach the Median city of Rages.

When they resumed their journey and the two of them walked along, Tobias asked the angel, "Tell me, brother Azariah, what are the heart, liver and gall of the fish good for which you made me keep?"

"A piece of the heart or liver roasted over coals," the angel replied, "gives off a smoke which if inhaled drives out every kind of evil humor from man or woman, never to return. The gall makes a good ointment for eyes which have become opaque with blotches of white, which it completely cures."

When they had entered the land of Media and were not far from Ecbatana, the angel said to the young man, "Tobias, my boy."

"Yes, what?"

"Tonight we're going to stay with Raguel. You know, he's a relative of yours and has a daughter called Sarah, but no sons or any other daughter besides this Sarah. You are the next of kin, so have first claim on her together with his whole estate. The girl is not only beautiful but intelligent; and the father is a good-looking man too. You definitely ought to marry her. So listen to me, young man: I'm going to talk to the father about the girl tonight about making her your bride, and we can have the wedding before we leave Rages. Raguel can't refuse you, that I know, or give her to somebody else because according to Mosaic law you have first claim on her. So take good note, my boy, we'll talk to the father this very evening and you can start courting her at once."

"That's all very well, brother Azariah," Tobias replied, "but I hear that she's been given to seven husbands and they're all dead. What's more, all were killed on the bridal night itself just as they were about to consummate the marriage. Now, I'm the only son of my father and I'm frightened that the same thing will happen to me because this demon is obviously in love with the girl. He never hurts *her*, but hurts every man who tries to come near her. So naturally I'm afraid of dying too. It would shatter my father's and mother's life. They'd follow me to the grave weighed down by sorrow. Besides, there's no other son to bury them."

"Don't you remember your father's order," the angel replied, "that you had to choose a wife from your own tribe? So, my friend, stop fretting about this devil, because this very night the girl is going to be your wife. Besides, let me point out to you the sort of people the devil has power over. They're the ones who shut God out from their marriage and from their minds, and mindlessly go to it with all the lust of horse and mule. That's whom the devil has power over. But you, when you wed her, keep yourself chaste for three whole nights and give yourself over to praying with her.

"On that first night, put some of the liver and heart of the fish on the glowing charcoals of the incense burner. The fumes will reek in the devil's nostrils. He'll rush out and never come near her again.

"On the second night you become admitted into the august company of the holy Patriarchs. And on the third night you earn the blessed pledge of healthy offspring.

"After that third night, you may in all reverence take your virgin bride and deflower her: moved more by the love of children than by common lust, and so be an honor to Abraham with your sons."

* * *

Finally they arrived at Raguel's and Raguel received them with joy. Gazing at Tobias, he remarked to Edna his wife, "How like my cousin this young man is!"

After this observation he asked, "Where are you two youths from?"

"We're of the tribe of Nephtali exiled in Nineveh," they said.

"Then do you know my cousin Tobit?" Raguel asked.

"Of course!" they said.

Raguel began to extol the virtues of Tobit, but Raphael interrupted with: "Tobit, about whom you are speaking, is this young man's father."

Raguel went straight over to him and kissed him, his eyes wet with tears. As he hugged him he said in a sobbing voice, "Every blessing on you, my boy, because you are the son of a good and virtuous man." His wife Edna and their daughter Sarah were crying too.

After this exchange, Raguel ordered a sheep slaughtered and a banquet prepared. However, when the time came to sit down to dinner, Tobias said, "I'm not going to eat or drink here unless first you grant me my request and give me your daughter Sarah."

The words struck Raguel with a twinge of fear. He was all too conscious of what had happened to the seven previous husbands on their wedding nights and feared that the same fate awaited Tobias. Caught off his guard, he was dumb.

Then Raphael spoke up. "Don't be afraid to give Sarah to this man," he said. "Your daughter has been reserved for a husband who fears God. That is why none of the others could have her."

At last Raguel said, "I don't doubt that God has heard my prayers and been moved by my tears. I believe that he has made you come to me so that this young woman might be married to one of her own clan, according to the law of Moses. So I've made up my mind to give her to Tobias."

At which, taking his daughter's right hand and putting it in the right hand of Tobias, he pronounced: "May the God of Abraham, the God of Isaac, the God of Jacob be with you. May he join you together himself and fill you with his blessings."

Then calling Edna his wife to his side, he took writing materials and together they made out the certificate of marriage. Afterward, with gratitude in their hearts, they opened the festivities, and Raguel told Edna to get ready yet again the nuptial chamber. This she did, and, weeping, led her daughter Sarah into it. "Darling daughter, be brave," she said, "the Lord of heaven is going to make it up to you for all you've suffered."

NOTES

1. As to the birds whose droppings fall into Tobit's eyes, the Septuagint has them as sparrows, St. Jerome as swallows. After the accident, the Septuagint has Tobit say: "White blotches began to form in my eyes. The more the physicians treated them with various ointments, the more blotches appeared. In the end I was completely blind." (It looks as though a cataract had formed.)

2. The Vulgate gives Edna's name as Anna. There are many differences between the Vulgate and Septuagint account. I have selected from both.

Tobias and Sarah's Nuptial Night

(Tobias 8:1-24)

WHEN dinner was over they brought the young man in to Sarah, and Tobias, remembering the angel's instructions, took out of his bag the fish bits of heart and liver and put them on the glowing charcoal of the incense burner. The moment the reek of the fumes reached the demon's nostrils he fled—he fled right to the deserts of Upper Egypt with Raphael hot on his heels, where he tied him up on the spot.

Tobias had shut the bedroom door and, with their complete union in mind, he stood by the bed and said, "Get up, sweet cousin, we must pray for the Lord to bless us and keep us safe."

They began to pour our earnest prayers together. "Lord God of our fathers," Tobias uttered, "let sky and earth, let oceans, fountains and rivers, and all creation adore you. Adam you created, and gave him Eve to be his wife, his helper and supporter, because you said: 'It is not good for man to be alone.' And from these two all mankind has come. So now, Lord, I take this girl my cousin not through lust but in true fellowship."

And Sarah added, "Have mercy on us, O Lord, keep us in health and let us reach a ripe old age together."

"Amen, amen!" they said in chorus. Then they lay down to sleep the night side by side.

* * *

Meanwhile, at cockcrow, Raguel roused himself, called the servants, and went off with them to dig a grave, thinking to himself, "I have no guarantee that the awful fate that happened to the other husbands hasn't happened to Tobias too."

It was not till after the grave was dug and he had returned to his wife that he suggested, "Perhaps you ought to send one of the maids to see if Tobias is dead so I can bury him before daylight."

She sent one of her maids, who tiptoed into the bedroom and found them both safe and sound, sleeping side by side.

When she returned with the good news, Raguel and Edna fell on their knees in gratitude. "How we bless you, Lord God of Israel," they prayed, "for not letting things happen as we feared! You have shown us great kindness and freed us at last from the curse that harassed us. You have taken pity on two only children, and they will overwhelm you with their thanks that they are safe, and will sacrifice to you and make it known among all nations that you alone in all the earth are God."

Then Raguel quickly told his servants to fill in the pit they had dug, before it was daylight. To his wife he gave instructions for the preparation of a tremendous wedding feast. The cowherd was told to walk two plump oxen to the slaughter, as well as four rams. So the preparations began. Then he called Tobias and said to him:

"Swear you won't think of leaving for another fourteen days—fourteen days of festivity for your wedding. You'll eat and drink here with us and make your wife, my daughter, happy. I want you to take half of all that I own so that you can go back to your father a very successful young man. The other half will be yours on the death of my wife and me. Be full of gladness, my boy: I'm a father to you now, and Edna a mother. From now on we will always and forever be behind you and your bride."

After this, Tobias called Raphael (who he still thought was a man), and said to him, "Brother Azariah, I have a favor to ask. You've already given me so much that even if I made myself your slave it would never be a proper return. All the same, I ask you now to go with servants and beasts of burden to Gabelus at Rages in Media and give him back my father's note of hand in return for the money of the loan. Also, invite him to my wedding celebrations. You know my father's days are numbered and each day that I'm away is anguish to him. Yet you see how Raguel has committed me to stay and I can't refuse him."

Raphael, accordingly, went off to Rages, the Median city, taking with him four of Raguel's servants and two camels. There he met Gabelus, gave him his note of hand, and got back from him all the money. He also told him about Tobit's son Tobias, and pressed him to come to the wedding festivities.

Gabelus came, and as he entered Raguel's home he caught sight of Tobias sitting at a table. The young man leapt up and they kissed: Gabelus weeping and praising God.

"The God of Israel reward you," he exclaimed: "the goodly son of a goodly holy man—a man devoted to God and to the poor. May every blessing be showered upon you and your bride, and on your parents. I hope that you will see your children and your children's children, on and on, till the third and fourth generation: offspring supremely blessed by the God of Israel, who reigns forever."

They all shouted, "Amen! Amen!" then fell to the wedding feast. And this they began to enjoy in a spirit of pious glee.

NOTE

Gabelus belonged to the same clan as Tobias, and the two families had obviously been very close to each other in the days when Tobit lived in Rages as a prosperous favorite of the king.

Tobias' Parents at Home

(Tobias 10:1-13)

BECAUSE Tobias was constrained by his wedding to delay his return, his father Tobit began to worry. "What do you think is keeping him?" he fretted. "Why is he still there? Is Gabelus dead, do you think, and no one will give him the money?"

A great sadness came over Tobit and over his wife. They began to cry on each other's shoulders because there was no sign of their son at the time arranged. His mother, beside herself with weeping and quite unconsolable, sobbed, "My poor boy! Why oh why, did we ever send you on that senseless trip: you the light of our eyes, the prop of our old age, the hope of our future? All our riches were fixed in you. We ought never to have let you go."

"Hush now!" Tobit scolded. "Don't torture yourself so. Our son is safe. That man we sent him with is as solid as a rock."

But nothing could console her. Every day she ran out looking in all directions. She would go down every byroad hoping for the sight of him in the distance.

Meanwhile Raguel was pressing Tobias to stay on. "I'll send a message to your father telling him that you are safe and well," he said.

"But my father and mother are counting the days for my return," Tobias protested. "By now they'll be sunk in misery."

Raguel pressed him further, inducing him with every kind of reason, and when Tobias would not hear of it, he finally let Sarah go and he signed away to Tobias half his estate—which included men and women servants, cattle, camels, pigs,* and a handsome sum of money. He sent him off a whole and happy man. Mother and father kissed their daughter goodbye and let her depart, urging her to be good to her father and mother-in-law, to care for her family, take charge of the home, and conduct herself without reproach.

Tobias' Homecoming

(Tobias 11:1-21, 12:1-22, 14:1-17)

ON the eleventh day after setting out they came to Charan, which is halfway to Nineveh, and Raphael said to Tobias, "Tobias, my young friend, you cannot be sure in what state your father is, so I suggest that you and I go on ahead to make things ready for your wife and all the rest, including the livestock. . . . Don't forget to have the gall of the fish with you," he added. "We shall need it."

So the two of them hurried on together, the dog faithfully at their heels. Anna, sitting by the roadside in her usual watchplace on top of a hill and scanning the distance, suddenly saw somebody coming from afar and presently she saw that it was her son. She ran shouting to her husband, "Our son is back, our son! And the man he went out with is with him."

*Probably kept only as scavengers.

Raphael had already told Tobias, "The moment you step over the threshold, adore the Lord your God and thank him. Then go straight to your father and kiss him. Have the fish gall ready and smear some of it over his eyes. It'll make them smart, but a film of whitish skin will begin to pull away from the pupils, and I promise you that your father's eyes will open to heaven's daylight and the sight of you."

The dog had already run ahead, wagging his tail and fawning as if it was he that had brought the news. Anna too had run forward, and now she fell into her son's embrace, crying out, "Oh my child, I'm actually seeing you! I don't mind dying now."

His blind father had got to his feet and was stumbling toward the door when Tobias ran forward and caught him. Immediately he smeared some of the fish gall on Tobit's eyes. "Don't worry, Father, it's all right!" he encouraged.

Soon a white skin, like the inside skin of an egg, began to droop from his pupils, which he was able to pull away. Then he threw his arms around his son, exclaiming, "I can see you, my boy: the light of my eyes! Praised be God, praised be his great name, praised be all the holy angels, because he chastised me and, look, now I see—Tobias, my precious son!"

Seven days later, Tobias' wife Sarah arrived safe and sound, together with the rest of the household, including cattle, camels, his wife's handsome dowry, and his own generous bequest from Gabelus. There arrived too a couple of other relatives of the family, Achior and Nabath, who joined in the rejoicing and the congratulations for all that God had done to them. Tobias then related to his parents the unceasing acts of kindness he had received from his escort.

The festivities went on for seven days. At the end of which Tobit called his son Tobias and said to him, "Son, what can we possibly give this good man that went with you?"

"No payment would be enough," Tobias replied. "What possible price could we put on all he's done? He took me out, he brought me safely home again; he gave me a bride, chased away her evil spirit, brought gladness to her parents, saved me from a voracious pike, got the money back from Gabelus, made you see the light of heaven once more. We are too overwhelmed by all the good he has done us. What reward could ever match it all? I would suggest, Father, that you beg him to accept one half of everything I've gained."

Father and son then called Raphael aside. They started by begging him to accept half of everything that Tobias had brought home, but he very quietly declined, preaching them this little sermon:

"Bless the God of heaven, glorify him in the sight of all, because he has been so kind to you. Maybe to keep the secrets of a king is desirable, but with God to blaze forth his works is better. Prayer, fasting, and the giving of alms are worth more than a mint of gold and call down the divine mercy of life everlasting. But the wicked, lost in their sins, are enemies of their own soul.

"Now let me discover the truth to you. In those days when you used to pray with tears, and leave your dinner uneaten to hide the dead in your house by day and bury them at night, it was I that proffered your prayers straight to the Almighty. And because God was pleased with you, it was then necessary for you to be proved by hardship. After which the Lord sent me to heal you and to save your son's wife Sarah from the evil spirit. For I am the Archangel Raphael, who stands before the Lord."

These words filled them with consternation, and in their panic they threw themselves to the floor. "Peace to you! Don't be afraid," the angel reassured them. "While I was with you I was there by God's will. Bless him and praise him. Though I seemed to eat and drink with you, my real meat and drink was not tangible, not visible to human eyes. . . . Now the time has come for me to go back to him who sent me. So bless our God and proclaim him everywhere and all his wondrous works."

Hardly had Raphael spoken these words when he was taken from their sight and they could see him no more. They were still prostrate on the ground, and there they stayed for full three hours, stunned by the sheer need to lie prone in reverent awe. Then they arose telling everyone the wonders God had done.

Tobit lived another forty years after getting back his sight. He lived to see the children of his grandchildren, and died at the age of one hundred and two. He was buried with pomp at Nineveh.

Tobit was fifty-six when he lost his eyes, and sixty when he got them back again. All the rest of his life was joy, and when he came to his peaceful end his love of God had immeasurably grown. At the hour of his death he called his son Tobias and Tobias' children around him—seven strapping sons, with their offspring too—and he said to them:

"The destruction of Nineveh is imminent, and the Lord's prophecy must be fulfilled. When this happens, our scattered exiles from the land of Israel will return to it. All that region which is now a wasteland will be filled with people. The House of God, now burnt to the ground, will be set up again, and the pious will once more flock there. Even the pagans will forsake their idols and come to Jerusalem to live. The kings of the earth shall rejoice there in homage to the King of Israel.

"My dear children, hear these counsels of your father: serve the Lord in truth, wanting always his will. Train your children to be honest and generous to the poor and full of the presence of God, blessing him at all times to their utmost power.

"Now, dear children, listen carefully: do not stay here. As soon as you have buried your mother by my side in a single grave, don't delay to hurry away from here, for I see the iniquity of this place beckoning to its destruction."

So it was. After the death of his mother, Tobias with his wife, children, and grandchildren left Nineveh and went back to his father and mother-in-law in Rages. He found them in good health at a ripe old age, and he took care of them till he closed their eyes in death. Raguel's full inheritance then fell to him, and he saw his children and children's children to the fifth generation. He lived to the age of one hundred and seventeen, pious to the end; and before he died he had the satisfaction of seeing Nineveh destroyed. They buried him with joy.

His descendants in all their generations led good and reverent lives, amiable both to God and man and to all who dwelt around them.

NOTE

The order of events as Tobias steps across his father's threshold is curiously different in the Vulgate from the Septuagint. It goes thus: first, family weeping, then general thanksgiving, followed by all sitting down, and finally the anointing: the healing taking presumably about half an hour.

Judith

This is a story from the Apocrypha, but included by St. Jerome in his Vulgate. It was written probably during the era of the Maccabees about 160 B.C. and intended as a quasi-fictional tale of encouragement for the Jews in their struggle against their Seleucid oppressors. (The Seleucids were a powerful Hellenistic line of kings that conquered much of the Middle East after the death of Alexander the Great in 323 B.C. They did their best to force a Greek culture on the Jews.)

The name Judith means "Jewess." Like the story of Deborah (with affinities to those of Esther and Susanna) it is an attempt on the part of the biblical writers to inject a note of feminism into their predominantly male, even chauvinistic, culture.

The first three chapters describe how Nebuchadnezzar, king of the Assyrians, with his powerful general, Holofernes, not only overcomes Arphaxad, king of Persia, but overruns the cities of Syria and Mesopotamia and is now poised to strike at Israel.

(Judith 4:1-9, 5:1-29, 6:1-13, 7:1-16, 23-25, 8:2-17, 28-34, 9:1-6, 12-15, 10:1-20, 11:1-21, 12:1-20, 13:1-23, 27-30, 14:1-18, 15:1-15, 16:1-11, 24-30)

WHEN the Israelites who lived in the land of Judah heard what threatened, they were terrified, convinced that Holofernes would do the same to Jerusalem as he had done to the other cities and their shrines. So they deployed troops in and around Samaria, and laid up grain and provisions against a war.

Eliakim the high priest sent dispatches to the whole region of Esdraelon, facing the great plain of Dothan, as well as to every spot where there was easy entry, urging the defenders to hold all the mountain approaches to Jerusalem, and to post sentries at all the passes.

The Israelites did what the Lord's high priest told them, and both men and women called desperately on the Lord, mortifying themselves by prayer and fasting. The priests put on haircloths and made even the little children prostrate themselves in the Lord's temple, where the altars too were draped in haircloth. A universal appeal went up to the Lord God of Israel that he not let their children become victims, their wives be carried off, their cities destroyed, their shrines profaned, and they a laughingstock to the heathens.

When it was reported to Holofernes the commander-in-chief of the Assyrian army that the Israelites were preparing to resist him and had closed the mountain passes, he flew into an ungovernable rage and summoned a meeting of the rulers of Moab and Ammon.

"Tell me about these people who are holding the mountain passes," he demanded. "What sort of cities do they have? Are they large? Is it a numerous people? What is their military strength and who is their commander? Why are they the only nation in the east that has not come out to parley with us and accept us peacefully?"

At this point, Achior, general of the Ammonites, replied, "Sir, if I may make so bold, I can tell you everything about this people who inhabit the hills. I can tell you their complete history. They stem from the Chaldeans, but long ago emigrated to Mesopotamia, being unwilling to worship the gods of the Chaldeans (though their ancestors), whose religion they abandoned because it was based on the worship of many gods. They believed in one God of heaven and that he commanded them to depart from Mesopotamia and live in Charan. But when that land was struck by famine they moved into Egypt and within four hundred years were so numerous that they could hardly be counted.

"When the king of Egypt began to oppress them and turn them into slaves to make bricks for his cities, they cried out to their Lord and he struck the whole of Egypt with a series of plagues.

"At which the Egyptians expelled them, but as soon as the plagues were over the Egyptians had second thoughts and wanted to go after them and bring them back into being their slaves.

"It was then that the God of heaven opened up the sea to the fleeing Israelites, dividing it into two walls of water between which they walked dryshod. But when the Egyptians chased after them, the sea closed in over them, and not one of them lived to tell the tale.

"Then, after the Israelites had emerged from the Red Sea, they dwelt in the deserts of Mount Sinai, which had never been inhabited by man because they were uninhabitable.

Brackish springs became sweet for them to drink, and for forty years they were fed from heaven. Moreover, at such times as they must give battle, they fought without bow and arrow, without shield and sword, yet their God fought for them and they won. Nobody was able to conquer them except when they were unfaithful to their God Yahweh. Every time they deserted their own God and took up with another, he handed them over to sword, rapine, and disgrace. And every time that they repented having abandoned the worship of their God, he, the God of heaven, gave them power again to stand their ground. This was the way they overturned the kingdoms of the Chanaanites, the Jebusites, the Hittites, the Hevites, and the Amorites, as well as the mighty ones of Heshbon, taking over their lands and occupying their towns.

"So long as they kept from sin in the sight of their God, everything went well with them because their God abhorred iniquity. Just some years ago when they fell away from the path God wanted them to follow, they were decimated in their wars with other nations, and large numbers of them were carted off to alien lands.

"At the moment, however, they have returned to their own God after having been scattered, and have come together. They command these mountains and have repossessed Jerusalem, where their sanctuaries are. So, sir, the thing to do is to watch for a time when they are committing sins against their God and then attack them. Then their God will let them fall into your hands and you can do what you like with them. On the other hand, if they are doing nothing wrong in the eyes of their God, it is quite useless to fight them because their God will defend them and make fools of us in front of everybody."

When Achior had finished speaking, there was a swell of condemnation from the ranks of Holofernes' officers. They would have liked to kill him on the spot. "Who is this upstart," they demanded, "who dares to suggest that the Israelites are a match for Nebuchadnezzar and his armies: these people with no arms, no proper troops, and quite untutored in the arts of war? We'll show this Achior what a liar he is. We'll march into those mountains and when we've captured their chief warriors we'll put him to the sword with the whole bunch of them. That will show all the nations that the only god around here is Nebuchadnezzar and no other."

After the officers had made their speeches, Holofernes himself—now in a towering rage—turned to Achior and stormed, "Yes, indeed, since you have dared to tell us that Israel is protected by their God, I'll have to show you that Nebuchadnezzar is the only god here. And when we slaughter the Israelites as one man, you too will be slaughtered by our Assyrians and you will go down with the rest of Israel. My soldiers' swords will thrust through your sides and when you are stabbed to the ground among the wounded Israelites, you will learn—though at your last gasp—that Nebuchadnezzar is lord of the world. Now if you really believe that what you say will come true, why the downcast head, why the ashen face? But just to make quite clear to you that you are going to suffer along with these people, I'm herding you together with them from this moment onward; and when they receive the thrashing they deserve, you will be given the same treatment."

Holofernes then commanded his guards to seize Achior, march him to Bethulia, and deposit him into the arms of the Israelites. Holofernes' soldiers, however, after traversing the plains with Achior, were attacked near the foothills by Israelite slingers, so they turned off the mountain road, bound Achior hand and foot to a tree, and, leaving him all trussed up, went back to their master.

The Israelites came down from the hills, found him, loosed him, and took him to Bethulia, where they stood him among an assembly of the people and asked him how it was that he came to be tied up and abandoned by the Assyrians. (The leaders of Israel at that time were Ozias son of Micah—the tribe of Simeon—and Charmi, also called Gothoniel.)

So Achior related to the elders and the citizens everything that he had told Holofernes and how the response of Holofernes' officers was to want to kill him. Also, how Holofernes himself, in a great rage, had ordered him to be handed over to the Israelites so that when he crushed them he might have the pleasure of seeing him tortured to death for having said that the God of heaven would protect Israel.

When the assembly broke up, Ozias invited Achior to a big dinner at his home, at which the elders were also guests. Since the long fast was over, they all enjoyed themselves. After which the people were called together and they prayed through the night in the temple, begging the help of the God of Israel.

The next day Holofernes gave the order to his troops to march on Bethulia. The army consisted of a hundred and twenty thousand infantry, twenty-two thousand cavalry, as well as all the recruits who had been taken from various provincial cities and trained.

This entire well-equipped force advanced against the Israelites through the defile that leads to Bethulia. The army stretched in width from Dothan to Belma, and in length from Bethulia to Keramon above Esdraelon. When the Israelites caught sight of the sheer numbers, they threw themselves on the ground, strewed ashes on their heads, and sent up a chorus of prayer to the God of Israel, pleading for mercy. Then they posted fully armed contingents night and day to guard the various passes.

Meanwhile Holofernes in the course of reconnoitering discovered the watercourse that supplied the Israelites with water and which ran through an aqueduct on the south side of the city. This he ordered to be cut. However, there were other wells not far from the walls, where the inhabitants were detected stealing out to draw water—just enough to take the edge off their thirst—and the Ammonite-Moabite spies reported this to Holofernes.

"You know that the Israelites don't rely on their spears and arrows," they told him, "but on the mountains that fence them in and on the ravines and precipices which are a natural protection. So if you want to overcome them without having to fight, station guards all around their wells so that they can't draw any water. This way you can destroy them without lifting a sword, or at the very least wear them down till they willingly give up their city, which at the moment they imagine because of the mountains to be impregnable."

Holofernes was glad of this information and he surrounded every well with a force of four hundred men. After twenty days of this supervision, the cisterns and reservoirs on which the Bethulians depended gave out and nowhere in the city was there a drop of water—not even a day's ration (water had been doled out to the people each day).

Then men and women, youths and children, set up a clamor around Ozias.

"God be our judge," they shouted. "You've ruined our chances. You should have negotiated with the Assyrians. Now God has sold us into their power and there is no one to come to our aid. We've reached rock bottom and are visibly dying of thirst. Call an assembly of the whole city so we can put to the vote our surrendering to Holofernes. It is better to be prisoners and live to praise the Lord than to die ignominiously after having had to watch our wives and children die before our eyes."

Ozias stood up, the tears streaming down his cheeks. "Don't give up, my friends," he pleaded. "Keep going at least for the next five days. Perhaps the Lord will come to our rescue. It may well be that he is no longer angry with us and is ready to magnify his own name. If after five days no help comes, we will do what you propose."

There was a young widow named Judith and she got to hear of this. Her husband had been Manasseh, who died during the barley harvest. (He was overseeing the sheaf binders out in the fields with the sun beating down on his head and he died of sunstroke in Bethulia, his hometown, where he was buried with his forefathers.) Judith had now been a widow for three years and six months. She had made herself a private apartment in the upper part of the house, and there she secluded herself with her maids. She wore a haircloth next to her skin and fasted every day except on Sabbaths, new moons, and the festivals of Israel.

Judith was exceedingly beautiful. Also, her husband had left her a rich woman, with a large staff of servants, an extensive estate, herds of cattle, and flocks of sheep. She was well known to all as dedicated to the Lord. No one had a bad word to say of her.

Now when Judith heard that Ozias had pledged to surrender the city to the Assyrians in five days, she asked the two elders Chabri and Charmi to come and see her. When they came she said to them, "What is this rumor I hear that Ozias has agreed to surrender the city to the Assyrians if no help comes within five days? Who are you to lay down conditions to God? This is hardly the way to draw down his mercy but rather his annoyance and wrath. To suit your pleasure you have given the Lord a deadline for his help. Since the Lord is abundantly patient, let us apologize and tearfully ask his forgiveness. God doesn't issue threats the way a man does, or go into a rage like us human beings. I suggest we humble ourselves before him and in that spirit of humility ask him in tears to show us—should he deign to—his loving kindness. Let us hope that the effrontery of our presumption will be matched by the beauty of our humility."

Ozias and the elders answered her, "Everything you say is true. We cannot fault you in a single word, and we ask you to pray for us because you are a pious and holy woman."

Judith went on, "As you know, whatever I have been able to say comes from God. So now please tell me if the plan I have conceived is of God too, and if it is, pray that God may strengthen my design. . . . Tonight you are to stand by the gates as I go out of the city with my maid, and you are to pray that the Lord will within five days—as you have proposed—come to the rescue of his people Israel. I ask you not to inquire into what I am about. Do nothing till you hear from me, but continue in your prayers for me to the Lord our God."

"Go in peace!" Ozias and the other leaders answered. "May the Lord be with you in your purpose to bring vengeance on our enemies." Then they turned and went away.

When they were gone, Judith walked into her oratory, clothed herself in haircloth, sprinkled ashes on her head and, falling prostrate before the Lord, she uttered this prayer:

"O Lord, God of my forefather Simeon, who put a sword in his hand, to avenge those heathens who violated the virginity of his sister Dinah, [Genesis 34], and gave over their wives as booty and their daughters as captives, and all their goods to be divided among your zealous people, come to my help now—my God, my God!—to me a widow. Often in the past you have exerted yourself for us and have always triumphed, because your designs are always well devised, well prepared, and well carried out. So now look down on the hosts of the Assyrians as you deigned to look down once on the hosts of the Egyptians in full armor trusting in their chariots, their horsemen, their enormous army as they pursued your children. Bring to pass that Holofernes' pride is severed with his own sword. Let him be snared in the net of his own lecherous gaze, and charmed by the syllables from my lips. Give me a steady mind that disdains him, and a strong heart that destroys him. This will be a monumental victory for your name: that he should fall by the hand of a woman."

When she had finished her prayers she rose from the floor, where she had been prostrate before the Lord, called her maid, went downstairs, took off her garments of haircloth, and put away her widow's weeds.

Then she bathed, anointed herself with the most alluring perfumes, coiled her hair in a coif, and arrayed herself in the lovely clothes she used to wear when her husband was alive. Then she put a bonnet on her head, sandals on her feet, and bedecked herself in bracelets, earrings, rings—all her best jewelry—and she wore a lily.

Because all this adornment was prompted by virtue, not vanity, the Lord doubled her beauty. Indeed, he made her so beautiful that she appeared in men's eyes as incomparably lovely.

She gave her maid a small skin of wine to carry and a flagon of olive oil, as well as barley griddle cakes, dried figs, bread, and cheese. When they reached the city gates they found Ozias and the two elders, Chabri and Charmi, were waiting for them, who when their eyes fell on her they were stunned by her beauty.

They asked no questions but simply let her pass as they prayed: "May the God of our fathers fill you with grace and strengthen your resolve. May all Jerusalem be proud of you and your name be written among the saints!"

"So be it! So be it!" they all responded.

Judith then asked for the gates to be opened so that she could proceed on her mission. The young men were ordered to open the gates, which they did, and Judith with a prayer on her lips passed out of the gates—she and her maid.

It was daybreak when she went down the hill, and the Assyrian sentries stopped and challenged her. "Where have you come from and where are you going?" they demanded.

"I am a Hebrew woman," she replied, "but I am running away from the Hebrews because I know that they are going to be fodder for your swords. They turned their backs on you instead of peaceably giving themselves up and trusting to your mercy. So I said to myself, 'I'll present myself to the general Holofernes. I'll disclose their secrets to him and show him how he can take them without the loss of a single man.' "

The sentries respectfully listened, staring at her dazzled and awed by her beauty. Then they said, "You have saved your life by this decision to go to our commander. You can be quite sure that when you stand before him he will treat you kindly. In fact, he will find you irresistible."

They escorted her to Holofernes' tent, explaining to him her mission. And the moment he set eyes on her he was trapped. His officers remarked, "How can we despise the Hebrews when their women are so beautiful? We ought to call off this fight just for the sake of the women."

Judith took one look at Holofernes, throned as he was under a canopy of woven purple and gold set with emeralds and precious stones, then she abased herself to the ground. But Holofernes' aides immediately raised her up at their general's command.

Then Holofernes addressed her, "Be reassured, madam,"

he said, "I have never hurt anyone who came willingly to serve Nebuchadnezzar, lord of the world. If only your people had not turned their backs on me I would never have lifted a spear against them. Now they've brought things on themselves. But tell me exactly why you have left them and come here into safety—because, my dear, you *are* safe, not only tonight but always."

Judith answered, "My lord, if you will deign to hear what your humble handmaid has to tell you and will follow it, God will grant you a great triumph. For it is certain that our God is so offended by my people's sins that he is giving them up. And because the Israelites know this, they are scared. Besides which, they have been struck by famine and are so short of water that they're already half dead. Indeed, they are planning to slaughter their animals to drink their blood. Even the sacred provender of grain, wine, and oil which is consecrated and expressly forbidden by the Lord for them to touch, they are prosposing to fall upon. Because they are doing all this they are certainly going to be destroyed, and it is this certainty which has made me get away from them. The Lord has sent me to let you know these things. For I, your humble servant, even here am in touch with God and pray to him. He will tell me exactly when he intends to punish them, and I shall come and let you know. Oh, I hope to see you parading through the heart of Jerusalem, with your enemies scattered like a flock without a shepherd, and not a dog so much as barking at you."

Judith's speech gratified Holofernes and his officers, and they admired her intelligence. "Where in the world is there a woman to match her for good looks and good sense?" they remarked to one another.

Holofernes said to her, "Your God has done a great thing to send you here and put your people in our hands. If he will really grant me the triumph that you promise, he shall be my God too, and you will be a great lady at the court of Nebuchadnezzar and renowned throughout the world."

Then Holofernes ordered them to conduct her to the emporium where all his treasures were displayed, after which they were commanded to offer her the full range of dishes from his table.

At which Judith said to him, "I must tell you, sir, that I cannot eat any of the food which you have kindly ordered to be put before me. For me it would be a sin. So I shall eat what I have brought with me."

"But, my dear," said Holofernes, "what are we to do when you've got through all that?"

"I promise you, my lord," she returned, "God will have accomplished his purpose through me long before I have used up my provisions."

As his servants escorted her to the tent that he had reserved for her, she asked him if she could be free to go every evening and morning to pray. He told his orderlies that for the next three days she must be allowed to come in and out as she pleased to adore her God.

So in the evening she would wander down to the vale of Bethulia, bathe in a spring and, as she climbed up again, pray to the Lord God of Israel to direct her toward the deliverance of his people. She would then return to her tent and eat her evening meal and keep her chastity intact.

On the fourth day Holofernes threw a banquet for his entire staff and he said to Bagoas, his eunuch, "Do go and coax that Hebrew damsel to come and live with me." (Incidentally, it is considered a disgrace among Assyrians for a woman to ignore a man's approach.) So Bagoas went to see Judith and said to her, "My dear beautiful girl, don't be afraid of accepting my lord's honorable invitation to eat and drink and have a good time with him. Indeed, this will lead to your becoming a fine Assyrian court lady at the palace of King Nebuchadnezzar."

"Who am I," Judith replied, "to say nay to my lord Holofernes? I will do whatever he wants, whatever he thinks best. Indeed, for the rest of my life, to please him will be my chief delight."

She went then and began to dress herself up, adorning herself with the utmost feminine art. Her maid walked before her, and spread out for her in front of Holofernes the sheepskin rugs which Bagoas had obtained for her daily use to lie on during meals, which was the custom.

So Judith came into the presence of Holofernes, and he at once was smitten to the heart—on flame with desire for her.

"Drink," he said, "and prepare to enjoy yourself."

"Of course, sir," she said, "because today my life is going to be magnified beyond anything since I was born."

Then in front of him she began to eat and drink the food which her maid had prepared for her, while Holofernes, wildly gloating on her presence, put away a great deal of wine: more wine than he had ever drunk before in a single day.

* * *

It was already late when he sent the servants to their quarters. Bagoas had closed the entrance to the general's pavilion and gone on his way. Judith was now alone in the tent, with Holofernes sprawled out on his bed in sodden slumber. (Everybody there had overdrunk.) She told her maid to stand on guard outside the tent, while she herself stood by Holofernes' bed, the tears streaming down her face and her lips moving in silent supplication.

"Give me strength, O Lord God of Israel," she pleaded. "In this hour of need, come to help my desperate act to save Jerusalem, your own special city, and make me succeed in my design, which I believe is your design."

With the words still on lips, she crept to the bedpost by Holofernes' head and unstrapped his short-sword that hung tied to the bedpost. Coming right up to the bed she took hold of Holofernes by the hair as she whispered, "O Lord God, give me strength in this moment of need!"

She lifted the sword and came down twice on his neck, completely severing the head, which she then wrapped in the curtains which hung from the bed posters. The headless body she rolled off the bed onto the floor.

When she had done all this, she went outside and gave the head to her maid to put into her haversack. Then the two of them simply walked out of the camp as if on their usual way to pray. They walked out, descended to the valley, and at length arrived at their own city gates.

Judith shouted up to the watchmen on the ramparts: "Open the gates! Open! God is with us and has shown his power in Israel."

They recognized her voice and [as soon as the gates were opened] they ran off to tell the elders of the city. A throng of people raced to meet her, from the greatest to the very least. They had given up hope that she would ever come back. All the lamps were lighted as people pressed around her and she mounted a platform and commanded silence. When there was quiet she called out: "Praised be our Lord God, who has not abandoned those who put their hope in him. He has used me to fulfill his mercy: that mercy which he promised the house of Israel. By my hand this very night he has slain the enemy of his people."

Saying which, she pulled out the head of Holofernes from her sack and displayed it to them.

"Look," she shouted, "the head of Holofernes, commander of the Assyrian army! Here is the curtain of the bed in which he lay in a drunken swoon and where God slew him by the hand of a woman. God's angel, by his grace, has been my guardian all the time I was there until my journey home. I was kept safe from sin with him and return to you unshamed, full of joy for this victory, for my escape, and your deliverance."

Then Achior the Ammonite was called for. He came hurrying out of the house of Ozias, and Judith said to him: "The God of Israel, who as you rightly testified avenges himself on his enemies, has this night cut off the heathen's head by this good right hand of mine. And if you want the evidence, here it is: Holofernes' head! In pride and contempt he dismissed the God of Israel and threatened you with death when you warned him, sneering that he'd have your flanks skewered with sword thrusts when the Israelites were his captives."

At the sight of Holofernes' head Achior fainted. His terror toppled him flat. Presently, however, he recovered and knelt at Judith's feet full of awe. (Later, convinced by the power of Israel's God, he was converted, had himself circumcised, and became an Israelite, which his descendants are to this day.)

At Judith's suggestion, they hung Holofernes' head at daybreak from the ramparts, and all the able-bodied men in full armor marched out of the city.

When the Assyrian lookouts saw what was happening, they ran to alert Holofernes' officers. The captains and tribunes and chief officers of the Assyrian army gathered outside the commander's pavilion and made a noise to rouse him, not daring to wake him directly by calling him, for it was unthinkable for anyone to knock or enter the bedroom of the commander-in-chief of the Assyrian army.

Eventually they said to the chamberlains, "Go in and wake him. Tell him that the mice have come out of their holes to challenge us."

Bagoas then went into the anteroom of his chamber, stood behind the curtain, and clapped his hands, thinking he was still in bed with Judith. He listened but there was dead quiet, so he took a step closer and parted the curtains. There he saw the headless body of Holofernes lying on the floor weltering in his own blood. He shrieked, broke into tears, tore at his clothes. Then he rushed over to Judith's tent and not finding her inside, ran back to tell the people.

"A lone Hebrew woman," he panted, "has wrecked the plans of Nebuchadnezzar king of Assyria. Holofernes is lying dead on the ground and there is no head on him."

When the military men of the Assyrian army heard this, fear gripped them. They ripped their clothes in despair and dread. A great wail went up from the whole Assyrian camp. The news of Holofernes' beheading made the troops dither with apprehension. Their only thought was to save themselves by flight. The soldiers hardly spoke to one another, but with hung heads full of misgiving they prepared to escape from the Hebrews, who, as they could hear, were advancing in full armor against them. So they dispersed in all directions across fields and through paths into the hills.

The Israelites, seeing this rout begin, pursued with a great hue and cry and bugles blaring. And because the Assyrian unity was shattered they fled higgledy-piggledy, while the closely knit Israelite forces found it easy to pick them off and destroy them.

Ozias sent messengers to alert the rest of Israel, and every province, every city, armed the flower of its young manhood and sent them to join the rout. They pursued the Assyrians with the edge of the sword right to their borders.

Meanwhile, the army in Bethulia swept into the Assyrian camp and looted all that the Assyrians had left behind, returning in triumph loaded with booty: not merely things but cattle and livestock beyond number, so much so that from the common foot-soldier to general everyone was rich.

Joachim the high priest traveled with his elders from Jerusalem to Bethulia to congratulate Judith.

"You are the luster of Jerusalem," they told her, "the joy of Israel and the glory of our people."

It took thirty days to sort out the spoils from the Assyrians. Whatever was proved to be the property of Holofernes—in gold, silver, clothes, precious stones, and furniture—they gave to Judith, and the people carried it to her.

There was universal rejoicing. Matrons, maidens, and youths played harps and musical instruments, and Judith sang this canticle of praise. [The first eleven verses out of a total of twenty-one.]

"Start up a tune to the Lord with your timbrels,
Sing out to him loudly with your cymbals:
Sing a new melody, sing a new psalm,
Extol and call on his glorious name.
For the Lord puts an end to all warring:
   And so he has saved us.

He encamped in the midst of his people, loosed them
From the grip of their foes. The Assyrian came

Down from the mountains, surged from the north,
Soaked up the streams with his hordes; smothered
The valleys with his horse.

But God the omnipotent struck him, felled him
By the hands of a woman: the mighty one fell
Not by the hands of our brave young men,
Nor by the stroke of a son of a Titan—
The tall stroke of a giant—no,
Judith, Merai's* daughter, made him
Limp with her beauty.

She put away her widow's mourning,
Assumed the garments of gladness and gave
Joy to the children of Israel.
In a fresh new linen gown she trapped him,
Ravished his eye with the gleam of her sandals,
Made him prisoner by her beauty.
Then with a short-sword severed his head."

For three months the people celebrated this victory with Judith, rejoicing at the shrines. After which they all returned to their homes.

Judith remained a great name in Bethulia. Her chastity, moreover, matched her bravery, because for the rest of her life she kept herself pure and never married again after the death of husband, Manasseh.

On festivals she would show herself and be acclaimed by the crowds; and she lived in her husband's house till her death at the age of a hundred and five, having granted her faithful maid her freedom. She was buried beside her husband in Bethulia and was mourned for seven days. During the remainder of her life, none dared harass Israel; nor did anyone for years afterward.

NOTES

1. Dothan, ten miles north of Samaria-Sebaste and on the edge of the plain of Esdraelon, is the present Tell Dotha. It was near here that Joseph and his brothers grazed their father's flocks (Genesis 37:17).

2. Heshbon was a powerful Moabite city near the present Jordanian village of Hesban. It was first captured by the Ammonites and then by the Israelites in their first battle across the Jordan.

3. The word "eunuch" can perhaps be rendered as chamberlain,

*The third son of Jacob's son Levi (Genesis 46:11)

steward, right-hand man, or even first secretary. Eunuchs (castrated males) were originally intended to supervise the harems, but they often became rich and important in their own right. Hence the supercilious and patronizing tone of Bagoas toward Judith.

Esther

The Book of Esther, known to Jews as the Megillah and read in the synagogues on the feast of Purim, dates probably from what is called the later Persian period (400 to 322 B.C.) though it may have been written as late as 130 B.C.

The story it tells has all the suspense, changes of fortune, and climax of a novella: one with some shaky history behind it, because though the general background is historically plausible, there is no mention outside the Bible of Esther herself or of any of the key figures.

In some ways the story of Esther is the obverse of the story of Ruth. The two together complete the picture of what it was like to be a Jew in a pagan world. Both Ruth and Esther marry outside their race. Ruth, a Moabite, marries a Jew and becomes the great-grandmother of David and therefore a progenitor of Christ (thus putting Jewry in debt to the Gentiles); whereas Esther, a Jew, marries a Gentile and is able to save the Jews from being exterminated in a fierce anti-Semitic pogrom. However, the tone of the two stories is very different. For the charm and tenderness of Ruth with its rural scene we are given the vicious political world of ambition and vindictiveness. And, as has been pointed out by more than one biblical scholar, Esther is the one book in the Bible where you will not find the word "God."

The setting of the story is Susa, or Shushan, the capital of the Persian empire, where some centuries later in 324 B.C. Alexander the Great was to marry Statira, daughter of Darius III, at a massive wedding celebration at which eighty of his officers took Persian brides. Ahasuerus, the Persian king in this story, is probably Xerxes I, who ruled the empire from 486 to 466 B.C. It was this Xerxes who attempted to conquer Greece and was defeated at the famous battles of Marathon and Salamis. He was a quirky man, grandiose but also childish.

The unfortunate Haman in this quasi-mythological tale was a descendant of that same Amalekite king Agag whom Saul spared contrary to Yahweh's injunctions and whom the prophet Samuel hewed to pieces (1 Samuel 15:32-33). Since Mordecai was of the same tribe as Saul, possibly even a descendant, the whole account would have an ironic echo for the well-read Jew.

(Esther 1:1-22, 2:1-23, 3:1-15, 4:1-17, 5:1-14, 6:1-14, 7:1-10, 8:1-17, 9:1-9, 22-23)

ONCE upon a time, in the third year of the reign of King Ahasuerus, who reigned over a hundred and twenty-seven countries from India to Ethiopia, and sat on his throne in Susa, capital of his empire, he arranged a great festival that lasted a hundred and eighty days.

To it he invited the royal princes, his chief ministers, Median and Persian nobility, and the provincial kings and governors of his far-flung realm. The purpose was to impress them all with the wide sway of his power and the wealth and glory of his empire.

When the festival was over, he gave an elaborate party for the entire staff of his palace at Susa, from the greatest to the least. The festivities (lasting seven days,) were held in the court of the royal gardens with their surrounding park, which the king himself had planted and supervised.

The place was festooned with green, blue, and violet hangings fastened with ribbons of linen and purple silk to rings of ivory set into marble columns. Gilded and silver couches were set out neatly on a floor paved with porphyry and colored marbles in wonderful designs.

The guests drank from golden goblets, and the dishes followed one another is unending profusion. Wine of the best vintage was in abundance—quite worthy of a king's munificence. No one, however, was compelled to drink. The king had arranged a wine steward for every table, instructed to pour out generously but only what was asked for.

Queen Vashti at the same time threw a banquet for the women of King Ahasuerus' palace; and on the seventh day, when the king was more than merry from all the wine he had drunk, he gave an order to seven of his eununchs—Methuman, Biztha, Harbona, Bigtha, Abagtha, Zethar, and Carkas—to go and fetch Queen Vashti, arrayed in her crown, into the royal presence. He wanted to display to all the dignitaries and people how beautiful she was (and she *was* extremely beautiful).

The queen, however, refused to gratify the royal whim conveyed to her by seven eunuchs. At which the king lost his temper and flew into a rage. He asked his counselors (always hovering near the royal presence ready with information and advice) what punishment should be meted out to Queen Vashti for refusing to honor the king's summons as brought to her by the seven eunuchs.

(These counselors were Persian nobles, their names being: Carshena, Shethar, Admatha, Tarshish, Meres, Marsena, and Memucan—all experts in Persian law and tradition, besides being favorites of the king.)

Memucan's answer before king, court, and ministers was this: "Sire, Vashti, the queen, has not only snubbed your majesty but all the rest of us in your realm: both high officials and simple citizens. Because once the other wives get to hear of the queen's behavior, they will look down on their husbands and say, 'King Ahasuerus summoned Queen Vashti into his presence and she refused.' The wives of governors and officials throughout Persia will take her as their model and begin to slight their husbands. The king therefore is quite justified in his anger. May I suggest, sire, that you issue an edict couched in the correct Persian and Median terms (which are inviolable) banishing Queen Vashti from your presence so that one better than she can take her place. Once this is published through every province of your wide empire, wives everywhere of both great and small will treat their husbands with respect."

This made sound sense to king and court, and he followed Memucan's counsel. He sent official letters to every province of his kingdom in the various local tongues enjoining that husbands everywhere assert their authority and be masters in their own house.

After a time the king forgot about his anger at Queen Vashti and could remember only that she was gone and how he had judged her. His aides and ministers decided to distract him by parading beautiful young women before him. "We'll send out a beauty scout through all the provinces," they said, "to search out lovely young women and bring them back to Susa for the king to look at. We'll lodge them in the royal harem in the care of Hegai the eunuch, who has charge of all the king's women. They can be given whatever they need in the way of clothes and jewelry to appear before the king, and the one that captivates him most will be queen instead of Vashti."

This idea pleased the king and he ordered it to be carried out.

Now in the palace at Susa there was a Jew named Mordecai (son of Jair, son of Shimei, son of Kish, a Benjaminite), who had been carried away from Jerusalem at the time that Nebuchadnezzar king of Babylon had taken Jeconiah king of Judah prisoner too. Mordecai had brought up his uncle's daughter Esther, an extremely beautiful girl who had lost both her parents. With mother and father dead, Mordecai raised her as his own daughter.

When the king's directive was made known, many beautiful girls were brought to Susa and put in the care of Hegai the eunuch, and Esther too found herself among the young women under his custody.

Hegai liked her at once and she became his favorite. He could hardly wait to let her deck herself out with the new jewelry and with her own ornaments. Moreover, he gave her seven maids to attend her, as well as the best rooms in the harem.

Every day Mordecai would walk up and down the courtyard of the harem where the girls where housed, wondering how she was and what kind of future lay in store for her. The procedure with the girls was this. Twelve months were spent grooming each of them before she was taken to the king. For the first six months her skin was regularly anointed with oil of myrrh, and for the next six months with a variety of perfumes and unguents.

When the girl's turn came to spend the night with the king, she was given whatever jewelry or accessory she asked for and then proceeded from the harem to the king's bedchamber. She would be inducted there in the evening and leave the next morning, to be lodged permanently in the second harem under the charge of the eunuch Shaashgaz, who looked after the royal concubines. She would not be called to the king again unless he had especially enjoyed her and asked for her by name.

In due course the day arrived for Esther—daughter of Abihail, the uncle of Mordecai, who had adopted her as his own child—to be presented to the king. Disdaining all ornament except what Hegai the eunuch pressed upon her, she nevertheless appeared to all who saw her ravishing beyond description. And so, in the month of January (known as the month of Tebeth), she was brought into the bedchamber of King Ahasuerus in the seventh year of his reign. The result was that he fell in love with her, forgot all about the other women, and set the royal crown upon her head, making her queen instead of Vashti.

He gave orders for a magnificent wedding feast for Esther, to which all his ministers and friends, and the leading subjects of his realm were invited. The nuptial celebrations lasted seven days. The king relieved the provinces of taxes and dispensed largesse in kingly style.

Esther had still not divulged her race and country, obeying Mordecai in this as she had in everything since she was a little girl. Mordecai himself meanwhile took to haunting the entrance of the palace—where he practically lived. And one day he overheard two of the king's eunuchs, Bigthan and Teresh (who sat in the porter's lodge at the first gate), plotting out of pique to assassinate the king. He went off immediately and reported this to Esther, the queen, who told the king what he had overheard. There was an investigation, the plot was exposed, and the two eunuchs were strung up on a gibbet. (This whole matter is recorded in "The Annals of the King.")

Some time later, King Ahasuerus promoted one of his officials—a certain Haman, son of Hammedatha, a descendant of Agag—to be his prime minister. Consequently, all the royal personnel at the palace gates saluted and bowed to him, as they had been so directed by the king—all, that is, except Mordecai, who refused to salute or bow.

This made the other members of the royal household at the gates ask him, "Why are you the only one who doesn't comply with the king's command?"

After pressing him several times on this point and receiving no answer, they reported the matter to Haman and waited to see if Mordecai would abide by his decision. When Haman himself verified the fact that Mordecai gave him no salute or sign of respect, he became very angry. So angry that, having heard that Mordecai was a Jew, he thought not only of destroying Mordecai, he wanted to exterminate the whole race of Jews in Ahasuerus' kingdom.

Accordingly, in April (called Nisan) of the twelfth year of Ahaseurus' reign, lots were cast into an urn (the Hebrew "phur") in Haman's presence to find out what day should be fixed for the extermination of the Jews. The month that came up was next February (called Adar).

Then Haman made the following report to the king: "There exists in your kingdom, sire, scattered through all the provinces, a race of people that has its own laws and religion and takes no notice of your royal ordinances. Your majesty must be well aware of the danger to your kingdom of allowing these people to go on like this with impunity. I suggest that you give the word for their extermination. I myself am ready to contribute ten thousand talents into the royal coffers for the purpose."

The king took the signet ring off his finger and handed it to Haman son of Hammedatha, descendant of Agag, saying, "Forget about the money. Keep it yourself. And as for these people, do whatever you think best."

On April 13th the king's secretaries were summoned, and Haman dictated a letter for dispatch to all the governors and officials of every province and principality throughout the empire. The letter, in the name of Ahasuerus, translated into every appropriate tongue and stamped with the royal signet ring, was sent by special courier to every province of the land. It decreed that on the 28th day of February of the following year, all Jews, young and old—whether women or children—were to be killed and their property distributed as spoils. Such was the purport of the letter. All provinces were alerted to be ready for the day.

The couriers lost no time in transmitting the royal mandate. In Susa itself the edict was at once hung up, where amid panic in the city the king and Haman sat down to carouse.

When Mordecai heard the news he rent his clothes in despair, put on sackcloth and ashes, and went out into the streets crying out with a loud and bitter cry: "A race massacre so undeserved!" He came and stood outside the palace gates (nobody in sackcloth and ashes would be allowed inside them), pouring out his anguish.

In every province and town where the king's decree had reached, there was mourning among the Jews: there was fasting, weeping, and lamentation. Many lay out in sackcloth and ashes. When Esther's maids and eunuchs came and told her what was happening, the news tore her apart. She sent clothes out to Mordecai to replace his sackcloth, but he would have none of it. So she called for Hatach, the eunuch the king had appointed as her personal attendant, and told him to go to Mordecai and find out more details.

Hatach went. Mordecai was still in the street outside the

palace. He related the whole story of how Haman had offered a contribution into the royal exchequer just to have the Jews destroyed. Mordecai also gave him a copy of the edict which was hanging up on display in Susa to show the queen, and he admonished her to go to the king and plead for her people.

Hardly had Hatach returned and made his report when Esther sent him out again, this time with the message to Mordecai: "Everyone knows, ministers and subjects all over the empire, that any person, man or woman, intruding into the royal presence without being summoned, courts instant death, unless the king holds out the golden scepter of clemency. But he hasn't called me for a whole month now, so how can I approach him?"

Mordecai immediately sent this reply: "Don't imagine that your life is any safer than the rest of us Jews just because you're in the palace. If you keep quiet now, a time will come when the Jews are saved some other way and then you and your relatives will be destroyed. Perhaps this is the very reason that fate has put you in the palace at a time like this."

Esther's message then to Mordecai was: "Go and assemble all the Jews you can find in Susa and fast for me. Eat nothing for three days and three nights, and I and my maids will fast with you. Then I shall go to the king, forbidden though it is; and if I perish, I perish."

Mordecai went on his way and did everything that Esther asked him.

Three days later Esther put on her full regalia and stood waiting in the inner court of the palace opposite the throne room, where the king himself was seated on his throne.

The appearance of Esther his queen standing in the inner court was a pleasing sight, and he held out the golden scepter toward her. She stepped forward and kissed the head of the scepter.

"Queen Esther," he said, "What would you have me do? What is your request? Were it half my kingdom, it would be yours."

"Sire, if it please your majesty," she said, "I have come to ask you and Haman to a banquet that I have arranged for you today."

The king immediately gave orders that Haman should be told to get himself ready for Esther's dinner, and that afternoon he and Haman came to the banquet which Esther had arranged. And after the king had well drunk he turned to Esther and said, "My dear, you haven't told me what you want. Whatever it is, even if you asked me for half my kingdom, it's yours."

"Sire, I do have a request," she replied: "I do have a petition. And if it please your majesty to consider it, will you and Haman come again to dinner tomorrow and I will tell you all about it."

Haman left the palace that day a happy man, quite full of himself, but when he passed Mordecai sitting by the palace gate and not only not rising and bowing but not budging an inch, his heart curdled with rage. However, he kept it hidden, and when he got home he called together his friends and his wife Zeresh and harangued them on how rich he was, how many children he had, how the king had showered distinctions on him and advanced him beyond every official and subject in the kingdom. And what's more," he went on, "Queen Esther invited no one else but me to her banquet for the king. She has even asked the king and me again tomorrow. . . . And yet—and yet, when I see that wretched Jew Mordecai squatting by the palace gate, all this is nothing."

"In that case, this is what we suggest," his wife and the others said. "Have a gigantic gallows built, seventy-five feet high, and tomorrow morning ask the king to hang Mordecai on it. Then you and the king can go off to the banquet with nothing to spoil your fun."

Haman thought this an excellent idea and forthwith ordered the gallows to be erected.

That night the king found it difficult to sleep, and he asked for the historical records to be read to him. When they came to the place which tells how Mordecai uncovered the treason of the two eunuchs Bigtha and Teresh, who were plotting to assassinate the king, the king interrupted:

"What reward or honor was ever given to Mordecai for his loyalty?" he asked.

"None at all," his attendants told him.

"Who is that in the outer court?" the king suddenly asked.

It so happened that Haman had just entered the outer court of the palace, come to get the king to send Mordecai to the gallows he had set up. And when his courtiers answered, "It's Haman standing out there," the king said, "Tell him to come in."

As soon as Haman had entered, the king asked him, "If there was someone the king really wanted to honor, how would he do it?"

Haman, thinking to himself: "Of course he must mean me. Whom else would he want to honor?" replied to the king, "The man the king really wants to honor should be clothed in king's clothing, mounted on the king's horse, and crowned with the king's crown. The first prince of the realm should robe him, hold his horse, and lead him through the streets proclaiming, 'This is how the king exalts a man he wants to honor.' "

"Perfect!" said the king to Haman. "Go and get some of my royal clothes and my horse, and do exactly what you have just described to Mordecai the Jew who sits by the palace gates. Be careful not to leave an item out."

So Haman had to go and dress up Mordecai in royal attire, mount him on the king's horse and walk along beside him proclaiming, "This is how the king exalts a man he wants to honor."

After which Mordecai returned to his place by the palace gate, while Haman hurried home hiding his face in mortification and shame. When he told his wife Zeresh and his friends what had happened, they and his wife shrewdly answered, "Once you've begun to give ground to the Jews, which this Mordecai appears to be, it's useless to resist."

They were still discussing this when the king's aides arrived and hustled Haman off to Esther's banquet.

So the king and Haman went in to banquet with the queen. And once again when the king was warm with wine he said to her, "Esther, my queen, are you never going to tell me your request? Whatever it is, I grant it—even if it's half my kingdom."

"Then, sire," she said, "if it please your majesty, I ask for my life and the life of my people. For we are under sentence of death. We are to be slaughtered—dismantled. If it were merely being sold into slavery, the disaster might be bearable and I would grieve in silence, but there is an enemy at large who is using the king for his own cruelty."

"And who is that?" asked King Ahasuerus. "Who would dare presume so much?"

"Haman, sitting right here," Esther replied. "He is our antagonist, our archenemy."

At this Haman blanched with fear, unable to face the king and queen. The king, quivering with rage, stomped off from the dinner table through the palace garden into the park, as Haman too got to his feet and began to importune Esther for his life, for he clearly saw that the king had doomed him.

When the king returned to the dining hall he found that

Haman had tripped over the couch Esther reclined on and lay sprawled there.

"What!" he roared, "would he even rape the queen in my own house?"

The words had scarcely left the king's lips when the death pall was draped over Haman's head. Then Harbonah, one of the eunuchs who attended the king, observed, "You know, sire, Haman has built a gallows seventy-five feet high in his yard for Mordecai, the man who saved your life."

"Hang him on it," said the king.

So they hanged Haman on the gallows he had erected for Mordecai. Then the king was pacified.

That same day King Ahasuerus gave over Haman's house to Queen Esther, and Mordecai was presented to the king, Esther having told him that they were related to each other. The king took off the ring which he had got back from Haman and placed it on Mordecai's finger, thus making him prime minister, and Esther put him in charge of Haman's estate.

Now once again she fell down at the king's feet, begging him with tears to annul the whole of Haman's vicious plot against the Jews. And once again the king held out the golden scepter to her, and Esther arose and stood before the king.

"If it please your majesty," she said, "and if you wish to please *me* and do not find my request too difficult, I ask you to abrogate the decree devised by Haman to exterminate the Jews inside your kingdom. How can I endure the slaughter of my own people? How can I watch my family being destroyed?"

King Ahasuerus' reply to Esther and to Mordecai the Jew was this: "I have given Haman's estate to Esther, and I have hanged Haman on a gibbet, all because he laid his hands upon the Jews. So you go ahead: compose whatsoever declaration you think best and send it out in my name, stamped with the seal of the king's ring, so that it becomes a royal decree which nothing can reverse."

Immediately the king's secretaries were called and in the month of July on the 23rd day, the document that Mordecai had drafted for the Jews was dispatched to all deputies, officials, and governors of the hundred and twenty-seven provinces stretching from India to Ethiopia. The people of every province and race were addressed in their own language, written in the characters they understood: this included Hebrew.

Copies of the decree, sent out in the king's name and sealed with his signet ring, were carried posthaste by couriers mounted on the swiftest horses, bred from the king's own stables. What the decree said was this: the Jews in every city were called to unite and stand up for their lives. They were to destroy, slay, plunder, and cause to perish whatsoever power or people came against them, not sparing women, children, or property. The day singled out for this act of vengeance was the 28th day of February (which is the month of Adar).

Copies of this edict were to be broadcast in every province and principality throughout the empire alerting the Jews to retaliate against their adversaries. So the messages were carried with all speed on mule and camel, hastened by the king's command. Mordecai himself went from the palace resplendent in princely robes of blue and white, with a cloak of purple silk and a golden diadem on his head. The city streets of Susa were thronged with cheering Jews beside themselves with joy, on whom a new sun seemed to have risen.

As the king's decree reached each province and city, there were celebrations, parties, banquets, and holidays. What is more, several of the other ethnic groups joined in the Jewish festivities and themselves became Jews: prompted no doubt by a certain awe of the Jews that now struck them.

So on the 28th day of February (which as we have said is called Adar), the day the king's two decrees took effect and the day the Jews were to have been destroyed in a bloodbath, they turned the tables on their enemies in a reverse massacre. They gathered themselves together in town and country throughout the provinces ready to retaliate with venom against any who attacked them. But no one tried because the Jews inspired such fear. Morever, the governors of the provinces and all their deputies and officials were now on the side of the Jews out of fear of Mordecai. For Mordecai was a mighty man at the king's court and his fame had spread: indeed, was daily spreading through every corner of the empire.

So the Jews began their own massacre, doing to their enemies what their enemies would have done to them. In Susa alone they slaughtered five hundred men, including the ten sons of Haman son of Hammedatha descendant of Agag. These sons were: Parshandatha, Dalphon, Aspatha, Poratha,

Adalia, Aridatha, Parmashta, Arisai, Aridai, and Vaisatha. They killed these men but did not take their property.

By evening a list of the slain in Susa was brought to the king and he exclaimed to the queen, "The Jews have killed five hundred men in the city of Susa, as well as Haman's ten sons. How many do you think they have killed in the rest of the country? Can I do any more for you? Just say the word and it shall be done."

"Sire, if it please you," she answered, "allow the Jews in Susa to repeat tomorrow what they have done today. Also, please hang up the bodies of Haman's ten sons on gibbets."

The king commanded both these proposals to be put into effect. A further announcement was posted up in Susa, and the ten bodies of the sons of Haman impaled on gibbets. That was on the 14th day of the month of Adar, when the Jews mustered again and slew another three hundred men, but did not take their property.

Meanwhile, the Jews in the provinces, who also had united to stand for their lives, killed a total of seventy-five thousand, but again kept their hands off their property.

So it was that in the provincial towns and villages the 28th day of February—i.e., the thirteenth day of the month of Adar—was the day of slaughter, and on the 14th they laid off, rested, and celebrated. But in Susa the Jews mobilized and slaughtered on both the 13th and 14th day of Adar, and therefore held their celebrations and parties on the 15th. In either case the holiday became known as the Feast of Purim, that is, "of lots," because *pur* is the Persian for a lot thrown into an urn. The feast commemorates the days that the Jews revenged themselves on their enemies and turned distress and lamentation into gladness and rejoicing. These were to be days of celebration and merriment when people send presents to one another and give alms to the poor.

NOTES

1. The Medes were a people closely akin to the Persians. At one time they had been a great empire with their capital at Ecbatana, north of the Persian Gulf. They took part with the Chaldeans (Babylonians) in the overthrow of the Assyrian empire, only to be overthrown in turn by Cyrus the Great of Persia in 549 B.C. and become incorporated into Persia.

2. Myrrh (*Commiphora myrrha*), with whose oil Esther was anointed, is a woody shrub not native to Palestine but found in Arabia and Ethiopia. The congealed gum which exuded from incisions in its branches was rendered into perfumes and ointments. Myrrh was not only a cosmetic for the living but a balm for the dead.

3. Ten thousand talents, the sum that Haman offers the king, is difficult to compute in modern terms. The Living Bible comes up with $20,000,000. If Haman had been that rich he would have been king himself. My own estimate is roughly $360,500—rich enough!

4. Though the ancient Israelites tended to eat dinner in the evening, about sunset, the Persians, Babylonians, and Greek were more likely to have their main meal at about 3 P.M., followed by a long siesta.

5. Verse 7:4, which I give as: ". . . there is an enemy at large who is using the king for his cruelty" is ambiguous in all versions. The Septuagint has: "But this monster is not worthy of your royal patronage." The Vulgate gives it as: "whose cruelties redound on the king." The Hebrew text: "Nothing will make up for the loss that the persecutor will cause the king."

The Story of Susanna

The Vulgate includes this masterly story in its canon, but in the Protestant versions of the Bible it is relegated to the Apocrypha. Though the locale of the story is not revealed, the time and setting are Babylon during the Exile, when a large Jewish community was twice carried away from Jerusalem (597 and 586 B.C.) by King Nebuchadnezzar and settled by him in Chaldea (i.e., Babylon). There they became so successful that most of them never returned to Jerusalem when the Exile was over in 538 B.C.

The young prophet Daniel lived at the court of Nebuchadnezzar, but that is several other stories.

(Daniel 13:1-64)

THERE was a man in Babylon called Joakim, married to Hilkiah's daughter Susanna: a very beautiful and God-fearing young woman who had been brought up by her devout parents according to the law of Moses.

Joakim was a wealthy man and he had a garden near his house. He was held in such respect by the Jews that they often came to consult him.

Now that year there were appointed as judges two elders whom these words of the Lord aptly fit: "Wickedness has come out of Babylon: wickedness in the very judges who are supposed to direct the people." These two men frequented the house of Joakim to hear the cases that litigants brought to them.

When everybody left at noon Susanna would go for a stroll in her husband's garden, and the two old men would watch her going into the garden every day and they began to lust for her, completely ignoring their conscience and turning their eyes away from heaven and from all right reason. Both of them were wounded by passion for her, but each kept his burning itch to enjoy her to himself—too ashamed to declare it.

Every day they used to watch for her eagerly. Then one day they said to each other, "It's time to go home for lunch," and off they went separately. But each turned back, so they ran into each other again. At which, after a question or two, each confessed his passion. So they decided jointly to look for a time when they could be with her alone.

A day came when they were waiting for the right moment and Susanna went into the garden as usual with just two of her maids, having decided to bathe, for it was a hot day. Nobody else was there but the two old men who had hidden themselves and were watching her. Susanna said to her maids, "Go and get me soap and my anointing oil, and shut the garden doors while I bathe."

The maids did as they were told. They shut the garden doors and went out by a back door to fetch what she had told them to, quite unaware that the elders were hidden inside the garden.

The moment the maids had gone the two old men jumped up and ran toward her. "Listen," they whispered, "the garden doors are shut and no one can see us. We are in love with you. So yield to our desire and lie with us. If you don't, we'll give evidence that you dismissed your maids because a young man was with you."

Susanna gasped, "Oh, I'm cornered! If I do this thing, it's the death of me; and if I don't, you have me trapped. But it is better for me to fall into your hands without giving in to you than to sin against the Lord."

Saying which, Susanna gave a scream as the old men too shouted out against her. And one of them ran to the garden door and opened it. The house servants, hearing the shouts coming from the garden, rushed in by the back door to see what was the matter, and when they heard the old men's accusations they were shocked. Nothing like that had ever been said of Susanna.

Next day when the people assembled at Joakim's house, the two elders were there seething with venom against Susanna, whom they had marked down for death. They publicly demanded that Susanna the daughter of Hilkiah and wife of Joakim be summoned. She was sent for and came with her parents, her children, and her relatives. Because of Susanna's exquisite beauty, the two lecherous old men ordered her to take her veil off (for she was veiled)* because they wanted to leer at her beauty. Susanna's friends and family wept to see this humiliation.

Then the two elders stood up in the center of the assembly and laid their hands on Susanna's head, as she—in tears—looked up to heaven, putting all her hope in the Lord.

The old men then began their indictment: "As we were walking alone in the garden, this woman came in with two maids, whom she dismissed after ordering them to shut the garden doors. Then out from cover stepped a young man, and he lay with her. The two of us, seeing this abomination from a corner of the garden, ran toward them. They were locked together. We couldn't catch the fellow—he was too strong for us and flung open the garden doors and bolted—but we grabbed the woman here and demanded who the young man was. Of course, she refused to tell us. This is our testimony."

Everybody in the courtroom believed them. They were elders, after all, and judges of the people. So Susanna was condemned to death. "O eternal God," she cried out, "you know all secrets, know everything even before it happens, you know too that I am convicted on false evidence and must die though I am innocent of the crime that these two monsters have maliciously fabricated."

The Lord heard her prayer and as she was being led to execution he stirred the heart of a youth named Daniel, who shouted out, "I will have no part in the murder of this woman."

Everybody turned toward him. "Explain what you mean," they clamored.

Standing where he was, he replied, "You sons of Israel, are you such fools that without a proper examination of the evidence you condemn a daughter of Israel? I demand a retrial. The evidence is false."

Everyone hurried back into court, and the old men said sarcastically to Daniel, "You'd better come and sit with us judges, seeing that God has bestowed on you the distinction of old age."

*Babylonian women were veiled in public.

Daniel said to the assembly, "Keep these two apart. I mean to cross-examine them separately."

When they were separated he called one of them over and said to him, "You ancient hypocrite, hardened in sin! All your other crimes will now come to light: your false verdicts, your condemnation of the innocent, your letting the guilty go free—as if the Lord had never said, 'The innocent and just you must not kill.' . . . Very well, if you saw her, tell me this: under what tree did you see them together?"

"Under a mastic tree," the man replied.

"Liar!" exclaimed Daniel. "This will cost you your head. God's angel is waiting for the nod to cut you in two."

Putting him on one side, he ordered the other elder to come forward. "You Canaan heathen!" he said, "no son of Judah! Beauty has led you astray, twisted your conscience. You may have got away with it with girls from Israel who yielded to you out of fear, but not this daughter of Judah. *She* would have nothing to do with your devilry. . . . Now then, tell me under what tree you saw them locked together?"

"Under a holm oak," the old man replied.

"Oh, excellent lie! That will cost your head too. The Lord's angel can't wait to cut you in two and blot you out."

There was a cheer from the whole assembly, blessing God for saving those who put their trust in him. Then they surged forward against the two elders so completely convicted by Daniel of perjury from their own mouths, and they inflicted on them the very punishment which they had viciously plotted for another. Innocent blood was not spilt that day, and the old men, according to the law of Moses, were put to death.

Hilkiah and his wife thanked God for such a daughter as Susanna (as did Joakim her husband and all her relatives), who was acquitted of all crime.

Daniel from that day onward became a name to conjure with among the people.

NOTE

Mastic tree (*Pistacia lentisca*): not so much a tree as a shrubby bush native to Palestine and Egypt. Also known as the balm tree, whose twigs and branches exude a resinous sap that is turned into balm.

Job

The Book of Job, written sometime between the seventh and fifth centuries B.C., is a dramatic poem whose theme is the trial of faith and the problem of evil. In the treatment of these, all simplistic answers and truisms are held up to scorn. Holy Job is made the mouthpiece of every stock objection to the existence of a God who cares. The wicked prosper, the poor are downtrodden, the guiltless suffer, and Job, in a seemingly sadistic spree on the part of Yahweh (who has made a bet with Satan), is rewarded for his blameless life with a litany of horrors.

Job eventually breaks down and delivers a diatribe against the Almighty so incalcitrant that it would satisfy the most diehard atheist. Then, after an endless set-to between Job and his three "comforters" (those who know all the answers), the answer is given: there is no answer. At least, the answer rests in the unfathomable nature of the Divine Being, in whom all seeming evil has a dynamic place and is ultimately resolved.

It cannot be denied that, at first sight, the denouement of Job's confrontation with Yahweh is both theologically and dramatically a disappointment. The facile deus ex machina ending seems to be tacked on, regardless of the fact that it virtually contradicts Yahweh's assertion that Job has spoken foolishly. Moreover, nowhere does Yahweh deal with the issue which Job poses. We are simply thrown back on the primacy of faith: a faith which exacts an agony of will and anguish of the spirit. Indeed, the subtitle of the Book of Job could well be: "Journey from Despair to Hope," for it speaks with a desperate beauty of that journey and that ordeal which every human being sometime in life must face.

The entire sequence of passages in the Book of Job is a masterpiece not only of Hebrew writing but of all literature. However, let it be said, the text in all versions, whether Hebrew, Greek, or Latin, so bristles with perplexities that even the experienced scholar is hard put to iron out some of the meanings. I have leaned heavily on The Authorized Version, The Anchor Bible, The Jerusalem Bible, and The Living Bible.

My personal recommendation is that this whole section (apart from the prose prologue and epilogue) be read aloud.

Otherwise, being poetry, the impetus of its language, and therefore its full message, may be largely missed.

What follows is roughly one third of the book of Job.

(Job: selections from all chapters)

THERE was a man in the land of Uz whose name was Job, and that man was perfect and upright. He feared God and shunned evil. Seven sons and three daughters were born to him. As to property, he owned seven thousand sheep, three thousand camels, five hundred yoke of oxen, and five hundred milking asses, as well as a very great household. He was indeed a man of consequence among the people of the East.

His sons took turns in giving banquets in their houses, inviting always their three sisters to come and eat and drink with them. When the time of these festivities was over, Job would always send for them to make them spiritual again, rising early and sacrificing burnt offerings for each of them. "For perhaps," he would say, "my sons have sinned in their hearts and offended God." This he did continually.

One day the Sons of God [the angels] who waited upon Yahweh came, including Satan, and Yahweh said to Satan, "Where have you been?"

"Oh, just roaming around—here and there—over the earth," Satan replied.

"Really!" said Yahweh. "And did you come across my servant Job? There is nobody like him on earth: a perfect and upright man. One that fears God and shuns evil."

"But he doesn't do it for nothing, I'll bet," sneered Satan. "Don't you hedge him around with your protection—his house and all that he possesses? You give your blessing to everything he does, and his wealth increases in all directions. But just you lay a finger on his goods and I warrant he'll curse you to your face."

"All right," Yahweh said to Satan, "everything he owns is in your power, but keep your hands off *him*."

Thereat Satan left Yahweh's presence.

A day came when Job's sons and daughters were eating and carousing in their eldest brother's house, and a messenger arrived at Job's, announcing, "Your oxen were plowing and the asses browsing near them, when the Sabeans [predatory nomads] fell upon them and carried them off.

What's more, they put your servants to the sword and only I have escaped to tell you."

While he was still speaking, another messenger came in to say, "God's lightning has just struck from heaven and frizzled to a cinder all your servants and your flocks, and only I have escaped to tell you."

Hardly had he finished speaking when yet another messenger arrived. "Three marauding bands of Chaldeans have just swept down upon your camels," he announced, "and carried them away. Only I have escaped to tell you."

He was still giving the news when another message was delivered: "Your sons and daughters were eating and drinking in their eldest brother's house, when a great wind swept out of the desert and blew the house down from all corners, killing the young people, and all are dead. Only I have escaped to tell you."

Job got to his feet, tore his gown in two, shaved off his hair, and fell to his knees in worship.

"Naked I came from my mother's womb," he prayed, "and naked shall I return. The Lord gave, and the Lord has taken away."

In all that had happened Job remained without fault and did not rail at God.

There came another day when the Sons of God were attending the Lord, and among them was Satan.

"Where have you been?" Yahweh asked Satan.

"Oh just roaming around the earth, going back and forth," Satan answered Yahweh.

"And did you come across my servant Job?" asked Yahweh. "There is no one like him on the earth: a perfect and an upright man, who fears God and shuns evil. All your attempts to destroy him have been in vain. They've made not the slightest dent in his integrity."

"Ah, but skin for skin," sneered Satan to Yahweh. "Everything a man possesses he'll surrender for his life. Just you lay a finger on his flesh and bone, and I guarantee he'll curse you to your face."

"Very well," Yahweh said to Satan, "he is in your hands. But spare his life."

So Satan left God's presence and struck Job down with a plague of boils from the soles of his feet to the crown of his head. Job sat among ashes, scraping himself with a piece of potsherd. His wife came to him and taunted:

"What! still devout? Curse God and die."

But he replied, "You talk like any foolish woman. Don't you know that if we receive happiness from God's hands we must also accept evil."

Through all this, Job uttered not a vicious syllable.

When three of Job's friends heard of the calamities that had fallen on him, they each set off from home: Eliphaz of Teman, Bildad of Shuah, and Zophar of Naamath. They had agreed among themselves to come and condole with him and comfort him. But when they saw him from a distance they could hardly recognize him. They wailed, wept, tore their garments, and sprinkled dust upon their heads. For seven days and seven nights they sat with him in his plight, never saying a word: so sorry was the spectacle he made. It was Job who broke the silence, cursing the day that he was born:

"Perish the day on which I was given birth
   and the night on which they said:
'A man child is conceived.'
Dark be that day. God disregard it.
Light of the sun, illumine it not.
Stain it with gloom and the shades of death.
Enshroud it in cloud; eclipse it in the darkest day.
Keep it solitary. Keep it silent. Empty it of joy.

Why did I not die from the womb,
Perish as I came from the belly?
Why was I not discarded like a stillborn child,
   never to see the light?
Down in Sheol [Hades], the wicked and their doings end.
And there the weary have their rest.
Down in Sheol, great and small are one,
   and all slaves free.
I have no appetite except for sighing,
Pouring out my groans like water.
All my fears grow real upon me.
All my dreads turn true before me."

Then Eliphaz of Teman spoke:

"If we commune with you, will you bear it?
Yet we cannot keep ourselves from speaking.
Many another you have schooled,
Strengthening the feeble hand,
Stiffening the tottering knee,
But now you faint when your own turn comes:
Overwhelmed when you yourself are touched.

Where is your piety, your faith?
Where is all the hope of your upright days?

Take note of this:
Who ever perished innocent,
Or, dedicated, was reduced to nothing?
Those who sow the seeds of evil—
  oh yes I have seen!—
Reap a harvest of the same.

Petition God—I would if I were you—
Lay before him all your cause.
Past reckoning are his mighty ways.
Past all counting are his wonders.
He sends his rain upon the earth,
He pours his waters on the fields,
He sets the lowly up on high,
He lifts the sorrowing to rejoicing,
He thwarts the conceits of the cunning
And brings to nothing their designs.
So, happy the man whom God corrects.
Do not spurn the Almighty's lessons.
He bruises, yes, but he bandages.
He wounds, but with a healing hand."

Job broke in and uttered:

"Oh that my grief were nicely weighed,
And my anguish heaped upon the scales!
How they would outbalance the sands of the sea!
What wonder, then, that my words are savage!
The barbs of the Almighty have bitten deep,
And my spirit saturates their venom.
All God's terrors are arrayed against me.
Does the wild ass bray when he sees green meadows?
Or the bull bellow in sight of fodder?
Can tasteless food be taken with no salt,
Or is there flavor in the white of an egg?
I disdain such fare, yet such the food
I am given in my malady.
Therefore, leave my mouth unmuzzled.
Let me speak the anguish of my heart.

Oh God, am I some monster of the deep
That you should watch me night and day?
If I say: "My bed will be a solace,
  my couch will ease my pain,"

Forthwith you scare me with dreams,
Appall me with apparitions.

Why must you rear mankind at all,
Or set your heart on him because you have?
Morning after morning, must you inspect him
And put him every moment to the test?
Will you never look away from me one instant—
Just long enough for me to gulp down my own spittal?
What harm, Man Watcher, have I ever done you?
Why aim your shaft at me? Why load me down?
Why not just forgive me? Let me off?
I shall be put to bed in the dirt, oh, soon enough!
And when you look for me, I shall be gone."

To these words Bildad the Shuhite answered:

"This blast of hot air, this gale of words,
How long will you maintain it?
Can God distort the course of law?
Does the great Almighty twist right to wrong?
Your offspring were a sinning lot
And he has paid them back in full.
If you would only cast your glance on God
And, pure and sound, implore El Shaddai's mercy,
He will surely rouse himself for you
And give you back again a happy home.
What you had before will seem as nothing.
What you *will* have will seem a new prosperity.

Can papyrus grow except in marshes?
Can reeds flourish except in water?
Even uncut they wilt at once.
So God does not forget the upright
Nor hold out his hand to the criminal.
Once again your cheeks would puff with laughter;
your lips would shout,
And your enemies be clothed in shame,
And the pavilion of the wicked be undone."

Job replied:

"I know all this. Of course I do.
How can a man outmatch God:
challenge him in court?
Such a one would hardly score
one point in a thousand.

God is too wise and too all powerful.
Who can take him on and come out whole?
Mountains he shifts before they even know it.
He turns them upside down just because he's angry.
He can give the earth a shake
  and tilt it from its axis;
Command the sun, forbid it to rise;
  seal up the stars.
How then dare I sue him
  or match my wits with his?
Even were I right,
  what use is my defense
When my prosecutor is my judge?
He would crush me for a hair,
  and wound and wound again.

My days flit by. I see
  no happiness in their flight.
As swift as frigates they fly,
  or like an eagle's fall.
If I be wicked, then,
  why struggle any more?
Were I to wash myself with snow
  or bleach my hands in lye,
He would toss me into the dung again
  till my very clothes disdained to touch me.
For he is not a man,
  and I am only that.

So let me say to God:
  'Do not condemn me, thou.
Show me why thou makest
  this onslaught on my soul.
Is it right for thee to spoil
  the thing that thou hast made?
Hast thou eyes of flesh?
  Dost see as humans see?
Thou hast modeled me, remember,
  made me out of clay.
Wouldst thou now reduce me
  once again to dust?
Didst thou not pour me out like milk,
  curdle me like cheese,
Clothe me with skin and flesh,
  knit me bone and sinew?

Life and love thou gavest me,
  and watched each breath of mine.
Wast thou just dissembling?
  I know thou didst just that:
Watching me to see
  when I would transgress:
Then like a lion thou'd hunt me down.' "

Zophar of Naamath exclaimed:

"Shouldn't someone stem this blathering?
Does all this talk prove you right?
All this babbling strike us dumb?
Shall you jeer at God and none rebuke?
Can you fathom the depth of God
And come to the confines of the infinite?
Oh how the dunce grows wise,
Like a wild ass born tame!

Come now, set your thinking straight
And stretch out your hands toward him.
If your hands are stained with sin,
  get rid of it.
In your tents let no evil dwell."

Job rounded on him:

"You, of course, know everything,
And when you die all wisdom goes.
But I have intelligence as well.
Who does not know these things?
The very beasts could teach you.
The fish of the sea could give you lessons.
No creature alive is ignorant of this:
That all is as it is
  because God makes it so.
In his hand is every living soul
And the breath of all mankind.

Yes, he makes fools of counselors, and judges dunces.
He undresses kings and gives them rags to wear.
He unfrocks priests and disestablishes.
The nimble speaker he strikes dumb,
Turns elders into chattering idiots,
Makes nations great, and then destroys them;
Strips rulers of all foresight
And lets them grope their way in darkness
  staggering like sots.

All this have I seen with my own eyes.
My ears have heard it and have understood.
As for you and these your curatives, you all are quacks.
I wish you would hold your peace.
That at least would show a little wisdom.
Listen to *me* now and hear my charge.

Do you speak for God? I ask.
Do you put your specious reasons in his mouth?
Does he need your help as advocate?
Is it wise to risk his scrutiny?
He can't be fooled, you know, as man is fooled.
Sharp will be the reprimand when he sees through
Your ashen platitudes, your defenses made of clay.

Let God kill me, I'll not waver
But defend my conduct to his face.
My very boldness perhaps will save me
Since no godless man would dare so much.
Two things, Lord, I ask, two things only:
Lift your heavy hand from off me
And stop my cringing in your presence."

Eliphaz of Teman then remarked:

"Are you the first man ever born?
Brought forth before the eternal hills?
Present at the Almighty's privy sessions?
The only wise man in creation?
What do you know that we do not?
What comprehend wherein we fail to grasp?
Among us too are gray and ancient heads
Much older even than your father.
Is God's gentleness too rough for you
That your tantrums carry you away?

How can any man be clean?
How, born of woman, be innocent?
Even God's angels he finds wanting;
The heavens themselves are dirty in his sight.
How much more abominable and filthy, then, is man—
Swilling his iniquity like water!"

To which Job gave answer:

"Oh, what sorry comforters you are!
I've heard it all before.

Is there to be no end to your wind of words?
What causes such a spate of verbiage?
If I were in your place and you in mine,
I too could prate like you,
Could sermonize and wag my head.
But I would encourage you instead;
Move my murmuring lips to soothe.

As it is, my grief remains, say what I may.
For God has turned me over to the vicious,
Tossed me into the embrace of sinners.
I lived at ease until he shattered me,
Grabbed me by the neck and mangled me.
His archers hedge me round. I am their target.
Their arrows fly at me from every side,
Piercing my vitals, pouring my guts out on the ground.
I pant for breath, my days are spent, my grave is dug.
My eyes are dim with tears,
  my limbs are like a shade.
So, set on me again, the pack of you,
Though not a single man of wisdom is among you.
No, my days are done, my plans in ruins, my heart broken.
I wait for Sheol as my only home.
Get ready there my bed in the dark.
Say to the abyss: "You are my father,"
And to the maggot: "You are my mother and my sisters."
Where oh where is my hope, or any happiness in sight?
Will they go down to Sheol with me?
Come, shall we descend to the dust together?"

At which Bildad the Shuhite interjected:

"Aha! The light of the wicked is put out;
His bright flare quenched, his tent dim.
No lamp burns above his head.
Crimped in his lusty stride,
  his own schemes trip him up.
The trap springs shut, his heel is caught.
Such is the fate of every evil house
  and every godless home."

Job replied:

"How long will you torment me
And break me into pieces with your words?

These ten times have you assaulted me,
  abused me without shame.
Even suppose that I have erred,
Must that error lodge with me?
Surely you must see
  that God has undermined me.
'Murder!' I scream, but no one answers.
I shout for help, but none comes.
He has fenced me in. I cannot pass.
He floods my path with dark;
  has stripped me of my name
And snatched the crown from off my head.
He has reduced me on every side:
Even my hope uprooted like a tree.
His anger smolders and flares,
  he counts me as his enemy.
My kinsfolk stand away,
  and all my friends have left.
Even my maids regard me as a stranger.
I call my servant, but he does not answer,
  though I go on my knees to beg.
My very breath is loathsome to my wife,
  and the stench of me to my own sons.
Even little children laugh behind my back.
My skin hangs on my bones;
  my teeth drop from my gums.
Pity me, pity me, oh you my friends,
  for the hand of God has touched me.
Would that this plea of mine were chiseled in stone,
  carved in monumental granite!
And yet I know that my redeemer lives
  and that he at last
Will stand beside me on this earth."

Then Zophar of Naamath said:

"Are you not aware since time began
And man was set upon the earth
That the mirth of the wicked is brief
  and the joy of the godless short?
Though his marrrow be fat with the lust of youth,
  it lies with him in the dirt.
The sweet of evil that he savored under his tongue,
Is changed to viper's venom in his bowels.
He cannot keep down the riches he gorged:
God spews them from his gut.

He forsook the poor, foreclosed their houses—
Houses that he never built—
So deluges shall sweep away his home,
And torrents on the day of wrath."

Job cried out:

"Oh, why do the wicked go on and on,
Growing old and getting richer?
Their offspring established in their sight,
Waxing big and strong before their eyes;
Their houses secure from fear,
While God withholds his big stick.
Their bullocks sire without mishap,
Their cows calve with never a loss,
Their flock of little children frisk and dance;
They carol away to timbrel and harp
And revel in the music of the flute.
They pass their days in affluent ease
And their passage to Sheol is smooth.
Yet these are the very ones who said to God:
  'Please go away!
We do not care to know your paths.
What is El Shaddai that we should serve him?
What good does praying to him do?' "

Eliphaz of Teman added:

"Surely a man is of little worth to God.
What does El Shaddai gain just because you're good?
Or does he punish you because you're pious?
Far from it: it is your wickedness.
You must have bled your debtors dry.
You must have stripped your brothers naked;
Begrudged water to the thirsty,
Withheld victuals from the hungry,
Dismissed widows empty-handed,
  twisted orphans' arms.
No wonder, then, that snares surround you,
  that sudden fears beset you!
Beware of that dark and ancient trail
  which worthless men have trod:
Plucked up in their prime; washed to oblivion;
The very ones who said to God: 'Please go away.
What can El Shaddai do for us?'
Forgetting that he had filled their homes with good.

Well then, make peace with God. Submit.
Welcome the lessons from his lips,
And lay his words up in your heart.
Return to the Almighty and be healed.
Then shall El Shaddai be your joy
And you will lift up your face to God.
You will pray and he will hear you."

Job answered:

"Oh that I knew where I might find him
And lay my case before his throne!
I go one way; he is not there.
I go another and cannot find him.
Northward I turn and do not see him.
Then to the south: there is no sign."

Bildad of Shuah then observed:

"What sovereignty and awe are his!
What tranquillity he keeps on high!
There is no counting his battalions,
And where in the world does his light not rise?
How can mere man be justified before him,
When even the moon hardly shines
And in his eyes the stars are murky.
How much less that maggot, man:
  the son of man, that worm!"

To which Job replied:

"What a support to the impotent you are!
How you have strengthened the stricken arm!
What wonders of wisdom for one unwise!
I swear by the living God who withholds my rights,
By the Almighty who has soured my life,
That so long as God's breath is in me,
My lips shall never utter lies,
Or a falsehood be found upon my tongue.
Till the day I die I *will* protest my innocence.

Oh for the months that have gone,
  the days when God was my keeper,
His candle bright at my head!
By his light I walked through the darkness,
  in those youthful years
When El Shaddai abode with me;
  when I bathed my feet in milk,

And the rocks poured rivers of oil.
  I went out of the city gate
And took my seat in the square.

The young men saw me and stepped aside;
The old stirred and stood to their feet.
Princes went quiet, put a finger to lips;
Statesmen went suddenly dumb.
For I was the one who came to the cry of the pauper
Or the fatherless who had no helper.
I was the eyes of the blind;
  I was the feet of the lame;
I was the father of the poor.

Surely, I thought, I shall die acclaimed,
My days as crowded as the sands;
My roots in water, and my leaves
  freshened by the dew.
But never this: jeered at by the young:
Sons whose fathers I would not
  have put among my sheepdogs:
A worthless progeny but the very ones
Who now make fun of me in songs.
I have become the jackal's brother,
Bosom crony to the ostrich.
My skin is blackened, my bones burn.
My harp is tuned to dirges
  and my flute to keening."

At this point, the three men Eliphaz, Bildad, and Zophar said no more because Job insisted on his innocence. But another man, Elihu, the son of Barachel the Busite, of the clan of Ram, flared out against Job because he made himself right and God wrong. He was furious with his companions too because they had failed to defend God on the charge of being unjust. The only reason that Elihu had waited out their speeches was that these men were older than he. But when he saw that they had nothing more to say, he lost his temper. So now, Elihu the son of Barachel the Busite declared:

"I am a young man and you are old.
I hesitated to assert my views.
For old age should speak, I thought,
And a wealth of years should lead to wisdom.
But now I know that it is the spirit of a man,
  the breath of the Almighty,

That makes a man intelligent.
Age is not always wise, nor an elder sage.
So hear now what I have to say.

I have listened to your arguments
  and probed your words,
But none of you has proved Job wrong.
None of you has answered his contention.
  And as for you, Job,
If you are able to answer me, prepare.
As you can see, I am no god
But, like you, only made of clay.
You need not, therefore, fear me,
And I shall not be hard on you.

How could you ever bring yourself to say—
  I heard the very words—
'I am pure and sinless,
  free of guilt or blame.
It's God who trumps up charges,
  considers me an enemy.
He's put me in the stocks,
  watches my every move'?

How wrong you are, I have to tell you:
  God is not a man.
How can you rail at him
For not spelling out an answer word by word?
He speaks again and again
  in ways that no one hears.
He speaks in dreams,
  visions of the night,
When in the depths of slumber
  we are cradled in our beds.
Then it is he whispers
  into the human ear;
Or shocks us with a nightmare
  warning us from evil.
Or he chastizes us
  on a couch of pain,
With a trembling in the bones.
  Then there is an angel,
Chosen out of thousands,
  to tell us where to turn.

* * *

But as for Job's asserting: 'I am right
And God has robbed me of all justice,'
And his: 'My judge is prejudiced
And lacerates a sinless man,'
Well, well, was there ever a man like Job?
He imbibes scurrility like water,
  consorts with ne'er-do-wells;
Asserts it a waste of time
  for mankind to serve God.
Surely, anyone unbiased would say:
'Job's pronouncements make no sense.
He should be hounded out of bounds
For giving the answer of atheists
And adding insubordination to his sins.
He says his own misdeeds are nothing
  and heaps abuse on God.' "

After a pause, Elihu went on:

"Bear with me a little longer.
There is more I want to say for God.
Let me illustrate my theme from far afield
  to prove my Maker just.
Don't you see, God is supreme.
There is no pedagogue like him.
Who has ever primed him how to act,
Or dared to say: 'You made a mistake'?
Great heavens! God is greater than we know.
Beyond computing are his centuries:
He who monitors the raindrops,
  squeezing them from clouds.
Who can understand the vagaries of the nebulae
And how the thunder crashes from God's tent
  when the storm winds surge
From the Mansions of the South?
God breathes, and there is ice,
The wide waters are congealed.

  Are you listening, Job?
Pause and ponder the wonders of God."

Then from the storm's center Yahweh gave Job his answer.

"Who is this that muddles up my providence
With outpourings of no intelligence?
  Where were you when I laid

The foundations of the firmament?
Tell me, since you know so much.
Who drafted the dimensions of the earth?
  Surely you must know.
On what drums do its pillars rest?
  Who laid the cornerstone
When the morning stars sang together
And all the sons of God shouted for joy?
Who locked up the sea behind closed doors
When it came bounding out of the womb
And I wrapped it in garments of cloud
And swaddled it in bands of blackest fog,
And ordered it: 'Thus far. No farther:
Here your wild waves halt'?

Did you ever give orders to the morning
  or wake up the dawn?
Have you found your way to the founts of the sea
Or walked in the enclaves of the deep?
Have the abodes of death been shown to you
And have you seen its gloomy portals?
Have you studied the compass of the earth?

Tell me, if you know all this.
Show me the way to the haunts of light
  and where the darkness dwells.
Perhaps you could direct them to their posts
Then put them on the path for home again.
Surely you know,
  because you were born with them
And must be very old by now.

Have you penetrated the treasury of the snow
Or seen where the stores of hail are housed?
    Has the rain a father?
And by whom are the dewdrops sired?
From whose womb issues the ice?
Heaven's hoarfrost? Who engenders it?
Can you rein in the Pleiades,
Or slacken the harness of Orion?
Can you bring the seasons out on time
Or guide Arcturus with his sons?
Can you holler to the clouds
And make the pent-up waters break?
Can you command lightning on the double?

* * *

Can you provide the lioness with quarry
And assuage the hunger of her cubs?
Who caters for the raven and his provider
When his fledglings squawk to God
Struggling up their little necks in famine?
Do you give the horse his mettle
And clothe his neck in quivering thunder?
Oh, how his imperious snort spreads terror
When he paws the ground exultingly
And gallops into the clash of arms!
'Aha!' he whinnies at the trumpet's sound
And smells the battle from afar . . .
The yells of the captains and the roaring.

Does the hawk take lessons from you how to soar,
Spreading his wings toward the South?
Or the eagle mount by your instructions
To make her aerie in the peaks?"

Then Yahweh turned to Job and said:

"Are you still ready to contend with the Almighty?
Does God's critic still have answers?"

And Job replied to Yahweh:

"Lord, I am nothing. What can I say?
I clap my hand on my mouth. I have spoken once.
Twice. Enough. I will not speak again."

But Yahweh continued from the center of the storm:

"Brace yourself and tell me this:
Would you really like to make my dispensation void:
To put me in the wrong and you right?
Have you an arm like God's?
  Or the thunder of his voice?
If you have, then deck yourself in robes of state.
Put on his majesty and mien.
Let loose your anger, let it flood,
To overwhelm the haughty with a glance.
Stamp on the wicked where they stand.
Then let me be the first to say
That you can save yourself by your own right arm.

And Job replied to Yahweh:

> "To you all things are possible, I know,
> And none can hinder your designs.
> I held forth on what I did not understand,
> On marvels far beyond my ken.
> I knew you only by what others said;
> But now with my own eyes I have perceived you.
> Therefore I recant and I repent—
> in dust and ashes.

After Yahweh had spoken his mind to Job, he turned to Eliphaz of Teman.

"I am angry with you and your two friends," he said, "because you have not been honest in the way you talked of me, as my servant Job has been. So now take seven bull calves and seven rams and go to my servant Job and make a burnt offering for yourselves while my servant Job intercedes for you—for he has my ear. Otherwise, I might turn upon you for your shallowness in representing me—unlike my servant Job."

So Eliphaz the Temanite, and Bildad the Shuhite, and Zophar the Naamathite went and did what Yahweh told them. And Yahweh accepted Job's intercession, and besides listening to Job's plea for his friends, he restored all Job's fortune. Indeed, he doubled it. All his brothers and sisters and former friends came to see him and celebrate with him in his home. They comforted him and condoled with him because of all the suffering that Yahweh had inflicted on him. Each of them gave him a silver piece and a gold ring.

Yahweh heaped more blessings on Job's life than ever before. Now he had fourteen thousand sheep, six thousand camels, a thousand yoke of oxen, and a thousand milking asses. He fathered seven more sons and three daughters. His daughters' names were: Yenimah, the first (Turtledove); Queziah next (Cinnamon); and thirdly Queren-happuk (Mascara). No women in the whole land could match Job's daughters for beauty. And their father gave them an inheritance equal to their brothers'.

Job went on to live one hundred and forty years. He saw his sons and his grandsons to the fourth generation. Job died an old man, having lived a very full life.

NOTES

1. Job's three Comforters were probably Idumean sages stemming from the Arab lands of the East.
2. El Shaddai was one of the names of God and is usually translated as "God Almighty."

The Prophet Ezekiel

Ezekiel ("God strengthens") was one of the three "Major Prophets," the others being Isaiah and Jeremiah. He was a young priest living in Jerusalem at the time of the assault of Nebuchadnezzar, king of Babylon, on Judah in 597 B.C., and he was carried off together with the young king, Jehoiachin, and ten thousand of the foremost inhabitants.

Ezekiel settled at Tell Abib near the river Chebar, a grand canal threading its way across the plains southward from Babylon, and he soon became the spokesman for a large colony of exiled Jews. These seem to have been fairly well treated by Nebuchadnezzar, many of them becoming successful farmers and traders—even prominent members of the king's court. They may indeed have indulged in the nostalgia of singing psalm 187 (as the King James version has it):

By the rivers of Babylon, there we sat down,
yea, we wept when we remembered Zion.
We hanged our harps on the willows in the midst thereof.
For there they that carried us away captive
required of us a song;
And they that wasted us required of us mirth,
saying, Sing us one of the songs of Zion.
How shall we sing the Lord's song in a strange land?

But when it came to the crunch and the exile was declared officially over in 538 B.C., the majority of them stayed and did not return to Jerusalem.

One of Ezekiel's functions as a prophet was to warn his people against too much of exactly this nostalgia as he flogged Judah mercilessly for its past sins. The other ten tribes of Israel had already been "lost" when in 722 B.C. the Assyrians swept down from Nineveh under Sargon II and put an end to the northern kingdom of Israel. These tribes had long since lost their identity among their pagan and more civilized conquerors; so one of Ezekiel's achievements was to warn the present exiles of becoming lost too. He has been called, if not the father, the grandfather of Judaism, because he taught the exiles of Judah—scattered throughout alien peoples—to maintain their identity and all the ritual requirements of the Law. He gave his compatriots hope and saved them from despondency by holding up before them the vision of their eventual return to Judah, even prescribing in detail how their life should then be lived.

Ezekiel was perhaps the most individual and original of all the Hebrew prophets, almost to the brink of confirming Dryden's lines (in Absalom and Achitophel):

> great wits are sure to madness near allied,
> And thin partitions do their bounds divide.

He lay on his left side for three hundred and ninety days as a symbol of the years that the northern kingdom of Israel would remain in exile, and then on his right side for forty days as a similar symbol for Judah. His visions were imaginative to the point of psychedelic and perhaps dangerous to the simple. In the words of the King James Bible:

> And I looked and behold a whirlwind came out of the north,
> A great cloud and a fire infolding itself,
> and a brightness was about it,
> And out of the midst thereof as the color of amber, out of the midst of the fire.
> Also out of the midst thereof came the likeness of four living creatures.
> And this was their appearance: they had the likeness of a man.
> And every one had four faces, and every one had four wings.
> And their feet were straight feet;
> And the sole of their feet was like the sole of a calf's foot;
> And they sparkled like the color of burnished brass.
> And they had the hands of a man under their wings on their four sides;
> And they four had their faces on their wings.
> As for the likeness of their faces, they four
> Had the face of man, and the face of a lion, on the right side;
> And they four had the face of an ox on the left side;
> They four also had the face of an Eagle.

Here Ezekiel tells of another famous vision.

(Ezekiel 37)

THE Lord's hand was upon me and carried me away in the power of his spirit and set me down in the midst of a valley that was strewn with bones. He walked me through them: bones were on every side, they covered the face of the plain—bones as dry as bones.

And he said to me, "Son of man, can these bones live?" And I answered, "Lord God, only you know that."

Then he said, "Prophesy to these bones and say to them, 'Listen, you dry bones, hear the word of the Lord. This is what the Lord God says to you—oh you dry bones! See, I am putting breath into you and you shall live. I am laying sinews on you and making flesh grow over you, and I will cover you with skin. I shall breathe into you and you shall live, and you shall know that I am the Lord.' "

So I prophesied as I was commanded. And as I prophesied there was a noise, the sound of rattling as the bones came together joint by joint. Then what did I see but sinews and flesh creeping over them, and the skin stretching upon them. Yet they had no life.

Then he said to me, "Prophesy to the wind. Prophesy, son of man, and say to the wind, 'The Lord God commands: Come from the four winds, O breath, and breathe upon these slain that they may live.' "

So I prophesied as he commanded, and breath came into them and they were alive and they stood up on their feet, an exceedingly great army.

Then he said to me, "Son of man, these bones are the whole house of Israel and what they are saying is this: 'We are bones, all dried up, our hope is lost and we are severed from our parts.' So, prophesy and tell them this, 'The Lord God declares: Listen, my people, I will open your graves and bring you out of your tombs back to the land of Israel. And when I have opened your graves and brought you out of your tombs, you shall know that I am the Lord, O my people. I shall put my spirit into you and you shall live. And I shall place you in your own land. Then will you know that what I have spoken I have done—I Yahweh, the Lord God.' "

The Three Young Men in the Fiery Furnace

The book of Daniel was written about 165 B.C. when the Jews were having a hard time of it at the hands of Antiochus IV, the Seleucid king. The author probably wanted to give them hope by telling stories of how long long ago the Jews were similarly oppressed but how God raised up the wise folk hero Daniel to keep their faith and courage from being quenched.

Daniel himself, like Ezekiel, was one of the young men carried from Jerusalem by Nebuchadnezzar in 597 B.C. to be given a Chaldean education in Babylon to fit them for the court. We are not told whether Ezekiel was destined for the same, though this is possible because he must have known Daniel and speaks of him with approbation no less than three times.

In Chapter 1, we are told how Nebuchadnezzar orders his First Secretary Ashpenaz to pick from among the captives youths who are suitable material for a palace education. These young men had to be from royal or aristocratic families. The king particularly specified that they should be good-looking, well set-up fellows, and intelligent. Their education was to last three years before they should be deemed ready to stand in the king's presence, and they were to be fed on food from the royal kitchens. Moreover, their Yahvist names were changed by Ashpenaz into names reflecting Babylonian deities. Thus Daniel, Hananiah, Mishael, and Azariah became Belteshazzar, Shadrach, Meshach, and Abednego.

Daniel, however, upstanding youth that he is and adhering to Jewish food restrictions, decides that he cannot eat any of the royal food or drink the royal wine (probably because it had been offered in idolatrous rituals), and he asks Ashpenaz—whose favorite he is already—to exempt them. This puts the first secretary on the spot and he answers:

(Daniel 1:10-21, 3:1-23, then 18 verses found only in the Septuagint, and 3:24-30)

"NO. The king has laid down what you should eat and drink, and I'm afraid of what he will say when he sees you looking paler and thinner than all the other boys in your group, and you'll make me risk losing my head."

Daniel then spoke to Melzar, the man that the first secretary had appointed to look after him and Hananiah, Mishael, and Azariah. "Sir," he said, "just try us for ten days. Give us only vegetables to eat and plain water to drink. At the end of that time compare us to the other boys who eat the king's food and deal with us accordingly."

The man agreed to the ten days' trial, and at the end of ten days he saw that they looked ruddier and robuster than all the other boys who were served from the king's kitchens. God too bestowed on these four boys exceptional proficiency in learning all the literature and science of the time. To Daniel he also gave the gift of interpreting dreams and visions.

When the training period that the king had fixed was over, the first secretary presented all the young men to Nebuchadnezzar, who interviewed them and found that Daniel, Hananiah, Mishael, and Azariah far outshone all the others and he made them his personal attendants. In the breadth of their knowledge and the comprehension of their understanding, he found that they were ten times wiser than all the clairvoyants and astrologers in his realm.

When King Nebuchadnezzar made a golden statue ninety feet high and set it up in the plain of Dura, he summoned all his satraps, prefects, governors, captains, treasurers, judges, mayors, and all the high officials of the provinces to come to its dedication.

Accordingly, all these satraps, prefects, governors, captains, treasurers, judges, mayors, and high officials of the provinces arrived for the dedication and stood around King Nebuchadnezzar's monument while a herald with a strong voice bawled: "Attention! you delegates from every nation, tribe, and tongue. When you hear the sound of the horn, the pipe, the lyre, the sackbut, the harp, the bagpipe, and every sort of instrument, you are to fall flat on the ground and pay homage to the golden statue which King Nebuchadnezzar has set up. Anyone who does not fall down in homage will be hurled forthwith into a blazing inferno."

As soon, therefore, as the people heard the sound of the horn, the pipe, the lyre, the sackbut, the harp, the bagpipe, and every sort of musical instrument, the delegates from every nation, tribe, and tongue fell to the ground and paid homage to the golden statue which King Nebuchadnezzar had set up.

It was then that certain Chaldeans [i.e., the Babylonian soothsayers and clairvoyants whom the four brilliant youths were displacing] came forward denouncing the Jews.

"O King, live forever!" they began. "Your majesty issued a decree that the moment we heard the sound of the horn, the pipe, the lyre, the sackbut, the harp, the bagpipe, and every sort of musical instrument, we were to fall down in homage to the golden statue which you have set up; and that anyone failing to prostrate himself in homage was to be hurled into a blazing inferno. Well, there are some Hebrews here whom you have made administrators in Babylon, namely Shadrach, Meshach, and Abednego, who have ignored your Majesty's edict. In fact they have no respect for your gods at all, and they do not pay homage to the golden statue which you have set up."

At this the king was very much annoyed and he ordered Shadrach, Meshach, and Abednego to be brought before him. He demanded:

"Is it true that you three, Shadrach, Meshach, and Abednego have no respect for my gods and do not pay homage to the golden statue which I have set up? . . . Very well, I hope that this time when you hear the sound of the horn, the pipe, the lyre, the sackbut, the harp, the bagpipe, and every sort of musical instrument, you will fall down in homage to the statue that I have set up. If you don't, you will be thrown immediately into the fires of a blazing inferno. Then what god will come forward and snatch you out of my hands?"

Shadrach, Meshach, and Abednego answered King Nebuchadnezzar: "Sire, it makes no difference to us whether we answer your question or not because if any god can save us and snatch us out of your hands, our God, the God we worship, can. In any case, even if he doesn't, your majesty can be quite sure that we will never serve your gods or pay homage to the golden statue you have set up."

At these words, Nebuchadnezzar flew into a rage and his whole demeanor changed toward Shadrach, Meshach, and Abednego. He ordered the furnace to be stoked up seven times hotter than it usually was, and he called on some of his most muscular soldiers to bind up Shadrach, Meshach, and Abednego and throw them into the blazing inferno. And they were bound up and hurled into the furnace still clothed in their trousers, shirts, and caps. So peremptory had been the king's command that the furnace was overheated to such a degree that the flames bursting out of it killed some of the men who threw them in. But Shadrach, Meshach, and Abednego in their fetters, having tumbled down into the white-hot furnace, walked about in the very heart of it singing to God and blessing the Lord.

Meanwhile, others of the soldiers who had thrown them in continued to stoke up the furnace with more brimstone, pitch, tow, and dry faggots so that the flames blasted seventy feet upward and around and seared to a cinder any Chaldeans in the offing. But the Lord's angel was down there right in the furnace with Shadrach and his companions, driving the scorching flames outward from the center and fanning through it a dew-laden breeze. The fire did not touch them or hurt them in the least, as with one mouth they sang a hymn to God in the depth of the inferno. [Fourteen verses out of forty-two].

> All you works of the Lord, bless the Lord,
> praise and exalt him above all forever.
> O you sun and you moon, bless the Lord,
> praise and exalt him above all forever.
> You showers and you dews, bless the Lord,
> praise and exalt him above all forever.
> You fire and heat, bless the Lord,
> praise and exalt him above all forever.
> You frost and cold, bless the Lord,
> praise and exalt him above all forever.
> You ice and snow, bless the Lord,
> praise and exalt him above all forever.
> You lightning and clouds, bless the Lord,
> praise and exalt him above all forever.
> You seas and rivers, bless the Lord,
> praise and exalt him above all forever.
> You dolphins and sea creatures, bless the Lord,
> praise and exalt him above all forever.
> You beasts, savage and tame, bless the Lord,
> praise and exalt him above all forever.
> And we, Hananiah, Azariah, and Mishael, bless the Lord,
> praise and exalt him above all forever.

King Nebuchadnezzar was dumbfounded. He leapt up, exclaiming to his aides, "Didn't we throw three bound men into the furnace?"

"We certainly did, sire," they answered.

"Then look," he said, "I see four men down there walking about freely in the heart of the fire, and the form of the fourth seems divine."

Nebuchadnezzar hurried over to the mouth of the raging furnace and called out, "Shadrach, Meshach, and Abednego, you servitors of the Most High God, come out, come out here!" At which Shadrach, Meshach, and Abednego walked out from the middle of the fire.

The satraps, prefects, and governors, as well as all the king's courtiers, crowded around them and saw that the fire had been powerless to touch them. Not a hair of their heads was even singed or their clothes scorched. Not even the smell of burning was on them.

Nebuchadnezzar broke out in praise: "Blessed be the God of Shadrach, Meshach, and Abednego. He has sent his angel to save these servants who trusted in him and who defied the king's decree and yielded up their persons rather than serve or worship any other god but their own. Therefore I herewith issue this edict, binding on every nation, tribe, and tongue: Whosoever utters a word against the God of Shadrach, Meshach, and Abednego shall be torn limb from limb and have his house razed to the ground, because there is no other god who can save like this one does."

The king then promoted Shadrach, Meshach, and Abednego in the province of Babylon.

NOTES

1. I have translated "chief eunuch" as first secretary. Eunuchs were not always castrated. See note on p. 295.

2. Daniel for some reason is not included among the three Hebrew youths thrown into the furnace.

3. Tow is coarse hemp fiber used for making ropes. It is particularly inflammable. Another word for it is oakum.

Belshazzar's Feast

Twenty-five years after the death of Nebuchadnezzar in 562 B.C., the Babylonian empire fell to the Persians under Cyrus the Great. Daniel then would have been about seventy-eight years old.

The last Babylonian ruler was the crown prince Belshazzar, son not of Nebuchadnezzar, as the author of the book of Daniel (writing some three hundred and seventy-three years later) says, but of Nabonidus, no relation whatever of Nebuchadnezzar. Nabonidus was more interested in refurbishing temples and researching antiquities than in being a monarch, and he handed over the government to his son, making him regent.

"Mene, Mene, Tekel, Upharsin," the famous "Writing on the Wall," which became a shibboleth for imminent disaster when all seems well, is a crytogram in Aramaic, a Semitic dialect related to Hebrew which gradually became (with Greek) the lingua franca of the Near East down to and including the time of Christ. The literal meaning of the words is: "A mina, a shekel, a half mina." These were weights for weighing precious metals. Each word is also a pun in Aramaic: "has numbered," "you have been weighed," "has been divided," "the Persians." It is thought by many modern scholars that the original text contained only one "mene." The repetition, however, makes the threat more ominous.

The name Belshazzar means: "O Bel, protect the king!" Bel (pronounced Bayl or Beel when by itself) was the chief Babylonian deity.

(Daniel 5:1-31)

BELSHAZZAR the king gave a great banquet for a thousand of his nobles, and in the midst of his carousing, when he was in his cups, he ordered the gold and silver goblets which his father Nebuchadnezzar had purloined from the Temple at Jerusalem to be brought in so that he and his nobles, with their wives and concubines, could drink from them.

The gold and silver goblets stolen from God's house in Jerusalem were accordingly fetched, and the king, with his nobles, wives, and concubines, drank from them, toasting their various idols of gold, silver, brass and iron, wood and stone.

Suddenly behind the candelabrum the fingers of a human hand appeared and began to scribble across the plastered wall of the palace. The king went pale at the vision of these writing fingers. Full of foreboding, his limbs turned to water and his knees knocked. He shouted for his Chaldean soothsayers and diviners. "If any of you can read this writing and decipher it for me," he told them pleadingly, "he is to be clothed in purple and a golden collar hung around his neck. And he'll rank third in the land."

The king's wise men arrived, but were unable to read the writing or decipher it; a fact that doubled the king's panic. His face went ashen, and his nobles too were shaken.

The queen mother, hearing of their disquiet, hurried into the banquet hall and after her formal greeting, "O king, live forever!" went on to say, "There's no need for you to be upset or look so pale. A man in your kingdom exists who is endowed with a divine spark. In the days of your father he manifested light and understanding to a godlike degree. So great was his genius in comprehending, interpreting, and solving every kind of dream, riddle, and problem, that your father King Nebuchadnezzar made him master of all his magicians, enchanters, astrologers, and diviners. His name is Daniel, which the king changed to Belteshazzar ["Bel guard his life!"]. Why don't you send for him so he can tell you what all this means?"

Daniel was then hustled before the king.

"Are you Daniel," the king asked him, "one of the Jewish captives my father brought here from Judah? I hear that you are endowed with a divine spark and are unsurpassed in the range and depth of your insight. Well, my wise men and clairvoyants were brought here to read and decode this writing for me, but they couldn't make head nor tail of it. Now, I hear that you are an expert at interpreting dreams and solving riddles. So if you can read this one and explain it to me, you shall be clothed in purple and have that gold collar hung about your neck, and you'll rank third in the realm."

"Sire, you may keep your presents," Daniel replied, "or give them to somebody else, but I will read the writing for your majesty and tell you what it means. So, King, listen to this: the Most High God gave your father Nebuchadnezzar a kingdom with majesty, glory, and honor: a majesty which commanded the respect and awe of every nation, tribe, and tongue, because he slew or let live whomsoever he would, and he promoted or put down whomsoever he chose. But when he became puffed up and his heart insolent, he was deposed from his kingly throne, stripped of his glory, and turned into an outcast. His mind dwindled to a beast's and he lived among wild asses, chewing grass like a cow, and his body was wet with the dew of heaven, until he learnt at last that the Most High God reigns over the kingdom of mankind and elects whom he will to rule them. But you, Belshazzar his son, have not been humble at heart though you knew all this. Instead you have reared up against the Lord of heaven. Yes, you had the sacred vessels of his house brought here so that you and your nobles and your wives and concubines could swill wine from them and drink toasts to idols made of silver and gold, of brass, iron, wood, and stone: things that can't hear or see or comprehend; but the God who fingers the very stops of your breathing and governs the whole course of your life—him you ignored. Therefore it is from him that this hand and this handwriting come. And this is what the writing says: 'Mene. Mene. Tekel. Upharsin.' And this is what the writing means: 'Mene: God has numbered the days of your reign. Tekel: You are weighed in the balance and found wanting. Upharsin: your kingdom is divided and given to the Medes and the Persians.' "

Then by Belshazzar's command Daniel was clothed in purple, a collar of gold put around his neck, and he proclaimed the third in rank within the realm.

That same night, Belshazzar king of Chaldea was slain, and Darius the Mede took over the kingdom.

NOTE

It was not "Darius the Mede" but Cyrus the Persian who captured Babylon. His troops had been besieging the city for some time and, unbeknown to the revelers, had already been let into it while the banquet was actually in progress.

Daniel in the Lions' Den

One must remember again that the author of the book of Daniel was writing his folk tales to impress and fortify the Jews of his own time, oppressed by the Hellenized Seleucids some four centuries after the Exile. Not surprisingly, his history is shaky and abounds in mistakes and anachronisms. Darius, for instance (pronounced Daríus), was not the son of Ahasuerus (supposedly Xerxes I of Persia) but the father. And Darius did not follow Cyrus on the throne, he preceded him. Further, no Persian or Hellenistic king ever issued a decree claiming divine honors. The author, however, is simply using Daniel as a symbol of the faithful Jew serving Yahweh, and the various pagan kings as the symbols of heathenism.

As to the savage retaliation visited not only on the culprits in this story but on their wives and children, a man's family was considered part of himself and therefore to be included in any punishment, even though in Deuteronomy 24:16 such inhumanity is expressly forbidden: "The fathers shall not be put to death for the children, neither shall the children be put to death for the fathers: every man shall be put to death for his own sins."

Daniel is now an old man.

(Daniel 6:1-21, 28)

DARIUS decided to appoint a hundred and twenty satraps over the different provinces of his realm, and over these satraps he set up three chief ministers, of whom Daniel was one. The satraps were to report to these ministers and ensure that the king's revenues were properly protected.

Daniel, however, with his divine-given character, so excelled the other chief ministers that the king was considering putting him in charge of the whole empire. Consequently, the other chief ministers and satraps watched for an occasion to catch him in some fault of administration, but when (because of his integrity) they failed to uncover a single flaw or false step in his conduct, they said to themselves, "Our only hope of tripping up this Daniel is through his religion." So these chief ministers and satraps put their heads together and craftily made this suggestion to the king: "King Darius, live forever! Your ministers, sire, including all the prefects, satraps, magistrates, and mayors, have come to the conclusion that your majesty should issue an imperial decree, lasting thirty days, by which everyone is prohibited under pain of being thrown to the lions from addressing any petition to any god or man save your majesty. Therefore, sire, may we have your signature on this law so that once it is published and becomes a law of the Medes and the Persians it automatically becomes irreversible?"

King Darius signed the document and it was published. Daniel, however, although he was aware of the new ordinance, continued to go to his house every day, open the windows of his upstairs bedroom which looked toward Jerusalem, and, three times a day, kneel down in prayer, praising and thanking God.

This address of praise and petition by Daniel to God was exactly what these men were watching for. They hurried to the king and reminded him of his imperial prohibition. "Didn't your majesty sign a decree," they said, "which prohibited anyone for thirty days from addressing a petition to any man or god except yourself—and that under pain of being thrown to the lions?"

"I did," the king answered, "and like all laws of the Medes and the Persians the decree ipso facto is irrevocable."

"Well then, sire," they continued, "this Daniel here, who is a Jewish exile, takes no notice of your majesty's decree. Three times a day he goes off and prays to his god."

When the king heard this he was very much distressed. He spent all that day till sunset trying to find a way to save him. But those people came back again in a delegation and said to him, "Your majesty, may we remind you that according to the law of the Medes and the Persians every royal decree is immutable?"

So the king at last gave orders for Daniel to be arrested and thrown into the lion pit, but he secretly whispered to him, "Your God to whom you are so loyal will come and save you." A stone was then hauled against the entrance of the den, which the king sealed with his signet ring and with the rings of his ministers, so that there was no chance of anyone's rescuing Daniel from his plight.

The king returned to his palace and without any dinner retired fasting to bed, but he spent a sleepless night. He got up early in the morning and hurried to the lions' den, and when he was near enough he called out to Daniel in an anguished voice, "Daniel, servant of the living God, has your God to whom you are so dedicated been able to save you from the lions?"

"King, live forever!" came Daniel's reply. "My God sent his angel to muzzle the lions' mouths, so they haven't touched me. Before God and before you I am seen to be innocent. Yes, before you, my king, whom I have never wronged."

The king was overjoyed and gave immediate orders for Daniel to be taken out of the lions' den, and when he was lifted out of the lion pit, not so much as a scratch was to be found on him, such was his trust in God.

Then by the king's command, those who had denounced Daniel were arrested and thrown into the lion pit with their wives and children. And even before they reached the bottom the lions got hold of them and tore their carcasses into ribbons.

Daniel went on to live through the reign of Darius, faring well, right into the reign of Cyrus the Persian.

Bel and the Dragon

These two stories are consigned to the Apochrypha in the Protestant Bible but included in the Catholic canon.

Dragons figured prominently and constantly in the mythology of the Near East, and in the Bible they are symbols of evil. Insofar as this dragon actually existed (in the second story), it was probably a giant snake, perhaps a python—a sacred animal in Greek mythology. (The author is writing in the Hellenized society of the Seleucids after the time of Alexander the Great.) This story is a variation of "Daniel in the Lions' Den." Both tales are tongue-in-cheek satires directed at the absurdity of worshiping idols; they are, however, more historically accurate. The Persian king is correctly named as Cyrus, who did indeed succeed (having defeated) Astyages. And the Babylonian temple of Marduk (another name for Bel) was indeed destroyed by Xerxes when he sacked the city early in the fifth century. As to the prophet Habakkuk in the second story, he would have been at least ninety years old, if he were still alive, and hardly vigorous enough to play the part which the author assigns to him.

(Daniel 14:1-42 in the Vulgate)

AFTER King Astyages was gathered to his fathers, Cyrus the Persian took over the kingdom; and Daniel was the king's favorite, more honored by him than any of his other friends.

Now, the Babylonians had an idol called Bel, and everyday they put before him six barrels of the finest flour, forty whole muttons, and fifty gallons of wine. The king worshiped him too and went every day to pay him homage. Daniel, of course, worshiped only his own God. So the king asked him, "Why don't you worship Bel?"

"Because, sire," he answered, "I do not worship idols made with hands. I worship only the living God who created heaven and earth and has dominion over all mankind."

"But," pressed the king, "what makes you think that Bel isn't a living god? Just look at how much he eats and drinks every day!"

Daniel began to laugh. "Don't be taken in, sire," he said. "This Bel is nothing but a lump of clay encased in bronze, and has never eaten or drunken a thing."

This made the king very cross and he summoned his priests. "Under pain of death," he said to them, "I want you to show me who consumes all these provisions. If you can prove that Bel consumes them, then Daniel will have to die for blaspheming him."

Daniel said to the king, "Good, let it be exactly as you say."

The priests of Bel numbered seventy, not counting their wives and children. When the king went into the temple with Daniel, the priests of Bel said, "See, we are now leaving, so your majesty can lay out all the food and set up the wine; then lock the door and seal it with your ring. If when you come in the morning you don't find that Bel has eaten up everything, we are ready to die; otherwise it must be Daniel for slandering us."

They were quite confident because under the table they had arranged a trapdoor and always used it to come in by and consume the provender. However, as soon as they had left and the king had set out the food before Bel, Daniel ordered the king's servants to bring in ashes and, in the king's presence, to scatter these over the temple floor. After which they all went outside and the door was locked and sealed with the king's ring.

Once they had departed, the priests came in by night as

usual with their wives and children and ate and drank up everything.

Early next morning the king went with Daniel to the temple. "Are the seals intact?" asked the king.

"They are, your majesty."

The king, catching sight of the empty table, burst out with: "O great Bel, so you are not a fraud!"

Daniel laughed and held the king back. "Look at the floor," he said. "Do you see the footprints?"

"I do," roared the king. "I see the footprints of men, women, and children."

Immediately he had the priests arrested, along with their wives and children, and they were forced to show him the trapdoor by which they used to enter and consume what was on the table. The king then put them to death and handed Bel over to Daniel, who made short work of the idol and its shrine.

In that place there also existed a dragon which the Babylonians worshiped. "Look at him!" said the king to Daniel. "You're not going to tell me that he is just made of bronze. He eats and drinks and is alive, so do him reverence."

"If your majesty will allow me," retorted Daniel, "I'll kill this dragon without sword or club."

"Very well," said the king, "I give you permission."

Daniel then got some pitch, fat, and hair, which he boiled together and made into dumplings. These he fed into the mouth of the dragon, which gobbled them up and promptly burst asunder.

"So that's what you worship!" he remarked to the king.

The Babylonians were furious when they heard what had happened and they turned against the king. "The king has become a Jew," they raved. "Not only has he destroyed Bel and put the priests to death, but now he has killed our dragon."

They went clamoring to the king. "Hand over Daniel, or we'll kill you and your whole family."

When the king saw that he was cornered by a violent mob, he was forced to hand over Daniel, whom they threw into the lion pit, where he remained for six days. There were seven lions in the pit and they were fed two whole sheep every day, but now they were fed nothing—to give them an appetite for Daniel.

While all this was going on, a prophet called Habakkuk in Judah was about to take a stew he had made, with pieces of bread in it, to some reapers in the field, when the Lord's angel came and told him, "Take this midday meal you have made to Daniel in the lions' den at Babylon."

"Babylon, sir?" Habakkuk protested. "I've never seen the place, and I know nothing about this den."

Whereupon the Lord's angel grabbed him by the hair of his head and wafted him with the speed of the wind to Babylon right over the lion pit.

"Look, Daniel," he called out, "God has sent you this lunch."

"Thank you, God, thank you!" Daniel exclaimed, "you have remembered me and not forsaken those who love you."

Daniel began to eat as the angel wafted Habakkuk back to his own place.

On the seventh day the king came to bewail Daniel. But when he arrived at the lion pit and looked down, there was Daniel sitting in the midst of the lions.

"Oh, how great you are, Lord, the God of Daniel!" The king burst out. "There is no other god besides you."

He immediately extracted Daniel from the lions' den and threw in those who had tried to destroy him. Then before the king's very eyes, the lions devoured them in a trice.

The Maccabees

After the golden age of Solomon, the Jews suffered an anguished history. Apart from the internecine strife between the two halves of Jewry, Israel and Judah, they were oppressed in turn by the Assyrians, the Babylonians, the Persians, and now the Seleucid kings of Syria. Seleucus, the founder of the dynasty, was one of Alexander the Great's generals and on Alexander's death in 323 B.C., with the breakup of his empire, acquired Palestine as his portion—Egypt falling to Ptolemy (another general and also founder of a dynasty).

There are four books of the Maccabees, all considered apocryphal in Protestant churches, but the first two of them canonical in the Catholic and Orthodox. These two books describe the resistance of the Jews to the Hellenization of their country under the Seleucid monarch: a Hellenization which had gone so far that even high priests succumbed to the allure of Greek culture and a gymnasium for youth was built within sight of the Temple itself. There young Hellenized Jews exercised naked in the Greek manner and even attempted to camouflage their circumcision.

The biblical writers describe with disgust the deterioration of Hebrew thought and religion under both the blandishments and the oppression of the Seleucids. They extol the various national champions that arose to defend orthodoxy, the chief of whom was Judas Maccabeus. He was the most successful member of the family of the Maccabees: a dynasty of high priests and kings founded by his father, Mattathias.

The following horror story was written to raise the spirit of the nation to a fever pitch of patriotism and holy zeal under the oppression of Antiochus IV Epiphanes, the most savage of the Seleucid kings. The events described follow the martyrdom of a prominent scribe called Eleazar, an old man of ninety who had refused to eat pig's flesh because it was against the law of Moses.

(2 Maccabees 7:1-31, 34-42)

WHAT happened next was the arrest of seven brothers with their mother, whom the king was trying to force to commit the sin of eating the flesh of swine. To this end, he whipped and tortured them.

The eldest of the brothers spoke up for the rest: "Do what you like with us, we'd rather die than break God's law which was handed down to us from our fathers."

The king in a fury ordered braziers and caldrons to be heated. When they were ready, he had the tongue of the young man who had spoken cut off, his head scalped, and the extremities of his hands and feet lopped off; all while his brothers and his mother looked on. When he was maimed in all parts but still breathing, the king had him brought to the fire to be fried alive in the pan. During this long torment, as the smoke rose from the pan, his mother and the others encouraged one another to die nobly. "The Lord sees us and will surely help us in this ordeal," they said, "as Moses immortalized in his famous hymn: God will never be oblivious to the plight of those who serve him."

When the first brother had departed from the world in this way, they brought in the second for their brutal sport. They scalped him, head of hair and all, then asked him, "Will you eat, or have your body gone through limb by limb?"

"Never will I eat," he answered in his ancestral tongue

[Aramaic]. Whereupon he was put through all the torments of the first. He gasped with his last breath, "You may destroy us in this life, you monster, but the king of this world will raise us up because we die for his laws. Yes, he will raise us up for all eternity."

After him, they made sport with the third, who before he was even asked, promptly put out his tongue and held out his hands. "These I had from heaven," he said with perfect composure, "but for the sake of God's Law I now let them go because I hope to receive them back from him again."

The king and his entourage were amazed at the young man's courage and his making nothing of his agonies. When he was dead in this way, they began on the fourth brother, who at his last cried out, "To be put to death by men is nothing compared to God's promise that we shall be raised up to life again: something you will never be."

While they were torturing the fifth boy, he looked at the king and said, "Just because you have power for the time being and can do whatever you like, don't imagine that our race is forsaken by God. Wait a little and you will see his power in the way he treats you and your descendants."

After him they brought forward the sixth, whose last words were: "Make no mistake, we suffer what we suffer for our sins, but we welcome what you do to us. Don't think that you'll go unscathed for trying to pit yourself against God."

The mother was a marvel, watching her seven sons slain on a single day. Great was her courage and her enormous faith in God. She exhorted each of her sons in his native tongue, imbued as she was with uplifting sentiments. Indeed, she infused her feelings as a woman with all the heroism of a man.

"How you were formed in my womb," she said to them, "is beyond my knowing, for it was not I that gave you breath, soul, and life. It was not I that shaped for each of you your limbs. It is the Creator of the world who ordains every human birth and knows the source of all. He will in his mercy assuredly give you back your life and breath, because you have thought nothing of these for the sake of his laws."

Antiochus, meanwhile, seeing himself despised and suspecting by the tone of her voice that he was being ridiculed, approached the youngest boy, who was still alive, and tried to entice him with promises on oath that he would make him a rich and happy man if he would turn away from the laws of his ancestors. He would even enlist him as his personal friend and give him everything he wanted.

When the youth was unmoved by this, he called his mother and asked her to appeal to the boy to save his life. When he pressed her further, she agreed to speak to her son. Bending close to him, her heart full of derision for the cruel tyrant, she said in the language of her ancestors:

"Son, think of me. For nine months I carried you in my womb, and for three years I nursed you at my breast, then reared you to your present age. And so, I implore you, my son, gaze upon heaven and earth and all that is in them, remembering that God made them out of nothing, and mankind in the same way. So have no fear of this tormentor, and be a worthy partner of your brothers. Accept your death, and one day, please God, I shall have you with me again and all your brothers."

While she was still speaking, the young man said, "What are you all waiting for? I am not going to obey the king's command but the commandments of the law given to us by Moses. And you, sir, who have inflicted so much pain on us Hebrews, will not escape God's hand. You are the most vile and vicious of men, but don't get carried away by what you are enjoying now in oppressing God's servants, because you won't escape the judgment of the Almighty, who sees everything. My brothers, after a short spurt of pain, now drink from the river of eternal life, but you will be judged by God and punished for your arrogance. And so I, like my brothers, offer up my body and my life for the laws of our fathers. We call upon God to come quickly and save our nation, and through our sufferings and our martyrdom to bring you to confess that he alone is God. Through my brothers and me, the Almighty's rightful anger with our nation will be assuaged."

The king, stung by the young man's scorn, vented his rage upon him more cruelly than all the rest. And so the last brother died undefiled, full of trust in the Lord. Lastly the mother met her end after all her sons.

But this is quite enough about forced sacrifices and bloody cruelties.

PART VII

PALESTINE UNDER THE ROMANS IN THE HELLENISTIC AGE

(C. 4 B.C. TO 67 A.D.)

Stories of Jesus and the Apostles from the Four Gospels and Acts

Introduction

In an anthology of this kind where the provenance of the stories is not given individual prominence, there seems little point in going into detail on the nature and style of each gospel. Perhaps it is enough to say that though by tradition Matthew, Mark, Luke, and John are the authors of the four gospels, we have no absolute assurance that they were and plenty of evidence that the order of their appearance was Mark, Matthew, Luke, and John.

Mark, the basis of both Matthew and Luke, wrote his account about A.D. 70, after the great fire in Rome in 64, which Nero blamed on the Christians, and after the Romans had crushed the Jewish rebellion and destroyed the temple at Jerusalem in 70.

All the gospels are written in Greek, the lingua franca of the Roman world, and Mark's Greek is the simplest of the four evangelists and larded with Hebrew idioms. His intention seems to have been to cater to those Christians of Jewish origin who needed to break away from the trammels of their background.

Mark was the disciple of St. Peter and the missionary companion of both Peter and Paul. It is possible that he was the young man (and tradition says that he was) who when Jesus was arrested fled from the clutches of the arresters naked, leaving the linen cloth he was wearing in their hands.

Matthew, writing about A.D. 80 to 85, includes most of Mark plus new material. It is possible that he wrote his gospel first in Aramaic, the language of Jesus and the Apostles. His Greek nonetheless is fluent and polished. He was obviously well educated, even a little pedantic: always at pains to quote from the Old Testament and by echoes and allusions show that the true evolution of God's purpose had passed through Israel to Jesus. Jesus was the Messiah, the Anointed One, for whom they had been waiting for centuries and who was to make a new covenant between God and man.

The audience that Matthew has in mind is the better educated Jew, to whom he wants to show that the new Israel (the Church) is not simply a collection of the righteous meticulously following the law of Moses, but a body of the worthy and the less worthy who believe in Christ and are called upon to go beyond the mere letter of the law and transcendentally fulfill it.

Matthew by tradition was one of the twelve Apostles. He was the tax collector whom Jesus calls in Matthew 9:9 and who immediately responds.

Luke, writing around A.D. 80 to 85, was probably not an eyewitness of the happenings which he relates. It is likely that he was not even a Jew. Tradition has it that he was the personal physician of St. Paul and faithfully accompanied him in his tireless missionary journeys. A long-standing legend, which may well be true, says that he was also a painter. Almost certainly he was the author of the Acts of the Apostles.

Luke was obviously well educated and writes in the most polished Greek of all four. The audience he aims at are not the Jews but the Gentiles, to whom his central message is: belief in Christ as the Messiah is now the true Judaism. Luke does not bother with quotations from the Old Testament the way Matthew does. He wants to show that Jesus brings salvation into the secular world, where it is most needed.

Lastly, John, by tradition the beloved disciple, Christ's favorite and the young man who leaned on Jesus' breast at the Last Supper, and whose brother James was also a disciple. Some seventy years or so after he had stood at the foot of the cross as little more than a stripling, when he was a very old man of at least ninety, roughly A.D. 100, he dictated his stupendous gospel in clear, simple Greek, often overwhelming in its unself-conscious poetry. His gospel is the loftiest and most inspired of all. In telling the story of Jesus he demonstrated his belief that Jesus was not only beautifully human, but also divine: the Father's eternally begotten Son made flesh.

The first three gospels are known as synoptic, the Greek for "with one glance," or "with the same eye," meaning that because they share so much of the same material and give a similar portrait of Jesus, they can be taken in by the same glance. It is John who breaks new ground.

The Conception of John the Baptist

At the time of these next four stories (a few months before the birth of Christ), Judea was governed by King Herod the Great—a man of robust propensities and violent whims—under the uneasy suzerainty of Rome. Herod, though Idumean by race, was a Jew by religion: pious enough to rebuild the temple and ruthless enough to execute his own wife, Mariamne, together with his son by her. (Isaac Asimov well describes him as the Henry VIII of his time, for Herod married ten times.)

The world into which John the Baptist and soon Christ were to be born had been torn by every kind of war and turmoil. Judea itself, only gradually healing from its own civil war, seethed with nationalistic impatience to cast off the foreign presence, even though that had brought peace—the Pax Romana—to the land. One must bear in mind, too, that the "whole" world then, even Rome itself (three hundred years after the empire of Alexander the Great had crumbled), was more than ever Hellenized. So it was largely a Greek culture into which these two babies were to be born.

(Luke 1:5-23)

IN the days of Herod king of Judea, there lived a priest named Zacharias (of the temple division called Abbijah), whose wife Elizabeth also belonged to the priestly line of Aaron. They were God-fearing people, keeping all the laws and commandments of the Lord; but they were childless, because Elizabeth was barren and they were advanced in years.

Then one day during Zacharias' term of office, when he had gone into the sanctuary to fulfill his priestly duties to God (having been given by lot, according to custom, the honor of burning incense), and while a throng of people prayed outside during the hour of incense, an angel of the Lord appeared to him, standing on the right-hand side of the altar of incense.

Zacharias was shaken, not to say frightened, but the angel said to him, "Have no fear, Zacharias. Your prayer has been answered: Elizabeth your wife will bear a son and you are to call him John. He will be your delight and pride, and many will rejoice in his birth because he will be great before the Lord, abstaining from all wine and strong drink, and filled with the Holy Spirit even from his mother's womb. He will move the hearts of many of the children of Israel again toward the Lord their God, and go before him in the spirit and power of Elijah, turning the hearts of fathers toward their children and of the rebellious toward the ways of the virtuous and so prepare a people fit for their Lord."

"But," said Zacharias, "How can I believe this? I am an old man and my wife is well advanced in years."

To which the angel replied, "I am Gabriel, who stands in the very presence of God. It was he that sent me here to tell you these glad tidings. And now you are to be struck dumb, unable to speak a word until the day these things happen, because you did not believe this my message—which is certainly going to be fulfilled."

Meanwhile the people outside were waiting and wondering why Zacharias stayed so long in the sanctuary. When he finally came out, he could not speak and they realized that he had seen a vision in the temple. He made signs to them but was dumb.

When Zacharias' term of office was over he went home and soon afterward his wife Elizabeth became pregnant and went into retirement for five months, saying, "These are the days when the Lord looked kindly on me and took away my disgrace in the eyes of the world."

The Annunciation and the Birth of John the Baptist

Nazareth, where the Annunciation took place, was a small town in Galilee about seventy miles north of Bethlehem and eighty from the priestly city of Hebron among the hills of southern Judea, where Zacharias and Elizabeth probably lived. Modern Nazareth lies halfway between the Mediterranean coast and the Sea of Galilee. Its present inhabitants are mostly Christian.

When St. Luke says that the angel Gabriel was sent to a virgin called Mary, he uses the Greek word for virgin, *parthenos*, which does indeed mean virgin. St. Matthew in his gospel uses the same word and he quotes Isaiah's prophecy of the birth of Christ. Isaiah, however, uses the Hebrew word *Almah* which simply means "young woman" whether virgin or not, though the Septuagint (the Greek version of the Old Testament) says *parthenos*. In Greek there are at least six words for "young woman," so it looks as though both Matthew and Luke really did mean virgin. The question is important when we come to the event of the "Virgin Birth."

(Incidentally, the Catholic doctrine of the Immaculate Conception has nothing to do with the virgin birth, but is about Mary's own conception in the womb of her mother, St. Anne. The Immaculate Conception means that Mary was conceived without the taint of original sin.)

"Jesus," the name that Mary's son is to be given, is the Greek form of the Hebrew *Yeshua*: a later form of Joshua, meaning "Yahweh saves."

Mary's song of thanksgiving which she breaks into when she visits her cousin Elizabeth (and which some manuscripts ascribe to Elizabeth) is known as the "Magnificat," that being the first word in St. Jerome's Latin translation c. A.D. 400 ("*Magnificat anima mea Dominum*"), and as such has been the vehicle of many musical masterpieces.

(Luke 1:26-80)

IN the sixth month the angel Gabriel was sent by God to a town in Galilee called Nazareth to a virgin engaged to a man called Joseph, of the house of David, and the virgin's name was Mary. The angel came in and greeted her with the words: "Hail, full of grace! The Lord is with you. Blessed are you among women."*

Mary was troubled by this salutation, wondering what such a greeting could mean. So the angel said to her, "Do not be afraid, Mary, because you have found favor with God. Indeed, you are to conceive and bear a son. You shall name him Jesus. He will be great and called Son of the Most High. The Lord God will give him the throne of David his forefather, and he will reign over the house of Jacob forever. Of his kingdom there will be no end."

*This last sentence is omitted in some manuscripts.

"And how will this be," Mary answered the angel, "since I am a virgin?"

"The Holy Spirit will come over you," the angel replied, "and the power of the Most High will overshadow you, and therefore the holy one to be born shall be called the Son of God. Furthermore, your cousin Elizabeth in her old age has also conceived a son: she who was called barren is now in her sixth month. With God nothing is impossible."

Then Mary said, "Take me as I am, Lord, your servant, and do with me whatever you will." And the angel left her.

Mary immediately made herself ready and hastened off to a certain town in Judah, where, as she entered the house of Zacharias and greeted Elizabeth—at the very moment of greeting—the child leapt in Elizabeth's womb and Elizabeth, filled with the Holy Spirit, burst out with a glad cry: "Oh, blessed are you among women, and blessed the fruit of your womb! . . . But what is this, that the mother of my Lord should come to me? The moment I heard your salutation—do you know—the baby in my womb gave a leap of joy . . . Oh, how blessed is she who believed that the Lord's message could be fulfilled!"

And Mary uttered:

My soul overflows with praise for the Lord
  and my spirit with gladness in God my savior.
Because he has noted his humble handmaid
  and made all generations call me blessed.
Because he has done great things for me:
  he the mighty one, holy is his name.
From generation to generation is his great mercy
  toward them that fear him.
His mighty arm has scattered the proud,
  oh, in the arrogance of their hearts.
Yes, he has plucked the powerful from their thrones
    and set up the little ones.
He has filled the starving with good food
  and sent away the rich ones empty.
He has come to the help of Israel his darling son
  and never forgotten his clemency . . .
Just as he promised our forefathers he would:
  promised Abraham and his scions forever.

Mary stayed with Elizabeth for about three months and then went back to her own home.

* * *

When Elizabeth's time of delivery came she gave birth to a son, and her neighbors and relations rejoiced with her at the news of God's great kindness. Eight days later they all came for the child's circumcision and were expecting him to be called by his father's name, Zacharias: "Not so," said his mother, "he is to be called John."

"But," they exclaimed, "none of your family is called by that name."

So they made signs to his father to find out what he wanted him called, and he asked for a writing pad and wrote on it: "John is his name."

Immediately his lips were unlocked and his tongue loosed and he began to speak, blessing God.

The Nativity

From St. Matthew's gospel we learn that when Joseph, to whom Mary was engaged, discovered that she was pregnant he wondered in dismay how he could break off the engagement without publicly disgracing her. (A betrothal in those days was hardly less than marriage and could include cohabitation). Then in a dream an angel told him not to hesitate to take Mary as his wife because the child in her womb had not been conceived through a man but by the Holy Spirit.

This brings up the whole question of the Virgin Birth. Both Luke and Matthew insist that Mary was a virgin though pregnant, and this idea would not have sounded all that strange in the Hellenistic world of the time, where heroes and pagan savior gods were often held to be of divine origin. But the difficult question remains: did Mary have other children after Jesus? Scholars differ and the gospel accounts are inconclusive. Jesus' "bretheren" are mentioned several times, but it was quite common then in the Near East (and still is) to call cousins brothers. Suffice it to say that the Christian tradition, at least from the second century if not earlier, insists that Mary was always a virgin. It should also be pointed out that "firstborn" was a title bestowed on the first son regardless of whether there were other children.

Another interesting question is how we ever came to celebrate Christ's birth on December 25th, when midwinter, even in Palestine, would not have been the best time for whole communities to be trekking to various towns to be registered, nor for shepherds to be out all night watching their flocks. Neither Matthew nor Luke gives us a clue as to when the Nativity really took place. December 25th nonetheless became gradually fixed (between A.D. 300 and 350) throughout the Roman empire as the feast of the Nativity.

The reason seems to have been (most lucidly conjectured by Isaac Asimov in his *Guide to the Bible*) that December 25th, or near that date, is the time of the winter solstice; that is, the time when the sun has passed its decline and with all nature is poised to climb back to warmth, birth, and growth. This point of "sunstop" (which is what "solstice" means in Latin) was an occasion for universal rejoicing. The Romans celebrated it in several days of holidaying called the "Saturnalia" in honor of Saturn the Titan—god of agriculture. When Julius Caesar reformed the Roman calendar, the winter solstice fell on December 25th. Later, in A.D. 244, at a time when the greatest rival to Christianity was the sun-worshipping cult of Mithraism, the emperor Aurelian fixed December 25th as the birthday of the sun.

Christians found it difficult and embarrassing to keep aloof from the explosion of celebration and partying that went on around them. So, very much in the spirit of "if you can't beat 'em join 'em," they gradually slid December 25th into their own celebrations to—as Asimov puts it—"greet the birth of the Son rather than the Sun."

The Roman emperor at the time of Christ's birth was Augustus, grand-nephew and heir of Julius Caesar: the same who as Octavian and a youth of nineteen contested the Roman empire with Mark Anthony and finally wrung it from him in a fourteen-year civil war. Thereafter began what was known as the Pax Romana, a period of comparative peace which settled on the large world which Rome had brought under its sway.

King David, from whom both Joseph and Mary (by tradition) were descended, was born in Bethlehem.

"Christ" is the Greek for the Hebrew "Mashiah" or Messiah. They both mean the "Anointed One."

(Luke 2:1-20)

AT this time a decree went out from Caesar Augustus for a census to be taken of the whole empire. (This census—the first of its kind—took place when Quirinius was governor of Syria.) And everyone had to go and register at his city of origin. So Joseph too went from Galilee out of the town of Nazareth up into Judea to the city of David called Bethlehem—to register with Mary his wife to be, who was with child.

It was while they were there that the time came for her to be delivered, and she gave birth to a firstborn son and wrapped him in swaddling clothes and laid him in a manger—because there was no room for them at the inn.

Meanwhile in the fields nearby, there were some shepherds watching their flocks through the night, and suddenly an angel of the Lord stood among them in the flooding light of God's glory and they were very much afraid.

"Have no fear," the angel said to them, "I bring you wonderful news: a joyous news for all people. This very day in the city of David your savior has been born: none other than the Messiah himself, the Lord. You will find an infant—this is your sign—wrapped in swaddling clothes and lying in a manger."

All at once a galaxy of celestial beings was with the angel in an outpouring of adoration: "Glory be to God in the highest, and peace on earth to all those of good will."

As soon as the angels had disappeared into the heavens, the shepherds began to say to one another, "Come, let us go into Bethlehem and see this marvel which the Lord has made known to us."

So they hurried off and found Mary and Joseph, and the baby lying in the manger. What they saw confirmed everything they had been told about this child; and the others hearing it were full of wonder at what the shepherds related. Mary meanwhile dwelt upon all these things, pondering them in her heart.

Then the shepherds went back, full of God's greatness, praising him for what they had heard and seen and been told.

The Circumcision and Presentation in the Temple

After being circumcised a firstborn child, having been "given" to God according to the Law, had to be bought back. This redemption was done by a purification ceremony performed by the mother, while the father made the offering. Luke has telescoped the two duties together.

Simeon's outpouring—"Now you can let your servant go"—is known as the *Nunc Dimittis* from its first words in Latin in St. Jerome's translation: "*Nunc dimittis servum tuum, Domine.*" It too, with the Magnificat and Ave Maria, has become the subject of masterly compositions.

As to the prophetess Anna's great age, she must have been over a hundred.

(Luke 2:21-40)

EIGHT days later when it was time for the child to be circumcised, he was called Jesus: the name given to him by the angel before he was conceived. Then when it was time for his parents' purification according to the Mosaic law, they took him up to Jerusalem to present him to the Lord (as prescribed by that same law: "Every male that openeth the womb shall be called holy to the Lord") and also to offer the required sacrifice ("A pair of turtledoves or two young pigeons").

Now, there was in Jerusalem a man named Simeon, an honest and devout soul who had long awaited the consolation of Israel. He was filled with the Holy Spirit and the Holy Spirit had revealed to him that he should not see death till he had laid eyes on the Lord's Messiah. Now, led by the Spirit, he came into the temple, and when the parents brought in the child Jesus to carry out for him what the Law prescribed, Simeon took him in his arms, praising God and exclaiming:

Now, my Master, you can let your servant go—in
peace at last—as you promised me,
Because these eyes of mine have seen the saving grace
you have prepared to shine upon all nations:
A light of revelation to the Gentiles,
and a glory to your own people, Israel.

While the child's father and mother were marveling at the things being spoken about him, Simeon blessed them and said to Mary, "I tell you, this child is set for the fall and the rising of many in Israel: a standard that will be withstood . . . (Ah! a sword shall pierce your own soul) . . . but because of whom the secrets of many will be revealed."

Another person there was Anna, a prophetess (the daughter of Phanuel of the tribe of Asher). She was a great age, having first lived with her husband as a young woman for seven years, and then on her own as a widow for another eighty-four years. She never left the temple but worshiped there night and day, praying and fasting. She came in just at that moment, and she too began to thank God and to hold forth about the child to all those who were longing for the redemption of Jerusalem.

When the parents of Jesus had done everything required by God's law, they returned to Nazareth, their hometown in Galilee, where the boy grew up into a strong lad, unusually wise and full of God's grace.

The Visit of the Magi and the Flight to Egypt

Jesus must have been about two when the wise men from the east found him. (The family had temporarily settled in Bethlehem.) Their gifts to the infant boy, besides having various significancies, are all symbols of royalty. Frankincense is what we would now call simply incense; both it and myrrh are the congealed resins of certain trees. Myrrh was used for embalming (see note on p. 307).

By tradition (or legend) the wise men or Magi have been numbered as three and described as kings. They have even been given names: Melchior, Gasper, and Balthazar.

As to the Star, no one really knows what it was or how its arbitrary appearance can be explained otherwise than miraculously. A supernova has been suggested, that is, a new star with a short blazing life of great brightness. Apparently, a comet or the conjunction of Jupiter and Saturn are also possibilities. It is known that Halley's Comet entered the inner solar system in the year 11 B.C., and that Jupiter and

Saturn came close together in 7 B.C. Since according to some modern calculations Christ was born sometime between 17 and 4 B.C., both dates are possible.

Herod, who has been ruling the Jews in Palestine for thirty-three years, is now an old man, more than ever cunning, superstitious, and irascible. His slaughter of the infants at Bethlehem, however (known as the slaughter of the Holy Innocents), was probably prompted not simply by a desire to protect himself but by a full awareness that the whole of Judea was sitting on a tinderbox of inflammable nationalism and that if the Romans were ordered in to put out the fire they would do it with characteristic thoroughness (as indeed was soon to be proved).

(Matthew 2:1-23)

WHEN Jesus was born at Bethlehem in Judea in the days of King Herod, there came all the way from the East a party of astrological wise men called Magi, inquiring: "Where is the newborn king of the Jews? For we have seen his star rise and have come to pay him homage."

When King Herod heard of this he was vastly perturbed, and all Jerusalem with him. He called together the chief priests and religious scholars of the people and asked them where the Messiah was to be born.

"At Bethlehem in Judea," they told him, "just as the prophet [Micah] wrote: 'And thou Bethlehem, in the land of Judah, art not least among the princes of Judah: for out of thee shall come a Governor that shall rule my people Israel.' "

Herod thereupon summoned the Magi to come to him privately, and he learned from them exactly when the star had appeared. Then he sent them on to Bethlehem, saying, "Discover where the child is and when you have found him bring me word so that I too can go and pay him homage."

They listened to the king and went on their way. Then, amazingly, the star which they had seen in its rising appeared in front of them, leading them on till it came to rest right over the spot where the child was. A thrill of joy went through them when they saw this star. On entering the house, there they beheld the infant boy with Mary his mother, and throwing themselves down they paid him homage. Then they opened up the treasures they had brought him: gold, frankincense, and myrhh. After that, having been warned in a dream not to return to Herod, they went back to their own country a different way.

* * *

When they were gone an angel of the Lord appeared to Joseph in a dream and said, "Get up at once and take the boy and his mother and flee to Egypt. Stay there till I tell you. Herod is searching for the child and wants to kill him."

So that same night Joseph got up and set off with the child and his mother for Egypt; and there they remained till Herod's death, thus fulfilling the Lord's words through another prophecy: "Out of Egypt have I called my son."

When Herod saw that he had been tricked by the Magi he flew into a passion, and he sent soldiers to kill all the boys in Bethlehem and thereabouts who were two years old and under (having calculated the time from the Magi). Thus were fulfilled the words of Jeremiah the prophet:

> In Rama was there a voice heard,
> lamentation and weeping and great mourning:
> Rachel weeping for her children
> and would not be comforted,
> because they are not.

As soon as Herod was dead, the angel of the Lord appeared in a dream to Joseph and said, "Rise now and take the child and his mother back to Israel, for those who wanted to kill him are dead."

So Joseph rose and set off with the child and his mother for Israel. But when he heard that Archelaus had succeeded his father Herod as king of Judea, he was afraid to go there, and being warned in a dream he turned aside into the province of Galilee, settling in a town called Nazareth; thus fulfilling the ancient prophecy about the Messiah that "He shall be called a Nazarene."

The Boy Jesus in the Temple

The following story is the only account in the Bible that we have of Christ's life before he began his public ministry. There are, to be sure, legends aplenty to be found in various apochryphal writings from the second century onward: sometimes enlightening and plausible but more often than not, coy, cute, and silly.

Be these as they may, Jesus at the age of twelve (a year

before the present bar mitzvah age) is lost to his parents in Jerusalem. Nazareth is some sixty-five miles from Jerusalem and we are told that Joseph and Mary had done a day's journey before they missed him, so we can suppose that they had traveled at least twenty miles by the close of the day. This means that if the search for him began then and lasted three days, Jesus was actually missing for four days.

As to the young Christ's seemingly precocious interest in rabbinical theology, it should be remembered that instructions in the Old Testament and the Law were regularly given to Hebrew boys at that time. By the age of twelve many of them probably knew most of the Old Testament by heart.

An important feature of this story is that Jesus boldly calls God his Father, thus not only establishing his future claim to be the Son of God, but inaugurating for the whole of humankind a new and vitally loving filiation.

(Luke 2:40-52)

JESUS' parents used to go every year to Jerusalem for the feast of the Passover, and when he was twelve years old they went [with him] to the customary festival.

When they had concluded their time and started for home, the boy Jesus stayed behind in Jerusalem. This they did not know and, supposing him to be among the traveling party, came a whole day's journey before they began to look for him among their friends and relatives. When they failed to find him they went back to Jerusalem to search for him there.

After three days they came upon him in the Temple in the midst of the professors, listening to them and asking them questions. Everyone who heard him was astonished at his understanding and his answers. His parents were amazed to see him there and his mother said to him, "Son, why have you done this to us? Do you know, your father and I have been looking for you in despair!"

"But why have you been looking for me?" he answered. "Did you not know that I had to be in my Father's house?"

They did not understand what he meant.

He traveled back with them and came to Nazareth, obedient in everything. And while his mother treasured all his sayings in her heart, Jesus grew in mind and body and graciousness before God and man.

The Coming of John the Baptist

The region where John the Baptist so austerely prepared himself for his ministry of preaching and baptizing was the barren wilderness stretching from the Jerusalem ridge to the Jordan valley where the river flows into the Dead Sea. The locusts he lived on were not the sweet dried beans of the locust tree (the carob, *Ceratonia siliqua*) but the insect: a kind of cricket or grasshopper, which is still relished in the east.

"Baptize" comes from the Greek *bapto*: to dip.

The Saduccees and Pharisees were rival religious sects with strong political leanings. The Saduccees at this time were in power and furnished the high priest. They tended to be more conservative in their interpretation of scripture—even puritanical—and yet, paradoxically, more sympathetic toward Hellenic culture. They did not believe in the resurrection of the body or of an afterlife of reward and punishment.

The Pharisees, on the other hand, were theologically more imaginative and when at their best promulgated a devotion to God and man not unlike Christ's own, but when at their worst they degenerated into mere casuists, encrusting the life of the spirit with such an overload of mechanical observances that they smothered it.

(Matthew 3:1-6, Luke 3:10-14, Matthew 3:7-17)

AT this time John the Baptist appeared, with a clarion call through the wilderness of Judea: "Change your hearts. The kingdom of heaven is near."

He was the man spoken of by Isaiah the prophet when he said:

A voice crying in the wilderness:
"Prepare ye the way of the Lord
And make straight his paths."

This John wore clothes of camel hair belted at the waist. His food was locusts and wild honey. People flocked to him from Jerusalem and all Judea and the Jordan valley, confessing their sins and being baptized by him in the river Jordan.

They asked him, "What must we do?"

He replied, "Let the one who has two coats share with the

one who has none. And let the one who has food act likewise."

Tax collectors also came to him to be baptized, asking, "Master, what must we do?"

"Exact no more than your due," he told them. And when soldiers on service asked, "And us too? What are we to do?"

"No extortion," he said to them. "No false accusations. And live on your pay."

But when he saw many Pharisees and Saduccees coming to him, he denounced them roundly, "You brood of vipers," he cried, "who has warned you to flee from the wrath that is to come? First you must produce fruit worthy of a change of heart. And do not imagine that you can glibly say: '[We are all right], we have Abraham for our father,' because, I tell you, God can raise up children to Abraham from these very stones . . . Already the ax is laid to the root of the trees, and every tree that does not bear good fruit is cut down and thrown into the fire. I baptize with water those who repent, but a more powerful than I is coming whose very sandals I am not fit to carry, who will baptize you in the Holy Spirit and in fire. His winnowing fan is in his hand. He will sort out his threshing floor, garnering the wheat into his granary but burning the chaff in unquenchable fire."

Then Jesus came to the Jordan from Galilee to John to be baptized by him, but John tried to dissuade him. "I need to be baptized by you," he protested, "and here you come to me?"

"Let it be so now," Jesus replied. "It is right for us to fulfill the plan."

So John consented. And when Jesus was dipped into the water he came straight up out of it, and at that moment the heavens opened and he [John] saw the Spirit of God come down like a dove and settle on him, while he heard a voice from the skies proclaiming: "This is my Son, the very much loved, and I am well pleased with him."

The Temptation in the Desert

Jesus is poised for the beginning of his public ministry, which in three years will terminate in his death. He prepares himself by a fundamental confrontation with evil.

There is a twist to this story that is not often thought of. It is this: the devil is not simply trying to get Christ to demean himself by succumbing to his suggestions, but he wants to find out for sure whether his present and future antagonist is really the Son of God. After all, even in the angelic world, there is no reason to suppose that spirit awareness of events comes independent of some kind of experience which builds up knowledge.

Which brings me to say, that in that world of the dynamic mind, if indeed it is the next rung in the ladder of being after human life, and if that plane of existence continues the pattern of subsuming all that is beneath it, plus something new (and there is no reason to suppose a break in the chain), then the angelic world comprises the very fabric of matter without itself being material.

Consequently, when part of this spirit world fell from grace (and a powerful part), it would not necessarily lose its natural hold and function in the workings of the universe.

So Christ here is dealing with an entity whose constitutional position in creation he in no way disavows, and whose powers he does not dispute, even while he repudiates all that that being stands for. And when Jesus refers to Satan as "the Prince of this world" (as he often does in the gospels), he is not using a derogatory epithet but bestowing on him his proper title.

Fundamentally, what Jesus rejects in the following encounter is the temptation to cheat. He will not use his divine powers to achieve success, even in converting the world (at least not at the behest of Satan). Otherwise, why should he ever have become man?

(Matthew 4:1-11)

THEN Jesus was led up into the wilderness by the Spirit to be tempted by the devil. And after fasting forty days and forty nights, he was hungry. Then came the tempter to him, saying, "If you are the Son of God, tell these stones to turn into bread." And Jesus answered, "It is written: 'Not by bread alone doth man live, but by every word that proceedeth from the mouth of God.' "

Then the devil took him into the holy city and set him on the pinnacle of the temple. "If you are the Son of God," he said to him, "hurl yourself down from here, for it is written: 'He shall put thee in his angels' charge, and in their hands they shall bear thee up, lest thou dash thy foot against a stone.' "

"It is also written," Jesus returned: " 'Thou shalt not tempt the Lord thy God.' "

Once more the devil took him to a very high mountain, and showed him all the kingdoms of the world and the glory of them. "All this will I give you," he said to him, "if you will fall down and adore me."

"Begone, Satan," Jesus replied to him, "for it is written: 'The Lord thy God shalt thou adore, and him only shalt thou serve.' "

Then the devil left him, and there came angels to tend on him.

Jesus Introduced by St. John

I thought it important to include the opening Hymn to Being of St. John's gospel with its amazing theological statement, and also because the description of the way Christ meets some of his first disciples is told with such artless charm that one almost misses the point that the grace of his human presence is irresistible. So there, in the first chapter are placed side by side Christ's divinity and his perfect humanity.

There is no way of putting into English all that is contained in the first sentence: "In the beginning was the *Logos*." Our "In the beginning was the Word" gets nowhere near it. The Greek *logos* does indeed mean word, but it also means reason, thought, conception. On top of that, the rich pedigree of *logos* stretching back to such philosophers as Thales, Heraclitus, and Philo, endowed the word with philosophical and theological connotations. *Logos* came to mean the expressed knowability of a thing, the dynamic rationale of its purpose. In philosophy one might call it the intrinsic finality of something: the knowable impetus of its existence.

Logos came to mean also the inherent intelligence, even wisdom, of all being; which of course immediately links up with the divine wisdom, the divine intention. So what St. John means in his first few lines is that Christ is the original blueprint of God's design: that design which is an image of his creative impulse—the eternally begotten Son.

(John 1:1-51)

IN the beginning was the Word, inseparable from God, because the Word *was* God, and existed always with God. Everything came into being through him, and without him nothing had any being at all. For the being that came through him was life and that life was the light of mankind: the light which shines in the darkness and which the darkness can never grasp.

There was a man sent from God whose name was John. He came as a witness, a witness to the light so that through him all should have belief. He himself was not the light, only the witness to the light: the true light that enlightens every person coming into this world.

He was in the world and the world had its being through him, but the world did not know him. He came to his own, and his own would not own him. But to those who did own to him, those that believed in his name, he gave the power to become the children of God. Such are born not through the will of flesh and blood, or any human wish, but from God.

So, the Word became flesh and set up in our midst. We have seen his perfection: the perfect expression of his Father's one and only Son—all grace and truth.

John testified to him (for he was his spokesman), crying out and saying, "He who comes after me is before me, because he *was* before me." And we have all received his abundance, grace on grace; because though the Law was given through Moses, grace and truth came through Jesus Christ. Nobody has ever seen God; that is why the one who is in the very lap of the Father, the Only Begotten One, why he has declared him.

The testimony of John was this, when the Jews sent priests and Levites from Jerusalem to ask him: "Who are you?" He confessed, "I am not the Christ." Yes, he confessed it with no denying.

"Who then?" they asked. "Are you Elijah?

"I am not," he said.

"Are you the prophet to come?"

"No," he replied.

"Then who are you?" they went on. "We must have an answer to give those who sent us. What do you say of yourself?"

Whereat he declared, "I am the voice of one crying in the wilderness: 'Make straight the way of the Lord,' as spoke the prophet Isaiah."

Now these people were sent by the Pharisees, and they went on to question him: "Why, if you are not the Christ, or Elijah, or the prophet, do you baptize?"

"I baptize with water," John replied, "but there stands among you one whom you do not know, who comes after me, whose very sandals I am not fit to unloose."

All these things happened in Bethany beyond the Jordan, where John was baptizing. The next day, seeing Jesus coming toward him, he said, "Look, there goes the lamb of God who takes away the sins of the world. This is he of whom I said, 'One comes after me who is before me, because he was before me.' I did not know him, but to manifest him to Israel is the reason I came here baptizing with water."

John continued in his testimony: "I saw the Spirit come down like a dove from heaven and settle upon him. I did not know him till the One who sent me to baptize with water declared, 'He on whom you see the Spirit come down and settle, he is the one who baptizes with the Holy Spirit.' And I saw it, and have testified: 'This is the Son of God.' "

The next day as John stood with two of his disciples, he saw Jesus walking and he said, "Look, the lamb of God!"

The two disciples, hearing this, followed Jesus, and Jesus, turning, saw them following him and said, "What are you looking for?"

"Rabbi," they answered (which means 'Teacher'), "where do you live?"

"Come and see," he said.

So they went and saw where he lived and stayed with him all that day. It was about four o'clock.

Andrew, one of the two who heard Jesus and followed him, was the brother of Simon Peter. Off he went to find his brother Simon and said to him, "We have found the Messiah" (which is translated, the Christ), and he took him to

Jesus. Jesus gazed at him and said, "So, you are Simon, the son of John! You shall be called Cephas" (which means "rock").

The next day, Jesus, wishing to go out into Galilee, found Philip and said to him, "Follow me." Philip was from Bethsaida, the town of Andrew and Peter. Philip found Nathaniel and said to him, "We have discovered the one Moses wrote about in the Law and the Prophets: Jesus the son of Joseph, from Nazareth."

"What!" replied Nathaniel. "Can any good come out of Nazareth."

"Come and see," said Philip.

As Jesus saw Nathaniel walking toward him, he remarked, "Look, an Israelite in whom there is no guile!"

"How do you know me?" Nathaniel said to him, and Jesus answered, "Before Philip called you, I saw you under the fig tree."

"Master, you are the Son of God," Nathaniel exclaimed. "You are the King of Israel."

"So! because I told you I saw you under the fig tree, you believe me?" Jesus answered. "You shall see much greater things." And he continued, "Oh yes, let me tell you: you will see the heavens open and the very angels of God ascending and descending about the Son of Man."

NOTE

Cephas is the Hebrew for the Greek πετρα (*petra*) and the Latin *petrus*, both meaning "rock."

The Marriage Feast of Cana

This miracle, Jesus' first, is given only in John. The account is not only a well-told vignette of the village wedding feast but is full of symbolism. The incident takes place "on the third day," a forehint of Christ's resurrection. The good wine that Jesus provides is not only a symbol of blood but is a foretaste of that wine to be drunk in the kingdom of heaven by the "blessed who are called to the marriage supper of the Lamb" (Revelation 19:9). The water pots of the Jewish purification ritual, like the old Dispensation, have to be emptied for the new Dispensation to be poured in. The wine that is offered, like the new life, is beyond measure abundant (the water pots had contained one hundred twenty gallons).

When Jesus' mother turns to him during the wedding celebrations and says, "They have no wine," his reply is, I believe, the most mistranslated sentence in the Bible, though St. Jerome, writing in A.D. 400 gets it right. Jesus's actual five words in the Greek are: Τι ἐμοι και σοι, γυναι (Ti emoi kai soi, gunai?), literally word for word: "What to me and you, woman?"

Let us take the "woman" first. "Woman" in this context in modern English would be plain rude, but "woman" in Greek was a term of respect and took its more specific meaning from the setting. It could mean madam, lady, mother, even my dear. Here I would choose "mother" even though the Anchor Bible with all its scholarship suggests that a symbolic import may be intended which the translation "mother" obscures.

Next we must tackle the *ti emoi kai soi*. The phrase is used several times in the Bible with meanings that range from "Must you be a nuisance to me?", "Mind your own business," "Does that concern us?" to "What do you want me to do about it?" and exactly what it says: "What is that to you and me?" St. Jerome is one of the few who translates the sentence word for word: "*Quid mihi et tibit est mulier?*" And that is what I prefer to do because the words happen to be contemporary English, the only difference being that we reverse the order: "What is that to you and me?"

Mary knows exactly the caliber of her son. For thirty years she has pondered his uniqueness. And he does not hesitate to please her, even though it means hastening his public ministry.

(John 2: 1-12)

ON the third day there was a wedding at Cana in Galilee, and the mother of Jesus was there. And Jesus too, with his disciples, was invited to the wedding. But the wine ran out, and the mother of Jesus said to him, "They have no wine."

"Mother, what is that to you and me?" Jesus replied. "My time has not yet come."

His mother said to the waiters, "Do whatever he tells you."

Now, there were six stone water pots standing there for the ritual washings of the Jews, each holding some twenty to thirty gallons.

Jesus said to them, "Fill the water pots with water."

They filled them to the brim.

"Now pour some out," he told them, "and take it to the master of ceremonies."

So they took some, and when the master of ceremonies had tasted the water now turned into wine—and he had no idea where it came from, though the waiters who had poured it knew—he called the bridegroom over and exclaimed, "Everyone puts out the good wine first, and the less good only after people have drunk well, but you have kept the best till last."

So did Jesus work his first miracle at Cana in Galilee and display the wonder of his power; and his disciples believed in him.

The Cleansing of the Temple

The Temple was the Second Temple, completed many hundreds of years before in 516 B.C. and now being restored: a restoration which, ironically, was finished only seven years before the whole edifice was destroyed by the Romans in A.D. 70.

What was offensive to Jesus about the Temple traffic was not so much that it happened (indeed, the economics of changing money to arrange for sacrifices could hardly proceed without it), but that the trading had intruded into the Temple itself. On top of that, there was the nasty element of profiteering and, undoubtedly, sharp practice at the cost of naive pilgrims coming into Jersualem from the country.

Significantly, Jesus expels not only the money changers but the innocent animals as well, thus perhaps symbolizing the worship to come, one of true spirituality which will not be dependent on mere material rites.

In the Synoptic gospels (Matthew, Mark, and Luke) this act takes place in the last week of Jesus' life, not at the beginning of his ministry. In Matthew, Jesus telescopes two quotations from the Old Testament together in justification of his bold move: "Has this shrine become a den of thieves? It is quite plain to me that it has, says the Lord" (Jeremiah 7:11), and: "My house shall be called a house of prayer for all peoples" (Isaiah 56:7). What Jesus actually says is: "It is written, 'My house shall be called the house of prayer, but you have made it a den of thieves.' " (Matthew 21:13)

Immediately after the wedding at Cana Jesus goes with his mother and family to Capernaum, a town on the Sea of Galilee, stays there a few days and then moves to Jerusalem in time for the Passover.

(John 2:13-25)

THERE in the Temple he found sellers of cattle and sheep and doves, and money changers sitting. He made a whip of cords and drove the lot of them out of the temple with all their sheep and oxen. He scattered the money changers' coins and overturned their tables. And to the sellers of doves he declared, "Take these things out of here and stop making my Father's house a house of trade." Then his disciples remembered the scripture which says: "The zeal of thy house hath eaten me up."

The Jews remonstrated with him and said, "What evidence can you give us to justify what you have done?"

"Pull this temple down," Jesus retorted, "and in three days I shall raise it up."

"This temple took forty-six years to build," they replied, "and you are going to raise it in three days!"

But he was speaking of the shrine of his body. Later when he rose from the dead, his disciples remembered this reply of his, and they believed the scriptures and the word of Jesus.

While he was in Jerusalem for the festival of the Passover, many saw the signs he did and believed in him. But Jesus did not trust himself to them, knowing mankind all too well without the help of others and what was in the human heart.

The Woman at the Well

Although John the Baptist was still preaching and baptizing, people were beginning to leave him and flock to Jesus, and Jesus, aware that a certain rivalry was springing up between the two sets of followers and also that he was drawing too much attention from the Pharisees, decided to leave Judea and go north into Galilee. To do this, the most direct route was through the province of Samaria.

Samaria, partly locked in by mountains, lay some forty miles north of Jerusalem. The Samaritans, though practicing Jews, were schismatic. They had their own temple, their own priests, and even their own canonical list of the scriptures, which was limited to the Pentateuch. The Jews and the Samaritans were not on speaking terms, and when the former wanted to go into Galilee (which was not schismatic) they chose a route that took them along the valley of the Jordan, thus bypassing Samaria altogether. Not so Jesus.

It had just turned afternoon, the hottest part of the day, when Jesus and his party reached Jacob's Well, and in any case they had had a long trek over the mountains and now down into the valley below Mt. Gerizim. St. John uses a curious little word when he describes how Jesus sat himself down by the well. He says that Jesus was weary from the journey and sat down οὕτως [houtōs], which means literally "thus" but by its order in the sentence here carries the connotation of "just as he was." In other words, he threw himself down without further ado. One might without irreverence say: he simply "flopped."

Jacob's Well—many centuries old in Christ's day—still exists and one can drink from it.

(John 4:5-42)

SO he came to a town in Samaria called Sechem, near the plot of land which Jacob once gave his son Joseph. And at Jacob's Well there, Jesus, weary from his trudging, just sat himself down as he was by the well. The time was about noon.

A Samaritan woman came to draw water and Jesus said to her, "Give me a drink" (his disciples having gone into the town to buy food).

"What!" exclaimed the woman, "do you, a Jew, ask me a woman and a Samaritan for a drink?" (the Jews having no dealings with the Samaritans).

"If only you knew God's free gift," Jesus answered, "and who it is that says to you, 'Give me a drink,' you might well have asked *him* for a drink instead, and he would have given you living water."

"Sir," said the woman, "you have no bucket to let down, and the well is deep. With what are you going to get this living water? Don't tell me you're greater than our forefather Jacob who gave us this well and drank from it himself with all his sons and his flocks?"

"Everyone who drinks this water will thirst again," Jesus replied to her, "but whoever drinks the water that I shall give will never thirst again—forever. For the water that I shall give will be a spring of water welling up into everlasting life."

"Sir," said the woman to him, "give me this water so I shan't ever be thirsty or have to plod out here to fetch it."

"Go and call your husband and come back here," Jesus answered.

"But I have no husband," said the woman.

"How right you are! 'I have no husband.' You have had five husbands and the one you have at present is not your husband. A correct statement, indeed!"

"Ah, sir," exclaimed the woman to him, "I see that you are a prophet! . . . Now, our forefathers worshiped on this mountain [Gerizim], but you Jews maintain that Jerusalem is the place to worship."

"Believe me, madam," Jesus answered, "the hour is coming when neither on this mountain nor in Jerusalem will you worship the Father. In the meantime, you people worship you know not what. We at least worship what we know, because salvation is with the Jews. But the time is coming, and is already here, when the true worshipers will adore the Father in spirit and in truth. Such are the worshipers the Father wants. For God is spirit, so his worshipers must worship him in spirit and in truth."

Then the woman said to him, "I know that the Messiah who is called the Christ is coming, and when he comes he will explain all this."

"I am he, talking to you," Jesus said to her.

Just then his disciples came, amazed to find him talking to a woman. But no one asked, "What do you want?" or "Why are you talking to her?" The woman put her pitcher down and hurried into the town, exclaiming to all: "Come and see a man who's been telling me everything I've ever done. Perhaps he is the Messiah." And out they flocked from the town to see him.

Meanwhile his disciples begged him, "Master, eat." "No," he said to them, "I have food to eat you know nothing of."

"Did someone bring something out here for him to eat?" they began to ask one another.

"No," said Jesus, "my food is to do the will of him who sent me and complete his work. There are still four months to the harvest, wouldn't you say? But look, I tell you: just raise your eyes and look at the fields: they are already white for the harvest. The reaper is paid his wage and gathers a crop for eternal life, so that sower and reaper celebrate together; which isn't usually true, as the proverb says: 'One sows and another reaps.' You, for instance, I have sent to reap where you have not toiled. Others have done the toiling and you have come into the fruits of their labors."

Many of the Samaritans from that town believed in him because of the woman's report and her declaration: "He told me everything I've ever done." And when they reached him they pressed him to stay with them, so he stayed there for two days, and many more believed in him because of his own words. They said to the woman, "Now we believe not because of what you said, but because we've heard him ourselves and know for certain that this is the savior of the world."

Jesus Cures the Centurion's Son

After a sojourn of two days with the Samaritans, Jesus passes into Galilee, arriving once more in Cana. The miracle described in this story may well be a variant of the healing of the centurion's son in the Synoptics (Matthew 8:5-13 and Luke 7:1-10). In any case, the man is a royal official at the court of King Herod, the tetrarch of Galilee, and is probably a Gentile.

This Herod is not, of course, the same as the Herod mentioned at Christ's birth who instigated the slaughter of the Holy Innocents, but one of his sons, Herod Antipas, the one who later beheads John the Baptist. The title "tetrarch" was bestowed upon rulers who had the power but not the official prestige of kings. It was a title favored by the Romans to fit rulers whom they promoted but could not quite trust enough to make monarchs—though that is what they were in fact.

A centurion was the commander of a hundred men (*centum* being the Latin for a hundred). The modern equivalent would perhaps be a company commander. There were sixty centurions to a legion.

Capernaum was a prosperous city on the northern shores of Lake Galilee, some twenty miles from Cana. Capernaum became the center of Jesus' Galilean ministry, perhaps because Peter had a house there. The Franciscans, who have been consistently excavating the ruins of Capernaum since the 1920s, have identified Peter's house on the basis of inscriptions and the accounts of early pilgrims. Recent archeological finds have also unearthed the ruins of a first-century synagogue, which is almost certainly the one in which Jesus preached.

(John 4:46-54)

SO once again Jesus came to Cana in Galilee, where he had turned the water into wine. And a royal official whose son was sick in Capernaum, hearing that Jesus had returned to Galilee from Judea, came pleading to him to come and heal his son who was on the point of death.

"Alas, unless you people see miracles and wonders," Jesus said to him, "you never will believe."

"I beg you, sir," the official pleaded, "come to my house before my little boy dies."

"Go back home," said Jesus. "Your son lives."

The man took Jesus at his word and started for home. As he was on his way his servants came to meet him with the news that his boy was alive and well.

"At what time did the crisis pass?" he asked them.

"Yesterday at about one in the afternoon the fever left him," they told him. The exact hour, the father realized, when Jesus had said to him: "Your son lives."

The officer and his whole household were now believers. . . . This was Jesus' second miracle after he returned from Judea to Galilee.

Jesus at Nazareth and Capernaum

One of the most quietly dramatic moments in the New Testament occurs about this time. Jesus, full of the power of the Holy Spirit, is touring Galilee, preaching in the synagogues, and people flock to hear him, drawn by the authority of his words and presence.

(Luke 4:16-21, 30-44)

HE came to Nazareth, where he had been reared and, according to his habit, on the Sabbath day entered the synagogue. As he stood up to read, the scroll of the prophet Isaiah was handed to him. Opening out the scroll, he found the place where it says:

The Spirit of the Lord is upon me,
Because the Lord hath anointed me to preach good tidings to the poor;
He hath sent me to bind up the brokenhearted,
To proclaim deliverance to the captives,
And recovering of sight to the blind,
To set at liberty them that are bruised,
To preach the acceptable year of the Lord.

Rolling up the scroll, he returned it to the server and sat down. Every eye in the synagogue was on him.

"This very day," he began, "this scripture is fulfilled in your hearing . . ."

At first the response of the congregation was enthusiastic, but when it dawned on his listeners that he was claiming to be the Messiah (whereas they knew him to be nothing more than the local carpenter's son), they became so enraged that they dragged him to a bluff on the edge of the village and tried to throw him down. But he walked straight through them and went on his way to Capernaum, a Galilean town, where on the Sabbath he taught in the synagogue, astounding people with what he said and the authority with which he said it.

There was a man there possessed by an unclean spirit who began shouting, "Aha, what do you and we have in common, Jesus of Nazareth? Have you come to destroy us? I know who you are: the holy one of God."

Jesus cut him short: "Be quiet!" he said, "and come out of him."

The devil flung the man to the middle of the floor, then went out of him without doing further harm. Everyone was amazed. "Such power in a word!" they exclaimed to one another: "Such authority that even unclean spirits obey his command to leave!"

Reports of Jesus flew around the countryside.

When he had left the synagogue Jesus went to Simon Peter's house, where Simon's mother-in-law lay stricken with a high fever. They begged him to do something for her. So he stood over her, scolding the fever, and it promptly left her. There and then she got up and began to serve them.

At sundown that evening, all those who had sick with them brought them to him with their assorted maladies, and laying his hands on each one of them he healed them. Devils too came wrenching out of many, shouting, "You are the son of God!" But he told them to stop blabbing and to keep it to themselves that he was the Christ.

When morning came he withdrew and retired to a desert place, but the mob went looking for him, and when they found him they restrained him from leaving them.

"Listen, there are other cities," he told them, "where I must take the good news of the kingdom of God. This is what I was sent for."

So he went preaching through the synagogues of Palestine.

The Miraculous Draft of Fishes

The wholehearted adherence of Jesus' first disciples to him was probably a gradual processs. The young men who had already come to him—Andrew and John, Peter, Philip and Nathaniel—did not at first abandon their homes or their trade. They were professional fishermen and continued to fish on the Sea of Galilee—until perhaps the present episode.

(Luke 5:1-11)

ONE day as Jesus stood by the Lake of Gennesaret [the Sea of Galilee] and the crowds were pressing on him to hear the word of God, he saw two boats standing near the shore whose fishermen had disembarked and were cleaning their nets. So he got into one of the boats, which was Simon's, and asked him to push out a little from the land; then, sitting down, he taught the crowds from the boat.

When he had finished speaking he said to Simon, "Put out into the deep and let down your nets for a catch."

"We've toiled all night, Master," Simon answered, "and haven't caught a thing, but if you say so, I'll let down our nets."

As soon as they had done it, they netted an enormous

haul of fish and their nets were near to breaking. They signaled to their partners in the other boat to come to their help, which they did, and both boats were so full that they were almost sinking.

When Simon Peter saw this he flung himself at Jesus' knees, protesting, "Don't stay near me, Lord. I am a sinful man." He was shaken, as was everyone with him, by the haul of fish they had netted. So too were the sons of Zebedee, James and John, who were Simon's partners.

"Don't be afraid," Jesus said to Simon. "From now on your catch will be humankind."

Beaching their boats they left everything and followed him.

The Leper and the Paralytic Let Down Through the Roof

The term "leprosy" in Biblical times could cover any number of skin diseases and did not necessarily mean leprosy as we know it. In this story, the reason Jesus tells the man not to broadcast his cure is not so much to keep his identity hidden as to shield Jesus himself from being swamped by crowds. (Though, of course, it was also essential for him to reveal his Messiahhood only with the utmost discretion.)

The scribes were an educated class, well read in the law and the scriptures; through them many of the functions of government and social intercourse at the higher levels operated. One might call them the intellectuals.

(Mark 1:40-45 and 2:1-12)

A leper once came to him, begging on his knees: "If only you will, you can make me clean." Jesus, moved with compassion, stretched out his hand and touched him, saying, "I will. Be clean."

Immediately the leprosy dropped from him and he was made clean. Jesus there and then dismissed him with this solemn warning: "See that you tell nobody, but go and show yourself to the priest and take him the offering for your cleansing which Moses prescribed as a token."

The man, however, went off and babbled the whole story to all and sundry, so that Jesus could no longer enter a city openly but had to remain outside in isolated places, where people came to him from all directions.

After Jesus had gone back to Capernaum, news spread in a few days that he was in a house there, and such a crowd gathered that the whole space before the front door was jammed.

As he was preaching the word to them, four men carrying a paralytic and failing to get to Jesus through the crowd, opened up the roof right over where Jesus was. They made a hole and let the paralytic down on his pallet.

When Jesus saw their faith he said to the paralytic, "Son, your sins are forgiven."

Some scribes sitting near thought to themselves, "How can this man talk like this? It's blasphemous. Surely only God can forgive sins!"

Jesus read their minds at once and said, "Why are you objecting? Which do you think is easier: to say to the paralytic 'Your sins are forgiven' or to say 'Get to your feet, pick up your pallet, and start walking'? Now, just to show you that the Son of Man is authorized on earth to forgive sins, I'm going to tell the paralytic: 'You there, I say, get to your feet, pick up your pallet, and go home.' "

The man stood up at once, picked up his mat and, right in front of everyone, walked out. They were all dumbfounded and burst into praise of God. "We have never seen anything like it," they avowed.

Jesus and the Sabbath

The next three stories concern Jesus' defense of the human being when confronted by religious pedantry: one that trammels men and women within strictures which have become purely legalistic and make no sense. All law, especially divine law, is a balanced equation between set principles: principles which emanate from the nature of reality itself as expressed in the dynamic of cause and effect. There can be no law where the effect is out of kilter with the cause; that is, where the reason for the law is not a true reflection of the real: in this case the needs and nature of mankind.

The first episode takes place soon after Jesus, while still in Cana, has cured the centurion's son in Capernaum. Now he has gone to Jerusalem to attend the festival.

Bethzatha ("House of Olives") or Bethesda ("House of Mercy") was a locale northeast of the Temple, which recent excavations have confirmed. The pool was surrounded by five porticoes or colonnades with one down the middle.

The phrase "Son of Man" is purposely ambiguous and ambivalent. It can mean simply human being, or this special human being, the Messiah, or even one who is Son of God, i.e., divine. Jesus is still at that stage of his ministry when he must be discreet about his claims (though in St. John's gospel discretion is thrown to the winds!).

(John 5:2-34, Mark 2:23-28, 3:1-4, Matthew 12:11-13)

NOW, in Jerusalem by the Sheep Gate there is a pool called in Hebrew Bethesda. It has five porticoes, where a crowd of sick people—the blind, the crippled, the paralyzed —used to lie.

There was a man there who had been ill for thirty-eight years, and when Jesus saw him lying there (knowing that he had been afflicted for a very long time), he asked him, "Would you like to be well?"

"Sir," answered the sick man, "when the water bubbles up I have no one to plunge me into the pool. For, the moment I am on my way someone else gets in ahead of me."

"Stand up," Jesus said to him. "Roll up your mat and start walking."

The man was cured on the spot. He picked up his pallet and began to walk.

Now, it was the Sabbath day and the Jewish authorities said to the cured man, "Today is the Sabbath. You are not allowed to carry your bed about."

"Oh," he retorted, "the man who cured me said, 'Pick up your mat and start walking.' "

"And who is this man that said to you, 'Pick up your mat and start walking'?" they queried.

The cured man had no idea who it was because Jesus had slipped away through the crowds. Later, however, Jesus came upon him in the Temple.

"Well, now that you are cured," he said to him, "don't sin any more or something worse may happen to you."

The man went off and told the Jewish authorities that it was Jesus who had made him well. The result was that they began to harry him for breaking the Sabbath. To which he answered, "My father never stops doing good, and I continuously work at it too."

This made the Jewish leaders all the more intent on killing him, because not only was he breaking the Sabbath but he called God his father as well, making himself equal to God.

"Let me solemnly tell you," Jesus replied to them, "the Son cannot act on his own but only as he sees the Father act. So he does exactly what the Father does, because the Father loves the Son and shows him everything he does. In fact, he will show him much more remarkable things than this for you to gape at. Yes, the Father can wake the dead, and the Son too can give life to anyone he wants."

It also happened one Sabbath that Jesus went walking through the fields of standing grain and his disciples were picking the ripe ears as they went.

"Look, they're sinning against the Sabbath!" the Pharisees exclaimed.

To which he replied, "Haven't you ever read what David and his companions did when they were hungry and had nothing to eat? How he went into the House of God (when Abiathar was high priest) and ate the consecrated loaves set aside for only the priests and distributed them to everyone with him?"

"The Sabbath," he continued, "was made for man, and not man for the Sabbath. The Son of Man consequently is lord even of the Sabbath."

Once when he was in the synagogue again [in Capernaum] and there was a man there with a shriveled hand, they were watching to see if he would heal him on the Sabbath day so that they could bring a charge against him.

Jesus called to the man with the shriveled hand: "Come over here, please."

Then he said to them, "Is one allowed to do good on the Sabbath or only evil? Is one to save life or only destroy it? . . . Is there a single one of you who wouldn't rescue his only sheep if it fell into a hole on the Sabbath? Wouldn't you grab it and pull it out? And how much more valuable is a human being than a sheep! So one *is* allowed to do good on the Sabbath."

They were silent. Then, glaring at them with anger, quite

exasperated at their callous hearts, he addressed the man, "Hold out your hand."

As he stretched it out, the hand became sound.

The Pharisees left and began immediately to plot with the Herodians on the best way of destroying him.

NOTES

1. John 5:4 "From time to time an angel of the Lord would come down into the pool and stir up the water, and the first to plunge into the water after this disturbance would be cured of whatever malady afflicted him." I have followed the Revised Standard Version in omitting this verse as a later gloss.

2. The Herodians were civil officials who constituted a link between Herod Antipas and the Romans. They had feet in both camps and, though despised among the higher echelons of orthodox Jewry, they could prove useful tools in maneuvering Jesus into a treasonable position as a danger to the state.

The Calling of Matthew and the Twelve Apostles

Jesus' calling of Matthew or Levi, the tax collector, is typical of his lack of concern for public opinion. Nobody was more despised than the tax collector: hardly a popular figure in our own day but not to be compared to one who not only collected taxes for Rome from his fellow Jews but as often as not was an extortioner in his own right. Moreover, since the sharing of food at a formal dinner was and is the symbol of human solidarity, Jesus' lending himself publicly to this intimate social contact with the class of person Levi represented was as courageous as it was outrageous.

In the following incident Jesus is just passing out of the gates of Capernaum on his way to the shores of Lake Galilee, with a horde of people behind him.

(Luke 5:27-39, 6:12-17)

ON his way Jesus noticed a tax collector called Levi sitting in his collecting booth and he said to him, "Follow me." The man got up, left everything, and followed him.

Then Levi threw a banquet in his house for Jesus, attended by a large number of tax collectors and others all at the same table. Soon the Pharisees and their officials came carping to his disciples: "Why do you eat and drink with tax collectors and sinners?"

To which Jesus answered, "It is not the healthy who need a physician but those who are sick. I have not come to call the virtuous to a change of heart but those beset with sin."

Then they objected: "John's disciples constantly go without food and they pray. So do the disciples of the Pharisees, but yours are always eating and drinking."

"Do you mean," retorted Jesus, "that members of the wedding ought to be fasting in the very face of the bridegroom? To be sure, a time will come when the bridegroom is taken from them. Then they can start fasting."

He went on to use this illustration: "No one tears a piece of cloth from a new garment to patch an old one, or he'll ruin the new one and put a [silly] patch that doesn't match on the old. Nor does anyone put new wine into old wineskins. If he does, the new wine will burst the wineskins and pour all over the place and the skins be ruined. No, new wine must be put into new wineskins. In any case, nobody wants new wine after drinking the old. The old is best."

One day Jesus went out to the mountain to pray and he spent the whole night in prayer to God. When morning came he called his disciples to him and out of them chose twelve, naming them apostles.

They were: Simon, whom he also called Peter, Andrew his brother, James and John, Philip and Bartholomew, Matthew and Thomas, James the son of Alphaeus, Simon (called the Zealot), Judas son of James, and Judas Iscariot, the one who turned traitor.

Then he came down the mountain with them on to the plain, where a huge crowd of followers and great numbers of people from all over Judea and from Jerusalem and even from the seaboard of Tyre and Sidon had come to hear him and be cured of their diseases.

NOTES

1. Scholars debate whether Matthew was the same person as Levi. I take the traditional view that he was.
2. The word "apostle" is a Greek word (ἀποστολος—from the verb ἀποστελλω—apostello—to send). It means one who is sent out to preach, in other words, a missionary.
3. The Zealots were a nationalistic party opposed to the Roman occupation.

The Sermon on the Mount

The Sermon on the Mount is not exactly a sermon, but more like an anthology of Christ's sayings on the inner spirit of all his teaching. The Beatitudes have often been taken as "timeless rules for the good life," but they are not really that. They have little to do with morals or the mere observance of ethical laws. They are promises made to those who, in this vale of tears, this human testing ground, make no boast of personal moral assets or resources, but stand bankrupt before the will of God, putting all their trust in him and seeking only his purposes.

The Sermon as given in St. Matthew's gospel was probably not spoken all at one time. Whether it was addressed to the besieging crowds or only to the disciples is also not clear, though more probably Christ was talking only to his disciples, with the rest of the world in mind.

The setting is this: Jesus has been touring Galilee, teaching in the synagogues, preaching and curing every kind of sickness. People are trekking from beyond the Jordan, from Syria, and even from outside Palestine to hear him. The crowds consequently are enormous and they dog his every footstep. To get away from them and have some peace he retreats into the hills, sits down, and lets the disciples gather around him. His mind is full of the sufferings of needy humanity.

(Matthew 5:1-16, 38-48, 6:5-13, 19-34, 7:1-12, 15-20 & 24-28)

. . . And when he was seated, his disciples came to him and opening his lips, this is what he said:

"Blessed are the diffident of soul,
theirs is the kingdom of heaven.
Blessed are the sorrowing,
they shall be comforted.
Blessed are the gentle,
they are the heirs of the earth.
Blessed are the hungry and thirsty for all that is right,
they shall have their fill.
Blessed are the compassionate,
they shall find compassion.

Blessed are the pure of heart,
they shall see God.
Blessed are the peacemakers,
they shall be called the children of God.
Blessed are they who are hounded because of their goodness, theirs is the kingdom of heaven.
And blessed are you when you are reviled and persecuted and lied about in every way because of me . . .
For then, be happy and celebrate,
because great is your reward in heaven:
in like manner they harassed the prophets before you.

You are the salt of the earth,
but salt gone insipid is salt that is useless: fit only to be thrown out and trodden on.
You are the light of the world,
but a city set on a hill cannot be hidden,
and no one lights a lamp and puts it under a basket but on a lampstand where it can shine on all in the house.
That is how your light must shine for everyone to see:
yes, everyone to see your beautiful deeds
and glorify your Father in heaven."

"You have heard it said: An eye for an eye and a tooth for a tooth, but I am telling you not to resist the violent man. If he hits you on the right cheek, offer him the left. And if somebody sues you for your shirt, present him with your jacket too. If somebody coerces you to go a mile, walk with him for two. Give to anyone who asks and do not turn your back on one who wants to borrow.

"You have heard it said: Love your friends and hate your enemies, but I say to you, love your enemies and pray for those that persecute you, and so be like true sons of your Father in heaven who makes his sun rise on both the bad and the good, and lets his rain fall on just and unjust alike. For if you love only those who love you, what merit is that? Do not even tax collectors do the same? And if you are nice to your brothers only, what more are you doing than everyone? Don't even heathens do the same? You must be perfect, just as your Father in heaven is perfect.

"When you pray, do not rattle off a heap of words the way the pagans do, imagining that if they say a lot they will be heard. Do not be like them. Your Father knows what you need even before you ask him. So pray like this:

Our Father who art in heaven,
  hallowed be thy name.
Thy kingdom come, thy will be done
  on earth as it is in heaven.
Give us this day our daily bread,
And forgive us our trespasses
  as we forgive them that trespass against us.
And lead us not into temptation,
  but deliver us from evil.

"Do not amass treasures for yourselves here on earth, where moth and rust whittle them away, where thieves break in and steal. No, amass your treasures in heaven, where neither moth nor rust consume, and no thieves break in and steal. For where your treasure is, there is your heart.

"The body's lamp is the eye. So if your eye is clear your whole body is lit up, but if your eye be clouded your whole body is in the dark; and when this light of yours within is dark, oh, how pitch black it is!

"Nobody can be a slave to two masters. For either he will hate the one and love the other, or dote on one and despise the other. You cannot serve God and Mammon.

"And so I say to you: Do not be anxious about your life, how to get your food and drink, how to clothe your body. Is not life itself much more than food, and the body much more than clothes? Look at the birds in the sky: they do not sow, they do not reap, they do not garner into barns, and yet your heavenly Father feeds them all. Are you not worth more than they? Which of you can add a single second to your life by worrying? And as to clothing, what good is worry? Learn from the wild lilies in the meadow, the way they grow: they do not toil, they do not spin, and yet I tell you that Solomon in all his glory was not bedecked like one of these. Why, when God so clothes even the grass of the fields—which flourishes today and tomorrow is thrown onto the bonfire—will he not all the more clothe *you*: you people of so little faith? So do not worry and say, 'What are we to eat? What are we to drink? What are we to put on?' All these things are what mere pagans want, and all these things your Father in heaven already knows you need. So, first go after the kingdom of God and his goodness, and all these other things will be heaped upon you. Do not then worry about tomorrow. Tomorrow can look after itself, for each day has worries enough.

"Do not pass censure, and you will not be censured; because the very censure that you pass will be the censure passed on you. Yes, you will be measured by the very measure with which you measure. Must you note the speck in your brother's eye and not see the log in your own? Will you dare tell your brother: 'Let me remove the speck in your eye,' when all the time a log is in yours? Hypocrite, first remove the log in your own eye, then you will see straight and be able to take the speck out of your brother's eye.

"Ask and you shall receive. Seek and you shall find. Knock and the door will be opened to you. Everyone who asks receives, and everyone who seeks finds, and everyone who knocks has the door opened to him.

"Or is there a man among you who offers his son a stone when he asks for a loaf, or offers him a snake when he asks for fish? Very well then, if you, bad as you are, know how to give your children only what is good, how much more will your Father in heaven give only what is good to those who ask?

"In all things do to others as you would have them do to you. This is the whole of the Law and the Prophets.

"Beware of false prophets, who come to you in sheep's clothing but inwardly are ravening wolves. By their fruits you shall know them. Do we gather grapes from thorns or figs from thistles? In no way. Every good tree bears good fruits, and every worthless tree worthless fruits. A good tree cannot produce bad fruits, or a worthless tree good fruits. And every tree that does not produce good fruits is to be cut down and thrown on the bonfire. And so, by their fruits you shall know them.

"Anybody here who takes heed of what I say and does it is like a wise man who builds his house on rock. When the rains fall and the rivers surge and the winds thrash, the buffeted house does not collapse, because its foundations are on rock. But anyone who hears my word and ignores what I say is like a rash man who builds his house on sand. And when the rains beat and the rivers rise and the gales rage, the buffeted house comes tumbling down, and great is its fall."

* * *

When Jesus had finished speaking, the crowds were amazed at his teaching, for he taught with authority—not like the ministers they were used to.

NOTES

1. As a possible new translation of the Our Father, I give the following:

> Our Father in heaven,
>   blessed be the fullness of your name.
> Your kingdom come, your will be done,
>   on earth as it is in heaven.
> Give us this day our daily bread.
> And forgive us our offenses
>   as we forgive our own offenders.
> Keep us from the ordeal of temptation
>   and free from every evil.

2. "Mammon" is a Semitic word meaning money and riches.
3. Matthew 6:27 can also be translated: "Which of you can add a single foot to his height by worrying?"

Jesus Raises the Widow's Son at Nain

This incident is recorded only by Luke. The background of the event is found in 1 Kings 17:17-24, where Elijah resurrects a widow's son by giving him what looks like the kiss of life, and also in 2 Kings 4:32-37, where Elisha performs a similar marvel on another widow's son. In each case, the restoration is a lengthy process with much calling upon the Lord and stretching over the prostrate child. Jesus, Luke insinuates, is a far greater prophet and gets his results immediately.

The village of Nain—sometimes called Naim—was six miles southeast of Nazareth, nestling at the foot of the mountains. It is identified with present-day Nein.

Jesus has been living at Capernaum and has just cured the centurion's son (or in Luke, his servant) from a distance.

(Luke 7:11-17)

SOON afterward he went to a town called Nain, accompanied by his disciples and a great crowd. What should come toward him as he drew near to the gates of the town but a dead man being carried out: the only son of his mother, and she a widow.

When he saw her, the Lord was moved to compassion. "Don't cry," he said to her, and stepping forward, he touched the bier and the bearers stood still.

"My boy, get up," he said. "I'm telling you."

Immediately the corpse sat up and started to talk. And Jesus gave him to his mother.

Everyone was shaken, but they were all loud in their praises of God.

"What a great prophet has risen among us!" they exclaimed. "God is certainly watching over his people."

Word of what he had done spread all over Judea and the surrounding countryside.

The Woman Taken in Adultery

Whether this woman is the same person as Mary Magdalene, and whether Mary Magdalene is the same person who anoints Jesus' feet in the next story, is a moot point too complicated to go into here. Suffice to say that the present account, though it conforms to all we know about Jesus' sympathy with sinners and his gentleness toward women, is today considered by scholars to be a non-Johannine interpolation.

Nonetheless, the drama of the passage with its picture of Jesus as both the serene defender of the weak and the utterly just judge, is as worthy of John as the delicacy of the parallelism is worthy of Luke. A single focus holds together the opposites: a sinful woman faces a sinless man, perfect justice meets perfect clemency, and no condoning of sin joins no condemnation of the sinner. In St. Augustine's beautifully succinct comment: "Just two were left—the miserable and the commiserating."

Jesus is in Jerusalem again for the Feast of the Tabernacles, a major Jewish festival held at the beginning of the autumn during which the celebrators lived in booths and tents to symbolize vintage and harvest conditions and to remind themselves that their passage through this life is but a pilgrimage.

Jesus has apparently been living on the Mount of Olives and going every day to the Temple to teach. It is there that the story opens.

(John 7:53, 8:1-11)

WHILE every man went to his own house, Jesus went to the Mount of Olives, but at daybreak he was back at the Temple and all the people flocked to him and he sat down and taught them.

Meanwhile the scribes and the Pharisees brought in a woman who had been caught in the act of adultery and they thrust her forward in full view of everyone.

"Master," they said to him, "this woman was caught in the very act of adultery. Now, by the law of Moses we are commanded to stone such a woman, but what do you say?" (The question, of course, was put to him just to trap him so that they could bring a charge against him.) Jesus simply stooped down and began scribbling with his finger in the dust. On their continuing to press him, he stood up.

"Then let the spotless one among you hurl the first stone at her," he said. And he stooped down again and scribbled in the dust.

Hearing this, they started to go out one by one, beginning with the eldest, and he was left alone, he and the woman in the middle. Straightening up, Jesus said to her, "Madam, where are they? Has no one condemned you?"

"No one, sir," she replied.

"Then neither do I condemn you," Jesus said. "Be on your way, and from now on sin no more."

NOTES

1. Unfaithfulness constituted adultery in Jewish law only on the part of the wife. Husbands were not penalized for affairs out of wedlock.

2. When Jesus wrote on the ground, we do not know whether this was writing or simply scrawling, i.e., doodling, and thus showing his contempt for the accusers.

The Anointing of Jesus at Dinner

All four evangelists recount this story but with so many variations that only with difficulty can one piece it together. In Mark the dinner is given in the house of Simon the leper, who in Luke becomes Simon the Pharisee. In Mark and John the dinner takes place in Bethany, the hometown of

Martha, Mary, and Lazarus, who are all present. Only in John is the woman named and she is none other than Mary the sister of Martha and Lazarus. In Luke she becomes "a woman of the town who was a sinner."

In Matthew it is the disciples who criticize the extravagance of the anointing. In Luke it is Simon the Pharisee, in Mark it is "some of them," and in John it is Judas Iscariot, "Simon's son."

Besides these differences, Mark and Matthew have the woman anoint Jesus' head, whereas Luke and John say that it was his feet. (Of course, it could have been both.) Luke is the only evangelist who does not mention the costliness of the ointment and he says that it is myrrh. John says that it was a pound of spikenard.

One cannot be certain that the woman in all four accounts is the same, or that Mary of Bethany is Mary Magdalene, or that any of them is the woman caught in adultery. Only in Luke is she called a sinner. My own guess is that Mary of Bethany and Mary Magdalene are the same because in Luke 8:1-3, where three women, including Mary Magdalene, are listed among those who accompanied Jesus and his disciples and "provided for them out of their own means," Mary of Bethany is not mentioned and yet she must have been one of them.

The Palestinians at this time had adopted the Greco-Roman custom of reclining at meals, supported on the left elbow and eating with the right hand. The diners lay diagonally across the couches, two or three to a couch, with their feet pointing away from the table; which could be circular or in the form of a horseshoe, or three tables placed in an open-sided rectangle.

Note that though Mary and Martha were present at this dinner, neither of them ate at the table; Martha served and Mary did her thing (John 12:2-3). It is doubtful if the women ever reclined in common with the men at meals.

The time and setting of this story is while Jesus is still on his preaching-healing mission through southern Galilee.

(Luke 7:36-50)

ONE of the Pharisees asked him to dine with him, so he went to the Pharisee's home and hardly had he taken his place at table when a woman of the town known for her immoral life, who had heard that he was eating at the Pharisee's house, came in with an alabaster jar of myrrh and stood behind his feet sobbing. Then she began to bathe his feet in her tears and to wipe them with her hair as she smothered his feet with kisses and anointed them with myrrh.

When the Pharisee who had invited him saw this he said to himself, "If this man was really a prophet he'd know what sort of woman it was who is handling him—a plain slut."

Jesus cut him short and said, "Simon, I have something to tell you."

"Say on, Master," he answered.

"Two men were in debt to a certain moneylender. One owed him five hundred denarii and the other fifty. When they were unable to repay this, he let them both off. Now which of them loved him most?"

"The one who was let off most, I suppose," Simon answered.

"Exactly," Jesus said. Then turning toward the woman, he went on, "Simon, do you see this woman? I came to your house and you gave me no water for my feet. But she has washed my feet in her tears and dried them with her hair. You gave me no kiss, but from the moment I came in she has not ceased to kiss my feet. You did not anoint my head with oil, but she has anointed my feet with myrrh. So let me tell you, her sins, her many sins, are now forgiven because she has loved so much. Where little is forgiven, little is loved."

Then he turned to her: "Your sins are forgiven."

The other guests at table with him began to ask themselves, "Who is this man who thinks he can forgive sins?"

But Jesus said to the woman, "Your faith has saved you. Go in peace."

NOTES

1. For note on myrrh see page 307. As to Spikenard or nard (*Nardostachys jatamansi*) it is a Himalayan plant of the Valerian family. Ointments and perfumes were made from dried portions of the root and stem, then sealed in jars which could only be opened by breaking the neck. The Phoenicians seem to have been the first to import spikenard preparations from India (where they are still favored), and naturally the great distance made them expensive.

2. The denarius was the equivalent to a day's wage.

Some Parables

The word "parable" comes from the Greek παραβαλλω (*paraballo*) which means to put side by side, to compare, also to hold out as bait.

The parables of the gospels are really extended metaphors or even proverbs that tell a story. As with fables, brevity is of their essence. One might call them very short stories or sometimes long riddles carrying a double meaning. Their surface meaning is merely a "come on" beckoning to a deeper meaning. The merit of parables is that they are swift and unforgettable; they provoke thought and even on their surface level are irresistible.

The parable form was widely used by rabbis, though in the surrounding Greek world (except for Aesop's ever popular fables) allegory was more common, i.e., using stories of the Olympian deities as symbols of the conflicts of mortals.

In the parable of the mustard seed, it may be worth noting that though the mustard seed is by no means "the smallest of all seeds," it is nevertheless very small. Jesus' point, of course, is that one can hardly believe that such a tiny seed will develop into a large, robust plant. But it does, so faith is justified, and faith too can grow.

The following parables were spoken by Jesus while he was still on his Galilean tour of teaching and healing. He has just told his listeners that those who do the will of his Father in heaven are as much his mother and his relations as his real kin (Matthew 12:46-50).

(Matthew 13:1-51)

THAT same day Jesus went out of the house and sat by the sea, and when large crowds congregated around him he got into a boat and sat down, while the crowd stood on the shore. There he told them many things in parables.

"Imagine a sower going out to sow," he said, "and as he sowed, some of the seed fell along the path and the birds came and ate it up. Other seed fell on stony ground where there was little soil, and though it shot up quickly because the earth had no depth, it was parched when the sun came out, and without roots soon dried up. Still other seed fell among thorns and the thorns sprang up and choked it. Some seed, however, fell upon good ground and this produced a crop a hundredfold and sixtyfold and thirtyfold over. . . . Whosoever has ears, let him hear."

His disciples then came to him and asked, "Why do you talk to them in parables?"

"Because," he replied, "to you it has been granted to know the secrets of the kingdom of heaven, but to them it has not been granted. For whosoever has, is given more till he superabounds; but whosoever has not, from him even that which he has will be taken. And so I talk to them in parables because they have eyes but do not see, ears and they do not hear, nor do they comprehend. There is a prophecy of Isaiah that fits them well.

> Hearing you hear and do not understand.
> Gazing you gaze and see not a thing.
> Oh, the heart of this people has grown numb.
> Their ears hardly hear,
> Their eyes they have shut
> Lest they see with their eyes,
> Lest they hear with their ears,
> Lest their hearts understand
> And they turn once again
> So that I may heal them.

"But you, blessed are your eyes because they see, and your ears because they hear. Many prophets and good men, I assure you, longed to see what you see, and did not see it, and to hear what you hear, and have not heard it."

"Listen, then, to the parable of the sower . . .

"When someone hears the word about the Kingdom but does not comprehend it, the evil one comes and snatches away that which was sown in his heart. This is the seed that falls along the path. The seed sown on the stony ground is the one who hears the word and accepts it at once with joy but has no roots in himself, no stamina, and when conflict and persecution come because of the word, he falls away. The seed sown among thorns is the one who hears the word, but the cares of the world and the blandishments of riches suffocate the word and make it barren. As for the seed that fell on good ground, this is the one who hears the word and discerns it, and bears a crop one a hundredfold, one sixty-fold, one thirtyfold over."

Jesus offered them another parable. "The kingdom of heaven," he said, "is like a man who sowed good seed in his field, but while his men were asleep his enemy came and sowed darnel among the wheat and went his way. When the plants came up and produced a crop, the darnel appeared too. At which the owner's laborers came to him and said, 'Sir, did you not sow good seed in your field? How then does it have darnel?'

'This is the work of an enemy,' he replied.

'Do you want us to go and pull it up?' his laborers asked.

'No,' he said, 'in case you pull the wheat up too when you gather the darnel. Let them both grow until the harvest and when harvest comes I shall tell the reapers, "Collect the darnel first and bind it in bundles for burning, then garner the wheat into my granary." ' "

He set another parable before them. "The kingdom of heaven," he said, "is like a grain of mustard seed which a man went and sowed in his field. It is the smallest of all seeds, but when full grown it is the largest of shrubs and becomes a tree in which the birds of the sky can come and nest in its branches."

Another parable he told them was: "The kingdom of heaven is like yeast which a woman took and sunk into three measures of dough till the whole batch rose."

Jesus spoke all these things to the crowds in parables. In fact, he told them nothing except in parables. And so the prophet's words were amply fulfilled:

> I shall open my mouth in parables.
> I shall utter things which have been kept secret
> from the foundation of the world.

When he had dismissed the crowds and gone to his house, his disciples came to him, asking, "Interpret for us the parable of the darnel in the field."

"This is it," he said: "the sower of the good seed is the Son of Man, and the field is the world. The good seed is the sons of the Kingdom, and the darnel is the sons of the wicked one. The enemy who sowed it is the devil. The harvest time is the end of the world, and the harvesters are the angels. The gathering of the darnel and throwing it into the bonfire—this is when the Son of Man at the end of the world sends forth his angels to weed out from his kingdom all that causes sin and all who do evil and to cast them into the flaming bonfire. Then shall be weeping and gnashing of teeth. Then shall the godly shine out like the sun in their Father's kingdom. . . . Oh, listen, you who have ears!

"The kingdom of heaven is like a treasure hidden in a field which a man finds and keeps buried while he goes off excitedly and sells all he has to buy that field.

"Again, the kingdom of heaven is like a merchant in quest of fine pearls, who finds one of superlative worth and sells all he has to buy it.

"And again, the kingdom of heaven is like a net let down into the sea, amassing every kind of fish. And when it is full they haul it ashore, then sit and sort the good ones into baskets, but throw the bad ones away.

"So will it be at the end of the world. The angels will go forth and sort the bad from the good, tossing them into the blazing furnace. There shall be weeping and gnashing of teeth."

NOTES

1. The common black mustard (*Brassica nigra*) was grown in fields and used as a condiment and for its oil. It does not exactly grow into a tree, but does sometimes achieve a sturdy bush up to six feet high with a stem as thick as a man's arm.

2. Darnel (*Zizanion* or *Lolium temulentem*) is a grass weed almost indistinguishable from wheat in its early stages. Its seed not only enjoys a germination potency of several years but is also poisonous. Eradicating darnel is impossible because its roots intertwine with the wheat.

The Storm at Sea and the Gadarene Swine

The storm at sea follows a typical day of Jesus as he heals on the shores of the Sea of Galilee. In the episode of the Gadarene swine, Matthew has the possessed as two men rather than one. As to the location of the incident, there is some doubt, but it must have been somewhere on the eastern shores of the lake. In any case, it was Gentile territory (the Jews did not keep pigs) and quite probably near the town of Gadara: a small, cultivated Greek town in a region known as the Decapolis, a federation of ten Hellenistic cities east of Samaria and Galilee. Gadara was the home of poets, orators, and philosophers. It is obvious from the gospel accounts that the citizens there did not relish any disturbance of their nucleus of culture by this young and disturbing do-gooder.

(Mark 4:35-41, 5:1-20)

THAT same day before evening he said to them, "Let's go across to the other side." So sending away the crowds they took him on the boat just as he was, with other boats accompanying.

Suddenly, down came a heavy squall and the waves beat into the boat till it was almost swamped. He was in the stern asleep with his head on a pillow, and they woke him, shouting, "Master, don't you care if we drown?"

Rousing himself, he rebuked the wind, and to the sea he said, "Quiet! Be muzzled!" And the wind dropped and there was a dead calm.

"Why are you such cowards?" he said to them. "Don't you trust me even now?"

They were terribly in awe and muttered to one another, "Who in the world is this that even the wind and the sea obey him?"

So they came across the sea to the land of the Gadarenes. There, just as he stepped from the boat, a man possessed by an unclean spirit rushed out at him from the tombs. The man had made his home there and nobody had been able to chain him up because every time they chained and fettered him, he simply wrenched the chains apart and smashed the fetters. Nobody was strong enough to control him. Day and night he haunted the tombs and the hills, howling away and gashing himself with stones.

As he caught sight of Jesus some way off he ran to him and flung himself down, bellowing, "What are you after, Jesus Son of the Most High God? In God's name, don't torture me!" (For Jesus had just issued the command: "Get out of this man, you unclean spirit!")

Jesus then asked him, "What is your name?"

"My name is Legion," he replied, "because there are a lot of us."

He began to plead with Jesus not to send them out into exile. Now, there was a large herd of swine rooting about on the hillside and the demons implored him, "Send us into the swine. Let us enter them."

So he let them, and the unclean spirits came rushing out and went into the swine, and the whole herd charged over the cliff into the sea—two thousand of them—and they drowned in the sea. The swineherds guarding them took to their heels, carrying the story through town and country. People hurried out to see what had happened, and when they approached Jesus they saw the possessed man—the man with the legions—sitting clothed and in his right mind, and they were very much in awe. Besides, those who had seen it described what had happened to the possessed man and the swine. Consequently they began to entreat Jesus to leave their territory.

As he boarded the boat, the man once possessed by demons begged to go with him, but Jesus would not let him. "No," he said to him, "go home to your own people and tell them what the Lord in his compassion did for you."

So the man went off broadcasting all through the Decapolis what Jesus had done for him—to the amazement of everyone.

NOTES

1. Both Mark and Luke have the location of this story as Gerasa, which cannot be right because Gerasa was situated thirty-three miles southeast of the Sea of Galilee in the mountains of Gilead. It was one of the three most important cities of Roman Arabia. In my translation I have therefore kept to Matthew's Gadara.
2. A Roman legion at full strength numbered six thousand men.
3. Luke makes clear that the exorcized man was naked.

Jairus' Daughter and the Woman Who Was Surreptitiously Healed

In this story within a story Jesus, having sailed across the lake after exorcising the man with the demons, has just landed at Capernaum.

(Mark 5:21-43)

HARDLY had Jesus crossed the lake again to the other side when a huge crowd gathered about him by the seaside. And one of the synagogue officials, a man called

Jairus, hurried up to him and as soon as he was in his presence threw himself before Jesus, desperately imploring, "My little girl is at death's door. Do come and lay your hands on her and make her better and save her life."

So Jesus went with him, followed by a great crowd that pressed upon him. And there was a woman who had been bleeding for twelve years and who had suffered much under a series of physicians, spending all she had and getting no better, but rather worse. She had heard all about Jesus and, edging up to him through the crowd, she touched his mantle. For she said to herself, "If only I can touch his mantle I shall be cured."

There and then the bleeding stopped, the flow dried up, and she knew in her body that she was healed. Jesus, however, immediately sensing that power had gone out of him, swung around in the crowd and asked, "Who touched my mantle?" "What!" exclaimed his disciples, "you see the press of people all around you and you ask, 'Who touched me'?"

As he was looking about to see who had done it, the woman, in fear and trembling, well aware of what had happened to her, threw herself at Jesus' feet and told him the whole truth.

"My daughter," he responded, "your faith has made you well. Go in peace healed of your affliction."

While he was still talking, a message came from Jairus' house: "Your daughter is dead. Why inconvenience the Master any further?"

Jesus, however, disregarding the babble of voices, said to the synagogue official, "Don't be anxious. Just trust me."

He would not let anyone accompany him except Peter and James, and John the brother of James. When they came into the home of the synagogue official, they were struck by a great commotion of weeping and moaning people, and Jesus exclaimed as they went inside: "Why all this commotion and weeping? The child is not dead but asleep." And they laughed at him.

He then turned them all out except for the child's father and mother and those who were with him, and he went into the room where the child lay. Taking the child by the hand, he said to her, "*Talitha cumi*," which means: "Little girl, I say to you, get up."

The little girl got up on the spot and began to walk about. She was twelve years old. Jesus, however, insisted again and again that they should tell nobody; and he commanded that something should be given her to eat.

The Beheading of John the Baptist

Herodias, the arch protagonist in this story, was the granddaughter of Herod the Great. She was a divorcee, having been married to a half uncle, the half brother of Herod Antipas. Now she was married to Herod Antipas himself, also a half uncle and divorcee. He was tetrarch of Galilee and Perea, a king in all but name under the suzerainty of Rome.

Herodias detested John the Baptist because he had denounced her new marriage as invalid and incestuous. Herod Antipas too, though he came to admire John for his honesty and courage, did not want him publicly prating about his family. Besides, the prophet could too easily become the focus of one of the subversive nationalistic factions that seethed with impatience under the firm yoke of Pax Romana.

Herod dared not execute him, for fear of the Baptist's zealous supporters, but at least in jail he could count on his silence. So, just before Jesus left Jerusalem on his yearlong tour of Galilee, Herod seized John and clapped him into the dungeon underneath his palace stronghold at Machaerus: a keep perched among the desolate hills overlooking the eastern shores of the Dead Sea.

Perhaps John's imprisonment was not so grim as it might appear. He seems to have been free to receive visits from his disciples. But what is a little baffling is why John, after having so wholeheartedly endorsed Jesus earlier on, should now think it necessary to send a delegation of two to quiz him and ask for proof of his authenticity. Perhaps he had been receiving conflicting reports about Jesus' activities; or he may simply have wanted to quell the ever present temptation on the part of some of his followers to rivalry and jealousy; or perhaps also (and most probably) because in the prophecies of Isaiah (and Jesus uses them indirectly in his reply), the note of joy which these prefigure is accompanied by a note of judgment and doom: a note that might seem singularly lacking in the reports about Jesus which John was receiving. If the role of the Messianic judge were not being fulfilled as he expected, he might have begun to wonder in the deranging solitude of his confinement if Jesus was really "He that is to come."

Salome, according to Josephus, was the name of the girl who charmed her great-uncle with her dancing. She was the daughter of Herodias by her former husband.

(Matthew 11:2-19, Mark 6:17-29)

NOW when John in prison heard what Christ was doing, he sent his disciples to ask him, "Are you the one who is to come, or must we look for another?"

Jesus' reply was: "Go and tell John what you hear and see. The blind have sight, the lame walk, lepers are made clean, the deaf hear, the dead are raised, and the downtrodden are given good news. . . . And blessed is he who because of me does not falter."

When the deputation had left, Jesus began to speak to the crowds about John. "What was it in the wilderness that you went out to see? A reed shaken by the wind? Then, what was it you went out to see? A man clothed in soft garments? In soft garments! Surely such are found only in the palaces of kings. Then what did you go out to see? A prophet? Yes, I tell you, and more than a prophet. He it is of whom the scripture says:

> Behold, I send my messenger before thy face
> which shall prepare thy way before thee.

"Believe me, no mother's son was ever born a greater man than John the Baptist. And yet the least in the Kingdom of heaven is greater than he. Since the coming of John the Baptist till this moment, the Kingdom of heaven is taken by storm and stormers bear it away. This is precisely what the whole Law and the prophets foretold—until this very coming of John. And if you can accept it, he is the Elijah that was destined to come. . . . So hearken, those of you who have ears to hear.

"Oh, to what can I compare this generation? They are like children sitting in the square and shouting to the others:

> We piped for you and you did not dance.
> We played at funerals for you and you did not cry.

For John came neither eating nor drinking and they said, 'He must be mad!' The Son of Man came eating and drinking, and they said, 'Look at him! A glutton and a drunkard! A friend of tax collectors and criminals!' So, no matter what, these clever ones always have the answer."

Meantime, Herod had dispatched soldiers to arrest John and had put him in prison: all on account of Herodias his brother Philip's wife, whom he had married. For John had told Herod, "It is not right for you to have your brother's wife."

Herodias could never forgive him and would have killed him if she dared, but Herod had a deep respect for John, knowing him to be a good and holy man, so he protected him. Indeed, he liked listening to John—though he listened with some perplexity.

Then came Herodias' chance. Herod on his birthday threw a party for his chief ministers, army officers, and the foremost dignitaries of Galilee. The daughter of the said Herodias came in and danced, giving enormous pleasure to Herod and his guests.

"Ask me for anything you like," said King Herod to the girl, "and I shall give it to you."

He said it again with an oath: "Whatever you ask for I shall give you, be it half my kingdom."

The girl went out and consulted her mother: "What shall I ask for?"

"The head of John the Baptist," came the reply.

So the girl hurried back to the king. "I want you to give me the head of John the Baptist," she said. "Yes, here and now—on a platter."

The king was struck with sadness, but had sworn an oath in front of guests and could not bring himself to refuse her. So he dispatched a guardsman with orders to bring back John's head. The man went and beheaded him in prison, then brought his head in on a platter and gave it to the girl, who gave it to her mother.

When John's disciples heard of this, they came and took the body and laid it in a tomb.

Jesus Feeds the Five Thousand And Walks on the Water

The following story is one of the few incidents recorded by all four evangelists. There have been many attempts to find a rationalistic explanation for the multiplication of the loaves and fishes, and all of them beside the point; the point being that Jesus as master of the universe is just as capable of multiplying loaves and fishes as he is of creating them. In John's gospel, theology is pushed to an extreme: either one believes in Jesus or one does not; and if one believes, then one must accept that he is the Son of God and that nothing is beyond his power: a conclusion which is clinched in the episode immediately following the walking on the water.

Loaves and fishes became an early Christian symbol of Christ and the Eucharist. The Greek word for fish ἰχθυς (*ichthus*) was a convenient anagram for Jesus himself.

Ιησους	Iēsous	Jesus
Χριστος	Christos	Christ
Θεος	Theou	Of God
Υιος	Uios	The Son
Σωτηρ	Sōtēr	The Savior

When the early Christians were persecuted in Rome and had to take to the catacombs, the *Chi Rho* (XP) sign of the fish and loaves could beckon them to their underground rendezvous for the celebration of the Eucharist without the authorities understanding.

While still in Galilee, Jesus had sent his disciples out in pairs through the town and villages on their first mission. He not only gave them authority to preach but power to heal the sick and to cast out devils. He said to them, "Take nothing for your journey: no stick, no pack, no food, no money, not even a change of clothes. Whatever house accepts you, stay there and make it the center of your travels" (Luke 9:3-4).

Now the disciples have returned, full of their exploits. But the crowds, swollen by the throng of those going to Jerusalem for the Passover, press upon Jesus thicker than ever, so that he and his disciples "have no time even to eat" (Mark 6:31). However, he manages to slip away with them by boat to a spot near Bethsaida, a fishing village on the northeastern shores of the Sea of Galilee, until the crowds detect their movements and follow on land. It is now evening. Jesus has gone up into the hills above the lake, and there the crowds find him sitting with his disciples.

(John 6:5-18, Matthew 14:23-33, John 6:22-71)

THEN Jesus, gazing out and seeing what a large crowd had come after him, said to Philip, "Where can we buy some bread for these people to eat?" (He said this to test him, for he knew very well what he would do.)

"Even two hundred denarii's worth of bread," answered Philip, "would not be enough for everyone to have just a little."

One of his disciples, Andrew the brother of Simon Peter, then said to him, "There is a boy here with five barley loaves and two small fish. But what is that among so many?"

"Make the people sit down," Jesus said.

The place was very grassy; so the men sat down, to the number of five thousand. Then Jesus took the loaves, gave thanks, and passed them among the people sitting there: as much as they wanted. And when everyone was satisfied, he said to his disciples, "Gather up what is left, the crumbs, so that nothing is wasted."

They gathered them up and filled twelve baskets with the scraps left over from the five barley loaves after everyone had eaten. And when the people saw what a miracle Jesus had done, they began to exclaim, "Surely this is the prophet who was to come into the world!"

Jesus, however, realizing that they were going to carry him off and make him king, retreated once again into the hills—alone.

The disciples meanwhile had gone down to the lake and embarked on a boat to cross over to Capernaum. It was getting dark and there was still no sign of Jesus. The boat by now was well out from shore and battling against a head wind and a heavy sea. Between four and six in the morning Jesus came toward them, walking on the surface of the sea. And the disciples, seeing him walking on the sea, were struck with terror, crying out that it was a ghost.

"It is only I," Jesus quickly reassured them, "bear up and don't be afraid!"

"Lord, if it is really you," Peter shouted, "make me come to you on the water."

"Come," he said.

So Peter stepped over the side of the boat and began walking on the water toward Jesus. But when he realized the full force of the gale, he panicked and began to sink.

"Lord save me!" he shrieked.

At once Jesus stretched out his hand and caught him.

"So little faith!" he remarked. "Why did you panic?"

Once they were both on board, the wind dropped, and those in the boat fell on their knees before him.

"Truly you are the Son of God," they declared.

* * *

The next day across the lake the crowds were waiting. They had seen only one ship leave there [the night before] and that Jesus had not gone aboard with his disciples, who had set off without him. However, when ships from Tiberias arrived near the place where they had eaten the bread after the Lord had given thanks, and the crowd now realized that neither Jesus nor his disciples were there, they themselves boarded these boats and made for Capernaum in search of Jesus.

When they found him there on the opposite shore, they exclaimed, "Rabbi, how did you get here?"

"The fact is," said Jesus, "you went in search of me not because you cared about my signs but because you were stuffed with bread. Try to be more concerned not for this perishable food but for the nourishment that takes you into eternal life: that life which the Son of God will give you: yes, he whom God the Father has solemnly sanctioned."

"What must we do, then," they asked him, "if we are to work for God?"

"To work for God is this," Jesus answered: "it is to believe in the one he sent."

"But what evidence can you give us as a clear sign," they said, "so that we can believe you? What feat can you accomplish? Our fathers ate manna in the desert, as the scripture says: 'He [Moses] gave them bread from heaven to eat.'"

"Let me tell you," Jesus answered, "it was not Moses who gave you bread from heaven, but my Father, and now he offers you the real bread from heaven: the bread of God that comes down from heaven and gives life to the world."

"Oh, sir," they cried out, "let us always have this bread."

"I am the bread of life," Jesus replied to them. "Whoever comes to me shall never go hungry; whoever believes in me shall never thirst . . . But, as I have told you, you see me and still don't believe. Only those that my Father gives me will come to me and never will I turn any such away. For I have not come down from heaven to do my own will but the will of him who sent me. And this is the will of him who sent me: that I should not lose a single one of those he gave me, but raise them all up on the last day. Yes, this is the will of my Father, that everyone that gazes on the Son and puts his faith in him shall have everlasting life, and I shall raise him up on the last day."

At this the Jews began to grumble because he claimed to be the bread that came down from heaven.

"Isn't this Jesus the son of Joseph," they objected, "whose

father and mother we know? How can he say he came down from heaven?"

"Stop grumbling among yourselves," Jesus answered. "Nobody can come to me unless the Father who sent me draws him, and at the last day I shall raise him up. . . . I tell you solemnly that whosoever believes, already has eternal life, for I am the bread of life. Your fathers ate manna in the desert and are dead, but this bread that comes down from heaven is a bread to eat and never die. I am that living bread which came down from heaven, and everyone who eats this bread shall live forever. For the bread that I am giving for the life of the world is my own flesh."

The Jews started to argue among themselves. "How can this man give us his flesh to eat?" they said, and Jesus answered: "Let me tell you in all earnestness that only if you eat the flesh of the Son of Man and drink his blood will you have any life in you. Whosoever eats my flesh and drinks my blood has everlasting life and I shall raise him up on the last day. For my flesh is real food and my blood real drink, and whosoever eats my flesh and drinks my blood assimilates me and I him. As the living Father sent me and I live by the Father, so too whosoever eats me shall live by me."

All this he expounded in the synagogue at Capernaum, and many of his disciples hearing it, muttered, "This is going too far. How can we accept it?"

Jesus was well aware of what his disciples were muttering and he asked them, "Does this shock you? Then what if you were to see the Son of Man ascending to where he was before? It is the spirit that gives life, the flesh gives nothing. The words I have spoken to you are spirit and life; yet some here do not believe me."

Of course, Jesus knew from the start who were the ones who did not believe him and who was the one who would betray him. So he said, "This is why I told you that no one can come to me except by a gift from the Father."

After this many of his disciples drew back and went with him no longer. Turning to the twelve, he said, "Do you want to leave me too?"

Simon Peter answered, "Lord, to whom shall we go? You have the words of eternal life. We believed and now we know that you are the Holy One of God."

"Yes, I have chosen you, all twelve," Jesus replied, "but one of you is a devil."

He meant Judas, the son of Simon Iscariot, the one out of the twelve who was going to betray him.

NOTES

1. "Two hundred denarii's worth of bread" would have been the equivalent of two hundred days' wages—in other words, a small fortune.

2. The five thousand who sat down on the grass did not apparently include the number of women and children.

3. In the twelve baskets of scraps, Mark includes remnants of the fish as well.

4. After dismissing the crowds Jesus had told the disciples to go by boat to Bethsaida. Meanwhile, the baffled crowds, having guessed that later the destination of the disciples in their boat was probably Capernaum (the center of Jesus' activites), seized the opportunity of embarking on the ships that had just come in from Tiberias and were headed for Capernaum. In point of fact, Jesus was at Gennesaret, just south of Capernaum.

Jesus Moves to the Coast, Makes a Second Visit to the Decapolis, Then Goes North to Caesaria Philippi

After the desertion of so many disciples Jesus must have felt himself rejected in Galilee. His mission there, which seemed to have been going so well and on which he had lavished so much energy, natural and supernatural, now appeared hollow. When the test of belief came, the results were no better than at Nazareth. So he abandons his headquarters in Capernaum and addresses his message to the Gentiles of Tyre and Sidon. Perhaps too, knowing that his time was running short (with less than a year to live), he wanted to get away from the crowds and be with the chosen twelve so as to train them.

Tyre and Sidon were prosperous Phoenician cities in northern Palestine on the Mediterranean: a territory which we would now call Lebanon. It was from Tyre early in the ninth century B.C. that colonists founded Carthage in North Africa.

It is interesting that the Gentile inhabitants of the Decapolis received Jesus much more cordially than when he sent the legion of devils into the swine. Probably the man who Jesus exorcised had obeyed his injunction to tell his people "what the Lord in his compassion did for you."

Caesaria Philippi was an Iturean town about thirty miles north of the Sea of Galilee and built on the slopes of Mount Hermon (from which the river Jordan rises). The town was Greek, famous in antiquity for its shrine to Pan the satyr god. Herod the Great's son Philip—brother of Herod Antipas of Galilee—named it after the Roman emperor and himself.

As to the manner of Peter's great confession of Christ at Caesaria Philippi, it is seldom if ever pointed out how much humor there is in the gospels, Christ himself being its prime exemplar. The immediate effect of Peter's outspoken declaration is that Jesus rewards him in a joyful play of words. Peter's name was Cephas in Aramaic, meaning rock or crag (the Geek *petra*), but the humor is not simply in the wordplay but in the well-known fact that of all people the impetuous, impulsive, unreliable Peter is most unlike a rock, though undoubtedly in some ways craggy. Who would not have smiled, if not broken into a guffaw, at the surprise comparison? (One can imagine the single-minded, ambitious sons of Zebedee, James and John, doing exactly that.)

(Mark 7:24-37, 8:22-37, Matthew 16:16-27)

SO he left Galilee and went to the district of Tyre, where he entered a certain house, not wishing to be recognized, but he could not remain hidden. A woman whose little daughter had an unclean spirit immediately got to hear of him, and she came in and threw herself at his feet. She was a Greek, or rather a Phoenician born in Syria. She begged him to drive the demon out of her daughter. Jesus' response was: "One's own children ought to be fed first. It is not fair to take our children's food and throw it to the puppies."

"Oh certainly, sir," she replied, "but even the puppies under the table get some of the children's scraps."

"Because of your reply," he told her, "go home. The demon has left your daughter."

When the woman got to her house she found the child lying on her bed, and the demon gone.

Leaving the region of Tyre, he returned by way of Sidon to the Sea of Galilee and then on through the territory of the Decapolis. There they brought him a man who was deaf and almost dumb, and they implored him to lay his hand on him.

Jesus, leading him off on his own away from the crowd, put his fingers into the man's ears, spat, and touched his tongue with spittle. Looking up into the heavens he drew a deep breath and said to him, "Ephphata," which means "Be opened."

Immediately, the man's ears were unclogged and the fetters of his tongue loosed. Jesus charged them not to tell anyone, but the more he charged them the more they published it abroad. For they were amazed. "Everything he does is unique," they said. "He even makes the deaf hear and the dumb speak."

When Jesus and his disciples came to Bethsaida, the people brought a blind man to him and begged him to touch him. Taking the blind man by the hand, Jesus led him away outside the village, then spat in his eyes, and laid his hands over them. "Can you see anything?" he asked him. Peering up, the man said, "I can see people. They look like trees walking." Jesus laid his hands over the man's eyes again, and this time he gazed out completely cured, seeing everything clearly. Jesus sent him home with the injunction: "Don't even go into the village."

Jesus and his disciples now set out for the villages round Caesaria Philippi and on the way he asked them, "Who do people say I am?"

"John the Baptist," they told him, "or Elijah, some say, and others, one of the prophets."

"And you," he asked, "who do you say I am?"

Then Simon Peter spoke up and said: "You are the Christ, the Son of the living God."

"Oh you are blessed, Simon son of Jonah!" Jesus exclaimed, "because flesh and blood have not revealed this to you but my Father in heaven. And now I tell you: Rock [Peter] you are, and on this rock I shall build my church, and the gates of hell shall be powerless against it. I am giving you the keys of the kingdom of heaven. Whatsoever you shall bind on earth shall be bound also in heaven, and whatsoever you shall loose on earth shall be thrown open in heaven."

Then he charged his disciples not to tell anyone that he was the Christ; and from that time on he began to warn them that he must go to Jerusalem and and undergo great suffering at the hands of the elders, the chief priests, and the scribes, and be put to death, and be raised on the third day.

At which Peter took him by the arm and began to scold

him. "God forbid, Lord!" he burst out. "Never shall this happen to you!"

Jesus turned on him. "Back, Satan!" he said. "You stumbling block—full of man's thoughts, not God's!

"If anyone wishes to go after me," Jesus continued to his disciples, "he must renounce himself and take up his cross and follow me. For whoever tries to preserve his life shall lose it, and whoever lets his life go for my sake shall find it. What gain is it for anybody to win the whole world at the cost of his life? Or what can anyone give worth his soul? For the Son of Man is going to come in the glory of his Father amid his angels; then he will reward each as each has done."

NOTE

Commentators in general have been bothered by the gratuitous rudeness Jesus appears to show to the woman when he says, "It is not right to throw the bread of the children to the dogs." The difficulty disappears if the word κυναφον (*kunarion*) is correctly translated. κυναριον does not simply mean dog but a pup, a little dog, a pet dog, even a lapdog. The whole point of the analogy is that the pets of the house must not be preferred to the children of the house. No pejorative sense is intended: even less so if one translates κυναριον as *puppy*, which it almost certainly means here.

As to the word "bread" (ἄρτος-*artos*), in this context it simply means "food."

The Transfiguration

Jesus' choice of Peter, James, and John to witness the glory of his transfiguration was prophetic: these three were later to become the pillars of the infant Church in Jerusalem. In Luke's gospel the three disciples are described as being "heavy with sleep," which indicates that the transfiguration probably took place at night . . . The mountaintop may well have been one of the peaks of Mount Hermon.

The possessed boy is called in Matthew (17:15) an epileptic—which obviously he was.

(Mark 9:2-10 and 14-29)

SIX days later, Jesus took with him Peter, James, and John and, with no one else but them, led them to the top of a mountain. There he was transfigured before them, and his garments shone with a whiteness no bleacher on earth could match. They saw, too, Elijah, and Moses with him, talking to Jesus.

Peter burst out, "Master, how wonderful to be here! We'll put up three tents: one for you, one for Moses, and one for Elijah." Of course, Peter did not know what he was saying—they were all so staggered. Then a cloud enveloped the figures, and from the cloud came a voice: "This is my beloved Son. Hearken to him."

All at once as they looked around there was no one to be seen but only Jesus.

Coming down from the mountain, he told them strictly not to divulge to anyone what they had seen until the Son of Man had risen from the dead. So they kept it to themselves, discussing, however, what it meant—this rising from the dead.

On returning to the other disciples they found them in the thick of a large crowd and scribes arguing with them. And as soon as the crowd saw him, they ran up to welcome him, very surprised.

"What is all the commotion about?" Jesus asked.

"Master," a man from the crowd responded, "I have brought my son to you. He is not able to talk because of a spirit, and when this comes over him it hurls him to the ground and he foams and grinds his teeth and becomes quite rigid. He is wasting away. I asked your disciples to drive out the spirit, but they could not."

"You faithless generation!" Jesus exclaimed. "How long shall I be with you? How long shall I put up with you?. . . . Bring me the boy."

They led the boy to him and the moment he saw Jesus, the spirit brought on the convulsions, felling him to the ground and making him thrash and foam.

"How long has he been like this?" Jesus asked the father.

"Since he was little," the man replied. "Often it throws him into the fire or into water, attempting to destroy him. Please, if you can do anything, have pity on us and help us."

"*If* I can do anything!" Jesus repeated. "Everything is do-able to one who has faith."

"I have faith, I have!" the man cried out. "Help me to have more."

Jesus saw how the crowd was increasing around him, so he issued this rebuke to the unclean spirit: "You demon of deafness and dumbness, I say to you, 'Get out of him and never come back.' "

At that, the spirit, with much shrieking and struggling, came out of the boy, who lay there like a corpse, and most of the people began muttering, "Look, he's dead!"

Jesus just took him by the hand and raised him to his feet.

Back at home, his disciples asked him privately, "Why were we not able to drive the spirit out?"

"This kind," Jesus told them, "can only be expelled by prayer."

Jesus and the Payment of Taxes —He Admonishes Against Ambition, Lack of Compassion, and Greed for Riches

Jesus' brilliant answer to those who thought they had cornered him on the question of paying the hated tax to Rome is another example of his sense of irony. Tiberius had begun his reign in A.D. 14 and had now been emperor for some twenty-three years and was nearing the age of eighty. It would have been his head stamped on the coin which Jesus asked to see. So, there displayed for all to goggle at was the grisly old visage of this symbol of Mammon.

The story of the coin found in the fish's mouth was probably included by Matthew in his account to clarify the question that was beginning to bother both Jews and converts to Christianity. Should they continue to pay the half-shekel tax (which was originally intended for the upkeep of the Temple in Jerusalem), now that there was no Temple: it having been destroyed by the Romans in A.D. 70? Moreover, their half-shekels were going to support the temple of Jupiter in Rome. The implied answer, adumbrated in Christ's masterful reply to the Pharisees, was that, as free children of the one true

God they had no moral obligation to pay such a tax, but as de facto members of a particular society it would be expedient to do so.

Much of this section of Matthew's gospel is colored by considerations arising in the early church, and it is difficult to determine how much of Jesus' conversation really stems from him and not from somebody representing his views. There is an intransigence in some of the language Jesus uses which is fierce with Semitic overstatement.

(Matthew 17:24-27, 22:15-22, Mark 9:33-37, Matthew 18:6-14, 21-35, Mark 10:13-31)

ON their arrival in Capernaum the collectors of the two-drachma tax came up to Peter and said, "Doesn't your master pay the temple tax?"

"Yes, he does," Peter answered, and Jesus, the moment he came home, anticipated him by asking, "What do you think, Simon? From whom do the kings of the earth levy duty and taxes—from their own subjects or from foreigners?"

When Peter answered, "From foreigners," Jesus went on, "In that case, their own subjects are exempt. However, not to cause trouble, go down to the lake and cast in a line and take the first fish you hook, open its mouth, and you will find a four-drachma piece. Give it to them for you and me."

Then the Pharisees got together in a plot to trip Jesus up in his speech, and along with the Herodians they sent their partisans to say, "Master, we know that you only speak the truth and in all honesty teach God's way; moreover, that you are not swayed by anyone and are no respecter of persons. So tell us what you think: Is it right or wrong for us to pay taxes to Caesar?"

Jesus, well aware of their evil machinations, replied, "You hypocrites, why must you try to trap me? . . . Show me a coin for the tax."

They handed him a denarius.

"Now," he asked them, "whose image and inscription is on this?"

"Caesar's," they said.

"Well then, render to Caesar the things that are Caesar's and to God the things that are God's."

This answer left them gaping. They stopped bothering him and went away.

When Jesus and his disciples reached home after returning

to Capernaum, he asked them, "What were you arguing about on the way?" They were silent because they had been arguing about who was the greatest. He sat down and called the twelve and said to them, "Anyone who wants to be first must be last of all and servant of all."

Then taking a little child, he stood him among them, hugged him, and said, "Whosoever welcomes a little child like this one, in my name, welcomes me, and whosoever welcomes me welcomes him who sent me."

Then he went on, "Anyone leading astray one of the little ones who believe in me should have a millstone strung to his neck and be tossed into the depths of the sea. Woe to the world because of all the occasions of sin! Of course, occasions of sin must come, but woe to the one who causes them. If your hand or your foot makes you sin, chop it off and throw it away. It is better to enter eternal life with one hand, or crippled, than with two hands and two feet to be cast into eternal fire. And if your eye makes you sin, gouge it out and throw it away. Far better to enter eternal life with one eye than with two to be cast into Gehenna.

"So be careful not to despise one of these little ones, because I say to you, their angels in heaven gaze forever on the face of my Father in heaven. . . . What do you think? If a man has a hundred sheep and one of them strays, won't he leave the ninety-nine on the hillside and go after the one that has strayed? And if he is lucky enough to find it, he is happier with that—believe me!—than with all the ninety-nine that never went astray. And so you see, it is not the will of my Father to lose a single one of these little ones."

Then Peter came to him and asked, "Lord, how many times should I forgive my brother when he wrongs me? Seven times?"

"Seven times?" Jesus replied. "Oh no—I tell you seventy times seven times. You see, the kingdom of heaven is like a certain king who wanted to settle accounts with his subjects and had hardly begun going through the lists when a man was brought in who owed him a thousand talents but couldn't pay it. The king therefore ordered him to be sold—he, his wife and children, and all he had—until the sum was paid. The man groveled before him, pleading, 'Be patient with me and I will pay you all.' So the king took pity on his subject and let him off his debt.

"This same subject forthwith went off and found a fellow subject who owed him a hundred *denarii.* He collared him by the throat, demanding, "Pay back what you owe me." When the fellow subject went on his knees, begging for time and promising to pay back every penny, the man would not hear of it and had him thrown into jail till he paid up everything.

"The man's friends were deeply distressed when they saw this, and they went to the king and told him what had happened. So the king summoned the man into his presence. 'You brute!' he said. 'I let you off the whole of your debt because you implored me; ought you not to have been as merciful to a fellow subject as I was merciful to you?'

"The king in his anger handed him over to the extortioners till he paid up everything. And that is what my heavenly Father will do to you if you don't forgive your brother from your heart."

People were bringing their children to Jesus to bless, and his disciples reproached them. This upset Jesus and he said to them, "Let the little children come to me. Don't stop them, for the kingdom of heaven is made of such. Indeed, let me tell you, anyone who doesn't accept the kingdom of heaven like a little child can never enter it."

Then he took the children into his arms and laid his hands on them and blessed them.

And now, who should accost him as Jesus was starting out on a journey but a young man who ran up and knelt before him, asking, "Good Master, what must I do to gain eternal life?"

"Why do you call me good?" Jesus replied. "No one is good except God. You know the commandments: do not murder, do not commit adultery, do not steal, do not give false evidence, do not cheat, honor your father and your mother."

"But Master," said he, "I have kept all these since I was a boy."

Jesus gazed on him and loved him. "There's one thing you lack," he said. "Go and sell everything you have and give it to the poor, and you shall have treasure in heaven. Then come and follow me."

At this the young man's face fell and he went away sad, for he was very rich.

Jesus, glancing around him, remarked to his disciples, "How hard it is for those with money to enter the kingdom of God!"

His disciples were surprised at this remark, but Jesus repeated it: "Yes, my children, how hard it is for such to enter God's kingdom! It's easier for a camel to pass through the eye of a needle than for a rich man to enter the kingdom of God."

They were all the more surprised at this and began to ask one another, "Who then can be saved?"

Jesus turned his eyes on them and said, "With man this is impossible, but not with God. With God all things are possible."

Peter began to say, "Look, we've given up everything to follow you—" but Jesus cut him short: "Let me solemnly reassure you," he said: "no one who has given up home or brothers and sisters or mother and father or children or lands, for my sake, will not get back a hundredfold in this present time and everlasting life in the time to come. . . . But many who are now first shall be last, and many who are last first."

NOTES

1. As to the eye of the needle, the image is a hyperbole of something completely impossible. The suggestion that it referred to a particular gate into Jerusalem which was exceedingly narrow is supported by no evidence and weakens the hyperbole.

2. The image of hellfire comes from the valley of Hinnom or Gehenna, which was the city of Jerusalem's rubbish dump. Anyone who has gone close to a town refuse dump will agree what a perfect symbol this is of the worthless and the discarded.

Dives and Lazarus

This parable is given only by Luke and is addressed to the Pharisees, to whom Jesus has been speaking about the Law, and who also are "fond of money" (Luke 16:14). Dives has come to be the name of the rich man because it is the Latin for "rich man" and was adopted from St. Jerome's translation, the Vulgate. Lazarus, because he is described as being covered in sores, has come to be synonymous with "leper."

Sheol, or the hell of the Old Testament, was not unlike the Greek Hades: a place where the souls of the dead wandered about in a dim half reality. Then the Greeks opened up a new wing, so to speak: a part of Hades reserved for serious offenders which they called Tartarus. There the most imaginative tortures were thought up for famous sinners.

Probably when the Jews came to believe that rewards and punishments were meted out not in this life but in the next, and when they were living in a Hellenistic world following the conquests of Alexander the Great, they also took over the Greak idea of Tartarus, but made it a place of fire rather than a rich terrain of versatile torments.

(Luke 16:19-31)

THERE was once a rich man clothed in purple and fine linen who feasted sumptuously every day, while a poor man called Lazarus was huddled outside his front door all covered in sores and yearning just to eat the scraps that fell from the rich man's table. The dogs would come and lick his sores.

In time the poor man died and was carried up by angels to Abraham's bosom. The rich man also died and, once dead and buried, gazed up from the pit of Hades in anguish toward Abraham a great distance away, with Lazarus reposing on his bosom.

"Father Abraham," he beseeched, "have pity and send Lazarus here just to dip his finger in water and cool my tongue, for I am in an agony of flame."

But Abraham replied, "My son, remember that all the good things fell to you in life and all the bad to Lazarus. Now he is comfortable while you are in pain. Besides, there is a huge chasm fixed between you and us, so that even those wanting to cross from us to you cannot do so, any more than you can come to us."

"At least, Father," the rich man begged, "send him to my father's house to warn my five brothers not to come to this place of torment."

"They have Moses and the prophets," Abraham replied. "They can listen to them."

"Oh no, Father Abraham, they'll only listen to someone who comes back to them from the dead."

"But if they won't listen to Abraham and the Prophets," Abraham replied, "they are not going to be convinced even by someone coming back from the dead."

NOTE

The color purple was exclusive to royalty and the very rich. It was extracted at great cost by the Phoenicians from two species of Mediterranean snail (*Murex brandaris* and *Murex trunculus*), whose habitat was restricted to the coastal waters of Lebanon.

The Feast of Tabernacles

The Feast of Tabernacles was held every year at Jerusalem in the autumn. It combined the idea of harvest festival with a memorial of the Israelites' forty years wandering in the desert without a home. The feast lasted a week and people flocked to the city from all parts, living in tents and also in huts made of branches and palm leaves, which as often as not were erected on the flat roofs of the houses. "Tabernacle" comes from the Latin word for "tent" or "hut" as used by St. Jerome. The focus of the festival was worship in the Temple, and the general air was one of piety and holiday.

Jesus was still in Galilee at the beginning of the festival and seems at first to have been reluctant to go to Jerusalem, though urged by his family. His reason may have been the growing hostility of the Jewish leaders, or possibly his desire to upstage them by arriving in the middle of the week when speculation about his movements was at its height.

In John's gospel it should be noted that the writer's generalized use of the term "the Jews" when he really means specific elements or parties in Jewry is peculiar to John. The other evangelists specify which Jews—scribes, Pharisees, or whatever. After all, Christ and his disciples were Jews too. This blanket reference has been the cause of much offense, as if the Jews in general were Christ's enemies and did him to death.

The air is charged with drama on the last day of the Feast, and when the ritual waters from the pool of Siloam begin to be poured in the Temple, there is a valedictory earnestness about Jesus' utterance, as if he were offering himself to the people for the last time.

(John 7:2-13, Luke 9:57-62, John 7:14-18, 25-38)

THE Jewish Feast of Tabernacles was near and his brothers said to him, "Leave here and go to Judea so that your disciples can see the wonders you are doing. No one, surely, wants to be in the public eye and at the same time keeps under cover. If you are going to do these things, at least show yourself to the world." (You see, even his brothers did not believe in him.) To which Jesus replied:

"For me it is not the right time. For you it is always the

right time and the world cannot hate you, but it hates me because I show up its evil doings. So you go along to the festival. I shan't go to this Feast till my time is right."

Having said this, he remained in Galilee. However, after his brothers had left for the festival he went himself, not publicly but more or less in secret. Meanwhile the Jews began to look for him at the festival, asking, "Where on earth is he?" And there was much discussion about him among the crowds. "He's a good man," some were saying. "Oh no," retorted others, "he's misleading the people." But nobody spoke openly about him for fear of the Jews.

Meanwhile, as Jesus and his disciples were traveling along the road, a man came up to him and said, "I want to follow you wherever you go," and Jesus replied, "The foxes have their holes, and the birds of the sky their roosting places, but the Son of Man has nowhere to lay his head."

To another he said, "Follow me," and when the man replied, "Lord, let me first go and bury my father," he said to him, "Let the dead bury their dead, you go and proclaim the kingdom of God."

When another exclaimed, "I will follow you, Lord, but first let me say goodbye to my people at home," Jesus replied to him, "Nobody who puts his hand to the plow and then looks back is fit for the kingdom of God."

The festival was already halfway through when Jesus went up into the Temple and taught. The Jews who heard him could not help wondering: "How does this man know so much when he has never studied?" Jesus' answer was: "My teaching is not mine but his who sent me. Only those who are ready to do his will are able to tell whether what I say comes from God or just from me. A person who speaks merely for himself has his eye on his own glory, but one whose eye is on the glory of him who sent him is true through and through and there is nothing false about him."

Some of the people of Jerusalem exclaimed among themselves, "Isn't this the man they want to kill, yet here he is preaching in public and no one says a thing to him? Can it be that our authorities after all have decided that this is the Christ? On the other hand, we know where this man comes from, but when the Christ appears, nobody will know where he comes from."

Jesus therefore in the middle of his preaching called out, "Even if you know me, even if you know where I come from, I come not of myself but from him who sent me, the truth himself, and him you do not know. But I do know him because I am from him and it was he who sent me."

Whereat the authorities tried to arrest him, but no one could lay a hand on him because his time had not yet come. Meanwhile, many of the crowds believed in him. "For no Christ when he appears," they said, "will ever outmatch the marvels this man does."

The Pharisees and chief priests, sensing the growing mood of the crowds toward him, dispatched police to make an arrest, but Jesus responded:

"I am staying with you a little longer yet before I go to him who sent me. Then you will look for me, and you will not find me, because where I am you cannot come."

"Where does he mean?" the Jews asked themselves. "Why shan't we be able to find him? Surely he doesn't plan to go to the Jews of the Diaspora among the Greeks or even teach the Greeks? And what in the world does he mean by: 'You'll look for me, but you will not find me, because where I am you cannot come'?"

Then on the last day of the Feast, the great day, Jesus stood up and called out to the crowds, "If anyone be thirsty, let him come to me and drink; whosoever believes in me, just as the scripture says: 'From the core of his being shall stream torrents of living water.' "

NOTES

1. Remember again that in the Near East the word "brothers" did not and does not necessarily mean brothers but close male relations.

2. Luke 9:58, "the birds of the sky have their roosting places." The word John uses, κατασκηνωσις (*kataskēnōsis*), has invariably been translated as "nest," but birds do not ordinarily sleep in their nests. A naturalist like Jesus would not have made such a mistake. The word here means home or resting place, hence for a bird its perch for the night. St. Jerome was the first to get this wrong, and everybody (except The New English Bible) has followed him.

3. Diaspora, the Greek word for "scattered abroad," was the term used for those Jews who lived outside Palestine after the Babylonian Exile in 586 B.C. It was for the Jews of Alexandria and elsewhere that the Greek translation of the Old Testament, known as the Septuagint or LXX, was undertaken in the third century B.C.

The Man Born Blind

This incident took place probably while Jesus was still in Jerusalem following or during the Feast of the Tabernacles. He could just as easily have healed the man born blind on any other day than the Sabbath, but he seems to have gone out of his way (as often before) to show that from now on the Sabbath was to be a day not of restrictions but fulfillment.

This account is truly one of the great short stories in the New Testament. The piecemeal doggedness and jaunty mettle of the man as he is challenged all the way through is a wonder. He has to deal with his own bewilderment, his parents' cowardice, the trappings of authority, the threat of excommunication, and he comes through it all without flinching. One must remember too that he had to feel his way all through the streets with mud smeared over both eyes before he could reach the pool of Siloam—which was a reservoir on the southeast of Jerusalem and outside the city walls—no wonder he caused comment!

(John 9:1-41)

AS Jesus was going along he saw a man who had been born blind. "Master," his disciples asked him, "who sinned, this man or his parents, for him to be born blind?"

"He didn't sin nor did his parents," Jesus answered. "It is all to manifest through him God's greatness. Our task is to fulfill the work of him who sent me while it is still day. Night comes and no one can work. But while I am in the world, I am the light of the world."

Saying which, he spat on the ground and made a paste out of the spittle. This he smeared over the man's eyes and told him to go and wash in the pool of Siloam (the name means "Sent").

The man accordingly went off, washed, and came away seeing. Then his neighbors, who had often noticed him begging, began to ask themselves. "Isn't this the man who sat and begged?"

"It certainly is," said some.

"No, it isn't, but someone like him," asserted others.

The man himself then said, "I am the one."

"But how were your eyes opened?" they asked.

"A man called Jesus made a paste of mud and smeared it on my eyes and told me to go and wash in the pool of Siloam. So I went and I washed and I saw."

"Where is he now?" they asked.

"I don't know."

They took the man who had once been blind to the Pharisees. Now, it had been the Sabbath when Jesus made the paste of clay and opened the man's eyes, and the Pharisees in their turn asked him how he had gotten his sight.

"He put mud on my eyes and I washed and I see," the fellow repeated.

"Ah," said one of the Pharisees, "this man who breaks the Sabbath can't be from God!"

"Perhaps, but how can a sinful man do such wonders?" others countered. So they were divided, and once again they questioned the blind man: "What do you yourself have to say about him and how he opened your eyes?"

"I think he is a prophet," he answered.

The Jews, however, were not willing to believe that he had ever been blind until they called in his parents and questioned them.

"Is this your son?" they asked, "who you say was born blind? How is it that he can now see?"

"He is certainly our son," the parents replied, "and he was certainly born blind. As to how he now sees, we have no idea nor who it was who opened his eyes. Ask him yourselves. He is old enough."

His parents said this out of fear of the Jews, who had agreed that anybody confessing Jesus to be the Christ should be put out of the synagogue. That was the sole reason his parents said, "He is old enough, ask him yourselves."

So for the second time they summoned the man who had been blind.

"Praise God," they said to him. "As for us, we know very well that this man is a sinner."

"Whether he is a sinner or not, I do not know," the man replied, "but there's one thing I do know: I was blind before and now I see."

"What did he do to you?" they asked. "How exactly did he open your eyes?"

"I've told you already," the man retorted, "or weren't you listening? Why do you wish to hear it again? Do you want to become his disciples as well?"

At that they began to abuse him: "*You* can be his disciple. *We* are the disciples of Moses. We know that God talked to Moses, but this fellow—we don't even know where he comes from."

"How extraordinary!" exclaimed the man. "You don't know where he comes from, yet he opened my eyes. Now we can be certain God doesn't listen to sinners. He listens only to the devout doers of his will. And since time began, never has it been heard that anybody opened the eyes of one born blind. This man couldn't do such a thing were he not from God."

"You son of a whore!" they shouted. "How dare you give us lessons!" And they threw him out.

When Jesus heard that they had thrown him out, he found him and said, "Do you believe in the Son of Man?"

"Lord, who is he," he asked, "so that I may believe in him?"

"You have not only seen him," Jesus answered, "but he is speaking with you now."

"Lord, I believe," he uttered, falling down before him.

Then Jesus said, "The reason I came into this world was to see justice done, so that those who do not see should see, and those who see should go blind."

Hearing this the Pharisees who were with him remarked, "You don't mean *we* are blind, surely?"

"If you were really blind," Jesus replied, "you would have no sin, but since you insist that you see, your sin is blatant."

The Good Shepherd and the Good Samaritan

These two parables were probably spoken by Jesus in different places. The first—given to the people of Jerusalem after the Feast of Tabernacles and at the Feast of Dedication (*Hanukkah*) in mid-December—so incensed some of the Jewish leaders that Jesus left Jerusalem and went across the Jordan to a region called Perea (meaning "Beyond"), where he gave the second.

The parable of the Good Shepherd is a direct echo of the prophet Ezekiel in chapter 34 of that book (from the King James Bible):

> Woe be to the shepherds of Israel that do feed themselves!
> Should not the shepherds feed the flocks?
> Ye eat the fat and ye clothe with the wool,
> ye kill them that are fed, but ye feed not the flock . . .
> And they are scattered because there is no shepherd,
> and they become meat to all the beasts of the field . . .
> Behold, I, even I, thus saith the Lord God,
> will both search my sheep, and seek them out . . .
> I will feed my flock and I will cause them to lie down . . .
> I will seek that which was lost, and bring again
> that which was driven away,
> and will bind up that which was broken,
> and will strengthen that which was sick.

As to the parable of the Good Samaritan, Isaac Asimov in his *Guide to the Bible* illustrates this in a telling analogy: "The point Jesus was making was that even a Samaritan could be a neighbor; how much more so, anyone else. The flavor of the parable would probably be best captured in modern America, if we had a white southern farmer left for dead, if then we had him ignored by a minister and a sheriff and saved by a Negro sharecropper."

Jesus had preceded his arrival in Perea by sending out seventy disciples with power to preach, exorcise, and heal, while he himself went via Bethany-beyond-Jordan into Perea. What is confusing is that this Bethany is not the same as the village of Bethany on the eastern slopes of the Mount of Olives just outside Jerusalem, where Jesus' friends Martha, Mary, and Lazarus (sisters and brother) lived.

The scene opens with Jesus addressing the people of Jerusalem.

(John 10:1-18, 37-40, Luke 10:25-42)

"INDEED, I have to tell you: whoever enters the sheepfold not through the door but climbs in some other way is a rustler and a robber. The shepherd of the flock enters by the door, and the doorkeeper opens to him and the sheep listen to his voice. For these are his own sheep and he calls them by name and leads them out. Yes, they are his own and when he has them all outside he walks ahead of them, and the sheep follow him because they know his voice. They will not follow a stranger, but run from him, because they do not recognize a stranger's voice."

Jesus told them this parable, but they had no idea what he was talking about, so he said to them again, "Indeed, I tell you I am the door of the sheepfold. All those who came before me were rustlers and robbers, and the sheep paid no heed to them. I am the door. Whosoever enters by me shall be saved and shall go in and out of green pastures. The thief comes only to steal, slaughter, and destroy. I come so that they may have life and have it more abundantly. I am the good shepherd. The good shepherd lays down his life for his sheep. The hired man who is no shepherd, whose sheep are not his own, sees the wolf coming and leaves them and runs, while the wolf ravages and scatters the flock—because he is only a hired man and has no care for the sheep. But I am the good shepherd, I know mine and mine know me, just as the Father knows me and I know the Father. And I lay down my life for my sheep.

"Other sheep I have not of this fold: them also I must bring, so there will be one flock and one shepherd. That is why the Father loves me, because I lay down my life, to take it up again. Nobody takes it from me. I lay it down of my own will. I have the power to lay it down, and the power to take it up. Such is the charge I have received from my Father."

These remarks caused yet another bout of dissension among the Jews. "He is possessed and raves. Why do you listen to him?" many of them said. "No, these are not the words of someone possessed," others asserted. "And can a devil open the eyes of the blind?"

Jesus went on to say, "If I am not doing my Father's works, do not believe me; but if I am doing them, believe at least the works even if you do not believe in me, so that you may see and realize that the Father is in me and I in the Father."

At which they again tried to arrest him, but he slipped through their hands and once more crossed the Jordan to the spot where John had once baptized. There he stayed.

One day a lawyer came forward wanting to try him with a question. "Master," he said, "what must I do to merit eternal life?"

"What do the scriptures say?" Jesus returned.

The man replied, " 'Thou shalt love the Lord thy God

with all thy heart, and with all thy soul, and with all thy strength, and with all thy mind, and thy neighbor as thyself.' "

"You have answered right," Jesus said to him. 'Do this and you will live."

The man, however, wishing to justify himself, asked, "And who is my neighbor?"

"A man once," Jesus began, "was on his way from Jerusalem down to Jericho, and he fell into the hands of brigands, who stripped him, beat him, then made off leaving him half dead. By chance a priest came down the road and, seeing him, passed by on the other side. Then a Levite came to the spot, saw him, and likewise passed by on the other side. But when a traveling Samaritan came upon him he was moved to pity by the sight. He went up to him and bandaged his wounds, bathing them with oil and wine. Then he lifted him on to his own beast, took him to an inn, and nursed him there. Next day he put aside two *denarii* for the innkeeper and said, 'Look after him. On my way back I'll make good any extra expense you may incur.' . . . Now which of these three do you think was a neighbor to the man who fell among brigands?"

"The one who took pity on him," the man replied.

"And you," Jesus said, "you go and do likewise."

Their travels then brought them to a village where a woman named Martha received him into her home. She had a sister called Mary, who sat at the Lord's feet drinking in his words while Martha bustled about seeing to the meal. So Martha stepped up to Jesus and said, "Lord, doesn't it interest you that my sister has left me to do all the serving? Please tell her to give me a hand."

"Martha, oh Martha," the Lord replied, "you are fussing and worrying about so many things when only one thing is necessary. Mary has chosen the better part, which shall not be taken from her."

Some More Parables and Miracles

We are to assume that after the episode with Martha and Mary in Bethany-beyond-Jordan, Jesus spent some time in the region of Perea preaching and healing. The crowds were great, swollen no doubt by the activity of the seventy disciples whom he had sent before him.

(Luke 12:1-7, 13-21, 13:10-35, 14:1-24, 15:1-32, 17:11-19, 18:9-14, 35-43, 19:1-10, 18:31-34)

AS the crowds gathered by tens of thousands, crushing one another, he had begun to speak first to his disciples, "Watch out for the ferment of the Pharisees, I mean their hypocrisy. There is nothing which is not under cover which won't be uncovered; nothing now secret which won't be wide open. Accordingly, everything you say in the dark will be heard in broad daylight; and everything you whisper in the ear in an inner chamber will be blazed from the housetops.

"So I tell you, my friends, do not be afraid of those who kill the body and after that can do no more. I'll show you whom to fear. Fear the one who kills and then can throw you into hell. Yes, I tell you, that is the one to fear.

"The price of five sparrows is a couple of coppers, is it not? Yet not one of them is absent from God's sight. Even the hairs of your head are numbered. So don't be afraid. You are worth more than a flock of sparrows."

A man in the crowd said to him, "Master, tell my brother to divide the family estate with me."

"My good man," he answered, "who gave me power of attorney for you or made me judge?" Then he turned to the people: "Beware of greed. Be on the watch for all its kinds. A man's life is not in the wealth of his possessions." Then he told them this parable.

"There was a rich man whose land bore profusely, and he wondered to himself, 'How am I going to store all this produce? Ah yes,' he thought, 'I know what I'll do. I'll pull down my barns and build bigger ones, and there I'll hoard all my grain and the good things of life. And I'll say to my soul, "Soul, you have many good things laid by for a good many years. Relax, eat, drink, and enjoy yourself.' "

" 'You fool,' " God said, " 'this very night your soul is wanted. And who will then enjoy this hoard of yours?' "

"So much for the person who heaps up riches for himself instead of being rich for God."

One Sabbath Jesus was teaching in a synagogue where a woman was present who for eighteen years had been affected by a disease of the spirit which bent her double so that she was quite unable to stand up straight. Jesus saw her and called her over. "Madam," he said, "you are freed from your affliction."

At once she straightened up, heaping praises on God. The head of the synagogue, however, was indignant that Jesus had healed on the Sabbath, and he observed to the congregation: "There are six working days on which you can come and be healed, but not the Sabbath."

"You hypocrites!" Jesus interjected, "doesn't every one of you untether his cow or his donkey on the Sabbath day and lead it to the water? Yet this woman, a daughter of Abraham, whom Satan has hooped up for eighteen years, is she not to be untethered on the Sabbath day?"

His words filled his opponents with embarrassment, but the crowds were delighted with all the splendid things that happened through him.

One day when he had gone to the house of a leading Pharisee for dinner and everyone was watching him closely, he saw the way the guests tried to put themselves in the places of honor, and he told them a parable.

"When someone invites you to a wedding, don't go and settle in the first place in case the host has invited somebody more distinguished than you and he has to come and tell you, 'Do you mind giving up your place?' and to your humiliation you begin to drop toward the bottom. No, when you are invited, settle yourself in the lowest place so that when your host comes to you he will say, 'My friend, move up higher.' Then you will be honored in the sight of all your fellow guests, because everyone who exalts himself shall be humbled and everyone who humbles himself shall be exalted."

And he said to the man who had invited him, "When you give a luncheon or a dinner, don't invite your friends or your brothers or your relatives or your rich neighbors; they will only ask you back again and so you will be repaid. Instead, when you invite, ask in the poor and the maimed, the crippled and the blind. So you will be blessed because they cannot pay you back; though you *will* be repaid at the resurrection of the godly."

Hearing this, one of the company exclaimed, "How happy is he who shall feast in the kingdom of God!"

Jesus turned to him and said, "A man once gave a great banquet and invited many. On the day of the banquet he sent out his servant to all the guests to say, 'Come. Everything is ready.' But one by one they all began to make excuses. The first said, 'I have bought a piece of land and I must go and look it over. I beg you excuse me.' The next one said, 'I have bought five yoke of oxen and I am off to try them. I beg you excuse me.' Another said, 'I have just got married and that makes it impossible for me to come.'

"When the servant returned and reported all this, the master of the house was indignant and said to his servant, 'Go out at once into the squares and alleys of the city and bring in the poor and the maimed, the blind and the crippled.' . . .

" 'Your orders are done, sir,' the servant reported, 'and there is still room.'

" 'Then go out into the highways and along the hedgerows,' said master to servant, 'and compel them to come in. I want my house filled with people. But I tell you, not one of those who were invited shall taste my banquet.' "

At this time Jesus was attracting around him all the tax collectors and bad characters, which set the Pharisees and scribes mumbling, "This fellow welcomes criminals and sups with them." So he aimed this parable at them:

"Is there a man among you who has a hundred sheep, loses one, and does not leave the ninety-nine in the wilds to go after the lost sheep until he finds it? And when he finds it, he slings it across his shoulders full of gladness. And he goes home and invites his friends and neighbors and announces to them, 'Share my happiness: I have found my lost sheep.'

"I tell you, there is more merriment in heaven over one repenting sinner than over ninety-nine honest folk who have nothing to repent.

"Or what housewife who has ten drachmas and loses one of them does not light up the house and diligently sweep until she finds it? And when she finds it she calls in her neighbors. 'Share my gladness,' she rejoices, 'I have found my lost drachma.' Such, I tell you, is the festivity among the angels of God over one repentant sinner."

Then he told them this: "There was a man who had two sons, and the younger said to his father, 'Father, give me now what is coming to me of the estate.' So his father divided his property between them, and not many days later the younger son packed up everything and left for a far country, where he squandered his inheritance in reckless living. And after he had spent everything, a severe famine hit the land and he began to be in want. So he went and attached himself to a farmer of the place, who sent him out into the fields to feed the pigs. He would gladly have filled himself with the carob pods on which the pigs fed, but no one gave him anything. At last he came to himself and said, 'How many paid menials my father has, all stuffed with as much food as they can eat—and here am I dying of hunger. I shall get up and go to my father and say to him, "Father, I have sinned against heaven and against you. I am not worthy any more to be called your son. Make me into one of your hired men.' So he roused himself and set off for his father, and when he was still a long way away, his father saw him and, filled with compassion, ran toward him and flung his arms around him and kissed him. Then his son said to him, 'Father, I have sinned against heaven and against you; I am not worthy any more to be called your son.' But his father called to the servants, 'Quick, bring out the best robe and put it on him; and put a ring on his finger and shoes on his feet. And go and get the fatted calf and slaughter it, for we must feast and celebrate, because this my son was dead and now has come to life; he was lost and is found.'

"And so they began to celebrate. But his elder brother, returning from the fields, heard the sounds of music and dancing as he approached the house; so he called one of the servants and asked him what was going on.

" 'Your brother has just come home,' the man said, 'and your father has killed the fatted calf because he has him back safe and sound.'

"The elder brother was angry and would not go in, so his father came out and pleaded with him, but he responded, 'Look, all these years I have slaved for you and you haven't given me so much as a young goat to make a dinner for my friends. But the moment this fellow comes back, this son of yours who has squandered your living among whores, you kill the fatted calf for him.'

" 'Son,' " his father answered, " 'you are with me always,

and all I have is yours, but we had to celebrate and rejoice because your brother was dead and is alive again, was lost and is found.' "

It happened that on his way to Jerusalem when Jesus was traveling along the borders of Samaria and Galilee, coming into a village he was met by ten lepers, who stood at a distance calling out, "Jesus, Master, have pity on us." When he saw them he said, "Go and show yourselves to the priests," and as they went they were made clean. One of them, when he saw that he was healed, turned back praising God at the top of his voice, and he threw himself on his face at Jesus' feet, thanking him.

"Were there not ten lepers made clean?" Jesus said to him. "Where are the other nine? Could none be found to turn back and give glory to God but this stranger?" Then he said to the man, "Rise up and go on your way. Your faith has made you whole."

Jesus also told this parable to some who prided themselves on being virtuous and looked down on everybody else. "Two men went up to the Temple to pray, one was a Pharisee, the other a tax collector. The Pharisee, standing erect, uttered this prayer within himself, 'O God, I thank you that I am not like the rest of men: greedy, dishonest, adulterous—in fact, like this tax collector here. I fast twice a week, I give tithes of all I possess . . .'

"Meanwhile the tax collector, standing far off and not even lifting his eyes to heaven, beat his breast and said, 'O God, be merciful to me a sinner.' I tell you, it was this man and not the other who returned home in God's favor. For everyone who exalts himself shall be humbled, and everyone who humbles himself shall be exalted."

As Jesus was approaching Jericho, a blind man sat by the road begging and when he heard the passing crowd he inquired what was happening. On being told, "Jesus of Nazareth is passing through," he called out, "Jesus Son of David, have pity on me." The people in front told him to hold his tongue, but he shouted all the louder, "Jesus Son of David, have pity on me."

Jesus stopped and asked for the man to be brought to him, and when he came up he said to him, "What do you want me to do for you?"

"Lord," he replied, "let me see again."

"Then, see again," Jesus said to him. "Your faith has cured you."

And immediately he could see again, and he followed him praising God. And all the people who witnessed it praised God too.

Entering Jericho, Jesus was passing through it when a curious thing happened. A man called Zacchaeus, a chief tax collector and very rich, was trying to pick Jesus out from the crowd, but could not see him because he was a little man. So he ran on ahead and climbed into a sycamore tree to see him as he passed.

When Jesus came to the spot he looked up and called out, "Zacchaeus, hurry on down because I must stay in your house today."

So he hurried down and welcomed Jesus with joy, which when people saw they murmured in disapproval, "He has gone to stay with a blatant sinner." Zacchaeus for his part stood before the Lord and said, "See, Lord, I am giving half my possessions to the poor, and if I have cheated anyone I'll make it up to him four times over."

Jesus said to him. "Salvation has come to this house today, because this man also is a son of Abraham, and the Son of Man came to search out and save that which was lost."

[About this time] Jesus, taking the Twelve aside, said to them, "You know, we are going to Jerusalem and everything written by the prophets concerning the Son of Man will come true. He will be handed over to the Gentiles. He will be mocked, abused, and spat on. They will flog him and put him to death, and on the third day he will rise again."

But the disciples could take none of this in. It was all hidden from them and his words meant nothing.

NOTES

1. Five sparrows: in both the Hebrew and the Greek the word for "sparrow" can also sometimes mean any small bird. The Mosaic law did not forbid the eating of the flesh of sparrows. Jesus used sparrows for his illustration of divine providence because it is the commonest and least distinguished of birds.

2. The drachma was a Greco-Roman coin worth roughly a day's wage.

3. The husks, or pods, that the prodigal son would gladly have filled himself with were the long, chocolate-colored beans of the carob or locust tree (*Ceratonia siliqua*). The carob is a drought-

resistant evergreen of the pea family. Its fruit ripen into long, brown sugary pods which can be ground into a sweet flour for making cakes or cocoa-like beverages. The beans are also often used as cattle fodder.

4. The sycamore tree that Zacchaeus climbed is not the same as the tree of that name in England or America. The biblical sycamore (*Ficus sycamorus*) belongs to the fig family. It is an easy tree to climb because its branches are low and strong. The English and American tree belongs to the maple family, though they are not the same: the American sycamore (Platanus occidentalis) being the London plane, and the English sycamore (Acer pseudoplatanus) a tree not indigenous to America.

The Raising of Lazarus

This surely must be the greatest of Christ's miracles, apart from that of his own resurrection, to which it points symbolically while also precipitating his death. Lazarus, after all, was not merely dead but buried and in the tomb four whole days.

Jesus was beyond the Jordan, possibly still in Perea, when news of Lazarus's illness reached him.

In verse 16 when Thomas says, "Let's all go and die with him," it is not clear whether he means: "Let's all go and join our beloved Lazarus," or whether, sensing the danger Jesus will run into if they return to Jerusalem, he means: "Let's all go and risk our lives with Jesus."

Once again, let readers be reminded that when John says, "the Jews" he means the Jewish authorities.

(John 11:1-54)

A man was sick, Lazarus of Bethany, the village of Mary and her sister Martha. This was the Mary who had anointed Jesus with unguent and wiped his feet with her hair. It was her brother Lazarus who was sick. So the sisters sent to him, saying, "Lord, please, the one you love is sick."

When Jesus heard this he remarked, "This sickness is not to death, but for the glory of God and for the Son of God to be glorified by it."

Now, Jesus loved Martha and her sister and Lazarus, yet hearing that he was sick, he stayed another two days in the place he was. After which he said to his disciples, "We are going into Judea again."

"What, Master!" the disciples protested. "Only just now the Jews wanted to stone you and are you going there again?"

"There are twelve hours in the day, are there not?" Jesus replied. "And if you go walking in the daytime you won't stumble, because you see the world's light; but if you go walking at night, you stumble because there is no light."

Having said which, he remarked, "Our beloved Lazarus has fallen asleep."

"Lord, if he has fallen asleep he'll get well," the disciples exclaimed. But Jesus meant that he was dead, whereas they thought he was talking about ordinary sleep. So then he told them plainly, "Lazarus is dead. But I am glad for your sakes and for the sake of your faith that I was not there. Come, let us go to him."

When Jesus arrived he found that Lazarus had already been four days in the tomb. Now, Bethany was near Jerusalem, only about two miles away, and many of the Jews had come to condole with Martha and Mary over their brother.

As soon as Martha heard that Jesus was on his way she went to meet him, while Mary sat in the house. "Lord, if only you had been here," Martha burst out to Jesus, "my brother would never have died. And yet even now I know that anything you ask of God, God will grant you."

"Your brother will rise again," Jesus said to her.

"I know," Martha retorted, "he will rise at the resurrection on the last day."

"I am the resurrection and the life," said Jesus to her. "Whosoever believes in me, even if he dies shall live. And everyone who lives and believes in me shall never die. Do you believe this?"

"Yes, Lord," she replied. "I believe that you are the Christ, the Son of God, who was to come into this world."

Having said which, she went and called her sister quietly. "The Master is here and asking for you." Mary, the moment she heard this, got up and hurried out to him. Jesus had not yet reached the village. He was still at the spot where Martha had met him. Consequently, when the Jews who were in the house with Mary consoling her saw her suddenly get up and go out, they followed her, thinking that she was going to the tomb to mourn there. When Mary came to where Jesus was, she gazed at him and fell at his feet, sobbing, "Lord, if only you had been here, my brother would not have died."

At the sight of her crying and the Jews around her crying,

his spirit was torn with emotion and he asked, "Where have you laid him?"

"Come and see, sir," they said. And Jesus wept.

"How he must have loved him!" the Jews commented. But some of them said, "He opened the eyes of that blind man; couldn't he have prevented this man from dying?"

Jesus, still choked with emotion, walked toward the tomb. It was a cave, with a stone sealing it.

"Heave aside the stone," Jesus ordered. At which Martha the deceased's sister murmured to him, "Lord, by now there'll be a stench. It's been four days."

"Did I not tell you," Jesus answered, "that if you believed, you would see God's glory?"

So they heaved aside the stone and Jesus, lifting up his eyes, uttered, "Father, I thank you for hearing me. And I know that you always hear me, but because of the people standing around I have spoken so that they may believe you have sent me."

Saying which, he called out in a loud voice, "Lazarus, come out!" And the dead man walked forward, his feet and hands swaddled in linen strips and his head swathed in a cloth.

"Unloose him," Jesus ordered, "and let him go."

Many of the people therefore who had gone with Mary [to the tomb] and saw what Jesus did believed in him; but some of them went to the Pharisees and reported what Jesus had done. Consequently, the chief priests and the Pharisees called together the Sanhedrin and they asked themselves, "What are we to do? This man is working so many marvels that if we let him go on like this everyone will believe in him and the Romans will come and sweep away our Temple and our nation."

Then one of them, Caiphas, who was high priest that year, declared, "You people know nothing. Can't you see that it is better for one man to die for the public than for the whole nation to be lost?"

This statement of his did not really come from him, but was like a prophesy from the high priest of that year that Jesus would die for the nation, and not merely for the nation but for all the scattered children of God so that they should be gathered into one. So from that day on they plotted to kill him, and Jesus no longer went about openly among the Jews but withdrew from there to a town near the desert called Ephraim, and there he remained with his disciples.

The Last Supper

The religious authorities in Jerusalem headed by Caiphas were more than ever outraged by Jesus' triumphal entry into the city on "Palm Sunday": a rage hardly appeased by his continued preaching in the Temple and by a new spate of healings on the Sabbath. So they decided that Jesus must die, but they were not sure how to bring this about. "Then one of the Twelve, a man called Judas Iscariot, went to the chief priests and said, 'How much will you give me if I hand him over to you?' They agreed to pay him thirty pieces of silver, and from then onward Judas looked for an opportunity to betray him" (Matthew 26:14-16).

We shall probably never know why Judas was ready to betray Christ. It surely could not have been simple cupidity. Thirty pieces of silver was worth no more than the life of a slave. If the reason was disappointment in Jesus for not being the crusading earthly Messiah many Jews were expecting, that too hardly seems a sufficient motive for betraying a man who had shown himself lovable and remarkable beyond imagining. No, we must fall back on the bald statement in Luke 22:3: "Then Satan entered Judas Iscariot, though one of the Twelve."

As to why the Jewish authorities needed a Judas is another question. Why could they not themselves have arrested Jesus any time they wanted? The answer is, because they were in a hurry. Jesus must be dispatched before the Passover when religious fervor and popular support for him might reach fever pitch. For the same reason, the arrest must be made by stealth and at night. Only a disciple with inside knowledge of Jesus' movements could lead them to their man at the right time and in the right way. After which a trial could be rushed through so that by the time of the Passover the people could be presented with a fait accompli.

As to the Last Supper itself, whether in fact this was a Passover meal or not, it became for Christians the ritual inauguration of the Eucharist, a Greek word meaning "thanksgiving": a thanksgiving for Christ's whole redemptive mission. The crucial words (known as the words of consecration) "This is my body . . . This is my blood . . ." have been understood by Christians either symbolically or as actual fact. In either case they proved a stumbling block to the

Jews and turned away many who would otherwise have been Christ's followers.

When we come to Jesus' farewell discourse to his disciples (of which I give only a part), the atmosphere in the supper room is tense with suppressed drama, and Jesus slips easily and naturally into a heightened kind of speech which readily falls into a verse form akin to the iambic trimeter line of Greek tragedy (twelve syllables divided into two sets of three stresses with a caesura after the sixth syllable).

It is now the Thursday of Jesus' final week, and he gives instructions to his disciples for the preparation of a meal with them which he knows will be his last.

(Mark 14:12-16, John 13:1-18, 21-26, Matt 26:25, John 13:27-32, Matt 26:26-29, John 13:33-38, 14:1-11, 23-24, 15:1-4, 12-14, 16:12-13, 17:1-6, 22-23)

ON the first day of Unleavened Bread, when the Passover lamb was sacrificed, his disciples asked him, "Where would you like us to prepare the Passover supper for you?"

Jesus replied as he dispatched two of his disciples: "When you enter the city you will meet a man carrying a pitcher of water. Follow him into the house he goes into and say to the householder, 'The Master wants you to show us the dining room which has been reserved for him to eat the Passover with his disciples.' He will show you a large room upstairs all furnished and ready. Make your preparations for us there."

His disciples set out for the city and found everything just as he said, and they prepared the Passover. And so it befell that Jesus before the Passover festival, knowing that his hour had come when he must leave this world and go to the Father, having loved his own who were in the world, he loved them to the end.

During supper, when the devil had already put it into the heart of Judas Iscariot son of Simon to betray him, Jesus, fully aware that the Father had entrusted all things into his hands and that he had come from God and was going back to God, got up from the table, laid aside his tunic, took a towel and wrapped it around him, then poured water into a basin, and began to wash the feet of his disciples, wiping them with the towel he had on. When he came to Simon Peter, Peter said to him, "Lord, you are not going to wash my feet, are you?"

"You may not understand now what I am doing," Jesus answered, "but one day you will."

"Never, ever, are you going to wash my feet," Peter protested.

"Unless I wash you," Jesus answered, "you can have no part with me."

"In that case, Lord," burst out Simon Peter, "not only my feet but my hands and my head as well."

"It is not necessary for a person to be washed again after bathing," Jesus replied, "only the feet, for he is clean all over. And you are all clean—all but one."

He added the words "all but one" because he knew who was going to betray him. After he had washed their feet and put his tunic on again, he returned to the table.

"Do you understand what I have just done?" he asked them. "You call me Master and Lord, and quite rightly, for so I am. If then I your Lord and Master have washed your feet, you too should wash one another's feet. I have set you an example to do as I have done to you. For I hardly need tell you that a servant is not greater than his master, nor a messenger than the one who sent him. You know these things well enough, and happy will you be if you follow them. However, I am not speaking about all of you. I know whom I have chosen and there is a scripture to be fulfilled: 'One who shares my table is a traitor.' "

After these words, Jesus in a voice quavering with anguish said, "Yes, it is true: one of you will betray me."

The disciples stared at one another, desperate to know whom he meant. Then Simon Peter made a sign to the disciple Jesus loved, who was reclining against Jesus' breast, and whispered, "Ask him whom he means." So, leaning back on Jesus' bosom, he asked, "Who is it, Lord?"

"The one I give this sop of bread to from the dish," Jesus answered as he dipped a morsel of bread into the dish and handed it to Judas the son of Iscariot. And this Judas who was to betray him exclaimed, "Surely not me, Rabbi?" And Jesus answered, "The decision is yours."

The moment Judas took the bread, Satan entered him and Jesus told him, "Do quickly what you have to do." No one at the table understood what he meant by this. Some thought that as Judas was in charge of the common purse, Jesus was telling him to buy whatever was necessary for the festival, or telling him to give something to the poor. Judas, as soon as he had accepted the bread, went out. It was night.

When he had gone, Jesus declared:

"Now is the Son of Man
glorified, and God
is glorified in him.
If God is glorified
in him, then God will also
glorify him in himself.
And God will glorify him soon."

Then, while they were at table, Jesus took bread, spoke a blessing, broke it, and gave it his disciples, saying, "Take this and eat it, for this is my body." Then holding up the cup and pronouncing a grace, he handed it to them, saying, "Drink from this, all of you, for this is my blood: the blood of the new order poured out for many to wash away their sins . . . This is the last time, let me tell you, that I shall drink the fruit of the vine until that day when I drink it new with you in the kingdom of my Father.

"Only a little longer,
children, am I with you.
Then you will look for me
and as I told the Jews,
where I am going you
cannot come after me.
A new commandment I
leave with you: love
One another. Yes,
you must love each other
just as I loved you.
And by this love
you have for one another,
everyone will know
you are followers of me."

Then Simon Peter said, "Lord, where are you going?"
Jesus replied, "Where I am going, you cannot follow me now, but one day you will."
"Why, Lord, can I not follow you at once?" Peter persisted. "I am ready to lay down my life for you."
"Are you so?" Jesus answered. "Ready to lay down your life for me? Alas, I tell you, before the cock has crowed, you will have disowned me three times.

"Don't let your hearts be troubled,
keep your trust in God,
and keep your trust in me.
There are many chambers

in my Father's mansion,
  and if there were not,
I would have told you so;
  for that is where I am going
to prepare a place for you.
  And after I am gone
to prepare that place, I shall
  return to take you with me,
so that where I am
  you may also be.
And the way to where I go,
  that you know already."

Thomas interrupted: "Lord, we do not know where you are going, so how can we know the way?"

To which Jesus replied:

"I am the way, the truth, and the life.
  No one comes to the Father
except through me.
  And if you had known *me*
you would have known my Father.
  But from now on
you do know him
  and have even seen him."

Then Philip said, "Lord, show us the Father and we shall be satisfied."

"What!" said Jesus to him, "have I been with you, Philip, all this time and still you do not know me?

"Whoever sees me,
  sees the Father too.
So how can you say,
  'Show us the Father'?
Do you not believe
  that I am in the Father
and the Father is in me?
  Even the words I speak
do not come from me
  but from the Father, who
lives in me and does
  his work in me.
So you must believe me
  when I say that I
am in the Father and
  the Father is in me . . .

Whoever loves me keeps my words,
  and my Father will love him,
and we shall come to him
  and make our home with him . . .
I am the true vine
  and my Father is the husbandman.
Every branch of mine
  that bears no fruit, he cuts away,
And every branch that fruits,
  he prunes to bear still more.
You by my spoken word
  are already pruned
and make your home in me,
  as I make mine in you.
No branch by itself bears fruit
  but only on the vine.
Nor can you unless
  you too remain in me . . .
So this is my commandment:
  to love one another
as I have loved you.
There is no greater love than this,
  to lay one's life down for one's friends.
You are my friends
  if you do what I command . . .
There are so many things
  I want to tell you still,
but you are not ready for them now.
  When the Spirit of Truth
comes to visit you,
  he will guide you to the truth—
yes, all the truth there is."

After speaking these words, Jesus looked up to heaven and said:

"Father, the hour has come
  to glorify your Son,
so that your Son
  may glorify you too.
For you have made him sovereign
  over all mankind
to grant eternal life
  to all whom you have given him.
And this is eternal life:
  to know you the one

true God and Jesus
  Christ whom you have sent.
I glorified you here
  on earth by finishing
the work you gave me to complete.
So glorify me, Father,
  with your own self now,
with that glory that I shared with you
  before the world began.
I have revealed your name
  to those you plucked for me
out of the world.
  Yours they were, and you
have made them mine. May they,
  with me in them and you
in me, be perfect in one.
  Then the world will know
that you it was who sent me,
  and that I have loved them
as much as you loved me.
  Father, I wish that these
who are your gift to me
  be where I am with me
so they may gaze upon
  the glory which you gave me,
because you loved me so,
  before the world began."

NOTES

1. It is clear from John's gospel that the Last Supper took place on the day before the eve of Passover, i.e., the Thursday. The paschal lamb was actually slaughtered the day after, on Good Friday, at about the time that Christ was put upon the cross. This year the Sabbath and Passover coincided.

2. Dining in the Greco-Roman fashion, the disciples would be reclining on the left elbow, two to a couch: the couches being grouped around low tables. There were probably three tables arranged in a rough horseshoe, with Jesus and the Beloved Disciple sharing a couch at the central table. Since there were thirteen diners to begin with and Jesus obviously had no difficulty in reaching Judas with the sop of bread in his right hand, and since Jesus and the Beloved Disciple would be conferring in private, it is possible that Judas occupied the next couch to the right at the center table, with one other disciple between him and Jesus. With such a grouping, of course, it was easy to maintain both private and general discourse. Peter must have been positioned far enough away to have to make a sign to the Beloved Disciple, but not so far away that he could not

speak to him. Second man down on the left-hand corner couch at right angles to the top table would be my guess . . . (The Beloved Disciple by tradition was John son of Zebedee, the brother of James, the youngest of the Apostles and at this time no more than nineteen or twenty years old.)

The Passion

In putting together this account of Jesus' Passion (and in the next chapter of his Resurrection), I have reproduced as much as possible of all four gospels. This was no easy task because there are so many differences, even discrepancies, of time and place that to make the narrative flow as a complete story I had to make several omissions. For instance, I was not able to include the episode of Pilate's sending Christ to Herod Antipas, the tetrarch of Judea, who happened to be in Jerusalem for the Passover (an event recorded only in Luke). Nevertheless, in spite of the lacunae, the resulting account is a far fuller description of what happened than is to be found in any one gospel.

Crucifixion was a form of execution which the Romans adopted from the Persians and Carthaginians. (The Jews favored stoning and the Greeks the taking of hemlock.) It was usually reserved for slaves and aliens and was often preceded by a scourging, which could be severe enough in itself to induce the victim's death: perhaps a blessing if it saved a man many hours and even days of slow expiring from thirst, exposure, and bleeding. Jesus died within three hours on the cross, which was considered unusual, but he had already suffered a whole night of brutalization.

"My God, my God, why hast thou forsaken me?" This cry from Jesus just before the end is given in Hebrew by Matthew and in Aramaic by Luke (*Eloi, Eloi, lama sabachthani*). They are the opening words of Psalm 22, a psalm which runs through a litany of symbols expressing despair and the direst suffering and moves toward hope, faith, and universal triumph. So too the psalm that Jesus uses for his last utterance: "Lord, into thy hands I commend my spirit" (Psalm 31:5), the next sentence of which runs: "O Lord, thou hast saved me."

Pontius Pilate was the fourth Procurator (i.e., "Caretaker" or Governor) of Judea and had been appointed from Rome in A.D. 26. He had the task of maintaining the Pax Romana in a highly inflammable region, where a false step would not only bring to boil the simmering nationalistic discontent, but worse, lead to the intervention of Rome's powerful enemy to the east, the Parthians, who had within living memory (53 B.C.) cut to pieces the Roman army at Carrhae.

Pilate remained Procurator of Judea till A.D. 36 when the emperor finally lost patience with his lack of tact in dealing with the Jews and with his inability to keep down revolts and quarrels, and he recalled him. Independent (non-biblical) confirmation of Pilate and his activities is to be found in the writings of both Philo (20 B.C.–A.D. 50) and Josephus (37 A.D.–c. 100). Besides which, in 1961, an important inscription was found at Caesarea Maritima in which Pilate is named and given the correct title of prefect rather than procurator.

Contradictory legends grew up about his later life, ranging from a death by execution or suicide, to conversion to Christianity and even (in the Coptic tradition of the Ethiopian church) canonization as a saint.

(John, 18:1-2, Matt 26:36-39, Luke 22:43-44, Matt 26:40-49, Luke 22:48-51, John 18:10-11, Matt 26:52-53, Mark 14:48-52, John 18:12-14, 19-24, Matt 26:57-69, Luke 22:54-62, John 18:28-37, Matt 27:19, John 18:39, Matt 27:20-21, John 18:40, 19:1-13, Matt 27:24-25, John 19:14-17, Luke 23:32-34, John 19:19-24, Matt 27:39-43, Luke 23:39-43, Matt 27:47, John 19:28, Matt 19:48-49, John 19:30, Matt 27:51-54, Luke 23:46, John 19:30, Matt 27:50)

AFTER these words Jesus went out with his disciples and crossed the Kedron valley. There was a garden there called Gethsemane ["Olive Press"], and he and his disciples entered it. The place was well known to Judas the betrayer because Jesus had often met his disciples there.

"Settle yourselves here," he said to them, "while I go over there to pray."

He took with him Peter and the two sons of Zebedee. An overwhelming sadness had come over him, a heaviness of soul. "I have a mortal sorrow," he said to them. "I could die of it . . . Wait here and keep awake with me."

Walking a little farther, he fell on his face. "My Father, if it be possible," he prayed, "let this cup of sorrow pass from me. Yet not my will but yours be done."

Then an angel of heaven appeared, strengthening him, and in his agony he prayed more earnestly till the sweat rolled off him to the ground like great drops of blood.

When he came back to the disciples he found them sleeping. "What!" he exclaimed to Peter, "could you not stay awake one hour with me? You should keep alert and pray: pray not to be put to the test. The spirit may be willing but the flesh is weak."

He went off again a second time. "My Father," he prayed, "if it is not possible for this cup to pass from me, and I must drink it, then your will be done."

He came back and again found them asleep, for their eyes were heavy. So he left them there and once more went away and for the third time prayed the selfsame prayer. Then on returning to his disciples he exclaimed, "Still asleep? Still taking it easy? Well, the hour has come for the Son of Man to be betrayed into the hands of sinners. So, rouse yourselves and let us go. The traitor is here."

While he was still speaking, Judas, one of the Twelve, appeared and with him a great crowd armed with swords and cudgels, sent by the chief priests and elders of the people. The betrayer had given them a sign: "The one I kiss is the man," he told them. "Grab him." So Judas went straight up to Jesus, saying, "Greetings, Master!" as he kissed him. "What! Judas," Jesus said to him, "do you betray the Son of Man with a kiss?"

His followers, seeing what was happening, exclaimed, "Lord, shall we use our swords?" And Simon Peter, who carried a sword, took a swipe at the high priest's servant and cut off his right ear. (The servant's name was Malchus.) "Enough!" Jesus said to them. "Put your sword back in its scabbard, for those who live by the sword, die by the sword. And do you imagine that I cannot appeal to my Father, who would send me at once more than twelve legions of angels? Am I not to drink the cup my Father proffers to me?" And he touched the man's ear and healed it.

Then addressing his arresters, Jesus said, "Why have you come out with swords and cudgels to seize me as though I were a common criminal? Day after day I was with you teaching in the Temple and you never lifted a finger against me. No matter, let the scriptures be fulfilled."

Then his disciples all deserted him and ran away. And a young man who had been following, wearing nothing but a piece of linen when they caught hold of him, left the cloth in their hands and bolted away naked.

The contingent of soldiers with their captain and the Jewish police, having seized Jesus, now bound him. They took him first to Annas, the father-in-law of Caiphas, the high priest for that year. It was Caiphas who had advised the Jews that it was expedient for one man to die for the people.

Annas began to question Jesus about his disciples and his teaching, but Jesus cut him short: "I have spoken openly to all the world. I have constantly taught in synagogue and temple where the Jews throng, and I have said nothing covertly. So why do you question me? Question my listeners if you want to know what I taught them. They certainly know what I said."

At this retort, an officer standing by slapped Jesus in the face. "Is that the way to talk to the high priest," he exclaimed. Jesus turned on him: "If I have said something wrong, show me," he said, "if to the point, why have you hit me?"

Annas forthwith sent him, still bound, to Caiphas the high priest. The party that had arrested Jesus led him off to Caiphas, where the scribes and elders were all assembled. Following him afar off was Peter—right into the courtyard of the high priest's palace. There he sat down with the attendants to see the matter through.

The chief priests and the entire Sanhedrin were struggling to find some charge that they could trump up against Jesus by which they might pass the death sentence. But even though many false witnesses came forward, nothing could be found. Finally two people came forward with this accusation: "This fellow claimed, 'I can pull down God's Temple and in three days build it up again.' " At which the chief priest rose to his feet and said, "Have you no answer to the charge these witnesses bring against you?" But Jesus was silent. Then the high priest declared: "I adjure you by the living God, tell us if you are the Christ, the Son of God."

Jesus answered, "It is as you say, and let me tell you this: a day will come when you shall see the Son of Man on God's right hand of power coming in the clouds of heaven."

At this the high priest rent his garments, declaring, "He has blasphemed. What further witnesses do we need? You have all just heard his blasphemy. What is your verdict?"

"Guilty," they shouted. "He must die."

They proceeded to spit in his face and to beat him, and

some as they struck him jeered, "Come on, prophet Christ, tell us who hit you!"

Meanwhile Peter was sitting outside in the courtyard, where the servants had made a fire and were seated around it. Peter in their midst. A servant girl, seeing him sitting in the firelight, peered at him and said, "This man was with him too." "No, girl," he insisted, "I do *not* know him." A little later someone else saw him and said, "You're one of them too." "Man, I am *not*," Peter replied. About an hour later another man remarked, "Of course, this fellow was with him—he's a Galilean." "Man, I have no idea what you are talking about," he protested. Just then, as he was still speaking, a cock crowed, and the Lord turned and looked at Peter, and Peter remembered the Lord's words: "Before the cock crows tonight you will disown me three times," and he walked outside weeping bitterly.

Jesus was then led away from Caiphas to the Praetorium [the Roman governor's headquarters]. Morning had dawned and the Jews did not go into the Praetorium themselves, so as not to be defiled and unable to eat the Passover dinner; Pilate therefore came out to them himself and asked them, "What charge do you bring against this man?"

"If he were not a criminal," they replied, "we should never have submitted him to you."

"In that case, take him away and try him by your own law," Pilate answered.

"But we are not allowed to put a man to death," they countered [by which they meant crucifixion], thus fulfilling Jesus' prediction about the way he would die.

Thereupon Pilate reentered the Praetorium and called Jesus to him. "I take it that you are king of the Jews?" he observed.

To which Jesus answered, "Are you saying this in your sense or as the Jews mean it?"

"The Jews?" Pilate retorted. "I'm hardly a Jew, am I? It's your own race and chief priests that have handed you over to me. What have you done?"

"My kingdom is not of this world," Jesus replied. "If my kingdom were of this world my own people would certainly have put up a fight to stop me from being surrendered to the Jews. No, my kingdom is not of this kind."

"You *are* a king, then?" Pilate exclaimed.

"A king, you say!" Jesus answered. "That is why I was born, that is why I came into this world: to attest the truth. Everyone whose being is in truth responds to my voice."

As Pilate sat in court, a message came from his wife: "Leave that innocent man alone. I had a terrible dream about him last night."

Pilate turned to Jesus: "What is truth?" he asked. Then with the question still on his lips, he stepped outside again to face the Jews. "I find no case against him," he told them. "However, you have a custom at Passover of my releasing to you a single prisoner. How would you like me to release the king of the Jews?"

Now, the chief priests and elders had already primed the crowd to demand the release of Barrabas and the death of Jesus. So when the Governor asked them: "Which of the two do you want me to release to you?", they shouted, "Not this man but Barrabas." (Barrabas was a thief.)

Pilate thereupon took Jesus and had him flogged. The soldiers then plaited a crown of thorns and thrust it on his head, and robed him in a purple cloak. They came up to him, taunting, "Hail, King of the Jews!" and slapped him in the face.

Then Pilate came out again and announced, "Look, I am bringing him out to you once more to make quite clear that I find him blameless." Whereat Jesus came out wearing the crown of thorns and the purple cloak, and Pilate said to them, "Just look at the man!"

At the very sight of him the chief priests and their henchmen screamed, "Crucify him! Crucify him!"

"*You* take him and crucify him," Pilate answered, "because I find no guilt in him."

"We have a law," the Jews replied, "and according to that law he ought to die because he made himself the Son of God."

When Pilate heard this his unease grew, and he went back into the Praetorium and said to Jesus, "Where are you from?"

Jesus, however, gave no answer. At which Pilate remarked, "Won't you speak to me? Don't you realize that I have power to free you or power to crucify you?"

Jesus answered, "You would have no power over me whatsoever unless given to you from above. For this reason, those who delivered me to you have the greater sin."

Upon this Pilate tried to release him, but the Jews clamored: "If you free this man you are not Caesar's friend, because anybody making himself a king is defying Caesar."

As soon as Pilate heard this he brought Jesus out and took his seat at the tribunal in the spot called "The Pavement" (or in Hebrew "Gabbatha"), and seeing that nothing was being gained, but on the contrary, that a riot was starting, had a bowl of water brought to him and in full view of the mob washed his hands, saying, "Look, I am innocent of the blood of this just man. See to it yourselves."

The entire concourse roared back: "His blood be on us and upon our children."

It was the day before Passover, the time about noon, when Pilate declared to the Jews, "Here then is your king!"

"Away with him! Away with him!" they yelled. "Crucify him."

"What! Crucify your king?" Pilate taunted.

"We have no king but Caesar," the chief priests shouted back.

So finally he handed Jesus over to be crucified. They took hold of him and, carrying his own cross, he made his way to the place called The Skull, or in Hebrew, Golgotha. Two others were led away with him for execution, two criminals, and when they had arrived at The Skull they crucified him there with the two criminals, one on his right and the other on his left, as Jesus murmured, "Father, forgive them, for they know not what they do."

Pilate had written a notice which was fixed to the cross; it ran: "Jesus of Nazareth King of the Jews." The notice was read by many of the Jews because the spot where Jesus was crucified was not far from the city. Moreover, it was written in Hebrew, Latin, and Greek. The chief priests of the Jews then complained to Pilate, "You ought not to write 'King of the Jews' but 'This man *said*, I am King of the Jews.' "

To which Pilate retorted, "What I have written, I have written."

When the soldiers had crucified Jesus, they fell upon his clothes, dividing them into four lots, one for each soldier, except for the tunic, which was a seamless garment woven in one piece from top to bottom. "Let's not tear this," they said to one another, "but we'll toss for it." So were the words of scripture fulfilled:

> They parted my raiment among them
> and for my vesture they did cast lots.

This is exactly what the soldiers did.

People passing by hurled abuse at him, wagging their heads and jeering, "Ready to pull down the Temple, eh, and in three days build it up again? Then come down from the cross and save yourself if you really are the Son of God."

The chief priests with the scribes and elders likewise mocked him. "He saved others but cannot save himself," they jeered. "King of Israel indeed! Then let him come down from the cross and we'll believe him. He trusts in God, so if God wants him, let God come to the rescue. After all, he said he was the Son of God."

One of the criminals hanging there insulted him too. "Aren't you the Christ?" he taunted. "Then save yourself and us." But the other one reproached him. "Have you no fear of God?" he said. "You got the same sentence as he did—and quite right in our case: we're paying for our crimes—but this man has done nothing . . . Remember me, Jesus," he said, "when you come into your kingdom." And Jesus replied, "Yes, indeed, I tell you you shall be with me today in paradise."

Standing close to the cross was his mother with her sister, Mary the wife of Clopas, and also Mary Magdalene. Jesus, seeing his mother and that disciple whom he loved standing beside her, said to her, "Mother, he is your son," and to the disciple he said, "Son, she is your mother." And from that moment the disciple took her to his own.

Darkness fell over the whole earth from midday till three in the afternoon, and at about three Jesus cried out in a loud voice: "*Eloi, Eloi, lama sabachthani?*" which means: "My God, my God, why hast thou forsaken me?"

Some of those who stood nearby, hearing this, exclaimed, "He is calling Elijah." Then Jesus, knowing that everything written in the scriptures had been fulfilled, uttered, "I thirst," and one of them ran and got a sponge, which he soaked in sour wine and mounted it on a stick for him to drink. Meanwhile the rest said, "Wait, let's see if Elijah will come to rescue him."

Having tasted the wine, Jesus said, "All is complete." Then in a loud voice he cried out, "Father, into thy hands I commend my spirit," and with these words he let his head drop and yielded up his spirit.

Suddenly the Temple curtain ripped in two from top to bottom, the earth quaked, rocks were shivered, graves opened, and the bodies of many of the holy ones rose from the dead. (After Jesus' resurrection they emerged from their tombs and came into the Holy City, appearing to many.)

When the centurion and his men who were keeping watch over Jesus saw the earthquake and all that was happening, they were filled with awe. "So he really was the Son of

God!" they muttered. When the crowds that had clustered around to see the spectacle witnessed what had happened, they retreated to their homes beating their breasts.

As soon as Judas the traitor found that Jesus had been condemned, he was overwhelmed with remorse and returned the thirty pieces of silver to the chief priests and elders. "I have sinned," he said. "I have betrayed innocent blood."

"What is that to us?" they replied. "That is your concern."

At which he flung the money down on the Temple floor and left them, then went and hanged himself.

NOTES

1. Annas had been high priest between A.D. 6 and 15. Caiphas began his much longer term of office in A.D. 18. Jesus was taken to Annas first possibly because of the latter's experience and prestige as high priest emeritus.

2. When Jesus looked at Peter after Peter had denied him three times, one must not assume that Jesus too had been in the courtyard but that he was being led through it.

3. The reason why Caiphas was able to regard Christ's declaration as clearly blasphemous was that Christ quoted a Messianic passage from Daniel 7:13-14, thereby equating himself with one who "like the Son of Man came with the clouds of heaven. And there was given him dominion, and glory and a kingdom."

4. In Caiphas' court when Jesus is struck and asked to prophesy who struck him, we learn from Luke that he had been blindfolded.

5. Pilate went out to the crowd because for a Jew to enter the house of a pagan was ipso facto to incur ritual excommunication.

6. Jesus' prediction of his passion and death is clearly given in Matthew 20:19: "and they will hand him over to the Gentiles to be mocked and scourged and crucified, and on the third day he will rise again."

7. Tradition has it that Pilate's wife was Claudia Procla (or Procula) and that she became a Christian. She is honored as a saint in the Greek Orthodox Church.

8. Pilate's decision to flog Jesus was a last attempt to save him. He was offering this as a substitute to crucifixion in the hope that the deplorable state of Jesus after it would move his adversaries to pity.

9. Matthew, Mark, and Luke say that Simon of Cyrene coming in from the country was made to carry Jesus' cross. Probably Jesus began by carrying his own cross, but was seen to be too weak to continue. We can be sure that he was spared the burden not out of compassion but through fear that his death en route would snatch him from the ignominy of being nailed to the cross.

10. The Synoptics call the two criminals executed beside Jesus "thieves," but it is possible that they were insurrectionists. The

Penitent Thief or the Good Thief is by tradition named Dismas and is honored as a saint in the Christian calendar.

11. When Jesus addressed his mother from the cross he used the word (*gunai*) ("woman"), a term of respect in Greek. See note on page 374.

12. The sour wine offered to Jesus at the end poses a problem. We learn from Mark 15:23 that just before Jesus was crucified he was offered wine mixed with myrrh (spiced wine), no doubt as a pain killer, but he refused it. Then just after he cried out, "I thirst," on the cross, someone ran and dipped a sponge in a jar standing near full of crude wine, sour wine, or vinegar. And this Jesus accepts. But whether it was offered out of compassion or derision, the evangelists do not seem to be clear about. Jesus himself had in mind the last prophecy that confirmed him in psalm 69: 20-21, which goes:

> Insults have broken my heart
> so that I am in despair.
> I looked for pity but there was none;
> and for comforters, but I found none.
> They gave me poison for food,
> and for my thirst they gave me vinegar to drink.

That is why his penultimate words, "after knowing that everything written in the scriptures had been fulfilled," were: "All is complete."

13. As to the Temple curtain that was ripped from top to bottom, there were two curtains: this was probably the inner curtain shrouding the Holy of Holies.

The Resurrection and After

One of the impressions one gets from all the Resurrection accounts, however much they differ in detail, is that the mood of the risen Christ is very different from that of the solemn and even sad Christ of the Last Supper and Passion. He seems to go out of his way to restore the confidence of the shattered Apostles, huddled together in an upper room for fear of the Jewish authorities. This Christ is brisk, optimistic, playful, even teasing; as nowhere seen better than at his first meeting with Mary Magdalene at the empty tomb, and later in the way he handles the doubting Thomas.

In the former encounter, it has always seemed to me a tragedy that almost every translator of the Bible up till now (and even now) has followed St. Jerome's lead in rendering Jesus' remark to Mary as: "*Noli me tangere*" ("Do not touch me"). What Jesus actually says is: "μη μου ἅπτου," (*Mē mou haptou*,"). Now the verb ἅπτω (*haptō*) can indeed mean "touch," but is also means to "take hold of, to clutch," and that is the only meaning here which makes sense. Imagine the scene: here is this distraught and headstrong woman, whose love of Christ is nothing less than passionate and who has just been pushed to desperation by the discovery that his body is missing. Is she merely going to stand there when Jesus reveals his identity? Not likely! She will throw herself at him and, in the manner of the times, grasp him by the knees. So what does Jesus do to calm her? He smiles down at her, possibly even laughs, as he says, "Stop clinging to me like this. I'm still here. I haven't gone up to my Father yet."

What a different picture this gives of the beautifully human Christ from the starchy, lugubrious being who utters, "Hands off! I'm too holy to touch." Those who think that this is what he said are hard put not to conclude that the resurrected body was somehow more ethereal than real: a conclusion which Jesus goes out of his way to demolish. Not only does he make his disciples touch the wounds in his hands and feet ("a spirit hath not flesh and bones as ye see me to have": Luke 24:39), but he asks for something to eat and devours a piece of broiled fish in front of their eyes, and a day or so later cooks them breakfast on the shores of the Sea of Galilee.

In the last chapter of John's gospel it is worthy of note that when Jesus exacts an affirmation of Peter's love for him, he makes Peter repeat his affirmation three times—as if to purge him forever of the shame of his threefold denial.

Readers are reminded that the Jewish Sabbath is the Christian Saturday.

(John 19:31-34, 36-37, Matt 27:57-66, Mark 15:47, John 20:1-18, Luke 23:55-56, Mark 15:16, John 20:1-18, Matt 28:11-15, Luke 24:13-43, John 20:21-29, 21:1-23)

SINCE it was the Friday before Passover and the Jews did not want the bodies to remain on the cross during the Sabbath—a Sabbath of special solemnity—they requested Pilate to have their legs broken and the bodies taken down.

Consequently the soldiers came and broke the legs of the first and then the second man crucified with Jesus, but when they came to Jesus they found him already dead and did not break his legs. One of the soldiers, however, lanced his side with a spear, and immediately there flowed out blood and water: an occurrence that fulfilled the scripture which says: "A bone of him shall not be broken," and another scripture: "They shall look on him whom they pierced."

When evening fell, Joseph of Arimathea came. He was a man of wealth as well as a follower of Jesus and he had gone to Pilate asking for Jesus' body, which Pilate then ordered to be given him. So Joseph took the body down, wrapped it in a clean linen shroud, and laid it in his own new sepulcher which he had hewn out of the rock. Then he rolled a large stone against the entrance of the tomb and left. The women who had come with Jesus from Galilee had been following; they included Mary Magdalene and that other Mary the mother of James, and now they were sitting opposite the sepulcher watching where he was laid. Then they went home to prepare balms and unguents, resting, however, all the Sabbath as the Law prescribed.

The morning after that Friday, the chief priests and the Pharisees had come in a delegation to Pilate and said, "Your Excellency, we remember how that imposter while he was still alive asserted, 'After three days I shall rise again.' Please, therefore, order the tomb to be guarded until the third day in case his disciples come and steal the body, then spread it abroad that he has risen from the dead: which would make the final fraud even worse than what went before."

"Very well, take a guard," Pilate replied, "and secure the place just as you want."

So they went off and made the sepulcher secure, sealing the stone and posting sentries.

Early on the first day of the week [Sunday morning] while it was still dark, Mary Magdalene and Mary the mother of James and Salome came to the sepulcher with spices to embalm him, but seeing that the stone had been rolled away from the entrance, Mary Magdalene went running to Simon Peter and the other disciple whom Jesus loved, exclaiming, "They have taken the Lord out of the sepulcher and we don't know where they have laid him."

So Peter and the other disciple set off and made for the tomb, and they both started to run, but the other disciple outran Peter and arrived first at the tomb. Peering in, he saw the linen wrappings lying there, but he did not go inside. Then Peter followed hard on his tracks and entered the sepulcher. He perceived the linen wrappings lying there, but the band that had swathed Jesus' head was not lying with them: it was rolled up in a bundle on its own. Then the other disciple who had arrived first at the tomb went in, and he saw and he believed. For up till then they had not grasped the import of scripture which said that Jesus had to rise from the dead. The two disciples then returned home.

Mary Magdalene meanwhile stood outside the sepulcher weeping, and as she wept she stooped to gaze into the tomb and saw two angels in white sitting one at the head and one at the feet of where the body of Jesus had lain.

"Madam, why are you crying?" they asked.

"Because they have taken away my Lord," she sobbed, "and I don't know where they have laid him."

As she said this she glanced back and her eyes fell on Jesus standing there, but she could not tell that it was Jesus.

"Madam, why are you weeping?" he said to her. "Whom are you looking for?"

Thinking that he was the gardener, she replied, "Sir, if you have carried him off, tell me where you have put him and I'll take him away."

"Mary!" said Jesus to her, and turning, she uttered in Hebrew, "*Rabbuni*!" (which means "Master").

"Don't cling to me so!" Jesus exclaimed. "I haven't gone up to my Father yet, but go and tell my family that I *am* going to ascend to my Father and your Father, to my God and your God."

So Mary Magdalene rushed back to the disciples with the news: "I have seen the Lord," and she told them what he said.

The women who had first gone to the sepulcher were on their way home when some of the sentries hurried to the city to report to the chief priests what had happened. These at once called a meeting with the elders at which they decided to bribe the soldiers with a considerable sum to say, "His followers came during the night and while we were asleep stole off with the body." "Should the governor hear of this," they added, "we promise not to let you come to any harm."

The soldiers took the money and did as they were told, and to this day this fiction is current among the Jews.

That same day two disciples were on their way to a village some seven miles from Jerusalem called Emmaus and they were discussing all the events that had recently happened, and as they talked and discussed with one another, Jesus himself drew near and walked along with them, but something kept them from recognizing him.

"What are you talking about so earnestly as you walk along?" he asked them. "And why are you so sad?"

They stood still, their faces full of gloom. Then the one who was called Cleopas replied, "You must be the only visitor in Jerusalem who doesn't know what has been going on there these last few days."

"Such as what?" he asked.

"All about Jesus of Nazareth," they answered: "a powerful man in word and deed, a prophet in God's eyes and the people's, whom our chief priests and rulers condemned to death and crucified. And we had hoped that he was the one to liberate Israel. On top of this, today is the third day that it all happened, and some of our women who went to the tomb early this morning have dumbfounded us by saying that his body was missing. They came back and told us that they'd seen a vision of angels, who told them that he was alive. Then some of us went off to the tomb and found things exactly as the women had described, but there was no sign of *him*."

"Oh, you slow-witted ones!" Jesus burst out, "so dull of heart, who can't believe all the things that the prophets have told you. Wasn't it laid down that the Christ had to suffer this way and so to enter his glory?"

Then beginning with Moses and going through all the prophets, he expounded to them every scripture that concerned him. When they drew near the village to which they were going he made as though he would push on further, but they pressed him, saying, "Stay with us. Evening approaches and the day is far spent."

So he went in to stay with them, and when he was at table with them he took bread, spoke a blessing, broke and gave to them, and suddenly their eyes were opened and they knew him—just as he vanished from their sight. They turned to one another exclaiming, "How our hearts were on fire all the time he talked to us on the road and opened up the scriptures for us!"

They set out at once and returned to Jerusalem, where they found the Eleven gathered together with some others and affirming, "Yes, the Lord really has risen and has appeared to Simon." Then they gave an account of what had happened on the road to Emmaus and how they recognized him in the breaking of bread.

While they were still talking about all this, Jesus himself stood among them. "Peace be with you!" he said, but they were frightened out of their minds and thought they were seeing a ghost.

"Why are you so startled?" he asked. "Why are your hearts so full of doubt? Look at my hands, and look at my feet. Yes, it is I. Touch me and see for yourselves. A ghost hasn't flesh and bones as you see me to have."

He showed them his hands and his feet, and they could hardly believe for surprise and joy.

"Do you have anything here to eat?" he asked them. They offered him a piece of broiled fish, and right in front of them he took and ate it.

"Peace be with you!" Jesus said to them again. "As the Father has sent me, so I send you." Saying which, he breathed on them and uttered, "Receive the Holy Spirit. Whose sins you shall forgive, they are forgiven them. Whose sins you shall withhold, they are withheld."

Thomas one of the Twelve, the one called Didymus [The Twin], was not with them when Jesus came, so when the rest of the disciples told him, "We have seen the Lord," he retorted, "Unless I see the actual nail holes in his hands and put my finger through those nail holes, and thrust my hand into his side, I am not going to believe."

Eight days later the disciples were inside again and Thomas with them. Although the doors were locked, Jesus came in and stood among them. "Peace be with you!" he greeted them. Then he said to Thomas, "Put your finger right here, look, into my hands. And here put your hand, thrust it into my side . . . Stop doubting and start believing."

"My Lord and my God!" Thomas broke out. Then Jesus went on, "You believed because you can see me. Blessed are those who have not seen, yet still believe."

After this Jesus showed himself to his disciples again by the Sea of Tiberias [Sea of Galilee], and this is how he showed himself. Simon Peter, Thomas the Twin, Nathanael from Cana in Galilee, the sons of Zebedee, and two other disciples were all together. Simon Peter said, "I am going out to fish." "We'll come with you," the others said. So they set out in the boat and all that night they caught nothing.

Just as day was breaking, Jesus stood on the shore. "Catch anything, lads?" Jesus called.

"No," they shouted back.

"Then throw out your net on the starboard side," he said, "and you'll get a catch."

So they did, and they could hardly haul the net in, it was so full of fish.

"It's the Lord," the disciple whom Jesus loved exclaimed to Peter.

The moment Simon Peter heard that it was the Lord he threw on his clothes (for he was stripped) and leapt into the sea. The other disciples meanwhile came in the boat tugging the net full of fish. They were not far from land—only about a hundred yards. As they stepped ashore they saw a charcoal fire with some fish laid on it and some bread.

"Bring me some of your catch," Jesus said to them. So Simon Peter went aboard and dragged the net on to the beach. It was full of large fish: a hundred and fifty-three. Yet in spite of such a number the net was not broken.

"Come and have breakfast," Jesus said. None of the disciples was bold enough to ask, "Who are you?" though they were quite sure it was the Lord. Then Jesus came, offered the bread around and likewise the fish. (This was the third time that Jesus showed himself to his disciples after rising from the dead.)

When they had breakfasted Jesus said to Simon Peter, "Simon son of John, do you love me more than all the rest?"

"Yes, Lord," he replied, "you know that I love you."

"Then feed my lambs."

A second time he asked, "Simon son of John, do you love me?"

"Yes, Lord, you know that I love you."

"Be shepherd to my flock."

Yet a third time he asked him, "Simon son of John, do you love me?"

Peter, hurt at being asked "Do you love me?" three times burst out, "Lord, you know everything: you know that I love you."

"Then feed my sheep . . . When you were young—let me tell you the truth—you fastened your belt and walked where you would. But when you grow old you will stretch out your arms, and another will fasten you and take you where you would not." (Jesus meant by this the death by which Peter would glorify God.) Then he added, "Follow me."

Peter turned and seeing the disciple whom Jesus loved coming after them—the one who had leaned against his breast at the Supper and asked, "Which of us, Lord, will betray you?"—seeing him, Peter said to Jesus, "What about *him*, Lord?"

To which Jesus replied, "And if I should want him to wait here till I come, what is that to you? Just follow me."

This gave rise to the rumor among the brotherhood that this disciple would not die. But Jesus never said that he would not die. He said only, "If I want him to wait until I come, what is that to you?"

This is the disciple who vouches for these things and has written them down, and he guarantees that his whole account is true. But there is so much more that Jesus did that if it were all recorded I doubt if the world itself could hold the books that would be written.

NOTES

1. The reason for breaking the legs of the crucified seems to have been twofold: (1) to hasten death, (2) to render them helpless should by chance they recover.

2. As for the blood and water that flowed from the side of Jesus, there appears to be no medical explanation of this phenomenon. For the evangelist, however, it obviously held a special significance because in John 19:35-37 he stresses the point and quotes two Old Testament prophecies as having been fulfilled: "A bone of him shall not be broken," and "They shall look on him whom they pierced." He prefaces this with the assertion: "He who saw this attests to its truth, and he knows for a fact that he is telling the truth so that you too can believe it." There has been much discussion as to what the symbolism of the blood and water stands for.

3. We learn from Luke that Joseph of Arimathea was a member of the Jewish Sanhedrin, but had voted against the condemnation of Jesus. The location of Arimathea has been variously suggested.

4. The tomb that Jesus was placed in was a new tomb never used before. It was in the same garden where the crucifixion took place (John 19:41). The stone was probably a large millstone that rolled on a groove.

5. As to the angels after the Resurrection, Mark has one, a young man robed in white; Matthew has one, "with a face like lightning and a robe white as snow"; Luke has "two men in dazzling garments."

6. When the women came to the tomb to embalm Jesus on Sunday morning, there is no mention of the sentries. Matthew in 28:11 says that "some of the guards" had gone to the authorities to report the missing body.

7. Why does Luke in 24:33 say that when the two disciples hurried back to Jerusalem from Emmaus "they found the Eleven gathered together," when in fact if Thomas was not there (John 20:24), there would have been only ten? I simply do not know.

8. Tradition has it that Peter met his death by crucifixion. At any rate the date was A.D. 64 in Rome under the persecution of Nero. It is said that he asked to be crucified upside down because he was not worthy to be crucified the same way as his Master.

The Day of Pentecost

The word Pentecost is the Greek for "fiftieth," meaning the seven weeks and a day after the Passover for the Jews, and for the Christians the fifty days after Christ's Resurrection. The day of Pentecost was ten days after his Ascension. Jesus, just before he ascended, promised his disciples, "Ye shall be baptized with the Holy Ghost not many days from now" (Acts 1:5).

"The gift of tongues" was and still is a mysterious phenomenon which nobody has really been able to explain. Suffice to say that it is akin to all those preternatural or paranormal expressions of the human psyche which have manifested themselves throughout history—from the drug-induced trances of the priestess of Apollo at Delphi to the ecstasies of dancing dervishes or Mexican flagellantes. The gift of tongues or *glossolalia* (the Greek for "tongue-talk") usually takes the form of outbursts of apparent gibberish which then have to be interpreted, but it can also manifest itself in a language wholly unknown to the speaker.

What is curious about the "tongues" with which the Apostles addressed their multiracial audience was that these tongues were understood in each of their hearers' native language. Whether this is unique or not, Pentecostal has come to be the word applied to all those charismatic religions whose chief feature is some form of emotional illumination.

(Acts 2:1-21)

IT was during the fiftieth day [after the Resurrection], when they were all assembled in one place, that suddenly out of the heavens came the rushing sound of a mighty wind which swept into every crevice of the house where they sat, and what looked like tongues of flame fanned out and settled severally on each of them. They were infused with the Holy Spirit and broke out into divers tongues according as the Spirit inspired them.

There were many pious Jews visiting Jerusalem at that time, from every nation under the sun, and crowds of them were drawn to the spot by the noise. Then they were amazed at hearing themselves addressed each in his own tongue.

"Aren't the speakers all Galileans?" they asked. "How is it that we all hear them speaking in our native tongues? . . . Parthians, Medes, Elamites, people from Mesopotamia, Judea and Cappadocia, from Pontus and Asia, Phrygia and Pamphylia, from out of Egypt and the regions of Libya around Cyrene, as well as visitors from Rome (both Jews and converts), Cretans and Arabs—we all hear them preaching to us in our own language about the astonishing things of God . . . How can one explain this?" they asked one another, amazed to the point of bafflement. Others merely sneered, "They've had too much to drink!"

Peter then, standing with the Eleven, called out to them in a loud voice: "Men of Judea and all you pilgrims to Jerusalem, take good note of what I am about to tell you. These men here are not, as you suppose, drunk. Surely not at nine in the morning! No, this is the event that the prophet Joel spoke of:

> It shall come to pass in the last days, saith God,
> I will pour out my Spirit upon all flesh;
> and your sons and your daughters shall prophesy,
> and your young men shall see visions,
> and your old men shall dream dreams:
> And on my servants and on my handmaidens
> I will pour out in those days of my spirit;
> and they shall prophesy: And I will show wonders
> in heaven above, and signs in the earth beneath;
> blood and fire, and vapor of smoke:
> The sun shall be turned into darkness, and the moon into blood,
> before the great and notable day of the Lord come:
> And it shall come to pass, that whosoever shall call on the name of the Lord shall be saved. (Joel 2:28-32)

"You men of Israel, listen: I speak of Jesus of Nazareth: a man displayed before you by God through miracles and portents and signs which God worked through him when he was among you, as well you know. This Jesus was put into your hands by the express will and plan of God. You used the heathens to crucify and slay him, but God raised him to life again and set him free from the pangs of Hades, because it was not possible for him to be held by it . . ."

The Stoning of Stephen

As was inevitable with believers multiplying rapidly, a certain friction began to show itself between the Jewish converts from Judea and Galilee, who spoke Aramaic, and those from Jewish communities elsewhere, whose language was Greek. Accordingly, to make sure that these latter were properly represented in the administration of the infant church, the Apostles appointed seven deacons or helpers from the Grecian party to carry out the distribution of food, clothes, and other necessities to the faithful, who at that time owned all things in common.

Of these, the most notable was Stephen (meaning in Greek "crown" or "garland"), a young man "with the face of an angel . . . full of faith and the Holy Spirit," who "did great wonders and signs among the people." Stephen, accused by other Greek-speaking Jews of "blasphemy, speaking words against Moses and God," and "saying that this Jesus of Nazareth will destroy this place and will change the customs which Moses delivered to us," is arraigned before the high priest, where he makes a tremendous speech surveying the whole religious history of Israel. Toward the end of his harangue he declares to the high priest and the entire Sanhedrin:

(Acts 7:51-60, 8:1-3)

"YOU stiff-necked people, uncircumcised in heart and ear, always resisting the Holy Spirit, always doing exactly what your fathers did—tell me, is there a single prophet whom your fathers did not hound? They murdered even those who foretold the coming of the Righteous One—the very one whom you have just betrayed and killed. . . . Yes, you, who received the Law from the hands of angels but never kept it."

Cut to the quick by these words, they ground their teeth in frenzy. Then Stephen, filled with the Holy Spirit and gazing up into heaven, saw the glory of God and Jesus standing at God's right hand. "Look!" he exclaimed, "I see the heavens opened and the Son of Man standing on the right hand of God."

At this they roared in outrage, stopping their ears, as in

one body they rushed upon him and dragged him out of the city, where they stoned him. And they heaped their clothes [so that they could throw better] at the feet of a young man named Saul. While they were stoning him, Stephen called out, "Lord Jesus, receive my soul." Then he fell to his knees crying in a loud voice, "Lord, do not hold this sin against them." And with these words on his lips he lay down and died.

Saul was there approving of the murder, which sparked the first day of a bitter persecution of the church in Jerusalem. Everybody except the Apostles scattered into the countryside of Judea and Samaria. Meanwhile some good men buried Stephen with much lamentation. But Saul proceeded to ravage the church, entering house after house and dragging off men and women to prison.

Philip and the Eunuch

One of the results of Saul's zeal in assaulting the first converts was that as they dispersed over the land they spread the word, exemplifying the dictum which was to be proved over and over again through the centuries: "The blood of martyrs is the seed of the church." Stephen was the first Christian martyr.

The Philip in this story is not Philip the Apostle but one of the seven Greek-speaking assistants that the Apostles had selected to help with the needs of the Faithful. This Philip exerted himself beyond the mundane call of administration and became a persuasive evangelist—as this incident shows.

Ethiopia (which in Greek means "Burnt Face") was the name of a country bordering the Nile south of Egypt and some five hundred miles northwest of the present-day Ethiopia. It was what we would now call Northern Sudan and was inhabited by a strong, swarthy race called Nubians.

The queen in this account was one of a series of single-minded monarchs who at times thumbed their noses at Rome itself, and usually to their cost. The present queen, Candace, ruled over a nation somewhat chastened by Rome after her predecessor had unsuccessfully attacked Egypt. Candace's treasurer, a eunuch, was almost certainly a Nubian Jew who had traveled to Jerusalem to pay his respects at the Temple.

(Acts 8:26-40)

AN angel of the Lord said to Philip, "Get ready to set out at noon along the desert road that goes from Jerusalem to Gaza." So he set out, and it happened that an Ethiopian, a eunuch and high official at the court of Candace queen of Ethiopia—in fact, her treasurer—was on his way home after having made a pilgrimage to Jerusalem. He was sitting in his chariot reading the prophet Isaiah.

The Spirit prompted Philip to catch up with the chariot, and as he ran alongside he heard the eunuch reading aloud from Isaiah, so he asked him, "Do you understand what you are reading?"

"How can I understand," he answered, "unless someone shows me."

He then invited Philip to get in and sit beside him. The passage he was reading was:

> He was led like a sheep to the slaughter;
> and like a lamb dumb before his shearer,
> so opened he not his mouth.

Turning to Philip, the eunuch asked, "Who, please, is the prophet talking about—himself or someone else?"

Beginning with this text, Philip began to expound the good news of Jesus, and as they traveled along the road they came to water. "Look, here is water," exclaimed the eunuch. "What is stopping me from being baptized?"

"If you believe with all your heart, you may be," Philip replied.

"I do," he said, "I believe that Jesus Christ is the Son of God."

The chariot driver was told to stop, and both Philip and the eunuch went down into the water, where he baptized him. No sooner had they come up out of the water than the spirit of the Lord wafted Philip away and the eunuch saw him no more and he continued his journey rejoicing. Philip, meanwhile, found himself at Azotus, and passing on from there he preached the good news in all the towns till he came to Caesarea.

NOTES

1. The queen's name was not actually Candace, which was the Roman rendering of the Nubian word for "queen," the Greek being *kandake*.

2. Gaza, on the southwestern coast of Palestine forty or fifty miles from Jerusalem, was one of the five royal cities of the ancient

Philistines. Samson died there. The present town on the same site has a population of some forty thousand.

3. Caesarea was a seaport town on the Samaritan coast fifty miles northwest of Jerusalem (not to be confused with several other Caesareas). At one time it was the capital of the Roman province of Palestine. Present population is about one hundred thousand.

The Conversion of Saul

The Acts of the Apostles (literally "the Doings") is mostly about St. Paul and his missionary journeys all over the Mediterranean and finally to Rome itself. Paul, or Saul as he was called originally, though probably the most Hellenized of all the Apostles, described himself as "a Hebrew of the Hebrews . . . a Pharisee and the son of a Pharisee." He was born and educated in the city of Tarsus in Asia Minor, a region which in language and culture was almost an extension of Greece. Tarsus was an important and flourishing city, boasting a famous university and a circle of influential philosophers. It was at Tarsus that Mark Anthony some thirty-two years earlier had set up his headquarters after being allotted the eastern half of the Roman empire as his sphere in 42 B.C. It was to Tarsus that he summoned Cleopatra, Queen of Egypt, to answer certain charges, when she, then twenty-nine years old and in the prime of her beauty, came at her own pace and in her own way, making her famous passage up the river Cydnus to meet him—and to ensnare him . . . immortalized by Plutarch and Shakespeare:

> The barge she sat in, like a burnished throne
> Burned on the water; the poop was beaten gold,
> Purple the sails, and so perfuméd that
> The winds were lovesick with them; the oars were silver
> Which to the tune of flutes kept stroke and made
> The water which did beat to follow faster. For her own person,
> It beggared all description, she did lie
> In her pavilion, cloth of gold, of tissue . . .*

**Anthony and Cleopatra*, Act 2, scene 2.

Saul's parents must have been people of consequence because though Jews they were Roman citizens, a distinction Saul was born with and which in those days carried something of the advantages that a green card carries in the United States today. Moreover, they could afford to send him to Jerusalem for part of his education. Though they probably did not also allow their son to attend the University of Tarsus, as being far too Hellenized for an orthodox Jew, there are indications that he was not unacquainted with Greek literature. The fact that he wrote his famous letters in a curious and involuted Greek may be because he dictated them and never seems to have revised them.

If Saul was born in A.D. 10 (a probability) he would have been about twenty-five at the time of his sudden conversion. In Acts 18:3 his occupation is given as tent maker, which could mean that his family was involved in the production of a tough cloth woven out of goat's hair, for which Tarsus was famous.

A single-minded, passionate man whom many would call a fanatic, Paul was yet capable of great tenderness and affection, though he seems never to have had either the time or the inclination to marry. As a theologian he was supreme and laid the foundation of all Christology.

The date of Paul's death is variously given, though it seems likely to have been in A.D. 64 under the same persecution of Nero that ended the life of Peter. There are scholars, however, who think that it was not till A.D. 67 that Nero had him executed. (Nero committed suicide the following year.)

(Acts 9:1-30)

MEANWHILE Saul was breathing out threats and slaughter against the Lord's disciples. He went to the high priest and asked him for letters to the synagogues at Damascus authorizing him to arrest and bring back to Jerusalem in fetters all those he discovered, be they men or women, who were followers of the Way.

While he was still on the road and nearing Damascus, all of a sudden a blaze out of the sky flooded around him. He fell to the ground as he heard a voice calling, "Saul, Saul, why do you persecute me?"

"Lord, who are you?" he cried out.

"I am Jesus, whom you are persecuting," the voice replied. "Get up now and go into the city, and you will be told what to do."

The men traveling with Saul stood there speechless. They heard a voice but saw no one. Saul picked himself up from the ground, but when he opened his eyes he could not see. So they led him by the hand and brought him into Damascus, where for three days he was without sight and did not eat or drink. Meanwhile a disciple in Damascus by the name of Ananias had a vision in which the Lord said to him, "Ananias!"

"Yes, Lord?"

"Go at once to the street called Straight and at the house of Judas ask for a man from Tarsus named Saul. Believe it or not, but he too has had a vision of a man called Ananias coming in and laying his hands on him to restore his sight. So you'll find him praying."

"Lord, several people have told me about this man," Ananias responded, "and the harm he has done to your Faithful in Jerusalem. Even now he is here with a warrant from the chief priests to arrest all those who call upon your name."

"All the same, go," the Lord replied, "because this is the man I have chosen as my channel to carry my name to the heathen and kings of the heathen, as well as to the people of Israel. I mean to show him how much he must endure for my name's sake."

So Ananias went, and once in the house he laid his hands on him and said, "Brother Saul, the Lord Jesus who appeared to you on your way here has sent me to make you see again and be filled with the Holy Spirit."

Immediately something like flakes fell from his eyes, and he saw again. He was baptized at once, took some food, regained his strength and, after only a few days with the disciples at Damascus, began to proclaim in the synagogues that Jesus was the Son of God. All who heard him were astounded. "Isn't this the man," they said, "who was in Jerusalem trying to kill everyone who invoked this name, and who came here on purpose to drag them off in fetters before the chief priests?"

Saul nonetheless went from strength to strength, quite confounding the Jews of Damascus with his proofs that Jesus was the Christ. As time went on they came to the conclusion that they must do away with him, but Saul got wind of their plot and although they watched the gates day and night for the chance to kill him, his supporters took him by night and lowered him down the walls in a basket. Arriving in Jerusalem, he tried to join the disciples, but they were all afraid of him and did not believe that his conversion was genuine. So Barnabas led him by the hand to the Apostles, recounting to them how the Lord had appeared to Saul on his journey and spoken to him, and how at Damascus Saul had boldly preached in the name of Jesus. After this he went around with them in Jerusalem, fearlessly preaching in the name of the Lord. However, after a certain sermon and an argument with some of the Hellenist party, these wanted to kill him; so when the brethren learned this they took him to Caesarea and sent him off from there to Tarsus.

NOTES

1. Damascus, one of the oldest cities in the world and once the capital of ancient Syria, is about one hundred and fifty miles northeast of Jerusalem. It was famous for its cloth and its armor. Present population is some three hundred thousand.
2. Barnabas ("Son of Consolation"), born on the island of Cyprus, was a friend of Paul and did missionary work with him until they quarrelled (Acts 15:39).

Peter's Vision at Joppa

The episodes of this story—Cornelius the centurion's vision, Peter's vision, the meeting of the two men, and finally Cornelius' baptism—were of tremendous importance in the evolution of the infant church because it marked the point at which the giant step was taken to free the new religion from the requirements of the Law. Up till then even the Hellenized converts had to be circumcised. Queen Candace's eunuch, for instance, whom Philip baptized, must already have been circumcised, otherwise he would never have been allowed into the Temple to worship.

Peter's decision to permit the Roman Cornelius into the fold could not have been easy. Indeed, he was in a dilemma: on the one hand, his action would come as a shock to the rest of the Apostles and might cause a schism; on the other, the conversion of a Roman soldier, a centurion at that, would have salutary consequences. Peter took the step, and it proved to be the right one, but he was hauled over the coals for it when he got back to Jerusalem. Though he managed to explain himself, pressure was put on him again later and he seems to have compromised. It was not till

Paul, fresh from the successes of his first missionary voyage, threw his weight behind Peter at the Council of Jerusalem in A.D. 48 that the full go-ahead was given for a Christianity free from the ritual and dietary requirements of Judaism.

(Acts 10:1-36, 43-48)

IN Caesarea there was a man called Cornelius, a centurion of what was known as the Italian Cohort, a pious man who with his whole household served God, gave alms liberally, and was devout in his prayers.

One day at about three in the afternoon he had a vision in which he distinctly saw an angel of God come in and say, "Cornelius!"

Startled and staring hard, he answered, "What is it, sir?"

"Your devotions and almsgiving have gone up to heaven and made their mark," the angel replied. "So now send someone to Joppa to fetch a man called Simon Peter, who is lodging with Simon the Tanner, whose house is by the sea."

After the angel had said this and had gone, the centurion sent for two of his servants and a devout orderly of his staff. He told them the story and dispatched them to Joppa.

The following day, as the party was still on its way and not far from Joppa, Peter, at about noon, went up on to the roof to pray, but, growing hungry, he sent for something to eat and while this was being prepared he fell into a trance. He saw the skies open and something like a giant sheet let down to the earth from its four corners and teeming with every kind of four-footed beast and creeping thing in the world, and bird of the air. Then a voice said, "Rouse yourself, Peter: kill and eat!"

"In no way, Lord," Peter retorted. "I have never eaten any unclean trash."

The voice spoke a second time: "What God has made clean you are not to call trash."

Three times this happened, then the sheet was jerked up to heaven again. While Peter was still puzzling over the meaning of this vision, the men sent by Cornelius arrived. They had been directed to Simon's house and were now standing at the gate calling out to ask if a Simon known as Peter was staying there. Peter, in the middle of pondering his vision, was interrupted by the Holy Spirit saying, "Some men have come to see you. Hurry on down and don't hesitate to go with them, because I have sent them."

Peter came downstairs and said to the men, "I am the one you want. But why have you come?"

"We are from Cornelius the centurion," they answered. "He is an upright, religious man held in esteem by the whole Jewish nation, and he has been directed by a holy angel to bring you to his house for us to hear what you have to say."

Peter invited them in to put up that night, and the next morning he went off with them and some of the faithful from Joppa. The day following they arrived at Caesarea, where Cornelius and a gathering of his relatives and close friends were expecting him. Cornelius met Peter at the threshold, falling at his feet in homage. "Get up," Peter said, "I too am only a man!"

Still talking with him, he entered the house and found a large gathering there.

"I need hardly tell you," he began, "that a Jew is not allowed to mix with or visit people of another race. God, however, has just made it clear to me that I must not call anybody common or unclean. That is why when you sent for me I came without a second thought. Now may I ask *why* you sent for me?"

"Four days ago at about this time," Cornelius answered, "I was at home saying my afternoon prayers when suddenly a man robed in dazzling white stood before me. 'Cornelius, your devotions have been noted,' he said, 'and your charities remembered before God. So send to Joppa for Simon Peter and request him to come. He is staying in the house of Simon the Tanner by the seaside.' So I sent for you at once. It was good of you to come. Here we all are in God's presence, ready to hear whatever you have to tell us from the Lord."

Peter then began his address. "The truth has just dawned on me," he said, "that God does not have favorites. Anyone of any race who fears God and does what is right is welcomed by him. Of course, it is true that God sent his word to the people of Israel and singled them out for hearing the good news of peace from Jesus Christ, but the same Jesus is Lord of all . . . Every prophet points to him as the one in whom and in whose name all those who believe will have their sins forgiven . . ."

While Peter was still speaking, the Holy Spirit came down on his hearers. Those of the faithful who were Jews and had come with Peter were amazed to see the Holy Spirit poured out on the pagans too, for they could hear them speaking in tongues and extolling God.

Then Peter announced, "Who would forbid these people, who have received the Holy Spirit no less than us, from receiving the waters of baptism?"

Then he gave orders for them to be baptized in the name of Jesus Christ. After which they begged him to stay a few more days.

NOTES

1. Joppa, the present-day Jaffa, was a seaport in Israel about thirty-three miles south of Caesarea.

2. In Peter's vision of "every kind of four-footed beast," the Greek word used is τετραποδα (*tetrapoda*), meaning literally a quadruped or four-footed animal. It is a pity, however, that nine out of ten of the current translations render the word as "animal" as distinct from reptile and bird, forgetting that reptile, bird, and even insect are all animals: otherwise we lose a word to the language.

Peter Escapes from Prison

In spite of the rumpus Peter had caused in Jerusalem by having entered the home of Cornelius in Caeseria and baptized him and his household, further proseletizing among Hellenized Jews and even Greeks could not be halted; and soon Antioch, in what we would now call southern Turkey, became a center of early Christianity. Indeed, it was there that the followers of Jesus were first called Christians—a name which began as a term of abuse.

Meanwhile, Herod Agrippa had become the new ruler under Rome of Judea and Galilee, including Samaria. This Herod, the grandson of Herod the Great (and, incidentally, the same age as Paul), was not only a serious practicing Jew but a friend of Rome, where he had been sent as a youth to get him out of the way of his chronically suspicious grandfather.

Now in A.D. 41 as king of the three united provinces of Jewry, Herod Agrippa was anxious to please both the Jews and the Romans.

(Acts 12:1-19)

ABOUT this time King Herod reached out his arm to strike down some of the church. He beheaded James the brother of John, and seeing how much this pleased the Jews he went on to seize Peter as well. This happened during the Festival of the Unleavened Bread. Having arrested him he clapped him into jail under a sixteen-man guard of four squads, intending to bring him before the people for trial after the Passover. However, while Peter was locked up in prison, incessant and earnest prayer was being made for him to God by the church.

On the very eve of the day that Herod intended to produce him, Peter, in double chains, was asleep between two soldiers when an angel of the Lord suddenly stood there flooding the cell with light. "Quick, get up!" he said, nudging Peter in the ribs to wake him. At which the manacles fell from his wrists. "Put on your clothes and your sandals," the angel told him. He did so. "Now wrap yourself up in your cloak and follow me."

Peter followed him out, with no idea that what the angel was doing was real; he thought he was seeing a vision. They passed the first and the second guards and came to the iron gate that led out into the city. It opened spontaneously, and they went through it and had walked the length of a whole street when the angel vanished.

"So it's all real!" Peter exclaimed, coming to himself. "The Lord has actually sent his angel to snatch me out of Herod's clutches and save me from the fate the Jewish populace are expecting."

Convinced of this he made his way to the house of Mary, the mother of John Mark, where a large group of people were praying. He knocked on the outside door and a maid called Rhoda came to answer it. The instant she recognized Peter's voice she was so overjoyed that instead of opening the door she raced back, calling out that Peter was standing outside.

"You're raving!" they said to her, but when she insisted, they said, "It must be his angel!"

Meanwhile Peter went on knocking and when, to their amazement, they saw that it was really he, he silenced them with a wave of the hand and described to them how the Lord brought him out of the prison. Concluding which, he said, "Tell this to James and the others," then he left for elsewhere.

When morning came there was no small stir among the soldiers over what had become of Peter. And when Herod after a thorough search could find no trace of him, he interrogated the guards and ordered them to be executed.

NOTES

1. This James was one of the two sons of Zebedee. Barring Judas, he was the first of the Apostles to die and, so far as we know, the second Christian martyr after Stephen.

2. John Mark: by tradition this Mark was the author of Mark's gospel and probably the young man who fled naked after being seized during Christ's arrest (cf. Mark 14:51-52).

3. "Tell this to James": probably James "the brother of Jesus," who became the leader of the Christians in Jerusalem. He was not one of the original Twelve. According to Josephus he was stoned to death by the Jews in A.D. 62.

Paul Is Shipwrecked

Twenty-seven years have passed since Paul was struck down by a bolt of light and compelled to serve that Jesus whom he had persecuted and who had been crucified six years earlier. It has been long since that he became known to the rapidly increasing Christian community as *Paul*.

Apart from a quiet sojourn in Tarsus lasting several years (after he had been rescued from his adversaries in Damascus by being let down the walls in a basket), these twenty-seven years have gone by in a blaze of Christianizing zeal. He has crossed and recrossed the Mediterranean and the Aegean. He has preached in most of the major cities of Asia Minor, and at Athens, Corinth, and all over northeastern Greece. During this time he has poured himself out in many of the letters that were to become the very fount of Christian theology.

Now, at the age of about fifty-one and with some years of life still left to him, he waits at the port of Caesarea for a ship to take him to Rome, where he is to be tried on a charge brought against him by the religious authorities in Jerusalem. Having played his trump card of claiming Roman citizenship (with the right to appeal to Caesar), he may not be tried by a Jewish court, which he knows full well would be as unfair to him as it was to his Master.

Luke, his personal physician and fellow traveler, takes up the story.

(Acts 27:1-44, 28:1-10)

WHEN it was decided that we should set sail for Italy, Paul and some other prisoners were put in the charge of a centurion named Julius—of the Augustan Cohort. We boarded a vessel hailing from Adramyttium and bound for ports along the coast of Asia Minor. So we put out to sea. (In our party was Aristarchus, a Macedonian from Thessalonica.)

The next day we landed at Sidon, where Julius most kindly allowed Paul to go and stay with friends. From there we put to sea, but headwinds forced us to crawl along under the lee of Cyprus, after which we crossed the open sea off the coast of Cilicia and Pamphylia till we came to Myra in Lycia, taking in all fourteen days. There the centurion found a ship from Alexandria bound for Italy and put us on board.

For several days we made little headway as we struggled to put into Cnidus, which the wind made impossible, so we sailed under the lee of Crete off Cape Salmone, hugging the coast and batting our way along until we reached a place called Fair Haven, near the town of Lasea.

Much time had been lost and it was now quite risky to continue the voyage because the autumn equinox was on us, so Paul said to the others, "Sirs, I can see that this voyage is going to end in disaster and ruin: the loss not only of the cargo but of our lives."

The centurion, however, paid more attention to the captain and to the ship's owner than to Paul's warning, and because the harbor was unsuitable for wintering, the vote went in favor of putting out to sea in the hope that they would get themselves willy-nilly to Phoenix, a Cretan harbor with only a southwest and northwest exposure.

Just then a southerly breeze sprang up, perfect they thought for their objective, and they weighed anchor and sailed along the Cretan coast close to the shore. But presently a fierce gale, known as the "Northeaster," tore down on them off the land. The ship was caught in a futile attempt to turn into the wind, so we had to give her her head and run before it.

We careered along under the lee of a small island called Cauda and managed with difficulty to secure the ship's lifeboat and hoist it aboard, then to reinforce the hull with cables. The sailors, fearful of running aground on the flats of Syrtis, dropped the mainsail and let her drive. Next day, however, we were still being so violently buffeted that the sailors began to throw the cargo overboard, and on the third day they went so far as to jettison the ship's gear and tackle.

For days on end there was not a trace of sun or stars as the storm raged, and we gave up all hope of coming out alive. They had gone without food for a long time when Paul stood up and addressed the crew: "Men, if only you had listened to me and not set sail from Crete, you would have avoided all this hardship and loss! Nevertheless, I now urge you to bear up, because not a single life is going to be lost—only the ship. Last night an angel of the God I belong to and serve stood before me and promised: 'Have no fear, Paul, you definitely *will* appear before Caesar; and because of this, God has granted you the lives of all those who sail with you.' So take heart, men! I have complete confidence in God and that everything will turn out exactly as I've been told, even though we have to be cast up on some island."

On the fourteenth night we were still being driven across the Adriatic Sea when at about midnight the crew sensed that we were nearing land. They took soundings which registered twenty fathoms, but when a little later they sounded again and found only fifteen fathoms they feared we might run on to the rocks, so they dropped four anchors from the stern and prayed for day.

Some of the crew were planning to abandon ship and lower the lifeboat into the sea, pretending to put down anchors from the prow, when Paul said to the centurion and his solders, "If those men want to be saved, they'd better stay on board with everyone else." So the soldiers slashed the ropes of the lifeboat and let it drop.

Just before dawn Paul urged them all to take some food. "For fourteen days now you've been living on tenterhooks and starving," he told them. "You haven't touched a thing! So I entreat you to eat something to build up your strength, because not a hair of your heads is going to be lost."

Saying which, he took bread, gave thanks to God in front of them all, broke, and began to eat. As a result they all plucked up courage and ate something too. (There were altogether two hundred and seventy-six passengers on board.) When people had eaten enough they lightened the ship by dumping the grain into the sea.

Though it was now daylight they did not recognize the land, but noted a strand of beach in the bay and planned to run the ship onto this if they could. They therefore cut the anchors and let them go in the sea, at the same time loosening the ropes that held the rudders. Then they hoisted the foresail to the wind and headed for the strand. But the crosscurrents swung the vessel onto a reef, where the bows were irremovably grounded while the stern was pounded to pieces by the surf.

It occurred to the soldiers to kill the prisoners to prevent them from swimming away and escaping, but the centurion wanted to save Paul, so he kept them from carrying out this design. He ordered those of us who could swim to jump overboard first and make for the shore, then for the rest to follow on planks and pieces of wreckage. And so it was that everybody reached land safe and sound.

After our escape we discovered that the island was called Malta. Its rugged inhabitants showed us uncommon kindness, and because it was cold and starting to rain they made us all feel at home by lighting a fire; but just as Paul was thrusting a bundle of sticks he had collected on to the flames, an adder, stirred by the heat, fastened on to his hand. When the islanders saw the creature dangling from his wrist they muttered to one another, "Look, he must be a murderer, because even though he's escaped from the sea, divine justice is not going to let him get away with it."

Paul simply shook the snake off him into the fire and came to no harm. They were expecting him to swell up and fall down dead, but after they had waited a long time and saw nothing terrible happen, they changed their minds and said that he was a god.

NOTES

1. Some approximate dates: Paul's birth A.D. 10
The Crucifixion 29
Paul's conversion 35
First missionary voyage 45
Second missionary voyage 49
Third missionary voyage 54
Shipwrecked 61
Executed 64 or 67

2. The Caesar whom Paul appealed to was Nero, who succeeded his adopted father, Claudius, as emperor in 54.

3. Adramyttium was a port in northwestern Asia Minor at the foot of Mount Ida.

4. Myra is the modern Dembre. It was a port of call for the grain trade between Egypt and Rome.

5. Cnidus in southwestern Asia Minor jutted out into the Aegean between the islands of Cos and Rhodes.

6. Fair Haven was a harbor in the middle of Crete's southern coast about ninety miles west of Cape Salmone.

7. The Greater Syrtis in the Gulf of Sidra was a shifting sandbank

that ran along the coast of North Africa for about a hundred and twenty-five miles west of Crete and opposite Sicily.

8. When the ship was "being driven across the Adriatic Sea," it would have been more or less at the juncture of the Adriatic with the Mediterranean.

9. Malta, called "Melitē" in the Greek text, lies between Africa and Sicily. The site of the shipwreck, by tradition, is the present-day "St. Paul's Bay," eight miles northwest of Valetta, the capital. Paul stayed on the island for three months before resuming his journey to Rome. He rewarded the natives for their kindness with many cures. Legend has it that Paul was the cause of there being no snakes in Malta today.